LIFE OF JAMES CARDINAL GIBBONS

Faithfully yrs.

J. Card. Gibbons.

LIFE OF

JAMES CARDINAL GIBBONS

By ALLEN S. WILL, A. M., Litt. D.

"Render therefore to Caesar the things that are Caesar's, and to God the things that are God's."—Matthew, xxii, 21.

JOHN MURPHY COMPANY

PUBLISHERS

BALTIMORE   NEW YORK

R. & T. WASHBOURNE, Ltd.,

1, 2 and 4 Paternoster Row, London.   248 Buchanan Street, Glasgow.

Press of JOHN MURPHY COMPANY, Baltimore

TO THE INSPIRER OF
MY LABORS
THIS BOOK IS DEDICATED.

PREFACE

Few men who exert great influence are able to see in their own times the fruition of their most cherished undertakings; but such has been the privilege bestowed by a benign Providence on Cardinal Gibbons. It seems not inappropriate, therefore, to pause on the occasion of his fiftieth anniversary as priest and his twenty-fifth anniversary as Cardinal and survey, when he is 77 years old, the broad outlines of his career. Not only is it true that the principal labors to which he has hitherto devoted himself have been concluded, but some of them, indeed, were finished so long ago that their details have been almost forgotten by a generation intent chiefly on the things of the present.

No comprehensive attempt has been made up to this time to tell the story of the Cardinal's life, crowded, as it has been, with events not only of deep significance to the world, but of absorbing interest. True, there is much in print, but it is fragmentary, tinged with the impressions of a moment, controversial or wholly lacking in the perspective with which his career may now be fairly viewed. These considerations, and the peculiar appropriateness of the double jubilee, have emboldened me to embark on the rather hazardous task of trying to write a biography while the subject of it is yet living. At the beginning I resolved that if any compromise with the standards which should govern an impartial biography were encountered, I would not proceed with the work; and I have fully satisfied myself, at least, that this obstacle did not arise.

In the preparation of this book, I have been especially solicitous to obtain accuracy. Unverified statements have been rejected, and I have wholly discarded unconfirmed tradition and reminiscence. The opinions expressed, except where they are attributed to others, are mine.

ALLEN S. WILL.

BALTIMORE, *July* 30, 1911.

CONTENTS

CHAPTER I.

EARLY LIFE AND STUDIES.

CHAPTER II.

AT ST. PATRICK'S AND ST. BRIDGET'S.

CHAPTER III.

SECRETARY TO ARCHBISHOP SPALDING.

CHAPTER IV.

VICAR APOSTOLIC OF NORTH CAROLINA.

CHAPTER V.

AT THE VATICAN COUNCIL OF 1870.

CHAPTER XI.

KNIGHTS OF LABOR QUESTION.

CHAPTER XII.

EARLY YEARS OF CARDINALATE.

CHAPTER XIII.

CENTENNIAL OF THE AMERICAN HIERARCHY.

CHAPTER XIV.

APOSTOLIC DELEGATE; THE SCHOOL QUESTION.

CHAPTER XV.

AMERICANISM; THE CAHENSLY QUESTION.

CHAPTER XVI.

THE WORLD'S FAIR; PARLIAMENT OF RELIGIONS.

CHAPTER XVII.

SPANISH-AMERICAN WAR.

CHAPTER XVIII.

THE STRENUOUS LIFE; LABORS AND REFORMS.

CHAPTER XIX.

PAPAL CONCLAVE OF 1903.

CHAPTER XX.

CENTENARY OF THE BALTIMORE CATHEDRAL.

CHAPTER XXI.

SYMPATHY WITH FRENCH CATHOLICS.

CHAPTER XXII.

EVENTS OF LATER YEARS.

CHAPTER XXIII.

GREAT CIVIC CELEBRATION IN HIS HONOR.

CHAPTER XXIV.

A SUMMARY OF HIS LABORS.

ILLUSTRATIONS

LIFE OF CARDINAL GIBBONS

CHAPTER I.

EARLY LIFE AND STUDIES.

Although the active life of Cardinal Gibbons has stretched well into the twentieth century, the twilight of the eighteenth still seemed to linger around his early home when he was born in Baltimore, July 23, 1834. The city of which he was to become the foremost citizen, identified with it throughout a long career, was then overgrown from the straggling outlines of a colonial town. On the east the peaked roofs and tall, thin chimneys of its residential streets extended barely to Fell's Point, a full mile inside of where the Lazaretto Light, now half hidden by the smoke of clamorous factories, blinked at the smart clipper ships which raced up the Patapsco with the trade of the world. To the westward the swinging sign of the General Wayne Inn, on Paca street, bearing a portrait of "Mad Anthony" in brilliant blue and buff, marked the dividing line between urban life and a peaceful vista of rural estates, soon to be devoured by the hungry giant whose spreading bulk was already beginning to crowd them.

Uptown one might see, in the stately parade of late Georgian fashion which passed on bright afternoons, the women who were giving the city a repute as the home of the loveliest of their sex in America; and here and there might be observed the raven hair and olive cheeks of the daughters of rich Santo Domingan planters, driven in a swarm by the revolution of L'Ouverture to find in Baltimore the home of exiles. Downtown, around the waterfront, the heart of the city throbbed. Grave merchants in sober dress, their throats wrapped in stiff black stocks, sat in counting-rooms fronting on narrow streets and traded ambitiously with Europe, South America and the Indies. Privateers, which twenty years before had scattered British commerce in a hundred ports, now anchored around the wharves to load the products of the West and South in peaceful commerce. Swift schooners, manned not infrequently by sailors who had proved that they could use a cutlass as well as trim a sail, were freighting the rich crops of the Chesapeake region to the metropolis of Maryland. Planters and merchants from half a dozen States drank the old wines of the Fountain Inn, or Barnum's, crowding to the gay and busy city to buy their supplies a year ahead.*

The name of Johns Hopkins might be seen on the sign of a wholesale grocery store on Lombard street, near Light street.† A few hundred yards distant, on German street, near Charles, was the dry-goods establishment of George Peabody. The alert young man who opened Mr. Peabody's store in the morning and wrote his laconic business letters was William Pinkney Whyte. On Charles street, near German, was the modest office of Enoch Pratt, iron merchant. Chief Justice Taney's handsome residence was on Lexington street, the second house from St. Paul street. The courts of law felt the inspiration of William Pinkney, Luther Martin, William Wirt and Reverdy Johnson. Edgar Allan Poe, recently dismissed from West Point, was walking the streets seeking employment as a writer or teacher. At the Adelphi Theatre Junius Brutus Booth, then in the noonday of his genius, was playing nightly. Two years before, a tottering old man had been an object of respectful interest as he used to enter his residence at Front and Lombard streets after attending mass. He was Charles Carroll, and the hand that turned the heavy brass door knob had signed the immortal Declaration.

---

* Scharf, Chronicles of Baltimore, pp. 405-408.
† Mr. Henry C. Wagner, antiquarian, of Baltimore, is authority for the locations of old buildings as given here.

The stately Cathedral, then lately erected on a bold hill in the newer part of the city, was the seat of Catholic influence in America. It had been the pride of John Carroll, first American archbishop, who had died before it was opened for worship; but he had lived to see the organization of the Church planted on a foundation that would stand the shock of the "Knownothing" times, soon to come, and prove firm and lasting in the marvelous career of development that was opening before the new republic. Carroll had been succeeded by Neale, and then Marechal and Whitfield; and in the year of the future Cardinal's birth, Eccleston was elevated to the episcopal chair, and sat beneath the canopy at mass. Besides the Cathedral, the churches of St. Peter, St. John, St. Patrick, St. Mary and St. James had been erected; and the aggressive spirit of the clergy was fast winning converts. The Catholic population of Maryland was estimated at 75,000 out of 500,000, a greater proportion than in any other American State.*

The house in which the Cardinal was born survived the changes of time until 1892, when it was torn down to make way for the widening of Lexington street into a plaza for public parades and outdoor meetings. It stood on the west side of Gay street, a short distance north of Fayette street, and was a substantial home of two stories, capped by a high-pitched roof, the type of many others to be seen in Baltimore in the first half of the nineteenth century. That part of the city, since given over almost wholly to trade, was then near the core of the residential district. In front of the Gibbons home streamed a picturesque tide of life—fashionable idlers, who maintained many of the traditions of the English aristocracy; folk of many sorts coming in from the northeastern outskirts of the town to the maze of rope and mast that covered the inner harbor; coaches of the rich, with liveried servants on the boxes; white-arched Conestoga wagons, rumbling in from

---

* Letter of Archbishop Eccleston to the Congregation of the Propaganda, quoted by Shea, History of the Catholic Church in the United States, Vol. 3, p. 447.

Pennsylvania with the crops of rich counties to barter for the city's wares. In later years, when the pallium and the red hat, and other honors had been heaped upon him, the primate of the American Church used sometimes to point out this quaint building to favored friends, who accompanied him in his long walks about the city.

Here, in 1834, lived Thomas Gibbons, father of the Cardinal, who was employed by Howell & Sons, a firm which for many years carried on an importing business on Gay street. He was one of thousands of young Irish farmers who had lately been swarming to America to seek their fortunes. The bloody days of 1798 were not long gone by; and Daniel O'Connell was even then spreading the propaganda which he hoped would free his prostrate country from her wretchedness, but which, like others, was to end in disaster. Thomas Gibbons was born in 1800, and grew up near Westport, County Mayo. There he married Bridget Walsh, a deeply religious young woman, of strong character, the daughter of a neighboring farmer. Shortly after their marriage the couple emigrated in a sailing vessel to Canada, and after a short stay there, settled in Baltimore, in search of a milder climate and fuller opportunities in life. Six children were born to them, the first three being daughters and the last three sons.

James was the eldest son. He was baptized in the Cathedral by Rev. Dr. Charles I. White. When Father White, after a long life spent in works of piety, died pastor of St. Matthew's Church, Washington, in 1878, it was Archbishop Gibbons who preached the sermon at his funeral.

Thomas Gibbons became a citizen of the United States, and, like many of his fellow-countrymen, was an intense admirer of Andrew Jackson, whose crushing defeat of the English at New Orleans had made him a hero in their eyes. His infant son, the Cardinal-to-be, was proudly held up in arms to see "Old Hickory" on one of the latter's triumphal visits to Baltimore. Though the young immigrant's affairs prospered fairly well in America, his health failed, and his physician advised a long trip. He took his family back to Ireland in 1837, when James was three years old, and there he decided to remain, buying land near Westport and settling down again to the life of a farmer.

The future Cardinal's education was begun at the age of seven years, when he was sent to a private classical school at Ballinrobe, near Westport, taught at first by a Mr. Jennings, and later by John J. Rooney. He was a slender lad, with clear blue eyes and brown hair, and, though his health was not the strongest, his ardent love of outdoor life helped to develop a vitality which in future years enabled him to sustain the greatest fatigues of mind and body. An eager intellect and the power of intense application made him an apt pupil. When the elements had been mastered, he began with avidity the study of history, languages and mathematics, unraveling, by the laborious methods of Irish schools in those days, the polished sentences of Virgil, Ovid, Cicero and Livy, and delving hard into Xenophon and Homer. The English classics particularly fascinated him. Addison, Goldsmith, Johnson and Moore were his favorites, and to his pronounced fondness for the study of such models was due, in large measure, that limpid clearness of expression which became a striking characteristic of his literary style in later years. A remarkable memory enabled him to quote off-hand many poems he had read. He received much help from his maternal grandfather, James Walsh, for whom he had been named—a scholarly man who taught him the principles of mathematics.

Among those strenuous Irish lads, bubbling with vitality, sports were rough when the stern discipline of long school hours was lifted. They wrestled and boxed, ran and jumped, played cricket, football, handball and prisoner's base, which later developed into the American game of baseball. Young Gibbons, though not so sturdy of frame as some of his companions, loved the rigor of their contests as much as any. He played as hard as he studied, and a mark which he carried on one of his fingers through life was left by an injury received in a game of cricket.

Among the fifty boys at the school were not a few who rose to distinction. One of them, Thomas Tighe, became a member of Parliament, and held other important offices. His two brothers, Robert and James Tighe, adopted the career of officers in the English army, as did another schoolmate of the Cardinal, General Sillery. The future Bishop MacCormack, of Galway, was also a pupil at Ballinrobe. Thomas Tighe lived to a ripe old age. He used to recall James as an amiable lad, very studious and talented, and a marked favorite in the school.*

James was confirmed by Archbishop McHale at such an early age that he was rejected on account of his youth when he sought the privilege in company with other children; but, mingling in the stream of the favored ones, he received the rite notwithstanding this obstacle, and was praised for his precocity. The deep piety of his mother exerted a marked influence on him in the impressionable period of his early life.

The Gibbons family might have remained in Ireland and the Cardinal's lot might not have been cast in his native country, had not the death of his father in 1847, when the lad was 13 years old, changed the whole outlook. The energetic mother, thus suddenly left with the responsibility of a young family, decided to return to America with her children, and they embarked on a sailing ship at Liverpool for New Orleans. It was a long trip, .destined to be marked by shipwreck and a providential escape for all on board. They sailed from Liverpool in January, 1853, and it was the middle of March before the islands skirting the American coast were sighted. Near midnight on March 17, in calm weather, the vessel went fast aground on a sand bar close to the Island of Great Bahama, and, had the wind proved treacherous, none might have escaped

---

* Extract from a letter written by Thomas Tighe, May 27, 1909.

the sea. But fate was favorable, and, after waiting in great anxiety for the dawn, they were transferred in small boats to the island, whence they were carried to Nassau and kindly treated until they could continue their journey.

Arriving in New Orleans, James obtained employment as clerk in a grocery store on Camp street, kept by William C. Raymond. It was one of the business establishments characteristic of New Orleans in those days, supplying the needs of Mississippi river steamers and plantations, as well as families of the city. Little did the rough river men, or the elegant country gentlemen who came in from their broad acres of cotton or sugar to buy for themselves and their slaves, think that the obliging youth who waited on them would some day rise to eminence attained by few Americans.

Young Gibbons' intelligence, industry and fidelity attracted the notice of Mr. Raymond, and he was soon offered promotion. He was seriously thinking at this time of the choice of a career; and a mission held at St. Joseph's Church in the spring of 1854 served to fix his aspirations in the channel from which they were never to swerve. This mission was conducted by three remarkable young Redemptorist priests from New York— Revs. Isaac Thomas Hecker, Clarence Walworth and Augustine Hewit. All were converts from Protestantism. Idealists by nature and gifted with brilliant talents, they had run the gamut of religious aspiration and had at last taken refuge within the fold of the Catholic Church as the haven where the eager inquiries of their restless natures might find satisfaction. Of the three, Hecker was easily the leader.* In earlier years he had been a member of the socialistic community at Brook Farm and a companion of Ralph Waldo Emerson and George William Curtis. A venture in business life had failed to satisfy him. Converted to the Catholic faith in 1844, he had been ordained a priest but five years before he began his mission in New Orleans. His magnetic preaching kindled a fire within

---

* Elliott, Life of Father Hecker.

the soul of young Gibbons, who joined in the devotions with a new fervor and spirit. The priesthood became his goal, in which determination he was also greatly influenced by his confessor, Father Dufoe, a Jesuit, and by Father Duffy, a Redemptorist.

Four years after this mission closed, Hecker, Walworth and Hewit, with two companions, obtained the papal permission to found the Congregation of Missionary Priests of St. Paul, in which they realized their zealous hope of devoting their lives to preaching for the conversion of Protestants. The great work of the "Paulist Fathers" since that time has been their monument; but not the least of the fruits of Hecker's ardent labors for the development of the Church in America was the accession of the young New Orleans clerk to the roll of "Ambassadors of Christ."*

Mr. Raymond was loath to see his youthful friend forsake a business career, in which the prospects of success seemed so bright. A warm friendship had sprung up between these two which was to end only with the death of Raymond, many years afterward. Mrs. Gibbons, too, was reluctant to part from her eldest son, on whom she had grown to lean more as his talents and character ripened with years and in whom the widowed mother hoped to find the prop of her old age. James' decision remained fixed, and at last all acquiesced in the step he was resolved to take.

In the summer of 1855, when he was 21 years old, he started for Baltimore, having decided to make his native city and state the scene of the labors upon which he was about to enter. His mother, his eldest sister, Mary, and his younger brother, John, who had already begun to climb the ladder of riches in the grain trade, remained in New Orleans, his sister Catherine having died in Ireland at the age of 17. His journey was beset with delays and difficulties in those days, before

---

* Hewit had been a clergyman of the Protestant Episcopal Church. Walworth was a son of Reuben H. Walworth, a distinguished Chancellor of the State of New York.

the conveniences of the railroad had been generally extended. He went by steamer up the Mississippi and the Ohio to Cincinnati, and thence by rail most of the way to Baltimore, though it was necessary to cross part of the Alleghenies by stage. Sixteen days after he left New Orleans he arrived in Baltimore, and soon entered St. Charles College, Ellicott City, Md., then recently erected on land given by Charles Carroll, where he began his classical studies in preparation for the priesthood.

The next two years were spent at St. Charles, where the keenness of his mind and the thoroughness of his earlier education at once made him a pupil of note. He took up again the study of the ancient and modern classics, and so zealous was he to pursue these, that he wanted to remain another year, but Rev. Oliver L. Jenkins, president of the college, refused permission on the ground that he was already thoroughly equipped to enter St. Mary's Seminary, in Baltimore, and begin the second stage of his course. His character in those early days of his manhood seems to have made an impression on his fellow-students at St. Charles; but it was too early to predict for him, among so many other bright young men, that he would rise to any extraordinary height. His modesty and amiability tended to keep him in the background. One of his comrades was John S. Foley, later Bishop of Detroit, a member of a noted Catholic family of Baltimore, who, after the lapse of many years, wrote thus of his recollections of the future Cardinal:

"The burdens of his high office have told upon his slender frame with advancing years, and yet as he rises before my mental retrospect I cannot see much change in the supple, trim figure that entered so ardently into our youthful sports. He still preserves the grace of movement of his early days, when with all his apparent delicacy he proved himself to be as elastic as tempered steel. Those were the days when the fixed rules of football a la Rugby were unknown or ignored, and I recall with an accelerated pulse the dash with which the Cardinal *in petto* broke into the melee around the elusive sphere and ruthlessly beat down all opponents.   Whatever he did was done with all his might, and that is the philosophy of his story. He engaged in his studies in the same earnest, indefatigable fashion that he exhibited at football or in the racquet court, and his mind was as active as his body, full of spring and resiliency.   He was a youth, too, of noble and generous impulses, and his unaffected modesty was a most charming trait of his character.   All these splendid attributes he has carried with him into the turbulent arena of life.   *   *   *   With him, life is real, life is earnest."

In September, 1857, he began his training at St. Mary's, under the presidency of Rev. Francois L'Homme, a French Sulpician.   Owing to the inadequate facilities in those days, many American priests were still educated abroad, and a large number of others who labored among the American people were of foreign birth.   The devoted fathers of St. Mary's had come to Baltimore in Bishop Carroll's time to begin the work of training a native priesthood, and French influence was still strong in the institution, whose mother house remained in Paris.   Since the Council of Trent, the Church had insisted on rigorously thorough preparation for the duties of the ministry, and young men who aspired to that calling were forced to go where they could obtain the training.   Protestant churches, which did not exact these requirements, early recruited their ministers from native soil, and accepted them with such education as they could obtain at home.   The Lutheran clergy, most of whom still spoke German in the pulpit, continued to be predominantly Teutonic; and not a few of the Protestant Episcopal priesthood were Englishmen, or graduates of English colleges.   A largely increasing number of Americans were seeking holy orders in the Catholic Church, and the tide was fast turning from Paris and Louvain.

The training of the future Cardinal at St. Mary's was as strict as at European seminaries—the stern course in phi-

---

* Reily, Collections in the Life and Times of Cardinal Gibbons, Vol. 3, pp. 82, 83.

St. Charles' College. Ellicott City. Md.. where Cardinal Gibbons Studied

losophy, theology, scripture, church history and canon law; the prolonged meditations and devotions; the searching scrutiny of character, and the Spartan rigor of labors that might not stop for fatigue.   Young Gibbons met every test, being described by his teachers as "having exceptional facility in his studies and as applying himself with great eagerness.*" He "possessed a cheerful and even temper, and gained the esteem and affection of all."   Despite the severity of the course, he customarily spent an hour each day in devotional reading of scripture, instead of twenty minutes, which were obligatory.   His success in philosophy was so marked that he was appointed master of the conferences held three times a week by the students to discuss the points covered by the lectures of the professor and to arrive at a fuller understanding of them.   The professor of philosophy at that time, Rev. Francois P. Dissez, survived to celebrate the fiftieth anniversary of his entrance into the seminary, and he recalled throughout his long life the zeal and industry of his distinguished pupil.

Young Gibbons received the tonsure September 15, 1858, at the hands of Archbishop Kenrick, who conferred upon him the four minor orders June 16 of the following year.   The same prelate promoted him to the subdiaconate June 28, 1861, to the diaconate June 29, and to the priesthood June 30.

Deep shadows were drawing over the country in those closing years at the seminary.   In their brief periods devoted to general conversation the students had anxiously discussed the exciting events of the time—the John Brown raid, the fugitive slave riots, and the formation of the Southern Confederacy. Blood was already being shed in civil war when the young priest was ordained.   His associations and sympathies were with the Southern people, among whom he had lived, but his judgment opposed secession as a political step.   He remained a Union man to the end, though taking no part by word or

* Records of St. Mary's Seminary.

deed in the struggle that was rending his unhappy country. His not to draw the sword, but to preach peace and mercy; not to stir the passions of men, but to point them to the example of their Divine Master.   He had chosen his path; where the cross led, he would follow.

CHAPTER II.

AT ST. PATRICK'S AND ST. BRIDGET'S.

One Sunday morning in July, 1861, the congregation of St. Patrick's Church, Baltimore, saw within the sanctuary a young priest, lightly built, yet graceful and well-proportioned, of medium height, with a strong face and a large, firm mouth, softened by a singularly sweet and winning expression. When he spoke, his voice was clear, almost perfectly toned and musical, like the notes of a silver bell. The fascination of his manner won the hearts of all. That day he was introduced to members of the congregation as Father Gibbons, newly appointed as assistant to Rev. James Dolan, the veteran pastor of St. Patrick's. Not a few of them lived to see him, so rapid was his advancement, a member of the Sacred College, famed in America and Europe both as a shepherd of souls and a leader of men.*

Father Dolan, known as "The Apostle of the Point"—St. Patrick's is situated on Fell's Point—was a priest of vigorous and aggressive activity, who had long carried on a notably successful work in East Baltimore, unaided, and did not want an assistant. He had managed to find a separate field of labor for every one who had been sent to him, and Father Gibbons was no exception. Seven years before, Father Dolan, in his missionary zeal, had built a little church on the edge of the city's eastern boundary, in a district called Canton, and named it St. Bridget's, after the patron saint of his mother. It was then temporarily under the jurisdiction of St. Patrick's Parish, and Father Gibbons had not been ordained more than six

---

* Mr. John Malloy, of Baltimore, who survives at a venerable age (1911), recalls distinctly the brief period of Father Gibbons' life when he was stationed at St. Patrick's and the impression he produced on the congregation, of which Mr. Malloy was a member at the time.

weeks when Father Dolan sent him there, saying, "Canton is a good school for a young priest." Toward the end of 1861 he was made full pastor of St. Bridget's by Archbishop Kenrick, and began in an independent field the only work as a parish priest he was destined to do.

The neighborhood was semi-rural, and, in the temper of the times, turbulent and dangerous. Maryland alone, of all the American States, had lately been carried by the Knownothing party, and Canton had been a favorite scene for the operations of the "Blood Tubs," a band composed of butchers and their lawless associates, who used to carry half-hogsheads of beef blood to the polling places and bespatter with the gory contents citizens who would not vote the anti-foreign ticket. The fury of this movement had not fully subsided when the Civil War, with its violent clashes of opinion in a border State, rent the city asunder with excitement. Federal troops had taken possession of Baltimore and erected a chain of fortifications, one of which, Fort Marshall, was thrown up in what is now Highlandtown, within the boundaries of St. Bridget's parish. Armed force took the place of law, and the volunteer soldiers, not yet trained to the restrictions of discipline, terrorized the community.*

It was under these trying circumstances that Father Gibbons began his pastorate. The Church was in a lonely place, surrounded by farms and market gardens. Only one dwelling— that of Mrs. Bridget Smyth, a devoted member of the congregation, four of whose grandsons became priests—was near. The rectory consisted of a few small rooms built against one end of the church, lacking in light and ventilation, the boards of the floor touching the ground. The good Mrs. Smyth pitied the hardships of the young pastor and sent him his first meal on the Saturday evening when he went to Canton to begin his labors.†

---

* Scharf, History of Baltimore City and County, p. 132.
† Surviving members of the Smyth family are authority for these statements.

ST. BRIDGET'S CHURCH, BALTIMORE., IN 1865

The congregation included some of the neighboring rural population, but was chiefly composed of laboring men from the copper works and rolling mills scattered along the Canton waterfront. With his tireless activity and remarkable faculty of making friends, Father Gibbons soon knew them all by name. So vivid was his memory for names and faces that the absorbing mental impressions of later years were never able to blot out his recollection of the devout flock of St. Bridget's, and his smile and instant recognition were theirs whenever he met them.

Soon after going to Canton, Archbishop Kenrick directed him to take charge of St. Lawrence's Church, since renamed for Our Lady of Good Counsel, on Locust Point, a mile across the Patapsco. In this capacity he served as volunteer chaplain at Fort McHenry, as well as at Fort Marshall. Every Sunday morning, in winter storms as well as summer calms, he left Canton about 6 o'clock, was rowed in a skiff across to Locust Point, heard confessions at St. Lawrence's, said mass, preached, baptized, attended sick calls; then recrossed the river to Canton, where he celebrated high mass at half-past 10 o'clock and preached again. No obstacle deterred him. His kindhearted housekeeper used to bundle him up in stormy weather and tie her shawl over his head, but many of his trips meant keen suffering. When the river was impassable, he would travel to St. Lawrence's in a sleigh or carriage, crossing at the head of the harbor by way of Light street, several miles up. As no Catholic clergyman may celebrate mass except while fasting, it was usually about 1 o'clock in the afternoon when, after a morning's arduous labor, he could eat. This ordeal seriously impaired his digestion and compelled him to observe great care in diet throughout his life. "It killed my stomach," he used to say.

The decline of his health caused some of his parishioners to express the opinion at one time that he "could not live two months." Tuberculosis was suspected; but one day he returned from an examination by his doctor and joyfully announced that his lungs were sound.* The living conditions of the rectory were bad enough, but he made them worse by devoting a part of his limited quarters to the purposes of a hall for fairs and church meetings, leaving only a small sleeping-room which he called his own. When a fair was in progress at a late hour he would sometimes pass through the hall, returning from a pastoral call, and bid the merrymakers a smiling goodnight, saying, "I must go to bed now," as he disappeared in his little apartment. Directly above his living-room he established a parochial school, and the noise and trampling overhead did not seem to diminish his satisfaction that the children of his parish were thus provided for.

When he was able to obtain sufficient means, he built a new and suitable rectory of brick, in conformity with the style of the church. In order to carry out this project, he had to raise a considerable sum of money. As a means to the end, he decided to secure a large building in the center of the city for a fair, and applied to the lessee of Carroll Hall, a noted place for public assemblies in those days. At first the lessee assumed an air of suspicious coldness and was far from inclined to grant the request. After Father Gibbons had explained the circumstances to him more fully, his attitude changed and he readily yielded, besides making ample apologies for what had seemed discourtesy. A few words explained all. "I thought you were a Yankee," said this stout-hearted sympathizer with the Confederacy.

The war feeling was so intense that part of the congregation of the Cathedral left on several occasions when the prayer for the authorities was said. This prayer had been framed by Archbishop Carroll, and, among other things, besought that

---

* Mr. John J. Donnelly and Mrs. Peter Hagan, members of St. Bridget's Congregation, 1861-65, who lived to old age, recalled distinctly a number of incidents of that period, which have been incorporated in this work. Many traditions linger from the same period, which have been rejected unless confirmed.

the people might be "preserved in union," which by no means accorded with the views of the secessionists.

Natural inclination developed in earlier years, and the large area of his parish, in which there were no street cars at the time, made Father Gibbons a pedestrian, and this tended to restore his health. His habit of taking long walks has continued through life, and has been, perhaps, the most potent means of sustaining him in the manifold and prolonged activities, the endurance of which so often created amazement in others. He seemed going all the time. No detail of the field was too small to receive his painstaking attention; no locality too dangerous to be penetrated by the devoted priest, bent on his mission of mercy and help.

His duties at Fort McHenry required courage and circumspection. This place, hallowed in American history, had been made a prison for Confederate soldiers and for civilians who fell under the ban. Members of the Maryland Legislature suspected of favoring secession were held there by the power of the bayonet. Among the noted prisoners were George William Brown, Severn Teackle Wallis, Ross Winans and George P. Kane. Father Gibbons ministered to Federal and Confederate alike. At one time there were in the fort four Confederates who had been sentenced to be hanged. Three of them— John R. H. Embert, Samuel B. Hearn and Braxton Lyon— had been with the army in Virginia, and, in a lull of the campaign, had succeeded in crossing the Chesapeake to visit their families on the Eastern Shore. Though not spies, they were arrested as such, court-martialed, and received the death sentence with another Confederate, William H. Rodgers, said to have been a blockade-runner.* Father Gibbons was called to attend Embert. The sentence was to be executed immediately after 12 o'clock Sunday night, August 29, 1864; but when the

---

* Official Records of the Union and Confederate Armies. Series 2, Vol. 7, pp. 792, 834, 1040, 1291; Vol. 8, pp. 87, 114, 115, 132, 395, 436, 650.

young priest arrived at the gate of the fort to prepare the prisoner for death, he was told that the penalty had been commuted by President Lincoln a few hours before to imprisonment during the war.   John W. Garrett, president of the Baltimore and Ohio Railroad, and other prominent men had interceded for the four Confederates and the merciful President had lent a ready ear.

The men thus snatched from the verge of the grave by executive clemency were sent to Albany.   After the close of the war, when Father Gibbons had been transferred to the Cathedral, he was surprised to receive a visit from Embert. Their greetings were warm, but were scarcely over before his caller said:

"Father, I am delighted to see you under more favorable circumstances than confronted us at Fort McHenry; and, as you did not have the opportunity of tying the knot around my neck on that occasion, I ask you now to tie a more pleasing knot."

He had come to be married, and Father Gibbons performed the ceremony.

The young clergyman's courage was repeatedly proved in those stirring times.   Returning to St. Bridget's rectory one night, he found a soldier asleep in the yard, and started to arouse him with an admonition to leave the church property. The soldier leaped to his feet, seized a paling from a broken fence and rushed at him with the fury of a tiger.   Father Gibbons turned and ran toward his door, but soon found himself trapped in an angle formed by wall and fence from which there was no escape.   The soldier had the paling raised to strike him a murderous blow, when, realizing that he must defend himself quickly, he summoned all his strength, knocked the man down and thoroughly subdued him.   When the big soldier came to his senses he realized that the frail young man in priestly dress was more than his match, and beat a precipitate retreat.

On another night, arriving at his rectory after collecting money for the church, he was met outside tne door by his housekeeper, in tears, who told him a crazy man was inside. It proved to be an intruder of herculean size, naked and raving, who had taken possession of the premises and was threatening everybody.   Father Gibbons found no weapon at hand but an umbrella, with which he belabored the man to such good effect that in a short time he forced him to dress and leave the house.

He was often in danger from drunken soldiers, and always avoided a conflict when he could do so, but when that was not possible, proved that he could defend himself against any.

The entries of Father Gibbons in the parish record of St. Bridget's, written in a delicate and well-proportioned but firm hand, have been carefully preserved by the pastors who have succeeded him.   They tell the ordinary story of a priest's life—baptisms, weddings, financial details.   He neglected nothing, and became as familiar a figure to the people of Canton as the smokestacks of their mills.   His own congregation was devoted to the young priest, and, as he was never heard to say anything distasteful to non-Catholics or to refuse his ministrations to any, he was almost as well liked by those of faiths different from his own.   Traits that were to mark him in later life were developing strongly.   He was an accurate judge of men and women, and had a remarkable faculty for organization, which he put to good use in stimulating the work of the church in every direction.   The young folk would walk miles to help him, and the older parishioners were charmed by his respectful and sincere attentions.   Not infrequently he was called to travel long distances out the suburban roads which led into Baltimore through the Canton district, for churches were few and priests fewer in those days, even in Maryland.   Sparse outlying communities were in many cases too poor to support pastors, and the political and economic confusion of the times arrested the spread of the gospel.

Baltimore was passing through a dreadful experience during the period of his pastorate at St. Bridget's.   Known to be predominantly in sympathy with the South, the city worked and slept at the mouths of cannon planted by General B. F. Butler on Federal Hill, a bold eminence in the southern part of the city.   Thousands of young Baltimoreans had passed the gauntlet of the Union lines and gone south to fight for the Confederacy, leaving their families behind, racked by anxiety and scanning with sickened hearts the latest bulletins of bloody losses at the front.   Other thousands had voluntarily entered or been drafted into the Federal army, and wife, son and daughter counted themselves fortunate if their loved ones came back wounded, but living.   When the Southern tide rose with the genius of Lee, precautions at Washington were doubled to prevent Maryland from falling into the hands of the Confederacy; and in the agonized waiting at the end, while the requiem of the new republic was being sounded by the artillery around Petersburg, none in Baltimore knew who was friend or foe.

On the night of Good Friday, April 14, 1865, Father Gibbons was preaching in St. Joseph's Church, Baltimore.   His topic was the crucifixion.   With one of those apt similes which were characteristic of his literary and oratorical style, he pictured a benevolent ruler, exercising his authority with clemency, suddenly stricken down by the hand of a subject.   A short time after the congregation had been dismissed the streets filled with people, and from lip to lip passed the fateful bulletin, "Lincoln has been shot!"   In the light of the tragedy which startled the world, the words of Father Gibbons took on a strange significance.   That night there was a terrible commotion in Baltimore.   A week later the body of the murdered President was brought to the city, and Father Gibbons, with some of the other clergy, marched in the procession which escorted it to the rotunda of the Exchange, where it lay in State.*

---

* Scharf, Chronicles of Baltimore, p. 634.

Among the congregations which he served there was deep sympathy with the South; but he went about his work without mingling in the polemics of the time, though his heart bled for the agonies of the helpless which are always the fruit of war, no matter what the issue to be decided, nor under what flag the sword be unsheathed.

CHAPTER III.

SECRETARY TO ARCHBISHOP SPALDING.

The talents of Father Gibbons, combined with his piety and indefatigable zeal, attracted the attention of Archbishop Spalding, who had been raised in 1864 from the Bishopric of Louisville to the See of Baltimore, after the death of Archbishop Kenrick. It had been remarked of the young priest, as his powers developed, that he seemed "destined for leadership," though he had scant opportunity to show his real mettle in the little field of St. Bridget's. The shock was great to the devoted congregation when it was announced in October, 1865, that he had been transferred to the Cathedral as the Archbishop's secretary, and the people of Canton could hardly realize that the smiling face and gentle ministrations which had become interwoven as a part of their daily lives were to be missed from among them. A petition to have him retained was started, but it was soon seen that this would be futile.

It was a time when the Church had need of her strong men. The passions following the Civil War were at their worst, and grew daily in ferocity. The United States Government had used pressure at Rome against the appointment of Archbishop Spalding, because it was feared that he was not sufficiently in accord with the policy of repression toward the South.* This had failed, and the Church had been able to proceed serenely on her mission, unclouded by the storms of the political atmosphere. Whole States were in ruin, and the ministrations of religion were more necessary, and at the same time much more

---

* O'Gorman. History of the Roman Catholic Church in the United States, p 433; Shea, History of the Catholic Church in the United States, Vol. 4, p. 493; Riordan, Cathedral Records, Baltimore, p. 77.

difficult to convey, than before the gigantic conflict. Hundreds of families in the Diocese of Baltimore. as elsewhere, were mourning the loss of father, brother, son. In the counties of Southern Maryland, the soil in which the Catholic faith had first taken root among English-speaking people in the Western Hemisphere, the slaves had been freed, and poverty spread its shadow where the refinements of an affluent aristocracy had lately flourished.

To meet the emergency by dealing comprehensively with all the pressing problems of the Church in America, the Second Plenary Council of Baltimore was convened in the Cathedral in October, 1866. Father Gibbons was made its assistant chancellor, and for the first time was thrown into an arena where the larger outlook of the Church immediately confronted him. He fitted into these surroundings as if they had always been a part of him. A natural statesman, who might have been a Richelieu in world politics had he been a typical Frenchman of the seventeenth century instead of a typical American of the nineteenth, men of lesser parts instinctively looked to him. Where others might be unprogressive, impractical, out of touch with the times, too ardent or controversial, he was cool, judicial, far-seeing, enlightened, inspired by sentiments of lofty patriotism, as well as by the brilliant fire of apostolic zeal. He was already formulating in his mind those grand ideas which he was one day to impress on the world; and his contact with the leading men of the American Church served to give him the bearings with which he might start on his real career.

Archbishop Spalding presided over the council, and to Father Gibbons, as his secretary and the assistant chancellor, fell a large share of the work of the gathering. Among its most important acts was the creation of a number of new dioceses, subject to confirmation by the Holy See, to stimulate the spread of the faith in the stricken South and the growing communities of the North and West. One of these was the vicariate apostolic of North Carolina. So strong an impression had Father Gibbons made on the assembled bishops that, though but 32 years old and only five years removed from the seminary, he was unanimously nominated for this important post.

The decrees of the council were signed by seven archbishops, thirty-nine bishops or their procurators, and two abbots. An important declaration, destined to be quoted as a precedent by the fathers of the Church in Rome itself in a few years, related to the office of the Supreme Pontiff. The council decreed that he spoke with "the living and infallible authority" of the whole Church, "which was built by Christ upon Peter, who is the head, body and pastor of the whole Church, whose faith Christ promised should never fail; which ever had legitimate pontiffs, dating their origin in unbroken line from Peter himself, being seated in his chair and being the inheritors and defenders of the like doctrine, dignity, office and power."

The other decrees of the council need not be cited at length here. Among the many subjects treated were the dissensions among Protestant sects, and zeal for their conversion. Unitarianism and Universalism were condemned, the one as denying the divinity of Christ, and the other as rejecting the doctrine of eternal punishment. Transcendentalism and Pantheism were defined as human systems, which, having dethroned God, would make a deity of man. Warnings were given against spiritism and magnetism. There was held to be little reason for doubt that some of the manifestations of spiritism were the works of Satan. It was pointed out that the leaders of the system deny the divinity of Christ and the supernatural in religion.

Preachers, it was declared, were to employ an explanatory, rather than a controversial, style in their sermons, and to adapt themselves to the capacity of their auditors. In reprehending vices, they were never to become personal. They should declare the truth fearlessly, without being influenced by human motives. Attacks were not to be made from the pulpit on public magistrates, nor were priests to mingle political and civic topics with religious doctrines. Care must be taken not to bestow undue praise in funeral orations. Prolixity in sermons was to be avoided. Priests should avoid recourse to civil tribunals when possible. They should abstain from all improper spectacles and games. Regarding money matters, they were not to be importunate in addressing their congregations. The practice of taking money on deposit, for which interest was to be paid, was condemned. The clergy should avoid idleness as a pest. Greater provision for the education of priests, and for the erection of preparatory schools as well as seminaries, was recommended.

It was decreed that mixed marriages were to be discouraged. Bishops should seek to use a uniform method in granting matrimonial dispensations. Catholics might be buried with sacred rites in a non-Catholic cemetery if they possessed a lot in such a place, provided it was not obtained in contempt of Church law. Free burial must be given the poor. Entrance money was not to be collected at churches.

Stress was laid on the proper education of youth. It was urged that parish schools should be erected by every congregation, and the instruction, when possible, should be by teachers belonging to religious congregations. Catechism classes were to be instituted in the churches for children who attended the public schools. A strong desire for the establishment of a Catholic University in the United States—a dream to be realized in the near future—was expressed.

In addition to the Masonic order, long previously condemned by the Church, the Odd Fellows and the Sons of Temperance were forbidden. The faithful, it was decreed, should not enter any society which, having designs against church or state, bound its members with an oath of secrecy.*

The council adjourned after a session of two weeks. Its closing ceremonies were attended by President Andrew John-

---

* Acta et Decreta Conc. Plen. II, Baltimore, 1868. Sermons and Pastoral Letter, Second Plenary Council, published by Kelly & Piet, Baltimore, 1866.

son, whom Father Gibbons met on that occasion, the first of a long line of Presidents whom he was to know and with many of whom he was to have close and important relations.*

The nominations of the new bishops were not confirmed until 1868, and in the meantime Father Gibbons continued his work at the Cathedral. In January, 1866, he had established the first Sunday-school there, and it became so popular that he was able to report, in a letter to the Secretary of the Maryland Senate calling attention to the work of the parochial schools, that its average attendance in 1867 was 500. He taught classes in catechism regularly at Calvert Hall School and St. Mary's Orphan Asylum. His sermons soon attracted attention, and he was in demand at churches throughout the city. At this period the rare gifts as an orator in the best sense, which were to make him one of the foremost preachers of his time, were being rapidly perfected by experience and matured thought. The classical simplicity and beauty of his English could not fail to charm; his logic was sound, his learning solid; and the clearness and sweetness of his voice, which could fill a large hall without effort, combined with magnetism of manner that gripped the attention instantly, formed a rare medium for the virile ideas with which his pulpit utterances teemed.

In a remarkable degree he had the confidence of Archbishop Spalding, as he had later of Bayley, the successor of Spalding. The Baltimore Cathedral has long been a cradle of bishops, and the young secretary in 1865-68 proved to be the brightest ornament of them all. The surroundings are singularly well adapted to bring out of priests their capacity for the executive work of the Church. They live in the Archbishop's house and sit at his table. Here not only the affairs of the diocese, but, to a large extent, those of the American Church center. All avenues lead to the seat of the primatial see, and in this sense Baltimore is the Rome of America. The parish contains some of the most important Catholic families of the United States,

---

* Shea, History of the Catholic Church in the United States, Vol. 4, p. 720.

CARDINAL GIBBONS AS PRIEST IN 1866

FATHER GIBBONS STANDING, REV HENRY B COSKERY. V G., IS SEATED

pillars of the Church since the days of Leonard Calvert. The clergy thus have under their spiritual care a highly cultivated element, in whose social life they mingle and from whose environment they draw a certain inspiration.

The archiepiscopal residence stands in dignified semi-isolation on a large lot on Charles street, in surroundings which in 1865-68 were almost Athenian in their refinement. It is of gray stone and brick, two stories high, with a large basement, and is constructed in the breadth of proportion characteristic of Baltimore homes of the better class in the early half of the nineteenth century, but without any trace of magnificence of architecture or ornament. At the rear a paved walk leads to the Cathedral, which stands, like the house, on a hill where the victorious troops of Rochambeau encamped on the return from Yorktown in 1782. A tall flight of steps leads to the front door of the house, which sets back in a recess of the wall. Inside is an English hallway extending the full length of the building, flanked on each side by spacious rooms, furnished with marked simplicity—almost scantily. Not a trace of luxury can be seen. On the walls are religious paintings and portraits of prelates identified with the archdiocese, with a bust or two here and there. A bay window, standing out boldly, is a vantage point for reviewing parades.

The residence was originally a small building, erected in the administration of Archbishop Whitfield and occupied by him for the first time in 1830. Captain William Kennedy and his wife contributed a large sum in 1865, by means of which two wings were built and another story added. A conspicuous tablet in the library commemorates this gift.

Here, when Father Gibbons was a member of Archbishop Spalding's household, was the heart of fashionable Baltimore. Across the street and up and down were the houses of the rich and cultured, the historic families of Maryland, and on the sidewalks trooped the belles and beaux of the town. Charles street at that point does not twist sharply like its neighbor,

St. Paul street, which is said to have followed the tracks of a cow-path originally; but so numerous are the hills that scarcely a level spot is to be found. Inside and outside the archiepiscopal residence the atmosphere is one of lofty things, and every priest who has lived there has felt its stimulus.

CHAPTER IV.

VICAR APOSTOLIC OF NORTH CAROLINA.

In the Baltimore Cathedral, where he had been baptized, ordained, and at whose altar he had served as priest, Father Gibbons was consecrated titular bishop of Adramyttum and vicar apostolic of North Carolina August 16, 1868. He stood among the venerable men there assembled the youngest member of the American hierarchy. Rev. Thomas A. Becker, who had also been a member of the "school of bishops"—the Cathedral household—was raised to the See of Wilmington, Del., at the same time. The two new prelates received the crozier, ring and miter at the hands of their friend and patron, Archbishop Spalding. Another Cathedral priest, Rev. Thomas Foley, chancellor of the diocese, and afterward Bishop of Chicago, delivered the sermon.*

It was a beautiful day, and a great crowd assembled to witness the imposing ecclesiastical ceremony. As always on important occasions at the Cathedral, the procession was long, including the students from St. Charles College and St. Mary's Seminary, immediately in the rear of the cross-bearer, acolytes and sanctuary boys. Then came the clergy of the diocese, the superiors of religious orders, the bishops and archbishops. The hierarchy of the day was well represented by Bishops O'Hara, of Scranton, and Shanahan, of Harrisburg, themselves newly consecrated; Bayley, of Newark, destined to succeed to the See of Baltimore and exercise a strong influence on Bishop Gibbons' life; McGill, of Richmond, whose chair he was to occupy four years later; Whelan, of Wheeling; Domenec, of Pitts-

---

* An extended account of these ceremonies was given in the *Catholic Mirror*, the church paper of the Baltimore Archdiocese, August 22, 1868, which is authority for many of the facts related here.

burg, and Lynch, of Charleston. Dr. Henry B. Coskery, vicar-general of the diocese, was a deacon-of-honor to the Arch-bishop and shared the regrets of the Cathedral household in losing such an agreeable and useful companion.

Father Foley spoke from an overflowing heart in the words of his sermon addressed to the new vicar apostolic. "And you, Right Reverend Sir," he said, "are to go to the large State of North Carolina. It appalls one to think of that State of more than a million inhabitants, with but a few altars and one or two priests to minister at them. This is the work which the Holy Ghost, which the Supreme Pontiff, which the united body of our bishops in council assembled, have cut out for you, a work which plainly bespeaks the character which you hold with them. It would not do for me to speak from personal observation and with the feelings which I bear toward you. You have been associated with us, like your Right Reverend companion, at this altar. You were of our household and home. We have had the opportunity of observing in both not only those great characteristics which ought to be found in every Christian priest, but also those interior traits of virtue which embellish and complete the man of God. We, then, who have lived with you for years, if our testimony be of avail, added to that which the Holy Spirit, the Supreme Pontiff and the prelates of our country have given, cheerfully and truth-fully offer it. We have seen you both doing the toil of the priesthood, helping the poor, instructing the ignorant, visiting the sick at all hours; thinking nothing too laborious or too fatiguing for yourself and always willing to take not only your share of the labors, but ready to take a larger portion, that you might relieve your brother priests.

"Again, I say to you, that I cannot congratulate you on going to North Carolina, but I do rejoice for the honor which the Church of God has conferred on you, and I congratulate your flock, few and scattered, upon the advantage they are to derive from the apostolic mission you are to establish in that

State, which, in a religious sense, may be called a desert. It will not be long, I predict, before that desert will be made to bloom and produce much fruit, and your vicariate, now so poor and uninviting, will be able to compare with other dioceses of longer existence in religious prosperity."

The young Bishop remained in Baltimore a short time, confirming a class at his former church, St. Bridget's, dedicating St. Joseph's Monastery, since noted as a center for the work of the Passionists, and otherwise assisting Archbishop Spalding.

The Archbishop and Rev. Bernard J. McManus, of St. John's Church, Baltimore, accompanied him to Wilmington, N. C., where he arrived on Friday evening, October 30. He was received with joy by a delegation of the laity, headed by Rev. Mark S. Gross, a beloved priest of St. Thomas' Church, the only sanctuary of the Catholic faith in the city. The Bishop and his companions were taken in carriages to the residence of Col. F. W. Kerchner, one of the principal residents, a parishioner of St. Thomas', who welcomed them with southern hospitality. Major Reilly made an address in behalf of the laity, expressing gratitude that at last a bishop had been sent to North Carolina to build up the work of the Church and pledging the co-operation of Catholics as far as their means would go.

The new bishop responded with deep sincerity, thanking the faithful for their reception and hoping that the future would strengthen the bonds already established between the diocese and himself. He knew that the Catholics in the State were few and far between. He had not come among them to seek personal comfort; sent by constituted authority, he had only one object—their spiritual good and the salvation of souls. Regardless of sacrifices and difficulties, he was ready to expend his utmost efforts in the work, and he did not doubt that he would receive cordial co-operation. Archbishop Spalding spoke briefly, encouraging the Carolinians with hopes for the spread of the faith.

But there was another side to the picture. On the night following Bishop Gibbons' arrival, he beheld for the first time a torchlight procession of negroes, who were then, by alliance with the "carpet-baggers" from the North, in political control of the State. As he described the scene, it appeared like an inferno. "Is my lot to be cast in these surroundings?" he thought, with dismay. These wild and ignorant elements, suddenly sprung from slavery to power, had shaken the political and social fabric of the state to its foundations. Power to them meant an opportunity for turning loose the impulses of savagery. They even seized churches and devoted them to any use that suited their whim.

Soon after the new bishop arrived he was told of how the Catholic Church at New Bern had been saved a short time before from destruction. Captain McNamara, of the Federal Army, was riding past the church, when he saw a body of persons gathered about the door, apparently in charge of it, and asked their business.

"We have occupied this church for school purposes," said one of them.

"What is your authority?" inquired the Captain.

"Our authority is that of the United States Government and of Jesus Christ," answered the school mistress.

"Well," remarked the Captain, "that is pretty good authority; but, as a Federal officer, I am accustomed to obey written authority. Can you show papers from the sources you have mentioned?"

The teacher was at a loss for words, and the Captain continued:

"As you cannot produce the papers, my order is that you vacate this church at once and enter it no more for such purposes."

The shadow of the negro and "carpet-bagger" regime stretched from the mountains to the sea. On the first occasion when the bishop went to vote in the State, a negro official demanded that he show naturalization papers, and he had difficulty in convincing the suspicious black that he was native born. Another negro official ordered him peremptorily to tear down a frame shed on the church property in Wilmington because a city ordinance provided that buildings should be of brick or stone. The bishop pointed out that wooden buildings were standing on city property, but the negro insisted, and he was forced to cover the shed with tin.

Writing later of his experiences at this period,* he expressed the view that, "While right-thinking men are ready to accord to the colored citizen all to which he is fairly entitled, yet to give him control over a highly intellectual and intricate civilization, in creating which he has borne no essential part, and for conducting which his antecedents have manifestly unfitted him, would be hurtful to the country as well as to himself." In a subsequent political campaign in Maryland† he declared himself publicly against taking the suffrage from the negroes, but he adhered consistently to the view that their domination in political affairs would be madness.

On the Sunday after his arrival, the Bishop was installed in St. Thomas' Church. A pouring autumn rain descended, but the Church was filled. Archbishop Spalding preached a sermon, which served as a cordial introduction of the new prelate to the vicariate. "Your Bishop," he said, "was recommended by the Council of Bishops held in Baltimore a few years ago. He received their unanimous vote and holds his commission from Rome. I know him well. He is beloved by all who know him in Baltimore. There are few Catholics here, and they are poor. We cannot expect much at first. The Kingdom of God, steady in its increase, is the work of more than 1,800 years. The apostles were poor. They enriched the world with their heroic deeds of Christianity. They never failed, nor will they ever fail in their successors. I recommend your

---

* Reminiscences of Cardinal Gibbons read before the United States Catholic Historical Society of New York, May 25, 1891.
† 1908.

Bishop to you, not only to Catholics, but to all good Christian men who have the spread of Christ's religion on earth at heart.   *   *   *   He has not yet chosen his seat.   For the present, he will reside among you.   He improves upon acquaintance.   Though he will be found uncompromising in his principles of faith, he will be charitable to all, assist all, irrespective of sect or creed."

Bishop Gibbons postponed his own address to the congregation until vespers the same day.   On that occasion he began with expressions of gratitude to the Archbishop, who had left many pressing duties in Baltimore, "at the call of friendship," to install him in his new diocese.   He had come among them as a stranger, and yet he could not look upon himself in that light, called, as he was, by the Supreme Head of the Church to be their spiritual father.   Although he knew scarcely a face among all those in front of him, he knew the people of the diocese as citizens and sons of the South, for so was he.   They were not only united to one another by the bonds of a common faith, but were brothers linked by the ties of a common country and having the same material interests.   He had not doubted that a welcome awaited him in North Carolina, and would do his best to prove worthy of it.*

The field, as Father Foley had intimated, was almost untilled.   In the whole vicariate there were but three priests—Father Gross, Rev. Lawrence P. O'Connell and Rev. H. P. Northrop—and about 800 Catholics.   The faith which Bishop Gibbons had come to teach was not understood, but his wide sympathies and singular freedom from prejudice well fitted him for his trying task.   Father O'Connell was stationed at Charlotte, and Father Northrop, afterward Bishop of Charleston, was at New Bern.   Undaunted by his difficulties, the young Bishop began his labors.   As in many Southern churches, four small rooms had been partitioned off behind the sanctuary in the rear of St. Thomas'—two on the ground

---

* *Catholic Mirror*, Nov. 14, 1868 ; *Wilmington Daily Journal*, Nov. 3, 1868.

ST THOMAS' CHURCH, WILMINGTON, N. C.

floor and two upstairs—and these formed the pastoral residence. Father Gross shared his narrow quarters with the Bishop, there being no means to provide an episcopal house. These two devoted men of God were attached to each other by the warmest personal ties. Father Gross' large-hearted charity led him to give away so much that Bishop Gibbons sometimes found himself hard pressed to supply the funds for their little establishment. It was said of this saintly priest that if he had more than one hat or pair of trousers, he was sure to bestow the extra one on some needy parishioner. On one occasion, when he entered a store, it was noticed that he wore a laced shoe on one foot and a buttoned shoe on the other. When asked about it, he replied that he had given a pair to a poor man and had not noticed that they were not alike.

The Bishop had raised $7,000 before he left Baltimore to buy additional ground adjoining St. Thomas' Church, which was a small building and which he designed to enlarge. He spent some time in consolidating the foundations of the work in Wilmington, and then started on a tour of his diocese. Throughout the State he traveled, preaching and teaching, studying each locality, and, wherever opportunity offered, planting the seeds of a Catholic congregation. The leading people of the State, Protestants as well as Catholics, received him in their homes. When no other means were available, he instructed and preached in Protestant churches, courthouses, public halls, and even in Masonic lodge rooms. On a visit to Greenville, which he reached early one morning by boat, he went to the hotel to register, and met Dr. O'Hagan, a Protestant physician, who insisted that the Bishop should be his guest. During the morning he held a sort of levee. When it was learned that he intended to preach, the local judge offered him the use of the courthouse, and the trustees of the Methodist church put their house of worship at his disposal. He chose the church, and preached there at night to a large congregation, nearly all of whom were Protestants. The people were summoned by the church bell; the choir was the regular one of the church; the Bishop read from a Protestant Bible, and the only part of the service which was of his own faith was the sermon.

Everywhere crowds flocked to hear this liberal and zealous apostle of the faith.   They felt a pride in the youthful prelate, their own Bishop, pre-eminently a man of the people, mingling with all and winning friends everywhere by his rare graces of manner.   His gifts as a preacher were enough in themselves to form an attraction in the communities to which he went. Aimed especially to win those who were full of hostility to his creed, his sermons were of the simple truths of the gospel, the brotherhood of man, duty to God and country.   Prejudice melted before his words.   In the broken condition of the South, it was recognized on every hand that where Bishop Gibbons founded a church, it was an element of stability, of spiritual, social and material improvement, an inspiration to hope and progress.   Carolinians knew that he felt their woes and shared in their struggle upward from the ruins left by war.   It was said of him that he came to know every Catholic in the State by name.

His hardships in his travels would have taxed the strongest frame.   One of his converts was Dr. J. C. Monk, a physician who lived at Newton Grove, nearly a hundred miles from Wilmington.   His own account of Dr. Monk's conversion was as follows:*

"While I was absent in Europe at the Vatican Council, in 1870, a letter came through the post addressed 'To Any Catholic Priest of Wilmington, N. C.'   Father Gross received the letter, which was one of inquiry about the doctrines of the Catholic Church, and from Dr. J. C. Monk.   A correspondence was opened between us after my return from Rome.   I recommended certain Catholic books.   Dr. Monk procured these, and, having more fully instructed himself and his family in

---

* Reminiscences of Cardinal Gibbons read before the United States Catholic Historical Society of New York.

the faith, he and his household were all received into the Church. He came to Wilmington to make a profession of faith. I baptized the family and learned, with the deepest interest, of the circumstances that had led to his conversion and of his hopes in regard to the community in which he had lived all his life as a prominent physician.

"This was a remarkable conversion. The finger of God was here. Nor was the conversion to be barren of results. Dr. Monk returned home, after receiving my promise of a visit to his family. In due time Father Gross visited Newton Grove, and to a great throng in the open air preached on the true faith. From that time an earnest inquiry into the tenets of the Catholic Church sprang up among the people. Dr. Monk was a providential man for the diffusion of the faith. He was highly respected, and as a physician had access to every family in all that region. His zeal to enlighten the people was surpassed only by his solid piety and good example. Possessed of means, he liberally aided in every way the spread of the faith.

"A few months later I redeemed my promise of a visit to Newton Grove. The trip came near imperiling my life. I remember it was the month of March. The day of my departure opened with difficulties. The railway train left very early in the morning. Rising at 4 o'clock, I found the weather cold and rainy. The carriage failing to call for me, I was compelled, with the help of a boy, to carry my large, heavy valise, packed with mission articles, the distance of a mile to the depot. As I traveled northward, the rain became a furious storm of sleet and snow. Reaching the station, I found the brother of Dr. Monk, who had come to meet me, and on horseback, too, with ax in hand, to cut our way through the forests. The sleet and snow had covered the country and bound to earth, in many places across our course, the pine saplings that grew in dense bodies up to the margin of the road. A neighbor was with him to take me in his buggy. We started. It was a journey to be remembered—a trip of 21 miles in the

teeth of wind, rain, sleet and snow.   After a short exposure,
I was all but frozen by the violence of the storm and the intense cold.   We had ridden a number of miles, when, to my
delight, my friend drew rein at his own house.   I entered the
hospitable door, and the change was most grateful—from
cold and misery to warmth and comfort.

"In a few moments the housewife had brought in a hot
bath for my frozen feet, and the husband a supplement in the
way of a hot drink.   The generous hospitality restored, in a
very short time, my almost perished frame.   They were both
strangers, but the closest friends could not have treated me
more kindly.   I remained for dinner, and, as the weather had
become clear, we proceeded on our journey.   The next morning being Sunday, I celebrated mass in Dr. Monk's house, and
preached there later in the day to an earnest audience.   The
religious interest was profound.   It promised to become, as
it truly did, a movement of the whole district toward the
Catholic Church.

"Regular appointments were made for a visit by the priest,
and in a short time the brother of Dr. Monk, with his family,
embraced the Catholic faith.   The congregations that met on
the occasions of the priest's visits to Newton Grove were so
large that it became necessary to erect a temporary structure of
rough boards for their accommodation.*   This tabernacle answered admirably for the services, which were arranged to
suit the primitive state of affairs in that section.   The priest
appeared on the rostrum in his secular dress, and, after prayer
and reading of the Scriptures, delivered a long instruction on
the Catholic Church or some one of its doctrines.   The preaching, directed at the conversion of the people, was necessarily
simple in its character, historical and didactic.   Catechisms
and books of instruction were freely distributed after the sermons.   An attractive feature of these services was the singing, by select voices, of beautiful hymns.

---

* The number soon grew to three hundred.

"The Catholic movement daily gathered strength by the accession of many of the most respectable families in the vicinity. Within a short time the number of conversions warranted the erection of a church and schoolhouse. On their completion, this apostolic mission became firmly established and continues to prosper."

Another church sprang from a visit by a priest to three Irish brothers, peddlers, who had settled 80 miles from a church. Their families were baptized, and conversions among the country folk multiplied. In a short time a flourishing parish was established.

A missionary found at Chinquepin, a village far in the recesses of the North Carolina pines, an old Irish woman who had not seen a priest in 45 years. She said her faith was still as fresh as her native sod, and that she had never omitted her prayers. A congregation of converts was founded, for whom a chapel and school were subsequently erected.

On his mission journeys remote from railways, the Bishop used to ride in a dilapidated wagon drawn by two horses. A young priest, or sometimes a negro driver, accompanied him. The vehicle carried packages of clothing, flour and medicines for the poor; clerical robes, mission literature, and food for the wayfarers, for often they ate their noonday meal under a great tree, far from a habitation. This old wagon finally became so unsafe that the Bishop's friends were afraid it would break down and leave him stranded in the wilderness. They repeatedly offered to buy him a carriage, but he always replied that he thought the wagon might last a little longer. "Friends," he used to say, "you can give me the money, if you will, for the Church needs it, but not for any vehicle for my own use."

Priests were so rare in North Carolina in those days that they sometimes had difficulty in proving their identity. While Father O'Connell was traveling near Asheville, worn out by a long journey, he arrived at the house of a Catholic family and presented himself. The woman of the house had been imposed upon by a pretended clergyman some time before, and refused to believe Father O'Connell. He showed her his missal, vestments and breviary, which he carried in a valise, but she was still unconvinced. In despair, the tired priest gave up the attempt and turned, heartsick, from the door. Seeking spiritual comfort, he sat down beside a fence and began saying his beads. The woman opened the door, saw him at his devotions and was convinced at last. "Now," she said, "I know your are a holy man of God. I could be deceived about other things, but not those beads!" She welcomed warmly to her home the stranger whom she had so lately rejected.

In making a visit to an outlying community with Father Northrop, the man whose guest the bishop was to be drove up in a carriage, sitting bolt upright with singular fixity and holding the reins tightly. As he approached, it became evident that he was intoxicated and was trying to discharge his function as driver without betraying himself. The bishop began a severe reprimand, saying that it was the first time in many years that a bishop had visited the locality, and it was incumbent upon him to conduct himself properly on such an occasion.

"Your Grace," was the ardent reply, "I felt so overjoyed that I just could not help getting tipsy!"

Making the best of circumstances, the Bishop and Father Northrop entered the carriage, and each took a position on one side of their host, holding him erect by their combined efforts while he drove them to their destination.

At New Bern the Bishop had some copies of a circular printed, prescribing the manner in which worship might be held on Sunday where there was no priest. The faithful were to assemble at a designated place, and one of them was to read the prayers for mass, after which a portion was to be read from one of the Catholic books appointed for such occasions. The children and others in need of catechetical instruction were then to be arranged in classes and taught prayers and Christian doctrine.

Leaving New Bern, the Bishop stopped at Swift Creek, where he confirmed Mr. and Mrs. Nelson in the garret, "the only unoccupied place at our disposal." After a short visit to the town of Washington, where he "said mass in Dr. Gallagher's house," he proceeded to Plymouth. There he was hospitably received by Captain McNamara, who had saved the Church at New Bern from being turned into a carpet-bag school. Driving five miles from that town, he baptized and confirmed Mr. Isaac Swift, who had been a rich planter, but was greatly reduced in fortune. "I started to pursue the journey 12 miles further, for the purpose of visiting a Catholic family," the Bishop wrote, "but the vehicle broke down and we were obliged to return."

At Edenton he was able to say mass in "the finest Catholic Church in the State"—St. Ann's. He preached there to a large congregation, composed chiefly of Protestants. No wonder! The Catholics of Edenton and vicinity then numbered eighteen, about half of whom were converts. They were anxious to have a resident priest, who might also attend the near-by missions, and Bishop Gibbons expressed the hope "that Providence will soon enable me to gratify their wishes."

He preached in the courthouse at Tarboro, and noted that "the most intelligent citizens of the town were present, including three judges." At Wilson, the next stop, he also preached in the courthouse, and found that many Protestants had promised to subscribe for the erection of a Catholic Church.

Arriving at Raleigh, he was entertained at the handsome residence of William Grimes. The Legislature was in session, and many of its members went to hear him preach in St. John's Church.

He returned to Wilmington December 17, after a trip of four weeks, the results of which he summarized as follows:

"Number of miles traveled by rail, stage and steamboat, 925.
"Number of towns and stations visited, 16.
"Number of Catholics in various places, 400.
"Converts confirmed, 16; total number, 64.
"Converts baptized, 10; total number, 16."

The need of money to carry on the work was pressing. In the same month he received a draft for 1,600 francs from the Society for the Propagation of the Faith, a total of 8,000 francs having been allotted to his vicariate for 1868.

In preparing his Lenten regulations for 1869, the Bishop wrote that they were about the same as in the Diocese of Baltimore, except that "milk is allowed in this vicariate, owing to the scarcity of tea and coffee in certain sections of the State."

Having received a circular asking a small subscription in behalf of the American College at Rome, he replied that "the impoverished condition of the State and the smallness of the Catholic population" made it impossible to contribute.

He installed Rev. J. V. McNamara as pastor of the Church in Raleigh, July 11. The Governor, Chief Justice, several of the associate judges and many prominent citizens were present. By this time there were 100 Catholics at the State capital.

At Charlotte, where he arrived July 16, he confirmed 43 persons and baptized Mrs. Mary E. Butler, wife of John T. Butler, his host during his stay in Charlotte, having received her profession of faith. A short time later he dedicated St. James' Church, at Concord, whose congregation, consisting of 60 persons, were all converts, with one exception.

He found three Catholics on a visit to Morgantown, one of whom, Mr. McGraw, had ten children, all Protestants, having been reared in the faith of their mother. From that place he traveled 26 miles, over a beautiful mountain country, to

Moore's, in McDowell county.   On August 8 he observed the total eclipse of the sun from the Blue Ridge.

He traveled 24 miles on horseback, August 9, and arrived at Asheville, where he preached in the courthouse and bought a lot for a church.

The Bishop set out in November, 1870, for a second trip over the eastern part of the State, visiting many towns.   Conversions were still numerous.   At Plymouth he found that a certain Irish Catholic had been induced to join the Baptists. Immersed, the convert was invited to say prayer.   He gave out "Hail, Holy Queen."   The astonishment of the audience was immense.   The convert afterward returned to the Catholic Church.

In August, 1871, the bishop started on a visitation to the western part of the State. From the town of Company Shops to Greensboro he was conveyed on a freight engine.   At Gaston he found a congregation of 80, where there had been but 36 on his first visit, two years before.   At Lincolnton he preached to a large audience in the courthouse, the people being, no doubt, moved by some curiosity to see the first bishop who was ever present in that town.   He found that a handsome church had been erected by this time at Asheville, which he dedicated September 24, preaching on "Charity."

Bishop Gibbons recognized early that schools were one of the greatest necessities of the stricken South and a potent means of propagating religion.   "We can testify," wrote Father Gross, "to his self-sacrificing zeal for the establishment of Catholic schools throughout the vicariate, under stress of direst poverty and the most adverse surroundings.   To this end he not only sacrificed money, and time, and labor in begging money, but descended to teach himself daily a class in the parochial school, to help and encourage the priests whose services, for the want of lay teachers, had to be gratuitously engaged."*

---

* Rev. Mark S. Gross, in the *Carmelite Review*, May, 1895.

In 1869 the Bishop brought to Wilmington a colony of Sisters of Mercy from the mother house in Charleston and established them in one of the old-fashioned Southern homes, called the Peyton mansion, which he bought for $16,000—a fortune in Carolina in those days. The people wondered whence the money had come. But a small part of it had been raised in the vicariate, the Bishop having obtained most of the sum through several visits to the Northern States. More than $5,000 was collected in Albany alone. The sisters founded schools at Charlotte and Hickory, as well as at Wilmington.

One of the most enduring works of the Bishop's administration was the establishment of Mary Help Abbey by the Benedictine Order at Belmont, near Charlotte. For this · urpose Rev. J. J. O'Connell gave his estate of 500 acres, to which he had returned after the war, and whence he attended the neighboring missions. Arch Abbot Wimmer, of St. Vincent's Abbey, Pennsylvania, was applied to for a colony for the vicariate. The devoted Abbot received at the same time a similar petition from a far more favorable diocese, but he chose North Carolina, and Rev. Herman Wolf, formerly a Lutheran minister, was sent there as prior.

The first shelter for the fathers was a frame tavern a hundred years old, of Revolutionary celebrity. For a time the outlook was so discouraging that the abandonment of the priory was debated in the chapter of the abbey in Pennsylvania. At this critical period a number of young Benedictines volunteered to go to Belmont if allowed to take with them an abbot of their own selection. This offer was accepted, and they chose Rev. Leo Haid to lead them in the undertaking. With his administration a new era began. Handsome and ample buildings were erected, and St. Mary's College was launched as one of the successful educational institutions of the South, a training school for a native Southern clergy, so much needed in the aggressive work of the Church.

It was difficult to get priests to keep up with the progress of the work in North Carolina. Their task was full of obstacles and they were altogether unsalaried. But the spiritual rewards which they won cheered them on, and, as the success of their labors became known in other dioceses, outside help was less difficult for Bishop Gibbons to obtain.

His experiences in North Carolina, coming as they did at a comparatively impressionable period of his life, exercised a great influence over him. Previous to that time his lot had been the ordinary one of a priest, schooled in the repressive discipline of the seminary, and then thrown out into the active and arduous labor of a parish, with little time to come in contact with the world, except as represented by his own flock. In North Carolina he was suddenly thrust into a different atmosphere. The people were not only nearly all Protestants, but tens of thousands of them had no conception of what the Catholic Church was or what it represented.

From the beginning his mission was, first, to calm antagonistic opinion, and then to lay a foundation for the spread of his faith. His work, being so largely among Protestants, gave him a far better comprehension than the average priest receives of what they stand for in matters of religion and their sincerity of view. By force of circumstances, he had to concede to them desire equal to his own for the truths of Christian faith. He was not less a Catholic when he left Carolina than when he went there. In fact, it seems that the foundations of his belief had been strengthened by opposition; but he had acquired a broad charity, a wide horizon of view, from which he never separated himself in later life, and which stamped him as a friend of men of other creeds. Impressions gained in country towns and secluded rural homes were felt later in the Vatican itself.

CHAPTER V.

At the Vatican Council of 1870.

It was but a step for this man of destiny in the Church from his pioneer work in the North Carolina forests to the august assemblage of the Vatican Council of 1870. He had served his vicariate scarcely more than a year, when that memorable gathering, the first general council of the Church since Trent, 300 years before, convened. When the bishops sat at Trent, America had been discovered but a short time, and not all of them were sure that it was not a part of the Indies. So secure was the papacy in its political power over a great part of the civilized world, that Alexander VI had but recently issued his bull of demarcation giving to Portugal all of the newly discovered lands east of a line 100 leagues west of the Azores, and to Spain all to the westward.

America had no episcopate, and only a few adventurous priests had gone forth as messengers of the faith to the unknown peoples spread over its vast area. Now it was the home of many millions of Catholics, and the pontiffs were beginning to see in its future the Church's brightest hope for the expansion of her spiritual influence. From Canada to Patagonia the bishops were called to Rome to deliberate, in the providence of God, upon the welfare of the souls of men; and the American element constituted a force unknown in the previous councils which had declared the judgment of the Church.

While the problems which led Pius IX to summon the council were chiefly of European origin, they were not confined to the Eastern Hemisphere. Wars had been flaming upon every hand, and the campaigns of Garibaldi had been carried almost to the doors of the Vatican. The Crimea had reeked with Russian, French and English blood. Austria had been humbled at Sadowa. In the United States the great Civil War was raging when Pius took the first steps toward convoking the council. The independence of the papacy itself was threatened, and none knew when there might be another Avignon. Troops of Napoleon III had been supporting the Pope in the midst of Italian hostility. Catholics throughout the world had become impatient to the bursting point from the continual restraints exercised upon the papacy. In their minds, from long habit, they associated its spiritual independence with the temporal power; and the prospects of the loss of this filled the bishops with alarm. Many could not, from the nature of things, conceive the possibility of a pontiff shorn of political power, yet able to exercise, despite all obstacles, the spiritual oversight of Catholics throughout the world and aggressively to press forward in the propagation of the faith.

Of 36 crowned heads, 24 were Protestant, and in almost every country there was a powerful current of public opinion in favor of the separation of church and state. Perhaps even more was to be feared from Catholic than non-Catholic sovereigns. Regalism—the interference of Catholic monarchs in the purely internal affairs of the Church—had grown to be an almost insupportable burden. Political meddling hampered the pontificate in the selection of bishops; and priests were interfered with almost at the steps of the altar. Private ambition and intrigue interwove every step in the adjustment of the direct relations between church and state. Ecclesiastical seminaries, basking in the favor of powerful rulers, taught what Rome called heresy.

In the first era of the Church, kings and nations had been gradually brought in harmony with the papacy, until the real union of Christendom had become a fact; but in the 300 years following the Council of Trent there had been a steady centrifugal force to which the constitution of the Church had never adapted itself.   Many of the decrees of Trent related to conditions which had disappeared; others needed radical modification.   Pope Pius was inclined to consider that the time was ripe for convoking the council as an "extraordinary remedy for the extraordinary evils of the Christian world."*

Nearly all the cardinals whom Pius consulted in December, 1864, when he first announced that he had been deliberating regarding an ecumenical council, strongly advised that it be convoked.   They declared it to be their opinion that the special character of the age was a tendency to overthrow the ancient Christian institutions, founded on a supernatural principle, and to erect a new order, based on natural reason alone. They ascribed this tendency to two errors—first, that society as such had no duties toward God, religion being considered to be for individual conscience only; second, that human reason was sufficient to guide man to a higher knowledge and destiny apart from the organization of the Church.

They pointed to the revolt from the authority of revelation and the growth of naturalism, rationalism, pantheism, socialism and communism.   Liberalism, leading to the declaration of the supremacy of the state rather than the church over education, marriage and consecrated property and to abridgment of the temporal power of the head of the Church, was set forth as the practical result of these tendencies.   The cardinals dwelt on the need of amending the discipline of the Church, untouched for 300 years; of better provision for the education of the clergy and the government of monastic orders, and of bringing the laity to a more general obedience to ecclesiastical laws, almost ignored in some countries.   From these general sources many specific developments were cited, such as laxity in the observance of the marriage tie, mixed marriages, secret societies, the haste to get rich by questionable methods, non-uniformity in the observance of feasts and fasts.   An ardent desire was expressed by the consultors for the reunion of

---

* Manning, True Story of the Vatican Council.

Protestants in the fold of the Catholic Church; and it was hoped that the acts of the council would open a way for this great undertaking.

Only two of the cardinals spoke of papal infallibility, which was destined to be the overshadowing question for the council. A few alluded to the preservation of the temporal power. By far the largest number of replies dealt with subjects embraced in the supernatural character of religion and the eternal destiny of man, leaving material topics out of consideration as worthy to be discussed, if at all, in the light of the spiritual progress of the world.

Pius deliberated long before finally deciding to convoke the council. The bull of indiction was dated June 29, 1868, and the tremendous work of preparing in detail for the labors of the gathering began.

In October, 1869, Bishop Gibbons sailed from Baltimore in the company of Archbishop Spalding and other American prelates.* Landing at Southampton, he proceeded by easy stages through France to Italy. What emotions swept his imagination as he beheld for the first time the Eternal City, the chosen seat of the successors of Peter! The ardor of youth, as well as the impulses of piety, must have tinged his view as he gazed on the storied Vatican, in whose basilica he was soon to sit with the fathers of the Church from every quarter of the world. He was the youngest bishop in that gathering of more than 700. "My youth and inexperience," he wrote, "imposed upon me a discreet silence among my elders. I do not remember to have missed a single session, and was an attentive listener at all debates."†

The American and English bishops had, perhaps, a greater stake in the decision of the question of papal infallibility than any others. It had been accepted as a doctrine of the Church

---

* *Catholic Mirror*, October 23, 1869.
† Personal Reminiscences of the Vatican Council, Cardinal Gibbons in the *North American Review* for April, 1894.

so long in continental Europe that the opposition to it which might arise there would subside, in all probability, as the true meaning of the definition was comprehended. In England, from the time of Henry VIII, this had been a subject which had aroused Protestants to defiant denial. Sovereigns, in their coronation oaths at Westminster, had abjured it as a heresy. In America the problem was to win non-Catholics to the Church, as well as to hold the allegiance of the faithful; and this could only be done in the clear light of public opinion. The chief obstacle to the spread of the Catholic Church on this side of the Atlantic had been the impression that it was subject to foreign control. Enlightened Americans of Protestant ancestry could not wholly reconcile themselves to papal supremacy of a universal church; and the spread-eagle type of patriotism was moved to explosion at the very thought of it.

The American bishops did not question the truth of the doctrine of infallibility; they unalterably adhered to it in both belief and practice. Some of them could see, however, no use in defining it at that time, and were strongly of the opinion that it would raise another cloud between them and the Protestants when their Church was at last piercing the mists of misrepresentation which had darkened her path so long. The doctrine sought to be defined with the weight of a general council was that the pontiff, when speaking *ex cathedra,* in the exercise of his office as the shepherd of all Christians, and declaring a doctrine of faith or morals to be held by the universal Church, was infallible. This was very different from a declaration of personal infallibility on all subjects, but it would be hard to get non-Catholics to understand it. To say that it had been held before and was merely the definition of a dogma containing nothing new might complicate the situation by raising added doubts.

When Bishop Gibbons arrived in Rome it did not appear that the question of infallibility was likely to come before the council. Anti-Catholic papers, it is true, had been filled with rumors that a Jesuitical conspiracy was on foot to clothe the Pope with this attribute.   The *schemata,* or list of topics to be treated by the council, had been prepared by a Commission of Direction, composed of five cardinals, an archbishop and eight bishops, with 102 consultors, of whom 10 were bishops, 69 secular priests and 23 regulars.   When the commission, in preparing the outline on the subject of the Roman pontiff and his temporal power, came to discuss infallibility, two questions were raised.   The first was, "Whether the infallibility of the Roman pontiff *can* be defined as an article of faith;" the second, "Whether it *ought* to be defined as an article of faith."* The commission voted affirmatively, with unanimous voice, in reply to the first question; concerning the second, all but one agreed in the view that the subject ought not to be proposed in the council unless it should be demanded by the bishops.   The subject was thus, for the time being, set aside.

Notwithstanding the action of the Commission of Direction, a majority of the American bishops saw, with dismay, a rapidly growing sentiment in favor of bringing the question before the council.   This might be done by a petition to the Commission of Postulates or Propositions, which could introduce new subjects into the *schemata.*   In a short time 450 of the 700 prelates had actually signed such a petition.   About a hundred, including many of the Americans, signed a counter petition; but it became clearly evident that it was more difficult to marshal influence on that side of the question.   The Americans held a consultation at their college in Rome, and a large majority declared that it would be inexpedient to bring up the question.

Bishop Gibbons, on account of his youth, did not feel justified in expressing any opinion.   Not five bishops in the whole council, said Cardinal Manning, could be justly thought to have opposed the truth of the doctrine.

---

* Manning, True Story of the Vatican Council, p. 82 *et seq.*

The council lasted from December 8, 1869, to July 18, 1870. In March the question of infallibility was formally presented. On the first vote 451 recorded themselves in favor of the decree, 88 against it, and 62 gave a conditional assent. The stage of argument, learned, logical and profound, was soon reached. It may be well to pause here for a brief survey of the reasons for and against the decree, as stated by the Archbishop of Florence, to whom Pius IX gave a commission to write the history of the council.

On the negative side it was held that as the whole episcopate and priesthood and the faithful, with few exceptions, had received with veneration and docility the doctrinal decisions of the pontiffs, no necessity for such a definition existed. In order to define the question of infallibility with exactness, it would be necessary to prescribe the form and manner in which infallibility was to be exercised. This would be difficult, and would involve the Holy See in complications. The hope of reuniting the Eastern churches and of the return of Protestants to the fold would be weakened. Dissensions might be produced among Catholics themselves.

"Let that suffice which has already been declared and has been believed by all," wrote a learned theologian of the opposition, "that the Church, whether congregated in council or dispersed throughout the world, is always infallible, and the Supreme Pontiff, according to the words of the Council of Florence, is the teacher of the whole Church and of all Christians. But as to the mysterious gift of infallibility which, by God, is bestowed upon the episcopate united to the Pope, and at the same time is bestowed in a special manner on the Supreme Pontiff, it may be left as it is. The Church, as all Catholics believe, whether in an ecumenical council or by the Pope alone without a council, guards and explains the truth of revelation. It is not expedient or opportune to make further declarations, unless a proved necessity demands it, which necessity at present does not appear to exist."

This about stated the case for the Americans. Their objections might be summed up in a sentence—the fear that their propaganda among non-Catholics would be hindered and that public opinion might revert to the conditions of "Knownothing" times.

Weighty and pious arguments were presented on the other side by devoted fathers of the Church. They held that such a definition would be opportune, because the doctrine was true; for, if true, how could it be said to be inopportune? Has not God revealed it, they asked, and can it be permitted us to think that what He has thought it opportune to reveal, it is not opportune for us to declare? In the minds of objectors, "opportune" must refer to something of a political or diplomatic character, some calculation of expediency relating to peoples or governments. This caution would be proper for legislatures or cabinets debating public questions of a secular nature; but the Church deals with the truths of revelation, and it is at all times opportune for her to declare what God has willed that man should know. It had been said that many revealed truths were not defined. This was true, and would be a strong argument if the truth had never been denied. The infallibility of the Roman Pontiff having been denied, its definition became necessary. Some persons, in order to throw doubt on the doctrine, or to prove it false, represented the denial of it to be ancient and widespread. This increased the need of declaring it by an authoritative decree. Protestants would say: "If you are not doubtful, why do you hesitate to declare it?" Antagonists hoped to find a division among Catholics in order to gain leverage for an opinion that the Church was not really united and, therefore, not the authoritative custodian of the deposit of Divine truth. All Catholics believed that the Church, by the assistance of the Holy Ghost, is infallible. If it were left open to doubt whether the teaching of the head of the Church were true, those who believed that he might err could always contradict his teaching. A fallible head to an infallible body would be contrary to the logic of common sense. The Church during eighteen centuries had done many acts of supreme importance by its head alone. Were these acts fallible or infallible? The question had been formally raised, and, for the sake of Divine truth, it was contended, must be as formally solved.

To the petition of the bishops, addressed to the Commission of Postulates or Propositions, was added an appendix, containing reasons for their view and a citation from the authorities of provincial councils in support of it. Among these was an extract from the declarations of the Second Plenary Council of Baltimore, of which Bishop Gibbons had been assistant chancellor, and which it was hoped would have weight with the American prelates assembled at the Vatican. This declaration was:

"The living and infallible authority flourishes in that Church alone which was built by Christ upon Peter, who is the head, leader and pastor of the whole Church, whose faith Christ promised should never fail; which ever had legitimate pontiffs, dating their origin in unbroken line from Peter himself, being seated in his chair and being the inheritors and defenders of the like doctrine, dignity, office and power. And because where Peter is, there also is the Church, and because Peter speaks in the person of the Roman Pontiff, ever lives in his successors, passes judgment and makes known the truths of faith to those who seek them, therefore, are the Divine declarations to be received in the manner in which they have been and are held by this Roman See of Blessed Peter, that mother and teacher of all churches, which has ever preserved whole the teachings delivered by Christ, and which has taught the faithful, showing to all men the paths of salvation and the doctrine of everlasting truth."*

The declaration by the Council of Florence in 1439 was the favorite citation of those who urged that a definition be pro-

---

* Acta et Decreta, Conc. Plen. II, Baltimore.

mulgated. It was that "the Roman Pontiff is the true vicar
of Christ and head of the whole church and is the father and
teacher of all Christians; and to him in blessed Peter the full
power was given by our Lord of feeding, ruling and governing the universal Church."

Nearly five hundred of the bishops, assembled in Rome in
1867 to observe the centenary of the martyrdom of St. Peter
and St. Paul, had addressed Pius IX in the following terms:
"Believing that Peter has spoken by the mouth of Pius, whatever has been said, confirmed and decreed by you to preserve
the deposit of faith, we also repeat, confirm and profess, and
with one mind and heart we reject all that you have judged it
necessary to reprove and condemn as contrary to Divine faith,
to the salvation of souls and to the good of society. For what
the fathers of Florence defined in their Decree of Union is
firmly and deeply impressed on our minds—that the Roman
Pontiff is the vicar of Christ, the head of the whole Church,
the father and teacher of all Christians."

None claimed personal infallibility for the pontiff. In order to exclude the possibility of this interpretation, the title of
the Vatican Council's decree was changed from *"De Romani
Pontificis Infallibilitate"* (on the infallibility of the Roman
Pontiff) to *"De Romani Pontificis Infallibili Magisterio"* (on
the infallible teaching office of the Roman Pontiff). The *mag-
isterium* or teaching office of the primacy was the doctrinal
authority of the supreme ruler and teacher. It was held to be
a Divine assistance inseparable from the office and not a quality
inherent in the person of the Pope.

The chapter on papal infallibility came to a vote in the
council in July. On the first vote 451 of the fathers answered
placet, or aye, 88 *non placet,* or no, and 62 *placet juxta modum,*
or aye, with modifications. Nearly two hundred amendments,
some of which were adopted, were offered. When the time
came for the final action in public session, 533 voted *placet,*
and only 2 *non placet;* 55 absented themselves, in order to

avoid being recorded on the negative side of a question whose decision they considered inopportune; 11 others were absent for unknown causes, and were supposed to have left Rome, as permission had been given several days before to begin the journey homeward. The two who voted *non placet* were Bishop Fitzgerald, of Little Rock, Ark., and the Bishop of the Italian Diocese of Caiazzo. They at once made their submission and subscribed to the decree.

Bishop Gibbons voted *placet* on the question on both occasions when it came before the council. As we have seen, his judgment was that the time for the definition was not opportune; but, seeing the irresistible drift of opinion among the fathers of the Church, he could not cast his vote against a doctrine which agreed with his own belief and practice.

So much doubt has been thrown upon the meaning of the declaration of infallibility that it may be well to quote its language. It read as follows:

"Therefore, faithfully adhering to the tradition received from the beginning of Christian faith, for the glory of God our Savior, the exaltation of the Catholic religion and the salvation of the Christian people, the sacred council approving, we teach and define that it is a dogma divinely revealed: That the Roman Pontiff, when he speaks *ex cathedra*—that is, when in the discharge of the office of pastor and teacher of all Christians, by virtue of his supreme apostolic authority, he defines a doctrine regarding faith or morals to be held by the Universal Church—is, by the Divine assistance promised to him in blessed Peter, possessed of that infallibility with which the Divine Redeemer willed that the Church should be endowed for defining doctrine regarding faith and morals; and that, therefore, such definitions of the Roman Pontiff are irreformable of themselves and not from the consent of the Church."

Of the monumental work of the council in dealing with the doctrinal, disciplinary and social problems which had arisen since Trent, nothing need be said here. In all questions except that of infallibility there was no sharp line of difference between a majority of the Americans and the other fathers who sat in the Vatican. It was the one declaration of the gathering which profoundly stirred the external world.

Contrary to expectation, this was less acutely evident in America than in Europe. Here there were no political bonds between church and state which might be unloosed by a declaration in Rome or anywhere else. No officeholder or politician in America had the vestige of authority to meddle in doctrinal definitions which in no way affected the civil government. There was no concordat to be debated in Congress.

The Franco-Prussian War broke out while the council was in session. In a short time Bismarck and Von Moltke had crushed the power of Napoleon III. French troops having been withdrawn from Rome, the city was seized by Victor Emmanuel and Pius IX was deprived of the last remnant of that temporal power which had endured since the time of Charlemagne. It is clearly evident that in the whole of Europe a gradual weakening of the pontiff's potency in political affairs has taken place. In America it is perhaps true that the spread of the Catholic faith was arrested for a time; but its marvelous development in the closing years of the nineteenth century is complete evidence that the declaration of papal infallibility was not a permanent obstacle to the increase of spiritual results west of the Atlantic. Aggressive anti-Catholicism has flared up once or twice, but has found its strongest enemy in enlightened public opinion. The liberality of the young vicar of North Carolina who sat in the Vatican Council has been one of the most powerful factors in this state of things.

Bishop Gibbons, at thirty-six, was naturally impressed in an extraordinary manner by the scenes through which he passed. He had been ordained but nine years before, and life was still fresh to him when he was projected in the midst of the wisdom and grandeur and solemnity of the greatest organization of the modern world. His own country and its political organization had not a hundred years of independence behind it; in Rome he sat in an assembly whose deliberations represented the accumulated experience and weight of an institution whose roots were planted in the beginnings of Christianity, and whose development had employed a large proportion of the master minds of the world, from St. Peter to Constantine, and down through the ages. He was the youngest bishop; many prelates of venerable years sat on an equality beside him. He met for the first time Cardinal Manning, who was destined to have a great influence on his life; and he was impressed at the outset by the brilliant Archbishop of Westminster perhaps more than by any other man he met. Manning delivered the longest oration of the council, which lasted hardly more than an hour. His emaciated form and incessant activity moved Archbishop Spalding to say to him: "I know not how you can work so much, for you neither eat, nor drink nor sleep."*

Of the American prelates, Archbishops Spalding and Kenrick were among the most influential. Bishop Gibbons was surprised at the memory of Kenrick, who reclined in his seat, with half-closed eyes, listening to the debates, taking no notes, and yet, when he came to speak, reviewed with remarkable accuracy what had been said by others. Archbishop McCloskey, of New York, destined to become, five years later, the first American Cardinal, was a "silent Solon;" Archbishop Leahy, of Cashel, had in an eminent degree the gifts of the Irish orator, recalling in his eloquent Latin the glories of the Schoolmen. He could flavor judgment with wit in the tongue of the Cæsars. Archbishop Darboy, of Paris, who shared the confidence and expressed the views of Napoleon III, made a deep impression. He had seen the assassination of two of his predecessors—Archbishops Affre and Sibour; and in less than a year after the council adjourned was himself shot to death in the prison of La Roquette amid the ravings of the Commune.

Bishop Dupanloup, of Orleans, was one of the Forty Immortals of the French Academy and the counsellor of Prince Talleyrand, whom he reconciled to the Church after a long estrangement. Cardinal Dechamps, Archbishop of Malines,

---

* Personal Reminiscences of the Vatican Council, Cardinal Gibbons in the *North American Review*, April, 1894.

was primate of Belgium, and his brother Adolphus was Prime Minister of that Kingdom.   Baron Von Ketteler, Bishop of Mainz, was disfigured by a scar on the face received in a duel of student days at Goettingen.   Bishop Gibbons saw the democracy of the Church strikingly exemplified in Cardinal Prince Schwarzenberg, primate of Bohemia, and Cardinal Simor, primate of Hungary, the two most influential churchmen of the Austrian Empire.   Schwarzenberg, a handsome man, of commanding presence, was a prince of the realm as well as of the Church.   Simor sprang from the people, and was proud of declaring it.   Bishop Strossmayer, of Bosnia, was reputed the most eloquent prelate in the council.   "His periods," wrote Bishop Gibbons, "flamed with the grace and majesty and musical rhythm of Cicero."

Cardinal Pecci, afterward Leo XIII, the most powerful friend of Bishop Gibbons in the career that was opening before him, said little in debate, but was potent and indefatigable in council.   The young American prelate thought he could see a design of Providence in the fact that the man who was to rule the whole Church should not have been involved in the disputes of the council.   Cardinal Pecci's learning and administrative experience were invaluable in the vital work of the gathering.

Every bishop knew at least two or three languages; some spoke ten or twelve.   Cardinal Simor told Bishop Gibbons that he employed four different tongues in the government of his diocese—Latin, German, Hungarian and Slavonian. Next to the young American prelate sat a vicar apostolic from China, who used six dialects in his vicariate.   A bishop of a Chinese diocese had traveled twenty-three thousand miles to attend the council.   One or two blind bishops had to be guided by servants as they took their places in the assemblage.   Some of the feeblest were so exhausted by their travels that they died in Rome or on the way, martyrs to their obedience to duty.

At Trent only four English-speaking prelates sat; at the Vatican Council there were more than one hundred and twenty.   Bishop Gibbons ventured to express the opinion that if the next ecumenical council should be held in fifty years, "the representatives of the English language would equal in numbers, if not surpass, those of any other tongue."   He agreed with Cardinal Manning that "the number of prelates who questioned the claim of papal infallibility could be counted on the fingers of one hand."   "Yet," Bishop Gibbons added, "many of the speakers, indeed, impugned the domga, not because they did not personally accept it, but with the view of pointing out the difficulties with which the teaching body of the Church would have to contend in vindicating it before the world.   I have listened in the council chamber to far more subtle, more plausible and more searching objections to this prerogative of the Pope than I have read or heard from the pen or tongue of the most learned or formidable Protestant assailant.   But all the objections were triumphantly answered.   Every dispassionate reader, whatever may be his religious convictions, must be profoundly impressed, as I was at the time, with the fearless and serene conduct of the great majority, who, spurning a temporizing policy or the dictates of human prudence, were deterred neither by specious arguments, nor imperial threats, nor by the fear of schism, from promulgating what they conceived to be a truth contained in the deposit of Divine revelation.   Since the last vote taken in the solemn session of July 18, 1870, all the bishops of Christendom, without a murmur of dissent, have accepted the decision as final and irrevocable."

Such was the Vatican Council, a product of the thought, the labor, the spiritual inspiration of three hundred years.   Father Hecker, who expressed the general view of American·Catholics, considered that it meant a new era, especially for the United States, the tendency of whose free institutions, he declared, was to make men Catholics.   The constitution of the Church having been fixed in permanent form and the capstone applied by the definition of papal infallibility, he held that in the wide radius left for liberty of thought and action the fullest development of the individual should be sought.

From his experience in the Olympian atmosphere of the Church, Bishop Gibbons returned to his task in North Carolina with a new light on the world-wide mission of the Catholic faith, which was to guide his footsteps along many a difficult path that would open before him.

CHAPTER VI.

BISHOP OF RICHMOND.

Bishop Gibbons had labored in North Carolina a little less than four years, when a new field opened for his versatile activity. This was the See of Richmond, Va., in which a vacancy was created by the death in January, 1872, of the beloved Bishop John McGill, who had guided the affairs of that diocese 22 years. The Vicar of North Carolina was now recognized on all sides as a coming man in the Church. His superiors in the hierarchy were glad to acknowledge his talents, and his brother bishops were ready to acclaim any promotion that might come to him. He was no less popular among the clergy, on account of his charming personal traits. Always ready to help a priest, as well as a layman, he could listen well as they told their difficulties, and, if occasion demanded, could administer effective correction in a manner which the recipient would have difficulty in distinguishing from praise.

Human nature seemed almost an open book to him, as to many other men who combine in themselves the elements of success. He could often form an instantaneous and accurate judgment of a man whom he met for the first time, and his almost instinctive trait of justice enabled him to modify it readily, as circumstances might require. His was a strong character, which was bound to dominate in the end, but a conciliatory one. Few could attain with greater ease a purpose in the face of obstacles. Those who were thrown in contact with him, in and out of the Church, formed the habit of following where he led; it seemed the natural order.

At first Bishop Gibbons was appointed administrator of the Richmond diocese, in addition to the duties of his vicariate, while time might be afforded for the prescribed procedure of the Church in the selection of a permanent successor to Mgr. McGill. The final choice of Rome fell on him, and it was decided that he should continue as administrator of North Carolina at the same time. The situation of Richmond was favorable to the management of both jurisdictions, and the energy and resourcefulness of Bishop Gibbons might be expected to be equal to the double task.

Here began the close interweaving of his life with that of another man who was to exert a marked influence on it. This was James Roosevelt Bayley, one of the most interesting figures whose impress has been left on the Catholic Church in America. Bayley was a near connection of the Roosevelt family of New York, from which an American President afterward sprang. He was a grandson of Dr. Richard Bayley, a celebrated anatomist and a pioneer of American medicine. Born to luxury and culture, he was a society man in New York in his younger days. His family were of the Protestant Episcopal faith, and, his thoughts turning to the ministry, he was ordained in that church, serving as rector of an influential congregation in Harlem. In time he became a Catholic and studied at the Seminary of St. Sulpice, in Paris. Archbishop Hughes, afterward famous as the head of the See of New York during the Civil War, ordained him. On account of his ripe scholarship, he was made president of St. John's College, Fordham, N. Y. His contributions to literature were considerable. He was serving as Bishop of Newark, when a warm friendship sprang up between him and Archbishop Spalding, who looked upon him as his successor. Several months before Archbishop Spalding's death, it is related, he put his pectoral chain and cross around Bishop Bayley's neck and said: "One day this will be yours."*

Bishop Bayley did not want to come to Baltimore, saying: "I am too old a tree to be transplanted." He refused to accept

---

* Riordan, Cathedral Records, p. 85.

the idea of the change until the papal decree had been issued. Archbishop Spalding died in February, 1872, and on October 13 Bishop Bayley was invested with the pallium in the Baltimore Cathedral, Bishop Gibbons taking part in the ceremony. The next Sunday the new Archbishop installed Bishop Gibbons in St. Peter's Cathedral, Richmond, as the head of that diocese.

These two warm friends had been thrown intimately together at the Vatican Council.   Bayley was then 56 years old, Gibbons 36, and during the long months of the council, when Americans were participating for the first time in a general synod of the Church, the elder prelate learned to admire both the talents and the graces of the younger.   Bishop Gibbons, in turn, was captivated by the intellectual powers, the broad and deep cultivation, the strong nature of Bishop Bayley; and their friendship continued during the two years immediately following their return to America, until unexpected fate threw them in closer contact.   Bayley's practical experience in life before his retirement into the semi-isolation of the Church had continued to be of the greatest use to him.   He was a keen judge of the capabilities of others, and saw in his friend traits that would adorn the most exalted positions in the Church.

Virginia was not fruitful soil for an increase in the harvest of the Catholic faith.   In that State more than any other lingered a trace of the atmosphere of Elizabethan England. On Jamestown Island, in May, 1607, Rev. Robert Hunt had spread a sail cloth between the boughs of trees and read the first service of the Church of England on American soil.* This remained the established church of Virginia, as much as of the mother country, until the Revolution.   The local vestries were entrusted by law with political as well as ecclesiastical functions, such as the care of orphans and the poor.   From public taxation the pay of the clergy was taken.   Neither Catholics, nor persons of any other religious faith, were ever actively persecuted in Virginia, though the anti-Catholic, anti-

---

* Lyon G. Tyler, Cradle of the Republic, p. 116.

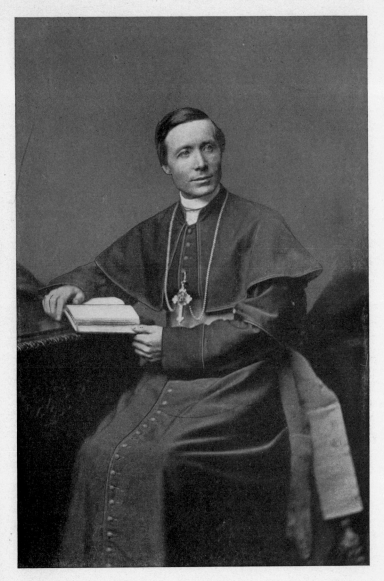

CARDINAL GIBBONS AS BISHOP OF RICHMOND

Puritan and anti-Quaker feeling among the people made it unpleasant at times to maintain open worship other than that of the English Church.

Even after the revolution marked impressions remained, especially in the tidewater counties, of the ecclesiastical and social predominance of the English Church in colonial times; it was too closely threaded in the life and institutions of the people to be withdrawn suddenly. Presbyterians and Lutherans entered the beautiful Shenandoah Valley, and other denominations, especially Baptists and Methodists, soon outnumbered the Episcopalians in the mountainous districts of the State.

In North Carolina there was scarcely any immigration to furnish a foothold for the Catholic Church. There was little more in Virginia, but still enough to plant a nucleus in each of the larger cities, like Richmond, Petersburg and Norfolk. The first mass in Richmond was said by Abbe Dubois, in 1791. Not until 1820 was the diocese created, and the outlook was so unpromising that it was abolished and united with Baltimore two years later. In 1840 it was re-established by Bishop Whelan, who administered it ten years, and was succeeded by Bishop McGill. Bishop Gibbons was, therefore, but the fourth in succession, counting from Bishop Kelly, who was in charge during the brief period 1820-22.

It is interesting to the student of American history to note that the Catholic faith and the Church of England were first planted on soil belonging to the English Crown, within the present limits of the United States, scarcely 100 miles from each other. Jamestown and St. Mary's are both within the segment of a circle of comparatively small radius whose center is at the mouth of the Chesapeake. In this strategic region, the key of America, Raleigh chose the base from which he would colonize the new empire; the Jamestown experiment succeeded, after Raleigh's head had fallen on the block; the Revolution was fired by the eloquence of Patrick Henry, and was consummated at Yorktown; the War of 1812 was settled by the victories of North Point and Fort McHenry; the crisis of the Civil War occurred; and seven Presidents of the United States were born. Maryland and Virginia, so closely akin in many things, are totally unlike in church antecedents and influences. One has been receptive, by tradition and feeling, to the Catholic faith; the other has been the opposite. In parts of Virginia a Catholic priest is unknown even at this day, and would be looked on as a curiosity should he come.

As in North Carolina, Bishop Gibbons' field of labor in the Richmond diocese was among a people broken by war and "reconstruction." Had public opinion been less unfavorable to the Catholic Church, the other difficulties in the way of building up the diocese would still have been tremendous; to a man of less resolution, they would have been appalling. There was scarcely money enough in circulation to supply the elementary needs of business transactions, and almost none to build churches, convents and schools. For four years great contending armies had struggled up and down the State. What escaped the seizure of the Federals, was willingly given to the half-starved Confederates. In the process of destroying the economic resources of the State, so as to prevent it from being made a highway for future military advances on Washington, crops had been laid waste, fruit trees torn up by the roots, horses taken for the cavalry, cattle and hogs bayonetted in the fields, mills and dwellings burned.

All able-bodied men had joined the army, and the corpses of thousands strewed the soil as the shock of conflict passed from the Alleghanies to the Potomac. The sudden freeing of the slaves had demoralized the supply of agricultural labor. Farmers could get no seed to plant, no man to sow or reap. Piled on this base of wholesale destruction, had been the weight of crushing taxation imposed by the "carpet-baggers" and their negro allies, who were bent on extracting the last ounce of blood from the helpless people suddenly cast under the evil spell of their power.

The diocese, which embraced nearly all of Virginia and several counties of West Virginia, contained at the time of Bishop Gibbons' arrival fifteen churches, the same number of chapels or stations, sixteen parochial schools and seventeen priests. A continuance of the aggressive methods employed in the vicariate resulted in winning many converts. The same liberality of view that had endeared Bishop Gibbons to the people of North Carolina, without regard to sect, appealed with equal strength to the predominantly Protestant population of Virginia. The Bishop's sermons in Richmond, Petersburg and throughout the State were attended by almost as many persons of other beliefs as Catholics, and were largely addressed to them. He could gauge his auditors. If they wanted an exposition of Catholic doctrine as a fortification to their own faith, few could give it as well as he; but, did they come to listen that they might disapprove, he won their attention at the outset by the presentation of the simple truths of Christianity, and then proceeded to a discussion of his theme with a breadth and charity of view that disarmed criticism. None could be offended; all were charmed. Protestants thanked him for visiting their towns, and Catholics looked upon him with pride.

Early in November, 1872, he went to Lynchburg, where he preached and confirmed, and then proceeded to Lexington. In that picturesque old town, where Robert E. Lee had died but two years before, the bishop confirmed ten persons in the engine-house, where Father Murray celebrated mass, no Catholic Church having then been erected there. He performed the ceremony of marriage for John B. Purcell and Miss Olympia Williamson, in the presence of a brilliant assemblage, including Gen. G. W. Custis Lee, son of the Confederate chieftain, and prominent persons from Washington and Lee University and the Virginia Military Institute, where "Stonewall" Jackson had taught.

Returning to Richmond, he contracted for the erection of a schoolhouse at the corner of Ninth and Marshall streets, at a cost of $17,695.

Early in 1873 he made a trip to North Carolina, preaching, lecturing, confirming and generally stimulating the work of the vicariate. At Raleigh he confirmed a class of nine, including the mayor and his wife, who were converts. Returning to his duties in Virginia, he visited Alexandria, Fairfax, Gordonsville, Warrenton, Middleburg, Winchester and other places in Northern Virginia, where almost every foot of ground had been trodden by armies but a few years before and where memories of Washington, Madison, Monroe, Marshall and other pillars of the republic abounded. In a short time he had inspected the work in practically every church in the diocese, and accessions to the faith in large numbers began.

At Culpeper, he preached in the town hall to a large congregation, most of whom were Protestants. The local judge adjourned court in order to enable those attending it to be present at the sermon.

While on a trip to North Carolina in 1874 the bishop preached in the Court-House at Halifax, where he was the guest of Mr. Conigland. About 4.30 o'clock the next morning, his sleep was disturbed by the barking of dogs. This enabled him to hear a noise in his room, which, he soon found, was made by a thief searching for plunder. Calling out "who's there?" he received no answer. He then leaped from bed to attack the robber, but the latter fled, leaving at the door the bishop's vest, containing about $150. His cross was lying on the table and his watch was under the pillow, but, after a hasty examination, he found that nothing was missing. "It was fortunate," he said, in relating the incident, "that I did not seize the man, as he probably would have overpowered me."

Wm. S. Caldwell, a wealthy resident of Richmond, deeded to the bishop a handsome residence, with its furniture, which

was converted into a home for the Little Sisters of the Poor.*
Both Houses of the Legislature, under a suspension of rules,
passed unanimously a bill incorporating the order in Virginia,
and it was promptly signed by the Governor. In a short time a
community of six, headed by Sister Virginia—appropriately
called—was installed. Two years later a community of the
Sisters of Charity was established at Petersburg.

Bishop Gibbons was constantly called upon to answer objections which sprang from the fact that the Protestant faiths
were the only ones known in many of the localities he visited.
When he returned after a time, he found the impressions produced by his sermons weakened, and the idea of supplementing
them by a printed treatise occurred to him. He suggested this
one day while visiting Father Gross, in Wilmington, in the
spring of 1876, and asked him to write it. Father Gross said:

"Bishop, why don't you write it?"

Seized with an inspiration, the Bishop replied:

"While the spirit is in me, give me paper and ink, and I will
jot down the first chapter."

Such was the beginning of "The Faith of Our Fathers," of
which nearly a million copies have been sold. The labor of
composing this book, one of the most remarkable religious
works which has appeared in any age or language, was
crowded into the indefatigable young Bishop's duties. He
meditated on each successive chapter while traveling on railway cars, or by other means, and confirmed his quotations
and references on his return. In clear, simple and classic
English he thus wrote the principles of the Catholic religion
and replied in detail to the arguments commonly urged against
it. No religious controversial book had ever been conceived in
a broader spirit. It leaves no sting with the reader, be his
convictions what they may, and as a concise explanation of the
Church, its history, doctrines and mission, it has never had an
equal. One may lay it down and say "I disagree," but never

---

* 1874.

"I do not understand." Its literary strength and grace gave it a permanent place in the libraries of the world almost immediately after its publication, late in 1876; priests found that it said what they wanted to say better than they could say it themselves, and its circulation by the thousands has ever since been a favorite means of reinforcing the efforts of the clergy. It has been translated into twelve languages.

The book takes up the leading doctrines of the Catholic Church, such as the trinity, the incarnation, unity of the Church, apostolicity, perpetuity, authority, the primacy of Peter, the supremacy of the popes, the temporal power, invocation of saints, the Blessed Virgin Mary, sacred images, purgatory, prayers for the dead, charges of religious persecution, the holy eucharist, the sacrifice of the mass, the use of religious ceremonies and the Latin language, penance, indulgences, and extreme unction. Regarding each of these, a clear and simple explanation is given. Objections are frankly and fully cited and answered in detail.

These doctrines, the author points out, are misunderstood by many Protestants; and where it serves the purpose of his exposition he employs dialogue. The following extract is in the form of a conversation between a Protestant minister and a convert to the Catholic Church, which he cites as an illustration:

Minister—"You can not deny that the Roman Catholic Church teaches gross errors—the worship of images, for instance."

Convert—"I admit no such charges, for I have been taught no such doctrines."

Minister—"But the priest who instructed you did not teach you all. He held back some points which he knew would be objectionable to you."

Convert—"He withheld nothing; for I am in possession of books treating thoroughly of all Catholic doctrines."

Minister—"Deluded soul! Do you not know that in Europe they are taught differently?"

Convert—"That can not be; for the Church teaches the same creed all over the world, and most of the doctrinal books which I read were originally published in Europe."

The author particularly urged that the Church should be judged by her own acts and declarations, and not by those of her enemies. Writing in the South, he asked if it would be fair, in order to obtain a correct estimate of the Southern people, to select for his only sources of information Northern periodicals which during the Civil War were bitterly opposed to the South. He defended with particular warmth the assertion that the Catholic Church had always been the zealous promoter of religious and civil liberty. Wherever encroachments on these rights of man were perpetrated by individual members of the faith, he argued, the wrongs, far from being sanctioned by the Church, were committed in palpable violation of her authority. He took up the old arguments about the Spanish Inquisition and the Massacre of St. Bartholomew, and discussed them fully from the Catholic point of view. The broad charity which shines through the pages of the book has been, perhaps, as potent as its logic in carrying conviction to the minds of tens of thousands of readers throughout the world.

In the five years during which Bishop Gibbons presided over the Richmond Diocese the number of churches increased from fifteen to twenty-four, with about the same number of chapels or stations, to which twenty-four priests ministered. The subject of education was always close to his heart, and under his vigorous efforts ten new parochial schools were established. There was a marked development in all directions, and the diocese was kept practically free from debt.*

He frequently visited Baltimore to assist Archbishop Bayley at ecclesiastical ceremonies, and, in fact, was identified almost as much with Baltimore as Richmond, the proximity of his diocese and his natural ties with the archiepiscopal see leading almost inevitably to this. The most notable of these occasions was the consecration May 25, 1876, of the Baltimore Cathedral,† whose corner-stone had been laid in 1806 by Bishop

---

* *Catholic Standard*, Philadelphia, October 27, 1877. Quoted by Reily, Vol. II, p. 113.
† *Catholic Mirror*, May 27, 1876.

Carroll, but which was not free of debt until seventy years later. Archbishop Bayley was the consecrator and Bishop Gibbons preached.

What thoughts welled up within him as he stood in the pulpit on that memorable occasion! The superb old pile had been a part of his life, and his life had been a part of it. Within two hundred feet of it had been old St. Peter's Church, the first of the Catholic religion in Baltimore, erected about 1770 on the north side of what is now Saratoga street, near Charles street, on land bought in 1764 from Charles Carroll, father of Charles Carroll of Carrollton. Archbishop Carroll had pontificated there, but he cherished the dream of a Cathedral and raised $225,000—a great sum in those days—by collections, subscriptions, and even by a lottery, which accorded with the custom of the times. Benjamin H. Latrobe, the architect of the Capitol in Washington, drew the plans. The Cathedral is a cruciform structure, Ionic in its general outlines, but now capped by Russo-Byzantine towers, which predominate the architectural tone. The great blocks of granite for its construction were hauled from Ellicott City, ten miles distant, by oxen. John Eager Howard, the hero of Cowpens, gave much of the large lot on which it stands. The War of 1812 stopped the work, and, while still unfinished, it was dedicated May 31, 1821, by Archbishop Marechal. Seven years later, Mgr. Marechal gave it a large bell, bought in his native France, and completed one of the towers. The altar was the gift of Marseilles priests, whose teacher he had been. Archbishop Eccleston finished the second tower, and Archbishops Kenrick and Spalding erected the noble portico, adorned with huge pillars. The bodies of Carroll and other archbishops find sepulture in this venerable church. Within its walls was held the Provincial Council of 1829, the first in any English-speaking country since the Reformation. Among the historic church edifices of

America the Baltimore Cathedral is easily first in importance, though not in antiquity.*

The consecration of the Cathedral was marked by a notable assemblage of prelates, clergy and laity. Bishop Gibbons, in his sermon, dwelt on the permanency of the Church, and then struck a note which was characteristic of him.

"It is charged," he said, "that the Church will shrink from the light of modern invention and discovery. Ah, no! She will welcome them and will use them to extend the knowledge of God. Yes, we bless you, men of genius! If, when railroads and steam vessels and telegraphs were not known, the Church carried the gospel to distant nations and unexplored regions, how much more can she do with their aid?

"Need it be repeated that the Church is slandered when it is charged that she is inimical to liberty! The Church flourishes only in the beams of liberty. She has received more harm from the tyranny and oppression of kings and rulers than any other of the victims of their power. We pray for the prosperity of this our young country. In this its centennial year we rejoice that it has lived to so sturdy a life of liberty and regard for right, and we raise the prayer '*Esto Perpetua.*' "

Only a little more than a year was to elapse before he would be preaching in this same Cathedral as Archbishop of the Province of Baltimore.

During his residence in Richmond, Bishop Gibbons was not able to obtain the appointment of a vicar for North Carolina. The faithful Father Gross wrote in February, 1876:

"When, on the death of the bishop of Richmond, Bishop Gibbons was *nolens volens*, introduced by His Holiness Pius IX into the see of Richmond, with the title of administrator apostolic over the vicariate of North Carolina, it was but the change of an additional new field, bringing an increase of the same arduous duties. The change was, and still is, keenly felt by the people and especially by the clergy of North Carolina. But the vicariate is not forgotten, nor is it neglected. Frequent

* Riordan, Cathedral Records, pp. 93-98.

visits are made in the State, when the bishop lectures upon Catholic truths and cheers the hearts of all, laity and clergy, by his presence. The citizens of Wilmington, Raleigh, Charlotte, Salisbury and Fayetteville frequently enjoy his strong and engaging discourses in explanation of Catholic doctrine. He has multiplied his help by the admission of priests for the missions in the work of the ministry. Every town in North Carolina of importance has its priests, its regular Sunday service. No hour of the day or night is there when Catholics may not receive the ministrations of their religion. If there is any regret, it comes from the Catholics themselves.

"But, thank God, if the field of North Carolina has been well worked, the fruit has been abundant. No Catholics are more fervent; no people are more easily won over to the faith. Of three missions, two of them can boast of a hundred converts each; the other of thirty. Male and female Catholic schools have been established. In a word, Rev. Dr. Gibbons found in North Carolina in 1868 three priests (one borrowed, since returned), now there are seven or eight; he found seven hundred Catholics, now there are sixteen hundred; seven churches, now there are eleven or twelve, with a convent-academy, conducted by the Sisters of Mercy, and located upon a handsome piece of property purchased for them by the bishop. The word is still 'onward' in North Carolina.

"An impression prevails that the Catholics could not support their vicar and bishop, hence his removal. They could not honor him, indeed, with those episcopal surroundings becoming, but not necessary to, his sublime office of bishop. Such wealth of catholicity North Carolina does not possess. The pope's vicar did not come to find and enjoy the becoming honors and dignity of an established diocese, but to accept and perform the duty of a bishop—to preach the gospel, to convert souls; to accept the poverty of a vicariate, and by his apostolic labor, to make it rich with the wealth of Catholic faith. The field of North Carolina, with its poverty and trials, and sparse Catholicity, was, and is yet, not too much for our vicar, nor for any one whom the Holy Father may judge to send. Everything has a beginning. Even the gospel of Christ has its seed. Others may enter into our labor and may enjoy its fruits. The more numerous and imperative wants of the Richmond diocese, widowed by the death of Rev. Dr. McGill, removed our vicar. Rather the spiritual poverty of the Richmond diocese caused the transfer than any failure in North Carolina.

"Our vicar was removed with the promise of another; but our bishop's zeal is so untiring, his charity so unselfish, that though we constantly regret, we feel the less his transfer. Catholicity is still advancing in

North Carolina, and rapidly, though our vicar's undivided efforts would, of course, produce still greater results."*

When Archbishop McCloskey was elevated to the Sacred College in 1875, the young bishop's thoughts were far from associating his own career with that honor. Nevertheless, it is interesting to note that he viewed it in much the same light as his own appointment afterward impressed him—an honor to his country, and to its non-Catholic as well as Catholic people. He thus expressed himself:

"The hierarchy of the United States will rejoice to hear that this eminent dignity has been conferred on an American prelate, who has endeared himself to the church by his long service in the cause of religion, his marked ability, his unostentatious piety and great suavity of manners. I am persuaded also that not only the Catholic body of this country, but our citizens at large, will receive, with just pride, the intelligence that the Holy Father has determined to associate an American Archbishop with the members of the Sacred College. There is no doubt that the venerable Archbishop of New York will fill with marked discretion and wisdom that exalted and responsible position."†

The Bishop's farewell sermon to the people of his diocese in St. Peter's Cathedral, October 14, 1877, was marked by characteristic modesty. Though he had done so much for them, he gave the human credit to his predecessor, Bishop McGill.

"Ever since I took charge of this portion of the Lord's vineyard," he said, "God has singularly blessed us. To Him be all the honor and glory. Every other cause of success is secondary to Him. Paul soweth, Apollo watereth, but God giveth the increase. Without Him, we would have made no progress. We would have fished all night, like Peter, and caught nothing. Next to God, you are indebted to my venerable and illustrious predecessor, who left the diocese in a solvent and healthy condition. He was a man of eminent prudence and discretion, and of caution verging on timidity. He might have gained

---

* Letter to the *Southern Cross*, February 9, 1876. Quoted by Reily, Vol. II, p. 106 *et seq.*
† New York *Herald*, March 14, 1875.

for himself a great name for enterprise and material progress by erecting churches and other institutions throughout the diocese, without regard to expense. But with all that, he might have bequeathed to his successor a load of debt which would have paralyzed his usefulness and crushed his heart. He left me few debts to pay and few scandals to heal. He left a diocese without incumbrance and a character without reproach. It was fortunate for this diocese that Bishop McGill presided over its destinies for upwards of twenty years, for he stamped his character upon the older clergy, who had the happiness of observing his edifying life and of being associated with him in the ministry.

"It is very gratifying to me, though this is the first occasion I have done so, to speak in terms of praise of the clergy of this diocese; other priests, indeed, I have met who have a greater reputation for learning and the graces of oratory, but, taken as a body, I have never met any priests to surpass those of this diocese in attachment to duty, in singleness of purpose, in personal virtue and obedience to the voice of authority. And if I be permitted to single out some of the clergy from among their colleagues, surely I can point with peculiar joy to the Cathedral clergy, who have lived with me as members of the same household, and who have always deported themselves in a manner becoming their sacred calling. * * * If I could lift the veil and reveal to you their domestic life, I could disclose to you a spirit of order, peace and brotherly concord which I hope to see imitated, but dare not hope to see surpassed.

"As for you, brethren of the laity, you can bear me witness that I never indulged you by vain flattery, but that I have always endeavored to propose to you your duty, no matter how distasteful it might have been to flesh and blood. But on the present occasion I would be doing violence to my own feelings if I did not express my deep sense of admiration for the piety of many of you, which edified me; for the obedience of all of

Old St. Peter's Cathedral and Bishop's Residence, Richmond, Va., in 1876.

you, which consoled me, and for your spirit of generosity, which strengthened my hands. I have never had occasion to rebuke you for any factious opposition, still less for any manifestation of a rebellious spirit, and I have always found you ready with heart and hand to second any effort I proposed for the advancement of religion. * * *

"I cannot without regret depart from a city to which I am bound by so many attachments, and from a people who have always manifested so much kindness toward me. I ask your prayers all the time. I do not ask you to pray that I may have a long life—that is immaterial—but pray that God may give light to my understanding, strength to my heart and rectitude to my will, in order to fulfill well the duties that may devolve upon me. I pray that God may send you a bishop according to His own heart—a man of zeal and mercy, who will cause virtue and religion and faith to flourish and bear fruit throughout the length of the diocese."*

His fellow-citizens of Richmond, without distinction of religious belief, viewed his departure with regret. Many testimonials of esteem brightened his last days in the diocese. On October 16, the clergy of the diocese dined with him, having come from their respective homes to say good-bye. After dinner, through Father O'Keefe, they presented him a beautiful chalice. The paten and cup were of solid gold; the other parts of silver gilt.

* *Catholic Mirror*, October 20, 1877.

CHAPTER VII.

ARCHBISHOP OF BALTIMORE.

Archbishop Bayley had presided over the See of Baltimore but a few years, when his health began to fail, and he sought the appointment of a coadjutor. The eyes of the people of the diocese, no less than the discriminating vision of the Archbishop himself, turned to the Bishop of Richmond. In Baltimore he had been born and baptized; studied for the ministry and been ordained; served as parish priest of St. Bridget's and as assistant at the Cathedral; and while in North Carolina and Virginia he had returned at times to aid the archbishops and share the labors of the clergy, who looked upon him both as a friend and a natural leader.

Archbishop Bayley wrote in his diary March 24, 1876:

"Two years ago the doctor advised me to obtain the assistance of a coadjutor. My health troubles me so much I find it difficult to attend to my duties. Today I wrote to his Eminence, Cardinal McCloskey, Archbishops Purcell, Kenrick, Wood and Williams, asking them to assist me in obtaining as my coadjutor *cum jure successionis* the bishop of Richmond."*

The time was ripe for the decisive change in Bishop Gibbons' career. In May, 1877, he was appointed titular Archbishop of Janopolis and coadjutor to the incumbent of the See of Baltimore, with the right of succession; and when that prelate died at Newark, October 3 of the same year, he succeeded to the exalted post at once. The funeral of Archbishop Bayley in the Cathedral, October 9, was marked by many tributes by clergy

---

* Rev. M. J. Riordan, in Volume II, The Catholic Church in the United States of America, p. 81.

and people to the work of this remarkable man. Cardinal Mc-
Closkey, of New York, who had been raised to the Sacred College two years before; Archbishop Wood, of Philadelphia;
Archbishop Gibbons, and many bishops and priests were present at the solemn and beautiful services. Bishop Thomas Foley,
of Chicago, delivered the funeral discourse, recalling the eminent contributions which Bayley had made to the progress of
the Catholic Church and the spiritual welfare of the American
people. The Archbishop had asked that when his labors were
over, his body should rest near the grave of his aunt, Mother
Seton, who introduced the Sisters of Charity into the United
States. It was taken to Emmitsburg, Md., and lowered into
the vault beside all that was mortal of that saintly woman.*

Archbishop Gibbons received with characteristic spirit the
new and great honor which had come to him. When he first
learned of his elevation, he exclaimed:

"Thy will be done. In Thy hand is my fate!"

The death of Pius IX caused him to hesitate about proceeding with the ceremonies of receiving the pallium, but Cardinal
McCloskey and other prelates and clergy advised him not to
postpone the event too long. This historic mark of his new rank
was placed upon his shoulders February 10 by Bishop Lynch,
of Charleston, in the Cathedral. The procession from the
archiepiscopal residence to the church embraced a distinguished
gathering of the hierarchy, many of them in the prime of life,
fruitful in their work for the harvest of souls, but scarcely
any of whom lived to see the full outlines of the career of
the man whom they had assembled to honor. Following the
picturesque seminarians of St. Mary's, came Bishops Moore,
of St. Augustine; Spalding, of Peoria, then full of his great
project of founding a Catholic university; Kain, of Wheeling,
afterward Archbishop of St. Louis; Corrigan, of Newark,
destined to succeed to the see presided over by the venerable
McCloskey, and to measure his strength against Archbishop

---

* Riordan, Cathedral Records, p. 85.

Gibbons in many a controversy regarding the vital problems of the American Church; Gross, of Savannah, soon to be Archbishop of Oregon; Foley, of Chicago, close friend from early days of the new Archbishop; Becker, of Wilmington, Del., also bound to him by ties of intimacy; Shannahan, of Harrisburg; Fitzgerald, of Little Rock, staunch opponent to the last of the decree of papal infallibility passed by the Vatican Council; Loughlin, of Brooklyn, venerable and beloved; Archbishop Williams, of Boston, strong upholder of the hands of Archbishop Gibbons on many a trying occasion; and, lastly, the new Archbishop, attended by two of his closest friends, Rev. Dwight E. Lyman, of Govanstown, Baltimore county, and Rev. Michael Dausch, of St. Vincent's Church, Baltimore. As the mass was beginning, Bishop Conroy, of Ardagh, Apostolic Delegate of the Holy See to Canada, entered the Cathedral and took a seat of honor opposite Archbishop Gibbons.

Such an eminent gathering of leaders of the Catholic faith in the old Cathedral could not fail to be inspired by its surroundings. Bishop Lynch, in his discourse, was moved to rehearse in outline what this Church, assembled in the plentitude of her power, had done for society, truth, virtue, and science. He recalled that men still lived who could remember when Carroll was the only American archbishop, while his successor could now count ten other archbishops and sixty bishops, whose authority stretched from ocean to ocean. Never, he said, had the Church in America been stronger, truer in the faith, or more united for aggressive work in pursuit of her great mission. Men were needed to control, like safe and devoted pilots, the progress of this vast undertaking, and it was a cause of congratulation that Baltimore had an archbishop who had already given promise of being a worthy successor of the eminent prelates who had gone before. He would not congratulate the new Archbishop, for those who had worn the mitre knew that he needed sympathy more than congratulation. Referring to the fact that he was placing upon Archbishop

Gibbons the last pallium bestowed by Pius IX, he paid an eloquent tribute to the fruitful labors of that pontiff.

As Archbishop Gibbons rose to reply, he gazed, not like a stranger sent into a new field, upon the faces of strangers; not, as in Wilmington and Richmond, upon men and women who had scarcely heard of him before, but upon a notable congregation of the leading people of Baltimore, whom for years he had counted as his friends.   Here, at last, he was at home. Here, in this venerable church, was the greatest work of his life to find expression.

"The See of Baltimore," he said, replying to Bishop Lynch, "is, indeed, replete with historical interest, whether we consider its venerable antiquity, as far as that term can be applied to a nation as young as ours, or whether we consider the illustrious line of prelates who have presided over its destinies. The morning of Bishop Carroll's consecration, in 1790, brings us back to the dawn of our American history, which followed the dark and eventful night of our American Revolution. Washington then occupied the Presidential chair.   The elder Adams, Jefferson and Madison were still in the full vigor of active political life; the United States as then constituted had a population short of four millions; the city of Baltimore, which now rejoices in its hundreds of thousands of souls, had only 13,500; while the Catholic population of the United States at that time may be estimated at twenty-five thousand souls, or less than one-fourth of the present Catholic population of Baltimore.

"But if this See of Baltimore is venerable for its antiquity, it is still more conspicuous for that bright constellation of prelates who diffused their light over the American Church, as well as over this diocese.   It is not necessary that I should enlarge upon the greatness of these eminent men; for many of them were personally known to yourselves by familiar acquaintance.   All are known to you by splendid reputations, their names are cherished as household words in your families, and their bright example is held up to the admiration and emulation of your children.

"Otherwise, I might speak of Bishop Carroll, who possessed the virtues of a Christian priest, with the patriotism of an American citizen; I might speak of a Neale, 'whose life was hidden with Christ in God;' of a Marechal, who united in his person the refined manners of a French gentleman with the sturdy virtues of a pioneer prelate; of a Whitfield, who expended a fortune in the promotion of piety and devotion; of the accomplished Eccleston, who presided with equal grace and dignity in the professor's chair, on this throne, and at the Council of Bishops; of a Kenrick, whose praise is in the churches—he has not only adorned this see by his virtues, but also, I might say, illuminated all Christendom by his vast learning. I might speak of a Spalding, whose paternal face is to this day stamped upon your memories and affections, whose paternal rule I myself had the privilege of experiencing, whose very name does not fail, even at this day, to evoke feelings of heartfelt emotion; of a Bayley, I can simply say that those who knew him best, loved him most. His was a soul of honor. He never hesitated to make any sacrifice when God's honor and his own conscience demanded."

The Archbishop alluded modestly to the alarm he felt when called to this important see; the fear with which he had taken up the lines, fallen from the hands of the illustrious man who had preceded him, and the sense he possessed of his own unworthiness. It would be, he said, a presumption on his part to hope to emulate these illustrious prelates, but he would make it the study of his life to copy their virtues, however imperfectly. If he was discouraged by the sense of the weight of the obligations resting upon him, he had also, thanks to God, great grounds of hope and confidence, and this confidence was in the clergy of the diocese. He could say of them, as he had said of the priests of Richmond, that they enjoyed an honored reputation among the clergy of the country.

In praising them, he would be doing violence to his own feelings and to his sense of justice, if he did not speak in commendation of that venerable institution, to which most of them owed their theological training and were so deeply indebted—St. Mary's Seminary, the fruitful mother of priests and bishops. The introduction of the Sulpician Fathers to the diocese had been almost coeval with the creation of the diocese itself. If the departed prelates to whom he had alluded were honored in public life, the names of a Nagot, a Tessier, a Deluol and others were not less revered. It would be difficult to say whether religion was more indebted to the active ministry of the former or the private, unpretentious labors of the latter.

He expressed his confidence in the religious orders with which the diocese abounded, from the Society of Jesus—the glorious pioneers of the Cross in this region—down to the last society founded. Different in their founders, in their dress and in their rules, they were all happily guided by the same spirit—one faith and one God. "There are diversities of graces, but the same spirit; diversities of ministries, but the same Lord; diversities of operation, but the same God, who worketh all in all." He wished to say that he confided in his brethren of the regular and secular clergy. He had unbounded confidence in their wisdom, devotion, learning, piety, zeal and hearty co-operation. United as a band of brothers, they were invincible. They would labor together in promoting the kingdom of Jesus Christ, in vindicating the claims of the Apostolic See, and in fostering faith, charity, religion, piety and pure patriotism, which would flourish still more in the favored State of Maryland, "the land of the sanctuary and the asylum of civil and religious liberty."

In conclusion, the new Archbishop asked his hearers to pray for the illustrious pontiff whose soul had just been released from the bonds of earth.*

Non-Catholics as well as Catholics applauded the selection of Archbishop Gibbons; all Baltimore seemed to look on it as a compliment. He was the first native of the city to fill that exalted office, so interwoven with the birth of religious liberty and of the Catholic faith and hierarchy among English-speaking people on this Continent.

He was but forty-three years old, the youngest of the archbishops, when he thus became the primate of the American Church. With Rev. William E. Starr as chancellor, and Rev. Alfred A. Curtis, afterward Bishop of Wilmington, as secretary, he began the work of the diocese with aggressive activity. The pioneer days of North Carolina were but a memory now. His task was to strengthen the foundations of the Church in the oldest diocese of America; to multiply its efforts in the city where it had found its most congenial home. At once he became a leading figure in the community, apart from his ecclesiastical office. It had not been the fashion for Catholic archbishops, nor, indeed, for prelates of any other faith, to take part in the complex activities of life in a modern American city. They had rather sought the seclusion of study, and had regarded the sharp boundary of ecclesiastical duty as one beyond which they ought not to trespass. Mingling with the world had seemed to them to be contamination or a compromise with the material life.

Not so with Archbishop Gibbons. He was among and of the people. His predecessors in the see had hardly been known to Protestants. He became so well known that in a short time he was as familiar to them and, perhaps, as much beloved by them, as by Catholics. It is related of him that on one occasion, when passing through the streets with a visitor,

---

Catholic Mirror, February 16, 1878.

they came to the door of a beautiful church, from which a large congregation was beginning to emerge.   Archbishop Gibbons was saluted so often, and gave so many salutes in return, that his companion was moved to remark:

"You seem to be well acquainted in this parish?"

"Ah!" he replied, "these are our Episcopalian friends!"

He felt from the beginning that the slight trace of distrust of the Catholic Church and hierarchy which was felt by certain elements of the people was due, in large part, to a lack of understanding.   One of his great purposes was to remove this cloud, to bring the Church out into the brilliant light of public observation among Americans, that all might see her mission and the mission of her priesthood as being a spiritual one.   He yielded to none in his devotion to American institutions and the Government of the United States, and he felt that the influence of the Church was for the perpetuity of law and order and constituted authority.   A student of history and an intense admirer of those grand figures in American life who had erected a magnificent nation where once the Indian had roamed through the forest or pushed his canoe along the stream, he was fond of recalling that Catholics had been among the most devoted pioneers who had helped to make the nation what it is.

In his own Maryland the faith which he held had been inseparably interwoven with the birth of the English province on the banks of the Potomac and the Chesapeake.   Jesuits, penetrating the wilderness from St. Mary's, had borne aloft the Cross to light the pathway of civilization.   Westward, along the Ohio and the Mississippi, down to the Gulf, near the shores of which part of his youth had been spent, these consecrated men of God had left enduring memorials of their sacrifices in the early days.   In the Revolution, Catholics had been eminent in the halls of statesmanship and on the field of battle. None craved more than they the full freedom of religion, the "government of the people, by the people and for the people," which, under Washington, had been won for the fringe of struggling colonies planted by adventurous Englishmen. They had felt more than Protestants the whip of oppression, the shackles of alien government. Almost simultaneously with the new nation, had come the consecration of Carroll, to found in free atmosphere at last the hierarchy of the Catholic Church. This Church had grown and prospered as the nation had become stronger. In every war and every time of stress its members had been one with their Protestant brethren in their examples of patriotism and devotion to the common country.

Still, in Baltimore as elsewhere, there was no denying that a trace of distrust remained. It had been too deep-seated a feeling to be erased in less than a century. The keynote of Archbishop Gibbons' attitude was liberality. As a churchman, none was more devoted to his Church; as an American, none was more devoted to America.

The month in which he received the pallium was marked also by the elevation to the papacy of Leo XIII, with whose career his own was to be so closely linked. These two men of advanced and liberal ideas, each a Catholic of Catholics and at the same time breathing the atmosphere of the times, alert, progressive, knowing how to "take occasion by the hand," labored concurrently in the most important periods of their lives. With a less sympathetic pontiff, the work of Gibbons would have been impossible; and Leo did not hesitate to say again and again that the encouragement and active help which he received from the Archbishop of Baltimore formed one of the potent influences that sustained him amid the hostility and misunderstanding with which he was often beset.

The bishop's former post at Richmond was filled by the elevation of the gifted and pious Dr. John J. Keane, then assistant pastor of St. Patrick's Church, Washington, to the bishopric. On the advice of the Archbishop, Rev. Mark S. Gross, his companion of other days in North Carolina, was appointed vicar apostolic there, but on account of ill health and dread of the responsibility, resigned at a meeting of the bishops of the province held in Baltimore November 24, 1880. Bishop Keane made a characteristic proposal to take up the work of the vicariate if the Holy See would release him from the Bishopric of Richmond, but this magnanimous offer was not accepted.

Bishop Keane continued for some years to perform the duties of both the bishopric and the vicariate, as Bishop Gibbons had done before him. The vicariate was finally filled by the appointment of Rev. H. P. Northrop, who had long labored as a priest in the field. Archbishop Gibbons consecrated him in the Baltimore Cathedral January 8, 1882, and installed him a week later in St. Thomas' Church, Wilmington.

Catholic bishops being required to go to Rome every ten years, unless excused by the Pope, Archbishop Gibbons made a visit *ad limina* in 1880. It was his first trip to the Eternal City since the Vatican Council, and his first meeting with Leo XIII as pontiff. Before his departure the clergy of the diocese, as a mark of their affection, presented $1,000 to him as a contribution toward his traveling expenses.

He spent 23 days in Rome, and had two "delightful audiences" (thus he wrote) with Leo XIII, besides several conferences with Cardinals Simeoni and Nina, upon whom largely fell the detailed oversight of American affairs. Returning, he stopped at Innspruck to witness the Passion Play; and in England visited Lulworth Castle, where Bishop Carroll had been consecrated. On his birthday, July 23, he met at the famous oratory of Edgbaston, near Birmingham, Cardinal Newman, upon whose wonderful life work the capstone of ecclesiastical approval—elevation to the Sacred College—had been placed a year before. He breakfasted as Newman's guest and was charmed with the brilliant conversation of that great English churchman, who presented to him several books bearing the autograph of the giver. The archbishop afterward spent a month in Ireland, and sailed from Queenstown August 25.

When he returned to Baltimore he found the city in a flutter of festal preparation for the observance of its one hundred and fiftieth anniversary, and he joined with hearty accord in the plans. He issued a circular to the clergy of the city, which he directed to be read at the masses on Sunday, October 10, of that year, advising that Catholic organizations should take an active part in the parades and other festivities, and that the clergy and the authorities of the parochial schools should march with them. At the same time, he exhorted the people to "avoid all sinful excess" during the celebration. A Te Deum was sung in the Catholic churches of Baltimore the following Sunday. Leading men of the city, who organized this celebration, never ceased to remember with gratitude the active and cordial help of the public-spirited Archbishop.

In common with all Americans, Archbishop Gibbons felt the shock when President Garfield was shot and fatally wounded by an assassin July 2, 1881. He promptly issued a circular letter to the clergy of the diocese, expressing his horror at the deed and directing prayer for the President's recovery. The following extracts show the tone of the circular:

"It is scarcely possible to imagine a deed more appalling to men or more iniquitous before God. For if it is such a crime to slay even a private citizen, what an enormity is it to attempt the death of one who, while representing the whole nation, is also as to matters temporal, the highest vice-gerent of God Himself in the land? * * * And our detestation of the wretch who has stricken down our head is yet more increased when we add to the official dignity of the sufferer his accessibility and affability to all and his committing, like all his predecessors, his personal safety entirely to the good will and good sense of those over whom he presides. * * * In the face, then, of this most hideous deed we are called upon to express at once our loathing of the crime and our deep sympathy with him whom this crime has placed in such great suffering and such imminent peril.

"For while the Catholic Church is happily above all parties and is far from the wish to take to herself the decision of the very transient, and as a rule not very momentous questions as to which these parties are at issue, yet none more than the Catholic Church inculcates respect for every duly constituted authority or more reprobates or threatens every thing by which such authority is assailed."*

The Archbishop sent a copy of his circular to Mrs. Garfield, with a letter of sympathy, for which she returned her grateful acknowledgments. When the president was informed of it, he exclaimed: "Bless the good will of the people." The Archbishop sent to Cardinal Simeoni an account of the attempted assassination, which occurred in his diocese.

After the death of Mr. Garfield, several months later, the Archbishop preached at the Cathedral, and took occasion to answer the doubts of the efficacy of prayer which had been raised in the minds of some by the fatal ending of the President's illness, despite the united petitions of the nation. He pointed out that "God answers our prayer in one of two ways, either directly or indirectly. Sometimes He grants us the direct and specified objects of our petitions; sometimes He denies us the direct object of our prayer, but grants us something equivalent or even better than we ask for. * * * In regard to the President: If God, in response to our prayers, did not save his life, He has done more—He has saved the life and preserved the peace of the nation. And the life of the nation is of more value than the life of any individual."

In addition, the Archbishop said God had been pleased to prolong the President's life until the popular excitement had subsided, saving the country from unknown dangers. He found in the subduing of party spirit and the increased respect for the Chief Magistracy of the nation additional cause for thanksgiving.†

In the autumn of the same year he issued what was, perhaps, the first official direction by a prelate of the Catholic Church in conformity with the national observance of Thanksgiving Day.

---

* Cathedral Archives.
† *Catholic Mirror*. October 8. 1881.

After citing in a circular to clergy and laity the admonition of St. Paul, that "prayers, intercessions and thanksgivings be made for kings and for all that are in high station," he continued:

"Surely it behooves us to pray with alacrity for the continued prosperity of our beloved country when we recall to mind the many advantages we enjoy as Christians and citizens under our system of government, which constantly holds over us the ægis of its protection. We should pray for all our public functionaries, both State and national, that they may discharge the important trusts confided to them with a due and conscientious regard for the interests of the people. We should also give thanks to the 'Giver of all good gifts,' not only for the spiritual blessings we have received at His hands, but also for the public peace and domestic tranquillity we enjoy and for the abundant harvests with which the land has been generally favored. * * * A fitting occasion will be presented to us for offering to God the homage of our adoration and gratitude on Thursday, November 24, a day especially recommended for public and national thanksgiving by the Chief Magistrate of the nation."*

The Archbishop was deeply affected by the death, in 1881, of Thomas C. Jenkins, the oldest pewholder of the Cathedral and the oldest member of its board of trustees, a scion of a family distinguished for generations by good works in the support of the Church no less than in the temporal activities of the community. Ten years later he consecrated the beautiful new church of Corpus Christi (Jenkins Memorial), built by the munificence of the children of this good man, who remained among his strongest props in the diocese. One of them, Michael Jenkins, was created a Knight of St. Gregory by a succeeding Pontiff.†

The Archbishop's mother, whom he had often visited in her declining years, and the struggles of whose untimely widowhood he vividly remembered, died at the home of his sister, Mrs. George Swarbrick, in New Orleans, May 7, 1883, at the age of eighty years. He continued to visit New Orleans at

---

* Cathedral Archives.
† Pius X, 1903.

intervals as the guest of his brother, John T. Gibbons, who had become a wealthy grain merchant.

The uncertainty of human events was strikingly illustrated by an experience of the Archbishop March 4, 1885, when Washington was resounding with the acclamations of a multitude assembled at the inauguration of President Cleveland, following the exciting campaign in which Mr. Blaine had been defeated. On that day he was in the sanctuary of the Cathedral taking part in the funeral of Mrs. Walker, sister of Mr. Blaine. The defeated candidate for the presidency came from Washington to attend the obsequies, while his late rival was being elevated to the office to which both had aspired.

In the same month the Archbishop paid his first visit to Mr. Cleveland in the White House, remaining half an hour. The President urged him to renew his visits from time to time. This was the beginning of a warm friendship, which continued during the life of Mr. Cleveland. He was a Presbyterian, but, like the Archbishop, was singularly free from prejudice regarding religion and was accustomed to "render to Cæsar the things that are Cæsar's, and to God, the things that are God's." On not a few occasions he leaned on the Archbishop's advice at critical periods of his career. Once, when the Baltimore prelate was visiting him in 1887, he remarked:

"Would you care to have me read to you my forthcoming message on the tariff?"

"I shall be much honored," was the reply.

The President then submitted to the judgment of his ecclesiastical friend, word by word, the famous message to Congress which cost him re-election in 1888, but brought about his triumph at the polls four years later. The Archbishop commended its frankness and statesmanlike character, but expressed doubt as to how it would be received by the public. History soon justified his viewpoint.

On another occasion great pressure was brought to bear on Mr. Cleveland to appoint a certain priest as chaplain in the Government service. This clergyman did not enjoy the confidence of his spiritual shepherd, the Archbishop of Baltimore, who declined to recommend him to Mr. Cleveland, though frequently importuned to do so. Without the Archbishop's sanction, the President positively refused to make the appointment. Threats were resorted to, and it was intimated that if Mr. Cleveland and the Archbishop did not recede from their attitude, they would be pictured in the pages of *Puck*. This showed a serious misjudgment of the characters of these two men, for both were so constituted that threats would only make them more fixed in any position they had assumed on a question of right and wrong. The clergyman was not appointed.

Mr. Cleveland frequently referred to his friend as one of the best types of the American citizen, and on meeting Baltimoreans was in the habit of saying:

"From Baltimore? Oh, that is Cardinal Gibbons' city! There are some men in Baltimore whom I particularly admire, and none more than the Cardinal!"

The anarchist riots in Chicago, May 4, 1886, profoundly moved the Archbishop with a sense of danger to the country. Preaching five days later at the dedication of the Church of the Holy Cross, Baltimore, a large number of whose members were of German birth, he declared that foreigners coming to these shores were generally an admirable addition to the population, but he denounced anarchism, socialism and nihilism. He said:

"They (the Chicago anarchists) have no conception of true liberty. They would retain for themselves the lion's share of freedom, leaving to others only a morsel. The citizens of the United States enjoy the amplest liberty, but it is a liberty of law, of order and of authority. Liberty without law degenerates into license."

Soon the Archbishop and future Cardinal came to be as much identified with Baltimore as Pericles with Athens. On the streets of the city his slender, graceful form, in somber black, relieved by a touch of purple, became familiar to passers-by as he took long walks, swinging a cane and chatting in animated fashion with a clerical companion.   In gatherings relating to the interests of the city or State, his aid was sought and freely given.   He sat on public platforms with Methodists, Jews and Quakers.   None spoke with more sincere patriotism, more progressive spirit.   Governor and Mayor regarded him as friend.

On a social occasion he could be charming.   When Baltimoreans have some particularly important business to transact, it is their custom to have a banquet.   It is characteristic of them that some of their greatest inspirations to public achievement are born amid the gastronomic delights of the diamond-back terrapin and the canvass-back duck.   It grew to be a familiar spectacle to see the Archbishop at the banquet board, in the place of honor, at the right of the presiding officer.   He seldom remained to the end, and took no part in the purely convivial aspect of the gathering.   When he spoke, it was as a patriot no less than a preacher.   His habit of gracefully fitting into his surroundings was nowhere more conspicuous than at the social board.   He opened conventions with prayer, and reviewed parades from his bay-window.

His sermons in the Cathedral became one of the attractions of the city.   Non-Catholics as well as Catholics crowded the spacious pews and aisles to hear him.   Rarely he preached on a controversial theme; never with a sensationalism designed to attract the unthinking.   He felt that the Gospel itself was strong enough to draw men, if it could be presented to them with clearness and simplicity.   He made no compromise with truth.   He palliated no sin because of the mightiness or the lowliness of those who practiced it.   He could unsparingly condemn a grievous fault.   He sustained his viewpoint from that of the apostles, and often Protestants found more spiritual sustenance in his discourses than in those of their own pastors.

In his visits to churches he made many converts. His whole attitude was a powerful appeal to Protestants. On an extremely hot Sunday in midsummer, while in Southern Maryland, he asked the priest accompanying him to preach. At the conclusion of the sermon, when the priest descended from the pulpit, almost exhausted by a vigorous discourse on the doctrine of absolution, he was surprised to see the Archbishop ascend the steps and preach again, but on a very different topic—one which appealed alike to persons of all creeds.

"I thought you asked me to preach?" exclaimed the astonished clergyman, when the congregation had been dismissed.

"Did you not see," replied the Archbishop, with one of his characteristic smiles, "that more than half the congregation were Protestants?"

His labors were incessant. Men of the most robust physique could hardly keep up with him. His health as he reached the noon of vigorous manhood showed much improvement, but his digestion remained weak, and at times he appeared almost emaciated. On one occasion it was said of him that his frame seemed barely substantial enough to hold the soul within. Regularity of habit, prudence in diet, a characteristic optimism, avoidance of the American sin of worry, and his habit of taking daily a long and vigorous walk sustained him in his most arduous activities.

Amid all the burdens which fell upon him, he practiced his devotions, which occupied several hours every day, with unfailing regularity. He was up at six o'clock every morning. Soon afterward he said mass, and, after a light breakfast, was alert for the business of the day. Callers were numerous. Some came for religious consolation; others, for advice; still others, to solicit alms, to invite his participation in public projects, to urge his presence in churches. He denied himself to none. He could turn from one to another with complete ease, as if the last visitor were the first whom he had seen. The breadth of his character and observation, together with the ready social faculty which seemed to be instinct with him, gave him the power of meeting almost all persons on a footing of congeniality.

His purse at this time was not over full. Though he was beginning to receive a considerable revenue from royalties on "The Faith of Our Fathers," this went almost as quickly as it came. He helped students with contributions, assisted the poor, subscribed to worthy undertakings, was a patron of literature and art. It was said of him that he was, perhaps, the easiest man in Baltimore from whom to get a response to an appeal for aid. With all his keen discrimination of character and his power of reading men, kindness of heart predominated in his impulses. His marvelous memory for names and faces, and his extraordinary acquaintance contributed greatly to swell the number of his visitors. He could identify children by their resemblance to their parents, and couples whom he had married were his friends forever.

Distinguished foreigners, visiting America for purposes of observation, made a practice of coming to Baltimore to call at the house of the Archbishop, the primate of the American Church. He could often speak to them in their own tongues. Not a few of them conveyed their impressions of him in the books which they subsequently wrote.

At his front door was usually an usher, who received the cards of visitors and escorted them to one of the reception rooms on the main floor of his residence. Often he was kept busy going from one room to another, and it seemed almost like a public reception. In a respite he would ascend the stairs to his study, where he would write or dictate; but at the next call he would descend again, with patience unruffled and a cheerful cordiality which made the last visitor feel thoroughly at home.

He dined about one o'clock; then he rested a while, perhaps received more callers, and about four o'clock came the daily walk or drive, when in the exhilaration of healthful exercise his cares were forgotten. After supper he studied, or made visits. At times he had a habit of dropping in on his parishioners or other friends, chatting half an hour, perhaps remaining for a cup of tea, and always the life of any party in which he happened to be. Through all these busy hours were scattered numerous devotional exercises. He spent more time reading the Scriptures than perhaps any clergyman of his diocese, and was always ready for the humblest duty of the priesthood. Marriages, baptisms and funerals found him every ready, if the time could be spared from his necessary episcopal duties. His discourses to bridal couples were particularly happy, and many of them kept his picture in their homes throughout life. The sacredness of marriage, its responsibilities and duties, was a favorite theme with him. He regarded this as the foundation of the social structure, and his influence was unceasingly and uncompromisingly bent toward maintaining the home life of the people. He never failed, when occasion offered, to exalt the nobility of wifehood, motherhood, womanhood. He valued the judgment of women, as well as their devotion to the cause of religion. In many a household he watched the home circle spring up, and now and then, by a visit or a word of encouragement, helped to strengthen its foundations.

Often he said high mass and preached on Sundays, and he was foremost in Lenten devotions. Once every year he went into retreat with the clergy of his diocese. While he could adapt himself to circumstances with rare tact, he never lost sight of his office as a minister of religion. He could laugh over a game of marbles with a small boy, or discuss theology with equal zest in a conference with a visiting archbishop.

A story is told of him by a friend who happened to see some angry boys disputing over a baseball game and a slender man standing in their midst trying to quiet them. On approaching, the friend was surprised to see that it was the Archbishop.   In a short time peace was restored and the game proceeded.

He frequently visited the institutions for the reformation of youth in Baltimore and its vicinity, speaking simple words of encouragement and vigorous common sense to the boys and girls.   He did not believe in severe restrictions, though firmness he considered thoroughly necessary.   His view was that in almost every person, young or old, there is much of good, which needs only to be awakened by proper influences.   It has been, perhaps, due as much to his personal guidance and frequent aid, as to any other cause, that the benevolent and reformatory institutions maintained by Catholics in the Diocese of Baltimore have taken a standard which has placed them conspicuously in the front rank.

CHAPTER VIII.

Third Plenary Council of Baltimore.

Archbishop Gibbons was near the noonday of his constructive activity when he embarked on one of the greatest projects of his life—the organization and guidance of the Third Plenary Council of Baltimore, over which he presided as Apostolic Delegate. This notable gathering, which served as a model for subsequent councils of the Church in Canada, Australia and Ireland, was held in the Baltimore Cathedral from November 9 to December 7, 1884.

The rapid growth of the American Church and the diversity of its new problems led to the decision to convoke the prelates for a general consideration of its needs. Since the Second Plenary Council of Baltimore, held in 1866, many questions of a highly important character had developed, simultaneously with the amazing expansion of the American people. Waste lands in the West, where only the Indian had roamed, or perhaps an adventurous miner had strayed in search of sudden wealth, had changed into prosperous and populous communities, which afforded fertile fields for the activities of the Church. The territory once embraced in the Louisiana Purchase, and subject to the ecclesiastical laws of Spain and France by turns, had become united by the railway and the telegraph with the older communities of the East, in which precedent had been largely obtained from the hierarchy of Great Britain. Still further toward the Pacific, States and Territories had been organized out of the immense region wrested from Mexico by the fortune of war. Here, too, the customs were, in many instances, different from those which prevailed in other parts of the nation, and there was no longer such a separation by distance that uniformity was not essential. Not long before, the Archbishop of St. Louis and the Bishop of San Francisco had rarely seen the Archbishop of Baltimore, because of the great distances and the physical obstacles which separated them; but now it had become easy to assemble the whole hierarchy for effective and concerted action.*

Wherever the Catholic Church goes, it organizes. From the nature of things, its methods necessitate concentration of authority and purpose. The mission which springs up in the primeval grove is as much subject to the spiritual oversight of the Supreme Pontiff as is the magnificent cathedral in one of the capitals of Europe. Its worship is not left to chance, nor circumstance, nor popular caprice; but must conform to the ritual of the universal Church, as decreed by the fathers assembled in the plentitude of their authority.

The priest may penetrate an unexplored country; he may journey over wild mountains, or along streams where the untutored native has never seen a white man; but he is bound as closely by faith and discipline to the great ecclesiastical organization of which he is a part as is the canon of a basilica in Rome. The language in which he may celebrate the mysteries of the mass is not the one which he learned from his mother, not the one which may be spoken in the locality where he happens to be, but the one which has formed the casket for the deposit of Catholic faith from the days of the martyrs.

The United States in 1884 was still, in the eyes of Rome, a missionary country, subject to the jurisdiction of the Congregation of the Propaganda. It had no comprehensive framework of canon law which would serve as an enduring basis for the multiplication of its activities. The gifted doctors of the Church in Europe, Asia and Africa had possessed such constitutions for their guidance from ancient times, modified to suit conditions as they arose from era to era. Much had been ac-

---

* Memorial Volume, Third Plenary Council, pp. 211-22.

complished by the first two plenary councils, which had assembled to deliberate upon the organization of the Church in America. The task, however, was far from complete, and the necessity for its accomplishment was one of the chief reasons which led to convoking the third council.

In a more conservative country, where population and social and political development proceeded at a less furious pace, many years might have elapsed before the comprehensive decrees of the second council would have become obsolete in any important particular. America had made precedent itself obsolete. Its statesmen had been no more able than its leaders in the religious world to penetrate the future. They had not seen that, in little more than a century, three millions of people would swell into a hundred millions. They had not known that the progress of invention would irritate the slavery question into a national sore which could be healed only by the knife. They had not seen that the rural communities of America, in which the framers of the Declaration of Independence expounded their sublime truths, would give place in a short time to vast cities, more populous and powerful than whole groups of independent States which had helped in times gone by to sway the world.

At first, Archbishop Gibbons took a conservative view of the proposal to hold a plenary council. At the instance of Cardinal McCloskey, Bishop Corrigan, of Newark, called on him in January, 1882, to consult in reference to the expediency of summoning such a gathering. Cardinal McCloskey's own views were rather adverse to it, and Archbishop Gibbons expressed the opinion that it would not be expedient to hold a council for some time to come. As a preliminary step, he suggested that provincial councils might be held, or the bishops of each province might assemble informally and consider what subjects might be discussed in a plenary council.

In time, as opinion among the American hierarchy crystallized, Leo XIII called a number of the archbishops to Rome to confer with him on the subject. Archbishop Gibbons left Baltimore in October, 1883, for the Eternal City. The conferences there continued during November and part of the following month, and the state of the Church in this country was carefully considered in the thorough manner characteristic of Rome. Cardinal McCloskey was in infirm health, and Leo, having finally decided to convoke the council, designated the Baltimore archbishop as Apostolic Delegate to preside over it in his name.

Archbishop Gibbons returned to Baltimore in March, 1884. He found that the clergy and laity had made extensive preparations for a public reception, which he declined. In a sermon at the Cathedral a few days later, he expressed his thanks for the offer, but added :

"I am myself opposed to such public demonstrations, and though they may be appropriate on some occasions, I felt that I had not the age nor the merits to deserve such. It would have taken place in the midst of Lent, and I would have felt very much mortified to consider myself conducted home in a procession of triumph at a time when the Church directs our minds to the spectacle of our Saviour conducted to suffering in a procession of shame."

The Archbishop, in the same discourse, spoke of his experiences in Rome. After saying that he had three private audiences with Leo XIII and two others in company with his brother prelates, he drew a picture of that pontiff which was significant of their future relations.

"No one can spend a half hour in the presence of Leo XIII," he said, "without giving thanks to God for granting to His Church so great a pontiff, and without being profoundly impressed with the breadth and elevation of sentiments that inspire him. In my first interview he remarked to me : 'I dislike severe and harsh measures; I dislike anathemas; I love to appeal to the good sense and intelligence and heart of the world. As the vicar and servant of Christ, I desire to draw all souls more closely to our common Master. To all I am a debtor. I have the solicitude of all the churches of Europe,

Asia, Africa, and especially of your own great and beloved country, whose spiritual progress gives me such consolation.'

"Notwithstanding his advanced age and delicate, I might say emaciated, frame, the Pope is indefatigable in his labors. In my first interview with him he informed me that he began his audiences that morning at half-past eight o'clock. They continued until his frugal meal at one o'clock, and were resumed and lasted probably until nine o'clock at night. I was informed by a member of his household that he allows himself but little repose, and that sometimes, when the city is buried in sleep, the aged pontiff is engaged until after midnight in writing his masterly encyclicals or in doing some other good work in the interests of the Christian commonwealth."

The Archbishop also spoke of the life of the cardinals—his future associates—saying that, "whatever may be the pomp which surrounds them on public occasions, the Roman cardinals, especially those engaged in congregations, are the hardest worked officials in the Eternal City. They are conspicuous for their learning and piety, and lead simple lives in the sanctuary of their homes, and, some of them, even lives of great austerity. If profound knowledge and clear insight into character and good common sense and sterling virtue and unwearied application to the duties of office form the essential elements of prudent counselors, the Roman cardinals constitute the most able senate of any deliberative body existing in the world."

Regarding his conferences at Rome, he said they were held at the College of the Propaganda, under the presidency of Cardinal Simeoni, assisted by Cardinals Franzelin and Jacobini. They were characterized by "the most ample freedom of discussion, joined with the most perfect harmony and good feeling."

The Archbishop also dwelt on his observations of general conditions abroad, and expressed a viewpoint which had already become characteristic of him, when he said:

"The oftener I go to Europe, the longer I remain there, and the more I study the political condition of its people, I return home filled with greater consideration for our country and more profoundly gratified that I am an American citizen. When I contemplate the standing armies of over a million soldiers in each of the principal countries of Europe; when I consider what an enormous drain these armies are on the resources of a country and what a frightful source of immorality; when I consider that they are a constant menace to their neighbors and an incentive to war, and when I consider that the subject of war engages so much of the attention of the cabinets of Europe; and when, on the other hand, I look at our own country, with its 55,000,000 of inhabitants and its little army of 25,000 men scattered along our frontiers, so that we might travel from Maine to California without meeting a soldier or a gendarme; and when I consider that, if need be, every citizen is a soldier without being confined to barracks and is ready to defend and to die for his country; when I consider that we have no entangling alliances; when I reflect on our material prosperity; above all, when I consider the happy blending with us of authority with civil and religious liberty; with all our political corruption, I bless God for the favors he has vouchsafed us and I pray that he may continue to hold over us the mantle of his protection."*

It was an immense task to prepare for a new plenary council. Archbishop Gibbons showed his rare judgment of men by selecting Dr. Dennis J. O'Connell as his assistant. He could not have chosen an ecclesiastic better fitted by keen insight into the workings of the universal Church and rare comprehension of the true spirit of the American people to help him in the undertaking. The archbishop himself was particularly adapted by experience, no less than by ability, for his work, having served as assistant chancellor at the Second Plenary Council of Baltimore and having been a participant as bishop in the

---

* *Catholic Mirror*, March 22, 1884.

Vatican Council of 1870.   He had seen the operations of the
Church in both Europe and America, and had studied her polity
at the fountain of the pontificate.   Her great men had been his
counselors.   The work was congenial to his natural bent, and
its prodigious labor did not deter him.

An outline was completed for numerous topics to be treated
by the council; and when his conferences in Rome were over,
the basis for all the deliberations of the prelates in Baltimore
had been accurately marked out.   On his return home, he
applied himself to a continuance of his preparation for the
council.   He was engaged on this arduous undertaking every
day up to the time for the gathering to assemble.

Soon after his return he issued a pastoral* on the confisca-
tion of the American College by the Italian Government.   The
college had been founded and maintained by contributions from
the American residents of Rome and the Catholics of this country.   The Government at Washington promptly protested
against its unwarranted seizure, and it was ultimately restored
to its rightful owners.

The work of Archbishop Gibbons in preparing for the council found a fitting climax in the deliberations of that body
itself.   It was natural that differences of opinion should develop, for its members represented diversified and widely separated communities.   They spoke with that full freedom which
is permissible even in the precincts of the Vatican, and which,
in the clash of ideas, develops the vital spark that fuses the
predominant judgment of learning, experience and piety.   The
ability and tact of Archbishop Gibbons were put to a severe
test, but seemed to respond more fully as greater demands were
made on them.   When debaters like Ireland, of St. Paul; Keane,
of Richmond; Spalding, of Peoria; Gilmour, of Cleveland;
Hennessy, of Dubuque, and Ryan, of Philadelphia, could not
agree, he found common ground on which all could stand.
Had his career been wholly different, and had he embarked on

---

* Cathedral Archives.

the uncertain sea of politics, he would probably have attained as conspicuous success as in the Church.   He understood, with rare comprehension of human nature, how to handle a large deliberative gathering.   He could say a word here, bestow a smile there, express a doubt at the right moment, and seize the psychological opportunity to press a point.

When the facts are considered, it is extraordinary that unity could have been obtained among men of such strong characteristics, whose opinions were inevitably influenced by great differences of initial viewpoint.   It was a "melting pot" in which the diverse tendencies of the American people were mingled; but, happily, the individual members of the gathering proved that they possessed within themselves resources enough for the construction of great national ideas.

The council ended in complete ·harmony; and the venerable Archbishop Kenrick, of St. Louis, wept at its close, as he expressed the thanks of the prelates to the Apostolic Delegate for the manner in which he had presided over their deliberations.*   "More than half a century," said he, "has ·passed since the First Plenary Council, when I stood beneath the dome of this Cathedral, a silent spectator of the deliberations of that body.   I had never seen a more sublime sight.   It was not this grand old building, nor the gorgeous vestments, nor the dulcet strains of the music that inspired me.   It was that assemblage of men from all parts of .the country, with different ideas and sentiments, but with one common end in view—the good .of our Church.

"When Xerxes beheld his army of a million men standing in their martial strength before him, he wept on reflecting that not one of that mighty host would survive a century; and so of us, venerable Fathers, in half that time death shall claim us all."

Tears flowed down the seams of his aged face as he referred to the pleasant memories of the two former plenary councils.

---

* *Catholic Mirror*, December 13, 1884.

Archbishop Gibbons was, naturally, moved to his inmost depths by this closing scene. "Whatever success has attended my part of the work," he said, with characteristic modesty, "I attribute, under God, to your kind forbearance and uniform benevolence toward me. Mindful of the words of the apostle, you have not despised my youth. I have witnessed the proceedings of the greatest deliberative bodies in the world; I have listened to debates in the House of Commons, the French Chambers, and both Houses of Congress; I have attended provincial, national and ecumenical councils; but never did I witness more uniform courtesy in debate, more hearty acquiescence in the opinions of the majority than in the Third Plenary Council of Baltimore.

"Venerable Fathers, we have met as bishops of a common faith; we part as brothers, bound by the closest ties of charity. Though differing in nationality, in language, in habits, in tastes, in local interests, we have met as members of the same immortal episcopate, having 'one Lord, one faith, one baptism, one God and Father of all;' and if the Holy Father, whose portrait adorns our council chamber, could speak from the canvas, well could he exclaim, 'Behold how good and how pleasant a thing it is for brethren to dwell together in unity!'

"The words you have spoken in council, like good seed, are yet hidden from the eyes of men; but they will one day arise and bring forth fruit of sanctification. The decrees you have formulated will foster discipline and piety; they will quicken the faith and cheer the hearts of millions of Catholics.

"This is the last time that we shall assemble under the dome of this venerable Cathedral, with the portraits of God's saints looking down upon us. The venerable Archbishop has reminded us of our short tenure of life; but we are immortal! God grant that the scene of today may be a presage of our future reunion in the temple above, not made with hands, in the company of God's saints, where, clothed in white robes

BALTIMORE CATHEDRAL

and with palms in our hands, we shall sing benediction and honor and glory to our God forever."*

The decrees of the council were taken to Rome by Dr. O'Connell and several of the American bishops. They were signed by 14 archbishops, 61 bishops or their representatives, 6 abbots and one general of a religious order. The decrees were approved and returned without material changes, and the highest praise was bestowed upon Archbishop Gibbons for the manner in which he had guided the assemblage of prelates. It was, indeed, a monumental work, and the Church throughout the world was quick to recognize it.

One of the principal outcomes of this council, as viewed in the light of later events, was the foundation of the Catholic University of America. The higher education of the American clergy and of Catholic youth had long engaged the deep attention of Archbishop Gibbons and other far-seeing members of the hierarchy. Notwithstanding the multiplication of schools for the advanced training of priests, many of them were still forced to go to the great universities abroad, and they returned, in some cases, with ideas which were not suited to the characteristics of the flocks they served. The development of a thoroughly American clergy, one in faith and discipline with their brethren throughout the world, but in touch with the spirit and aspirations of their own people, was a favorite project with the Baltimore Archbishop and other discerning men in the Church.

Naturally, the Church became the shepherd of a large portion of the immigrants from countries where English was not spoken, and she consistently pursued the policy of selecting priests for these people who could speak their own language, who could sympathize with and help them in their homes on an intimate footing. But the greatest obstacle of all was that a number of the clergy who served English-speaking congrega-

---

* Memorial Volume, Third Plenary Council, pp. 65-67.

tions were of foreign birth and training. In part, this could not have been avoided, as the Catholic Church insists upon a rigorous schooling of her priests, in accordance with the decrees of the Council of Trent and of the Vatican Council; they could not be content with the moderate education which often sufficed for clergymen of some Protestant faiths. Until the birth of the American republic, practically all the priests who labored in English-speaking America were foreigners. Almost simultaneously with the foundation of the hierarchy in the person of Bishop Carroll, the devoted fathers of St. Sulpice had come from Paris to found in Baltimore a college for the training of priests. This was, naturally, under French influences for many years. As other schools developed, they were all of European origin, and it had been difficult to send forth for ordination Catholic ministers of religion who had been associated with no educational training except that of their own country.

In colonial times the American priesthood had a French tinge, just as the priesthood of the Church of England had an English origin. Later, when the wave of Irish immigration set in, the priests were largely of Irish birth; and as Germans began to swarm to the shores of America, there was another introduction of foreign influence.

Archbishop Gibbons, a native American, an intense admirer of the land of his birth, an optimist regarding the American people, felt that this should be changed. While a priest could execute his Divine mission without being one in language or social environment with the recipients of his ministrations, it was far better to have an American clergy for Americans. It was also highly important to have a cultured clergy—men who, while able to penetrate among the homes of the poor, to carry their evangel into the nurseries of vice and degradation, could also meet the higher types of the people on a footing of perfect equality. Tens of thousands of Catholics were men and women of culture, refined in their social instincts, moving in the best circles of city, town and country. The priests ministering to them should have some polish, some versatility of education and association, some measure of the impulses of those with whom they came in contact.

In an incredibly short time a wonderful system of Catholic education had been established throughout the United States. Still, it needed a capstone. American universities, up to 1876, had been little more than advanced colleges; but with the establishment of the Johns Hopkins University, at Baltimore, in the centennial year, European methods of post-graduate education were introduced, and soon the whole American system of higher culture was being shifted to this base. It was no longer the under-graduate, but the post-graduate, work of an educational system which faithfully expressed its essential character. The one thing needed to surmount the structure already raised by the Catholic Church was the active help of devoted and wealthy laymen in founding a university where the loftiest ideals of the Church for the training of her priesthood and laity should be fitly expressed. At first this was only a dream. At the Second Plenary Council of Baltimore the question was seriously debated, whether the time had not come to establish a university; but means were lacking, and it was felt that the moment was not opportune to embark satisfactorily upon this undertaking. There was unanimity of opinion among the prelates who then expressed themselves on the subject that the day was not far distant when the university could be founded, and they resolved always to keep in sight this climax of their educational efforts.

Bishop Spalding was the apostle of the project. A Kentuckian by birth, he had studied at Mount St. Mary's College, Emmitsburg, Md., and also in Cincinnati; but to obtain the ample training which he sought for his life work, he had been compelled to spend five years at Louvain.* He saw the grievous need for a great university in America, and he early embarked

---

* Reily, Collections in the Life of Cardinal Gibbons, Vol. I, p. 151.

on a life of effort to bring about a realization of this fond hope. His brilliant talents and the ardor of youth combined to equip him admirably for his mission.   In 1882 he visited Rome and obtained the papal approval for the plan of organizing the university.   Archbishop Gibbons, and the other prelates who met in Rome in the autumn of 1883 to frame the outlines for the work of the Third Plenary Council, discussed the project with eager hopes, and resolved to embrace it in their program. When the council met, Bishop Spalding was able to announce a triumph.   He presented an offer from Miss Mary Gwendoline Caldwell of $300,000 to form the nucleus for a university fund.   Her father, William Shakespeare Caldwell, had inherited a large fortune, which he increased by his own business skill.   While living in Richmond, Va., as we have previously seen, he had munificently endowed the Little Sisters of the Poor, and bestowed with open hand other benefactions on the Church.*

The offer was gladly accepted, and the council appointed a board of trustees to take charge of the university project. Archbishop Gibbons headed this board, and for many years devoted himself with unceasing solicitude and activity to the realization of the plan.   An appeal was issued to the Catholics of the United States to provide the means for the endowment of eight professorships, with which it was decided that the university could begin its work, and also to erect the necessary buildings.   On all sides the idea was welcomed.   In a short time an admirable group of buildings had been erected at Washington, and the aspirations of years were bearing abundant fruit.†

Provision for the careful government of the Church was notable in the other acts of the council.‡   It was declared that when a see became vacant, the archbishop should assemble the

---

* Page 68.
† Riordan, in the Catholic Church in the United States of America, Vol. II, p 35.
‡ *Acta et Decreta Conc. Plen. III* (Baltimore, 1886).

consultors and irremovable rectors of the diocese, and they should choose three names to be forwarded to Rome and to the other bishops of the province. The bishops of the province, under the presidency of the archbishop, were to meet and discuss the candidates; if they desired, they might reject all the names proposed and substitute others, but must give their reasons for the change in forwarding their recommendation to Rome, where the pontiff was to make the final selection.

It was recommended that there should be six diocesan consultors, but two would suffice. Half of these were to be chosen by the bishop at his own option; the other half, after nomination by the clergy. The advice of these consultors should be asked by the clergy regarding the holding of a diocesan synod, dividing a parish, committing a parish to a religious society, and in transactions relating to Church property where the sum involved was more than $5,000. Consultors were to hold office three years, and could not be removed except for grave reasons. Each bishop was to appoint six examiners of diocesan clergy. They were to examine the junior clergy and the candidates for irremovable rectorships.

A parish, in order to have an irremovable rector, must possess a proper church, a school for boys and girls, and stable revenues for the support of priest, church and school. In each diocese every tenth rector should be irremovable, if the needed conditions obtained. A candidate for such a post must have been in the ministry ten years and have shown himself a satisfactory administrator in spiritual and temporal affairs. The examination for irremovable rectorships must take place before the bishop or vicar-general and three examiners. Each candidate was required to answer questions on dogmatic and moral theology, liturgy and canon law, and to give specimens of catechetical exposition and preaching.

Priests ordained for a diocese were bound by oath to remain in it. If an alien priest brought satisfactory testimonials from a former bishop, he might be admitted only after a probation of from three to five years. Infirm clergy were to be cared for. Unworthy priests, it was decreed, had no just claims to support, but, if they wished to amend, a house governed by regulars should be provided for them.

All priests should make a spiritual retreat once a year, or at least every two years. They should give themselves to solid reading and study, and avoid conduct that could raise the least suspicion of evil.

In all dioceses of the United States, it was ordered, there were to be the following six feasts of obligation and no others: The Immaculate Conception, Christmas, Circumcision of Our Lord (New Year's Day), Ascension, Assumption and All Saints' Day. The faithful were exhorted to a proper observance of Sunday. Music in church should accord with the sacredness of the time and place.

As the Church considers marriage one of the seven sacraments, it must be administered by a duly authorized priest. Mixed marriages were not to be contracted unless it were promised that the Catholic party to the union was in no danger of being turned from the Church and would strive to convert the non-Catholic party. Promises must also be given that the children of the union were to be brought up as Catholics. No dispensation from these obligations was permitted.

Preparatory seminaries for the education of clerics were to be organized. The students should be taught Christian doctrine, English, and at least one other modern language, according to the necessities of the diocese. They must learn to speak and write Latin, and instruction in Greek was also to be given. The teaching was to embrace the usual branches of profane learning, including the natural sciences, besides music and the Gregorian chant. Care must be taken in admitting candidates to the greater seminaries, and they must be zealously trained in virtue and learning. They were to take two years' work in philosophy and four years in theology. In theology were to be included the dogmatic and moral branches of the subject, biblical exercises, church history, canon law, liturgy and sacred eloquence. Great care must be taken in the appointment of the spiritual directors and the professors of the seminaries. Clerical students must spend their vacations in a manner becoming their profession.

For five years after ordination priests must take an examination every year in Scripture, dogmatic and moral theology, canon law, Church history and liturgy. Priests having the care of souls were to attend ecclesiastical meetings for the consideration of questions of doctrine and discipline; such meetings were to be held four times yearly in urban and twice yearly in rural districts.

Parochial schools were declared to be an absolute necessity, and pastors were directed to establish them. Parents must send their children to such schools, unless the bishop judged that there was sufficient reason for sending them elsewhere. It was held to be desirable that instruction in the schools should be free. Colleges and academies for the higher education of youth trained in parochial schools were to be encouraged by all possible means.

The council appointed a commission to prepare a catechism for general use, which was made obligatory after its publication. Another commission framed, with exacting care and the labor of years, a manual of prayers, which is a model of its kind and is the standard for American Catholics. Still another commission was appointed to aid the missions among the Indians and negroes.

Regarding secret societies, it was decreed that if Rome had not condemned a particular one, a commission composed of all the archbishops of the country was to decide whether or not it properly came under the laws relating to forbidden organizations. If the archbishops could not agree, the matter was to be referred to Rome.   This point later proved to be of the highest importance in the Knights of Labor controversy.

The bishop was decreed to be the guardian and supreme administrator of ecclesiastical property.   In all churches some seats must be provided for the poor.   Warning was given regarding abuses incident to such means of raising money as picnics, fairs and excursions.   Balls for religious purposes were not to be given.

Each diocese was to have an episcopal tribunal.   In disciplinary cases it was to consist of a judge, a fiscal procurator, a diocesan attorney, an attorney for the accused and a chancellor.   An auditor and a notary might be added.   In matrimonial cases the officers of the tribunal were to be an auditor, a defender of the marriage tie and a notary; the interested persons might employ advocates.

The pastoral letter issued by the Fathers of the Council at the close of their sessions expressed clearly the objects which they had sought to accomplish, as well as defined briefly their principal decrees.   The influence of Archbishop Gibbons was plainly seen in a number of its most important declarations. Perhaps most significant of all was its definition of the harmony between the Catholic Church and the American people. On this point the following extract may be quoted :*

"We think we can claim to be acquainted with the laws, institutions and spirit of the Catholic Church, and with the laws, institutions and spirit of our country; and we emphatically declare that there is no antagonism between them.   A Catholic finds himself at home in the United States; for the influence of his Church has constantly been exercised in behalf of individual rights and popular liberties.   And the right-minded American nowhere finds himself more at home than in the Catholic Church, for nowhere else can he breathe more freely that atmosphere of Divine truth, which alone can make him free.

---

* Memorial Volume, Third Plenary Council, Part. 3.

"We repudiate with earnestness the assertion that we need to lay aside any of our devotedness to our Church, to be true Americans; the insinuation that we need to abate any of our love for our country's principles and institutions, to be faithful Catholics.   To argue that the Catholic Church is hostile to our great Republic, because she teaches that 'there is no power but from God;' because, back of the events which led to the formation of the Republic she sees the Providence of God leading to that issue, and back of our country's laws the authority of God as their sanction—this is evidently so illogical and contradictory an accusation, that we are astonished to hear it advanced by persons of ordinary intelligence.   We believe that our country's heroes were the instruments of the God of Nations in establishing this home of freedom; to both the Almighty and to His instruments in the work we look with grateful reverence; and to maintain the inheritance of freedom which they have left us, should it ever—which God forbid—be imperiled, our Catholic citizens will be found to stand forward, as one man, ready to pledge anew 'their lives, their fortunes and their sacred honor.'

"No less illogical would be the notion, that there is aught in the free spirit of our American institutions incompatible with perfect docility to the Church of Christ.   The spirit of American freedom is not one of anarchy or license.   It essentially involves love of order, respect for rightful authority and obedience to just laws.   There is nothing in the character of the most liberty-loving American which could hinder his reverential submission to the Divine authority of our Lord, or to the like authority delegated by Him to His Apostles and His Church.   Nor are there in the world more devoted adherents of the Catholic Church, the See of Peter and the Vicar of Christ, than the Catholics of the United States.   Narrow, insular, national views and jealousies concerning ecclesiastical authority and Church organization may have sprung naturally enough from the selfish policy of certain rulers and nations in by-gone times; but they find no sympathy in the spirit of the true American Catholic. His natural instincts, no less than his religious training, would forbid him to submit in matters of faith to the dictation of the state or to any merely human authority whatsoever. He accepts the religion and the Church that are from God, and he knows well that these are universal, not national or local—for all the children of men, not for any special tribe or tongue. We glory that we are, and with God's blessing shall continue to be, not the American church, nor the church of the United States, nor a church in any other sense exclusive or limited, but an integral part of the one holy Catholic and Apostolic Church of Jesus Christ, which is the Body of Christ, in which there is no distinction of classes and nationalities—in which all are one in Christ Jesus."

The fathers stated that one of their first cares had been to provide for the education of aspirants to the priesthood. "It has always been the Church's endeavor," says the pastoral letter, "that her clergy should be eminent in learning, for she has always considered that nothing less than this is required by their sacred office of guarding and dispensing Divine truth. 'The lips of the priest shall keep knowledge,' says the Most High, 'and the people shall seek the law at his mouth.' This is true at all times; for no advance in secular knowledge, no diffusion of popular education, can do away with the office of the teaching ministry, which Our Lord has declared shall last forever.

"In every age it is and shall be the duty of God's priests to proclaim the salutary truths which our Heavenly Father has given to the world through his Divine Son; to present them to each generation in the way that will move minds and hearts to embrace and love them; to defend them, when necessary, against every attack of error. From this it is obvious that the priest should have a wide acquaintance with every department of learning that has a bearing on religious truth. Hence in our age, when so many misleading theories are put forth on every side, when every department of natural truth and fact is actively explored for objections against revealed religion, it is evident how extensive and thorough should be the knowledge of the minister of the Divine Word, that he may be able to show forth worthily the beauty, the superiority, the necessity of the Christian religion, and to prove that there is nothing in all that God has made to contradict anything that God has taught.

"Hence the priest who has the noble ambition of attaining to the high level of his holy office, may well consider himself a student all his life; and of the leisure hours which he can find amid the duties of his ministry, he will have very few that he can spare for miscellaneous reading, and none at all to waste. And hence, too, the evident duty devolving on us, to see that the course of education in our ecclesiastical colleges and seminaries be as perfect as it can be made. During the century of extraordinary growth now closing, the care of the Church in this country has been to send forth as rapidly as possible holy, zealous, hard-working priests, to supply the needs of the multitudes calling for the ministrations of religion. She has not, on that account, neglected to prepare them for their Divine work, as her numerous and admirable seminaries testify; but the course of study was often more rapid and restricted than she desired. At present our improved circumstances make it practicable both to lengthen and widen the course, and for this the council has duly provided."

The question of popular education, which had been fully discussed by the council, is treated of in the pastoral letter as one of supreme importance. The declarations of this council are particularly noteworthy as furnishing the basis on which the school question was afterward worked out by American Catholics.

"Popular education," the letter declares, "has always been a chief object of the Church's care; in fact, it is not too much to say that the history of civilization and education is the history of the Church's work. In the rude ages, when semi-barbarous chieftains boasted of their illiteracy, she succeeded in diffusing that love of learning which covered Europe with schools and universities; and thus from the barbarous tribes of the early Middle Ages she built up the civilized nations of modern times. Even subsequent to the religious dissensions of the sixteenth century, whatever progress has been made in education is mainly due to the impetus which she had previously given. In our country, notwithstanding the many difficulties attendant on first beginnings and unexampled growth, we already find her schools, academies and colleges everywhere, built and sustained by voluntary contributions, even at the cost of great sacrifices, and comparing favorably with the best educational institutions in the land.

"These facts abundantly attest the Church's desire for popular instruction. The beauty of truth, the refining and elevating influences of knowledge, are meant for all, and she wishes them to be brought within the reach of all. Knowledge enlarges our capacity both for self-improvement and for promoting the welfare of our fellow-men; and in so noble a work the Church wishes every hand to be busy. Knowledge, too, is the best weapon against pernicious errors. It is only 'a little learning' that is 'a dangerous thing.' In days like ours, when error is so pretentious and aggressive, every one needs to be as completely armed as possible with sound knowledge—not only the clergy, but the people also—that they may be able to withstand the noxious influences of popularized irreligion. In the great coming combat between truth and error, between faith and agnosticism, an important part of the fray must be borne by the laity, and woe to them if they are not well prepared! And if, in the olden days of vassalage and serfdom, the Church honored every individual, no matter how humble his position, and labored to give him the enlightenment that would qualify him for future responsibilities, much more now, in the era of popular rights and liberties, when every individual is an active and influential factor in the body politic, does she desire that all should be fitted by suitable training for an intelligent and conscientious discharge of the important duties that will devolve upon them.

"Few, if any, will deny that a sound civilization must depend upon sound popular education. But education, in order to be sound and to produce beneficial results, must develop what is best in man, and make him not only clever, but good. A one-sided education will develop a one-sided life; and such a life will surely topple over, and so will every social system that is built up of such lives. True civilization requires that not only the physical and intellectual, but also the moral and religious well-being of the people should be promoted, and at least with equal care. Take away religion from a people, and morality would soon follow; morality gone, even their physical condition would ere long degenerate into corruption, which breeds decrepitude, while their intellectual attainments would only serve as a light to guide them to greater depths of vice and ruin.

"This has been so often demonstrated in the history of the past, and is, in fact, so self-evident, that one is amazed to find any difference of opinion about it. A civilization without religion would be a civilization of 'the struggle for existence and the survival of the fittest,' in which cunning and strength would become the substitutes for principle, virtue, conscience and duty. As a matter of fact, there never has been a civilization worthy of the name without religion; and from the facts of history the laws of human nature can easily be inferred.

"Hence education, in order to foster civilization, must foster religion. But many, unfortunately, while avowing that religion should be the light and the atmosphere of the home and of the Church, are content to see it excluded from the school, and even advocate as the best school system that which necessarily excludes religion. Few surely will deny that childhood and youth are the periods of life when the character ought especially to be subjected to religious influences. Nor can we ignore the palpable fact that the school system is an important factor in the forming of childhood and youth—so important that its influence often outweighs that of home and Church.

"It cannot, therefore, be desirable or advantageous that religion should be excluded from the school. On the contrary, it ought there to be one of the chief agencies for molding the young life to all that is true and virtuous and holy. To shut religion out of the school and keep it for home and the Church, is, logically, to train up a generation that will consider religion good for home and the Church, but not for the practical business of real life. But a more false and pernicious notion could not be imagined. Religion, in order to elevate a people, should inspire their whole life and rule their relations with one another. A life is not dwarfed, but ennobled, by being lived in the presence of God. Therefore, the school, which principally gives the knowledge fitting for practical life, ought to be pre-eminently under the holy influence of religion. From the shelter of home and school the youth must soon go out into the busy ways of trade or traffic or professional practice. In all these, the principles of religion should animate and direct him. But he cannot expect to learn these principles in the workshop or the office, or the counting-room. Therefore, let him be well and thoroughly imbued with them by the joint influences of home and school before he is launched out on the dangerous sea of life.

"All denominations of Christians are now awakening to this great truth, which the Catholic Church has never ceased to maintain. Reason and experience are forcing them to recognize that the only practical way to secure a Christian people is to give the youth a Christian education. The avowed enemies of Christianity in some European countries are banishing religion from the schools, in order, gradually, to eliminate it from among the people. In this they are logical, and we may well profit by the lesson. Hence the cry for Christian education is going up from all religious bodies throughout the land. And this is no narrowness and 'sectarianism' on their part; it is an honest and logical endeavor to preserve Christian truth and morality among the people by fostering religion in the young.

"Nor is it any antagonism to the State; on the contrary, it is an honest endeavor to give to the State better citizens, by making them better Christians. The friends of Christian education do not condemn the state for not imparting religious instruction in the public schools as they are now organized; because they well know it does not lie within the province of the state to teach religion. They simply follow their conscience by sending their children to denominational schools, where religion can have its rightful place and influence.

"Two objects, therefore, dear brethren, we have in view— to multiply our schools, and to perfect them. We must multiply them till every Catholic child in the land shall have within its reach the means of education. There is still much to do ere this be attained. There are still thousands of Catholic children in the United States deprived of the benefit of a Catholic school. Pastors and parents should not rest till this defect be remedied. No parish is complete till it has schools adequate to the needs of its children, and the pastor and people of such a parish should feel that they have not accomplished their entire duty until the want is supplied.

"But, then, we must also perfect our schools. We repudiate the idea that the Catholic school need be in any respect inferior to any other school whatsoever. And if hitherto, in some places, our people have acted on the principle that it is better to have an imperfect Catholic school than to have none, let them now push their praiseworthy ambition still further, and not relax their efforts till their schools be elevated to the highest educational excellence. And we implore parents not to hasten to take their children from school, but to give them all the time and all the advantages by which they have the capacity to profit, so that in after life their children may 'rise up and call them blessed.' "

Another portion of the pastoral letter which was destined to be frequently referred to in impending controversies was that relating to forbidden societies. It should be remembered that these decrees were to be binding, unless revoked by a subsequent council. "One of the most striking characteristics of our times," says the letter, "is the universal tendency to band together in societies for all sorts of purposes. This tendency is the natural outgrowth of an age of popular rights and representative institutions. It is also in accordance with the spirit of the Church, whose aim, as indicated by her name Catholic, is to unite all mankind in brotherhood. It is consonant also with the spirit of Christ, who came to break down all walls of division, and to gather all in the one family of the one Heavenly Father.

"From the hilltop of her Divine mission and her worldwide experience, she sees events and their consequences far more clearly than they who are down in the tangled plain of daily life. She has seen associations that were once praiseworthy become pernicious by change of circumstances. She has seen others which won the admiration of the world by their early achievements corrupted by power or passion, or evil guidance, and she has been forced to condemn them. She has beheld associations which had their origin in the spirit of the ages of faith transformed by lapse of time and loss of faith, and the manipulation of designing leaders, into the open or hidden enemies of religion and human weal.

"Thus our Holy Father, Leo XIII, has lately shown that the Masonic and kindred societies—although the offspring of the ancient Guilds, which aimed at sanctifying trades and tradesmen with the blessings of religion; and, although retaining, perhaps, in their 'ritual' much that tells of the religiousness of their origin, and although in some countries still professing entire friendliness toward the Christian religion—

have, nevertheless, already gone so far, in many countries, as to array themselves in avowed hostility against Christianity and against the Catholic Church as its embodiment, so that they virtually aim at substituting a world-wide fraternity of their own for the universal brotherhood of Jesus Christ, and at disseminating mere naturalism for the supernatural revealed religion bestowed upon mankind by the Saviour of the world. He has shown, too, that, even in countries where they are as yet far from acknowledging such purposes, they, nevertheless, have in them the germs which, under favorable circumstances, would inevitably blossom forth in similar results.

"The Church, consequently, forbids her children to have any connection with such societies, because they are either an open evil to be shunned, or a hidden danger to be avoided. She would fail in her duty if she did not speak the word of warning, and her children would equally fail in theirs if they did not heed it.

"Whenever, therefore, the Church has spoken authoritatively with regard to any society, her decision ought to be final for every Catholic. He ought to know that the Church has not acted hastily, or unwisely, or mistakenly; he should be convinced that any worldly advantages which he might derive from the membership of such society would be a poor substitute for the membership, the sacraments and the blessings of the Church of Christ; he should have the courage of his religious convictions, and stand firm to faith and conscience. But if he be inclined or asked to join a society on which the Church has passed no sentence, then let him, as a reasonable and Christian man, examine into it carefully, and not join the society until he is satisfied of its lawful character.

"There is one characteristic which is always a strong presumption against a society, and that is secrecy. Our Divine Lord Himself has laid down the rule: 'Every one that doeth evil, hateth the light and cometh not to the light, that his works may not be reproved. But he that doeth truth cometh to the light that his works may be made manifest, because they are done in God.' When, therefore, associations veil themselves in secrecy and darkness, the presumption is against them, and it rests with them to prove that there is nothing evil in them.

"But if any society's obligation be such as to bind its members to secrecy, even when rightly questioned by competent authority, then such a society puts itself outside the limits of approval; and no one can be a member of it and at the same time be admitted to the sacraments of the Catholic Church. The same is true of any organization that binds its members to a promise of blind obedience—to accept in advance and to obey whatsoever orders, lawful or unlawful, may emanate from its chief authorities; because such a promise is contrary both to reason and conscience. And if a society works or plots, either openly or in secret, against the Church, or against lawful authorities, then to be a member of it is to be excluded from the membership of the Catholic Church."*

The council sent a letter of sympathy to the bishops of Germany, whose people were then groaning under the May laws. The Archbishop of Cologne replied, recounting the difficulties of the Church in his own country, and adding: "We congratulate you, venerable brethren in the Lord, because in your republic the Church rejoices in the fullness of liberty, so essential to her and her due by right Divine."

---

* Memorial Volume, Third Plenary Council.

CHAPTER IX.

CREATED A CARDINAL.

The discerning judgment of Rome in selecting the Archbishop of Baltimore to pilot the Third Plenary Council on its difficult path was fully sustained by the outcome. Now that the council had erased ecclesiastical complexities due to the diverse racial and political origin of the American people and had given the Church in the United States a complete and unified organization on which might be made the impress of a truly national character, the field of opportunity immensely broadened. Social and economic questions, always the deepest which move a nation, were beginning to throb. It was no longer true that all Americans might find work. Men were crowding to the cities, where stupendous aggregations of capital were tightening their grip on the means of employment. Labor was organizing to struggle for its own interests; financial exploitation threatened panic in the midst of prosperity. Immigration was unprecedentedly large. The assimilative power of the American Church was to be tested, no less than that of the body politic; for both it was to be a time of trial.

Cardinal McCloskey died October 10, 1885, having been a member of the Church's most exalted council ten years. Archbishop Gibbons was selected to preach the funeral sermon in St. Patrick's Cathedral, New York, on which occasion he thus aptly compared the Cardinal and his famous predecessor:

"McCloskey, meek, gentle, retiring from the world, reminds us of Moses with uplifted hands praying on the mountains; Hughes, active, bold, vigorous, aggressive, was, as it were, another Joshua fighting in the valley, armed with the Christian panoply of faith, truth, justice."

When, in time, speculation turned to the choice of a new cardinal, it soon became evident that, except for local preferences, Archbishop Gibbons was the favorite of prelates and people.   Friends of Archbishop Corrigan, who had been elevated from the Bishopric of Newark to the See of New York, hoped that he might receive the honor; or that, if a red hat were bestowed elsewhere, the representation of America in the Sacred College might be increased, and New York, the most populous Catholic diocese in the world, might continue to have a resident cardinal also.   In Boston, the wise and clear-sighted Archbishop Williams was considered worthy of the highest place in the gift of the papacy.

Leo XIII, always keenly observant, did not delay his choice long.   Private advices from Rome soon announced that the elevation of Archbishop Gibbons had been finally decided upon.

When the archbishop heard of these, he exclaimed:

"Should the report be verified, may God give me, as he gave to his servant David, an humble heart, that I may bear the honor with becoming modesty and a profound sense of my own unworthiness."

On May 18 he received from Cardinal Jacobini, Papal Secretary of State, the biglietto, an official document informing him of the Pontiff's intention to raise him to the cardinalatial dignity at the next consistory.

"The Sovereign Pontiff," wrote Cardinal Jacobini, "wishes in a particular manner to attest the high esteem and consideration he has for the virtues which adorn your Grace, and for the many claims you already have on account of your merits, as well as to increase the luster of the Metropolitan See of Baltimore, first among all the churches of the vast republic of the United States, and on that account adorned with the honorable title of primatial see."[*]

Baltimore has sometimes been compared, in certain rather striking aspects, to a European city, and one instance in which the parallel might be traced is the warm-hearted interest and pride with which the people, as a whole, regard the Catholic

---

* Letter of Cardinal Jacobini to Archbishop Gibbons, May 4, 1886 (Cathedral Archives).

archbishopric and the old Cathedral.   Perhaps there is in this an echo of the story of St. Mary's and the beginnings of the American hierarchy in the days of Carroll; but there is no doubt that the lofty character of an influential portion of the Catholic laity from early times has had much to do with the feeling.   Governor and mayor, merchant and laborer, talked with eagerness of the approaching ceremonial.   The novelty of seeing in a democratic community the ancient rite of the investiture of a cardinal excited popular expectation to a high pitch.   The city prepared for a fete and wrote the name of Gibbons on the roll of its most distinguished sons.

The consistory at which the new cardinal was created was held in Rome June 7; twenty-three days later would come the twenty-fifth anniversary of his ordination to the priesthood. Would the messengers of the papal court arrive in time for a double celebration?   Baltimore began to take an eager interest in this also, and lay committees which were making ready for a gala occasion redoubled their efforts.

Monsignor Straniero, the pontifical representative bearing the red zuchetta and biretta, accompanied by Count Muccioli, of the Noble Guards, and Rev. Thomas S. Lee, rector of the Baltimore Cathedral, who had been a guest of the American College in Rome, started for Liverpool promptly.

"Present to Cardinal Gibbons our affectionate paternal benediction," said Leo to them at parting.   "We remember him with the most cordial esteem, and believe we could not confer the hat on a more worthy prelate.   We cordially hope that during his cardinalate our most holy faith may be blessed by great increase of strength among the Catholics of the United States."

A fast steamer bore the messengers to New York, and they landed on American soil June 21.   Hurrying by train to Baltimore, a large gathering of clergy and laity met them at the railroad station.   That evening at the archiepiscopal residence, on Charles street, Count Muccioli, in clattering sword and brilliant uniform, giving a picturesque reminder of the temporal power, presented the red zuchetta to the new prince of the Church; and Monsignor Straniero, who bore the biretta to be conferred June 30, announced his mission in the presence of a distinguished assemblage.

Prelates, priests and laymen began to crowd into the city for the coming event. By the thirtieth nearly the whole American hierarchy had assembled. On the morning of that day, after an ecclesiastical procession, witnessed by an immense crowd of people, the venerable Archbishop Kenrick, of St. Louis, as the Pontiff's representative, bestowed the red biretta on Archbishop Gibbons in the Cathedral, where Mgr. Kenrick's famous brother, then Archbishop of Baltimore, had ordained the young priest a quarter of a century before.*

In no other American city, and indeed, in few cities of the world, can ecclesiastical processions be witnessed comparable with those in Baltimore. Though the people are accustomed to them, they regard each new one with intense interest. For the elevation of their cardinal, a spectacle of this kind unprecedented in the United States was arranged. On account of its rarity and picturesqueness, it deserves a brief description.

First, came a detachment of policemen; then, the processional cross-bearer, preceded by a lad bearing an incense urn, wafting the perfume to right and left; following were one hundred and seventy students of St. Charles College, where the new Cardinal as a youth had alternated the classics and football. An equal number of seminarians from St. Mary's, marching with steady tread, in white surplices, came next; they, too, acclaimed him as an alumnus. Afterward came nearly two hundred and fifty of the regular and secular clergy, wearing white surplices over their black cassocks; monsignori, abbots and bishops followed in line, preceded by the Capuchin Fathers, members of the Benedictine Order, Lazarists, Dominicans, Jesuits and Franciscans. Following the bishops—in a Catholic procession the post of honor is always at the end, following the

---

* *Catholic Mirror,* July 3, 1886.

Biblical rule that "the first shall be last and the last first"—came the archbishops. The herculean forms of Ryan and Feehan, clad in episcopal purple, towered above the rest like great trees in a forest. Archbishop Kenrick, so feeble that every step seemed an effort, tottered along; on his left was Mgr. Straniero, the Papal Delegate, bareheaded, and clothed in a purple robe, Count Muccioli, the Noble Guard, wore his full uniform. Last of all, came the new Cardinal, bearing himself with the simple dignity which seemed to fit him like a garment.

Protestants as well as Catholics reverently uncovered their heads as the procession passed through immense crowds congregated on the streets. Within the Cathedral, as this wonderful assemblage of the Church passed up the broad aisles, was a congregation which included many of the most distinguished men in the cardinal's native city and state.

Archbishop Williams celebrated pontifical high mass. The eloquent Archbishop Ryan was selected to preach the sermon. His strength as a pulpit orator, no less than his dignity and perfect self-possession on public occasions, were never more noticeable. With the new Cardinal he was in thorough sympathy, not only through the bonds of the closest personal friendship, but those of concurrent judgment regarding the weighty problems of Church and nation.

He began by treating the Church as a kingdom, not of this world, but "visible, universal and perpetual." "Behold that kingdom," he said, "under one king, Jesus Christ, and His visible representative on earth, the Sovereign Pontiff, with judicial and legislative departments spread throughout the whole earth, with more discordant elements than any kingdom that ever existed, and yet with more union of action and conviction and affection—a kingdom that extends farther than all others, and claims the tribute of intellect and heart. Men acknowledge, indeed, its power and wisdom, and try to account for both on purely human theories. Some regard it as the perfection of the monarchical system; others, as a great republic, whose officers, from the pope to the humblest abbot, are elected by the governed, and whose religious orders are the model in great part for our own form of government. But the truth is that the Church is, strictly speaking, neither of these, nor a wondrous combination of both; but a new and Divine institution, a kingdom of God on earth, as the Scripture calls it.   *   *   *

"The simple forms by which a few thousand converted Jews were ruled in Jerusalem would be insufficient to govern the children of every tribe and tongue and people, numbering over two hundred millions, ruled from Rome as a center of unity. Hence we find that the Sovereign Pontiff selected a body of ecclesiastics in Rome whom he constituted his chief or cardinal counselors in the great affairs of his spiritual kingdom.   *   *   *

"These cardinals form, as it were, a senate of the Church, and what a magnificent senate!   *   *   *   The selection of these counselors of the Pope is left to his own judgment; but the Fathers of the Council of Trent presumed to suggest that the Roman Pontiff select them, as much as possible, out of all the nations of the earth, when suitable persons can be found. The wisdom of this is evident. The central governing body ought to understand thoroughly the peoples whom they govern. The present Pontiff, who is remarkable for his knowledge of the outside world and of the genius of this century, has, more than any other, perhaps, acted on this great and most wise principle.

"To the exalted dignity which I have been describing the venerated and beloved Archbishop of Baltimore is now promoted. Providence has fitted him for the position. He is in perfect harmony with the spirit of the Church, and can represent it to the American people; he is also in entire harmony with the spirit of the country, and can represent it in the councils of the Church. He knows and feels that there is no antagonism between the Catholic Church and our political insti-

CARDINAL GIBBONS IN ROBES AS MEMBER OF SACRED COLLEGE

tutions; but, on the contrary, she is nowhere on earth today more perfectly at home than in this free land. * * *

"On this day twenty-five years ago the present Cardinal was ordained to the priesthood by the greatest ecclesiastic whom the American Church has yet seen—Archbishop Francis Patrick Kenrick, of this city. Today the brother of that great prelate, venerable in years and merits, after traveling over a thousand miles, appears in this sanctuary to crown with the scarlet of the cardinalate the young priest of that day. The former prelate prayed that 'God might bless and sanctify and consecrate' the prostrate young Levite; today his brother prays that the same God may illumine and fortify the exalted prince of the Church. In this Cathedral, where the new Cardinal was baptized, officiated as a priest and was consecrated bishop, and presided so wisely over the late plenary council, he receives today the highest honors of the Church of God. It is an honor not only to him, but to the American Church; to this great State of Maryland, which, Catholic in its origin, proclaimed from the beginning the great doctrine of religious liberty. It is an honor to this Catholic and hospitable city of Baltimore, and I rejoice to learn that her non-Catholic citizens appreciate it."

Mgr. Straniero, in conferring the scarlet biretta, spoke of the amazement which the growth of the Catholic Church in America had created at Rome. "Its hierarchy," he said, "has had scarce one hundred years of existence, and yet it is daily growing in splendor, both from its broad increase and the great virtues of the venerable men who make up its number. Witness those illustrious American prelates returning two years ago from Rome, whither they had gone to manifest their veneration and love toward the See of Saint Peter, and, again, when all were gathered at the late council at Baltimore to give that shape and life to ecclesiastical discipline and for the care of the faithful which existing circumstances required.

"All this could not escape the provident notice of the Roman Pontiff. Consequently, that he might give more proof of his fatherly care and love to the faithful of these States, and to their chief pastors, he determined to admit another of the prominent bishops of America to the Sacred College of Cardinals. Influenced by these motives, the Holy Father, in a secret consistory lately held at the Vatican, selected you, most eminent prince, who, bearing the dignity of the episcopate, have these many years ruled the Church of Baltimore. Your writings have been universally read, and all have admired the depth of your learning, your zeal, and your many virtues. Those who have known you intimately have been deeply impressed by your remarkable qualities of heart and powers of mind. Waiving all else, it is enough for me to recall that when the American bishops assembled in plenary council, the Roman Pontiff appointed you to preside therein and to discharge the office of Apostolic Delegate.

"To your Eminence may God grant a life of many years for the service and adornment of the Holy See and the welfare of the loving flock entrusted to your care. And as today is, moreover, the twenty-fifth anniversary of your ordination to the priesthood, on this account also, do I congratulate you. From the bottom of my heart I pray that God may grant you yet many anniversaries of this day."

Archbishop Kenrick, addressing the Cardinal, said that the honor which had come to him was one which American Catholics had a right to expect, on account of their number and the importance of the Church in the United States. "We also had a right to expect it," he continued, " on account of the greatness of our country, the position it occupies among the nations of the earth, the influence it is to exert over the future destinies of the human race. It is nothing anomalous or contrary to the principles of the republic that we should have in our midst a cardinal of the Holy Roman Catholic Church, and we are confident that your appointment will continue to be regarded as it is now regarded—a new element of strength and harmony for all.

"We congratulate your Eminence on your appointment to so high an office. It will increase your cares and responsibilities, but it will also increase your means of usefulness as an honored citizen of the republic and a faithful bishop of the Church of God."

The Cardinal responded, in turn, to the addresses of Archbishop Kenrick and Mgr. Straniero, and then addressed the prelates, clergy and laity. He spoke of the associations which clustered around the old Cathedral in which they were all assembled. "Many temples there are," he said, "more spacious and stately, indeed, than this; but none in our country which has seen within its sanctuary so many illustrious prelates. Within these walls were held ten provincial, and the three national councils—those of 1852, 1866 and 1884. How often has the voice of an England, a Hughes, a McCloskey, a Purcell, a Fitzpatrick, a McGill and an O'Connor resounded here!

"The corner-stone of this Cathedral was laid by the patriarch of the American Church, the immortal Carroll. Archbishop Neale passed away before its completion; and in that chair have sat in luminous succession a Marechal, a Whitfield, an Eccleston, a Spalding and a Bayley—great names of imperishable renown in the annals of the Church in America.

"Traditions such as these are so many links in the golden chain of love which binds your hearts to this ancient see. Another strong link which touches, as it were, and gathers up all the links that holds us, is the bond that draws us close to the See of Peter. I feel assured, therefore, that your hearts will go forth with mine in a message of thanks to our beloved Pontiff for the event we are celebrating today. It is an honor not personal to myself. It is an honor which he confers on this venerable see, which you all love so well, and on the whole Church in America. It is a signal mark of admiration and high esteem for our beloved country, in whose spiritual welfare from the first day of his accession to the Chair of St. Peter he has taken so enlightened an interest.

"God raises up men in every age to meet the emergencies of the occasion. He has providentially raised up our present illustrious Pontiff to meet the special wants of these times. As the first Leo, by his majestic bearing and fearless eloquence, arrested the march of an all-conquering warrior and saved Rome from destruction, so has the thirteenth of his great name conciliated one of the mightiest empires of modern times, giving back peace and liberty to the Church of Germany. He has been chosen umpire of two great nations of the eastern world; and his impartial decision, gratefully acquiesced in by their rulers, has hushed the clamor of strife and restored peace and harmony.

"Never, perhaps, in the history of the Church has the moral influence of the papacy been more strongly marked and beneficently exerted than during the reign of Leo XIII; never have the true relations of church and state been more clearly enunciated than in his ever-memorable encyclical letter, *Immortale Dei*.

"In no country of all the nations of the earth does he find more loyal and devoted spiritual children than among the clergy and laity of this free republic. And I am happy to add that our separated brethren, while not sharing in our faith, have shared in our profound admiration for the benevolent character and enlightened statesmanship of the present Supreme Pontiff.

"Beloved brethren of the laity, I say from my heart of hearts that earth has for me no place dearer than the sanctuary where I now stand and the diocese which I serve. And how could it be otherwise? It was in this Cathedral that I first breathed the breath of life as a Christian. At yonder font I was regenerated in the waters of baptism. Almost beneath the shadow of this temple, in old St. Mary's Seminary, I was raised to the dignity of the priesthood by the hands of the venerable Archbishop Kenrick, the illustrious brother of him from whom I have the honor of receiving the biretta today. It was at this very altar that I was consecrated bishop by my predecessor and father in Christ, the venerated Spalding.

"We of this diocese down to the humblest priest hold it an honor as well as a duty to labor in the sacred soil of Maryland, where your forefathers, two hundred and fifty years ago, planted the cross and raised the banner of religious liberty and called forth the oppressed of other lands to take their shelter beneath its protecting folds. What holy enthusiasm should not these memories evoke! What zeal should they not arouse for religion and country! May it be the study of my life to walk in the footprints of my illustrious predecessors in this ancient see, and in the footprints of the first cardinal archbishop in these United States, who has lately passed to his reward, and whose sterling merit was surpassed only by his modesty and humility. And may it be your good fortune also, dearly beloved brethren, to emulate the faith and civic virtues of your ancestors, and to hand down that faith and those virtues untarnished as precious heirlooms to the generations yet to be."

Following the long and magnificent ecclesiastical ceremony, there was a dinner at St. Mary's Seminary. The venerable institution had suddenly turned red. Bands of cardinal cloth adorned the building, and mingled with the American flag was the banner of the papacy. The Cardinal, in the brilliant robes of his new office, presided at the feast. In front of him was an archiepiscopal cross of flowers, and on each side of the cross were mitres of white roses. All who could get near him were eager to congratulate him. His winning smile and thorough modesty captivated all. Among priests he could be a leader as well as among people.

At night the seminary was brilliantly illuminated in emblematic designs. Red fire blazed along the streets, and there was a parade of Catholic Knights and young men's societies, many of them in uniform.   Again all Baltimore was out of doors to watch; and, characteristically, there was the utmost good nature and decorum.

A purely social touch was given the festivities by a reception in the evening to the visiting prelates, given by Miss Emily Harper, the granddaughter of Charles Carroll of Carrollton, at her home, on Cathedral street, in the center of fashionable Baltimore.

At ten o'clock the National Marine Band, then under the leadership of the afterwards famous Sousa, serenaded the Cardinal at his residence, as a final touch to a memorable day. So dense were the throngs in the streets that police had to clear a space for the band to approach.   The Cardinal appeared at his famous bay-window, where he was instantly recognized, and the multitude broke into resounding cheers.   Men threw their hats in the air, and women waved their handkerchiefs. It was almost like a candidate for the Presidency addressing a great mass-meeting in the height of an American political campaign.   Attired in his red cassock, partly covered by a black robe, the center of all eyes, the Cardinal walked out on the portico of the building when quiet had been restored and briefly expressed his thanks, concluding with a prayer for a blessing on all.   Amid another deafening din, he retired, and the throngs dispersed.

The next day, with many of the visiting prelates, the Cardinal attended the annual commencement of St. Charles College, where thirty-one years before, a youth just from New Orleans, he had pursued his classical studies in preparation for the priesthood.   He spoke with affection of the memories of those days and the panorama of life since.   "With respect to the references made in the course of the addresses here to our Sovereign Pontiff, Leo XIII," he said, "I wish to say in all simplicity and sincerity that the predilection he has appeared uniformly to evince toward me and the favorable appreciation he has made of what I have been able to do in the cause of religion, has been a constant source of embarrassment to me in his presence and of wonder when distant from him."

The devoted interest which the Cardinal had always taken in education wherever his lot happened to be cast had made him a prime favorite among the teaching orders. Such an occasion as his elevation to the Sacred College could not be permitted by them to pass unnoticed. A large body of the Christian Brothers, representing the Province of Baltimore, visited him at his residence and presented an address, printed on satin, accompanied by a sum of money in a silk purse made by the Sisters of St. Mary's Orphan Asylum. Brother Azarias, of Rock Hill College, known throughout the English-speaking world as a literary critic in the front rank, read the address, expressing their thankfulness at his interest in and zeal for education.

In such congenial company, the Cardinal responded from the fullness of his heart. "It is a source of inexpressible satisfaction to us," he said, "to feel the most perfect assurance of how free from friction are the relations of the Catholic Church and the giant republic of the West. It proves the elasticity, if we may so speak, of Catholic doctrine. It proves that it is Catholic indeed, and has the capacity to adapt itself to all that is good in the many forms of governments and persons. Breathing the pure air of liberty, the Church expands with its finest strength, and grows in beauty and power.

"We would find yet more occasion to approve and love it if we could contrast its state here with its condition in other countries less happy in their government and laws. Here the government extends over us the ægis of equal laws without interfering with the just rights of any.

"How much can you not accomplish, dear brothers, in that spirit of self-sacrifice displayed by you on so many fields of untiring effort! We see around us now the monuments of those labors in the many young men reared in the faith, in intelligence and learning, fitted for the duties of citizenship, making them noble representatives of the State of Maryland. You carry out the principles of your founder, or rather, of the Gospel, for, after all, everything must be referred to the Gospel. The secret of your success is found in humility, piety and intelligence; they form a triple cord which cannot be broken. Acting upon these principles in molding the minds, hearts and souls of youth, you do more than the great artists, whose genius brought out those beautiful images in marble or on canvas which have for centuries been the admiration and delight of every land and people.

"It is not a slight debt that this archdiocese and this great city of Baltimore—the first great field of your labors in this country—owe you. The clergy have experienced the benefit of your labors. You have many reasons to be proud of your mission in this archdiocese, for that mission is the high one of instilling virtue into young hearts and training their minds in knowledge."

By the press of the United States, that potent pilot of public opinion in which many foreign observers have found the real governing power of the country, the elevation of Cardinal Gibbons was commended with practical unanimity. Protestant as well as Catholic newspapers discussed it at length, expressing their sense of the honor done the whole United States, as well as that portion of it embraced within the Catholic Church. Cardinal Gibbons had not yet risen to the full height of his popularity; but already some knowledge of the traits which distinguished him as a man and a prelate had penetrated every part of the country. The newspapers saw in his selection for the Sacred College a recognition of the most progressive tendencies in the American Church and a hopeful sign of the complete understanding of the United States by the leaders of the Church in Europe. They felt that as an American by birth, training and public experience, no less than by sympathy and aspiration, he was well fitted to represent this country in the highest councils at Rome.   The favor with which he was regarded by Leo XIII was hailed as an augury of benefit to America.

The venerable Leo was then well past three score and ten; and none could foresee the remarkable age to which Providence was destined to spare him.

CHAPTER X.

SPEECH IN ROME ON THE RELATIONS BETWEEN CHURCH AND STATE IN THE UNITED STATES.

Rome was the next step. From the hand of the Supreme Pontiff alone could the new Cardinal receive the red hat, and there, among his brethren of the Sacred College, his words and acts would be fraught for the first time with the weight of a prince speaking to princes in the world-wide council of the Church. Would he remain only a national figure, of whom it would be said that he was a leader among a new people, but in the ancient forum of the pontificate had no mission to humanity as a whole? It was the greatest test he had yet been called upon to meet.

He left Baltimore January 26, 1887, accompanied by his chancellor, Rev. P. J. Donahue, afterward Bishop of Wheeling, and by his consultors—Revs. John S. Foley, Thomas S. Lee, John T. Gaitley, A. L. Magnien and J. A. Walter. New demonstrations of popular esteem marked his departure from New York, and in Paris he was extensively entertained. Arriving in Rome, he became the center of an influential American representation there assembled, including Mgr. O'Connell, then rector of the American College; Archbishop Ireland, Bishop Keane and others. Among such churchmen he was at home as leader and friend.

Conferences with the Pope ensued, at which conditions in America were discussed; and on St. Patrick's Day, at a public consistory in the Sala Regia, the Pontiff bestowed the hat and ring and performed the ceremony of sealing and opening the lips.

Archbishop Taschereau, of Quebec, was elevated at the same time, as were several European cardinals. To Cardinal Gibbons was committed, as his titular church, the ancient edifice of Santa Maria in Trastevere, the first temple raised in the world in honor of the Mother of Christ.

Standing in this church, March 25, 1887, the past and the future met. It was the day of his installation. He wore the scarlet cassock, signifying that he would defend the faith even to the shedding of his blood, as in the days when Christians were thrown to the lions in the Colosseum, not far distant. Surrounding him was the centuried magnificence of architecture, painting, statue, mosaic. The long ceremonial eloquently typified the story of Christianity from the era of Constantine, through the glories of Charlemagne, the brilliancy of the Italian renaissance and the reconstruction of modern Europe. It was carried out with the precise formalism of early Rome and in the majestic tongue in which martyrs praised God as they went to their death. The atmosphere was rich with incense and quivered with reverent music. Vestment and altar bespoke antiquity. It was an occasion to overpower the senses, to hush the voice of the present in the great shadow of the accumulated grandeur and wisdom of the past.

All this must have profoundly affected the American Cardinal as he stood in his gorgeous robes while bishops, canons and priests performed their parts. He had not intended to make an address, beyond the brief responses necessary to his participation in the ceremony. But a few days before Mgr. O'Connell had suggested to him that he should speak on such an occasion, and he had coincided in this view. The Cardinal spoke as follows:

"The assignment to me by the Holy Father of this beautiful basilica as my titular church fills me with feelings of joy and gratitude which any words of mine are inadequate to express. For, as here in Rome I stand within the first temple raised in honor of the ever-blessed Virgin Mary, so in my far-off home, my own Cathedral Church, the oldest in the United States, is also dedicated to the Mother of God. This venerable edifice in which we are gathered leads us back in contemplation to the days of the catacombs. Its foundation was laid by Pope Calixtus in the year of our Lord, 224. It was restored by Pope Julius in the fourth century, and renovated by another Supreme Pontiff in the twelfth.

"That never-ceasing solicitude which the Sovereign Pontiffs have exhibited in erecting these material temples, which are the glory of this city, they have also manifested on a larger scale in rearing spiritual walls to Zion throughout Christendom in every age. Scarcely were the United States formed into an independent government, when Pope Pius VII established a Catholic hierarchy and appointed the illustrious John Carroll the first Bishop of Baltimore. Our Catholic community in those days numbered a few thousand souls, and they were scattered chiefly through the States of New York, Pennsylvania and Maryland. They were served by a mere handful of priests. But now, thanks to the fructifying grace of God, the grain of mustard seed then planted has grown to a large tree, spreading its branches through the length and breadth of our fair land. Where only one bishop was found in the beginning of this century, there are now seventy-five exercising spiritual jurisdiction. *For this great progress we are indebted, under God and the fostering vigilance of the Holy See, to the civil liberty we enjoy in our enlightened republic.*

"Our Holy Father, Leo XIII, in his luminous encyclical on the constitution of Christian states, declares that the Church is not committed to any form of civil government. *She adapts herself to all.* She leavens all with the sacred leaven of the Gospel. She has lived under absolute monarchies, under constitutional monarchies, in free republics, and everywhere she grows and expands. She has often, indeed, been hampered in her Divine mission. She has even been forced to struggle for her existence wherever despotism has cast its dark shadow,

INTERIOR OF THE CHURCH OF SANTA MARIA IN TRASTEVERE, ROME

like a plant shut out from the blessed light of heaven. *But in the genial atmosphere of liberty she blossoms like a rose.*

"For myself, as a citizen of the United States, and without closing my eyes to our shortcomings as a nation, I say, with a deep sense of pride and gratitude, that *I belong to a country where the civil government holds over us the ægis of its protection, without interfering with us in the legitimate exercise of our sublime mission as ministers of the Gospel of Christ. Our country has liberty without license, and authority without despotism.* She rears no wall to exclude the stranger from among us. She has few frowning fortifications to repel the invader, for she is at peace with all the world. She rests secure in the consciousness of her stength and her good will toward all. Her harbors are open to welcome the honest emigrant who comes to advance his temporal interests and find a peaceful home.

"But, while we are acknowledged to have a free government, *perhaps we do not receive the credit that belongs to us for having, also, a strong government.* Yes, our nation is strong, and her strength lies, under the overruling guidance of Providence, in the majesty and supremacy of the law, in the loyalty of her citizens and in the affection of her people for her free institutions. There are, indeed, grave social problems now employing the earnest attention of the citizens of the United States, but I have no doubt that, with God's blessing, these problems will be solved by the calm judgment and sound sense of the American people, without violence or revolution, or any injury to individual right.

"As an evidence of his good will for the great republic in the West, as a mark of his appreciation of the venerable hierarchy of the United States, and as an expression of his kind consideration for the ancient See of Baltimore, our Holy Father has been graciously pleased to elevate its present incumbent, in my humble person, to the dignity of the purple. For this mark of his exalted favor I beg to tender the Holy Father my profound thanks in my own name and in the name of the clergy and faithful. I venture to thank him also in the name of my venerable colleagues, the bishops, as well as the clergy and Catholic laity of the United States. *I presume also to thank him in the name of our separated brethren in America, who, though not sharing our faith, have shown that they are not insensible—indeed, that they are deeply sensible—of the honor conferred upon our common country,* and have again and again expressed their admiration for the enlightened statesmanship and apostolic virtues and benevolent character of the illustrious Pontiff who now sits in the Chair of St. Peter."*

The speech was read in Europe and America with intense interest. It was characteristically American, they said in Rome. Here was a cardinal, barely out of his first consistory, daring to assert, in the very citadel of the Church, that separation in the United States did not mean hostility by the state to the Church, but protection, and that in the air of perfect freedom, unhampered by political bonds, the Church could work out her Divine mission better; that union of church and state often meant interference, and that American liberty meant the opportunity to win men to the faith free from the vexations of human complications. The message which the Cardinal had sought to convey, as he often said, was that "our duty is to preach the Gospel and save souls;" that it is wisest to separate entirely the ministry of Christ from politics, unless some great moral question is involved; that this course is better for the Church everywhere. He felt that in time comprehension of the American system would grow at Rome; but some one must be considered radical in launching the first official declaration of it, and he did not shrink from fulfilling this trying mission.

In the twentieth century, Europe understands America as never before, and not only tolerates, but imitates it in many

---

* *Catholic Mirror,* April 2, 1887.

things.   Two great influences have chiefly contributed to this:
The speech of Cardinal Gibbons in the Church of Santa Maria
in Trastavere, and the victories of the United States navy in the
Spanish-American War.   The turning point was in getting the
world to understand that liberty in America does not mean
license; nor authority, despotism.   Rome, the center of Catholic thought, was the best place in which to plant the idea, and
Europe rubbed its unwilling eyes and saw.

CHAPTER XI.

KNIGHTS OF LABOR QUESTION.

When the new Cardinal was boldly raising his voice for the institutions of his country in the ancient Church of Santa Maria in Trastevere, he had but recently penned a document which had the remarkable effect of causing the Congregation of the Holy Office—the "inquisition"—to reverse its attitude of opposition to the Knights of Labor. Foremost of the "grave social problems" to which he had alluded in that address and in the settlement of which he had expressed his complete faith, was the labor question. Mr. Cleveland was then President, and both the Executive and Congress were principally concerned with the urgent demands of labor. The law against bringing workingmen under contract from abroad had just been passed; the Interstate Commerce Act, a measure almost forced on the Government by labor organizations, and an extension of the Chinese Exclusion Act, were being debated and were soon to be adopted. The Administration had committed itself to the establishment of a Department of Labor as a unit in its executive system at Washington. The anarchist riots in Chicago, with their bloody climax, had shocked the nation but a few months before.

European pessimism, not yet fully awake to the truth, began to predict the downfall of America. It was believed that a government which maintained a standing army scarcely large enough to man its coast defenses, and a navy which at that time was archaic, could not withstand the shock of a popular tumult. Political equality, it was feared, had no corrective within itself for a sudden rising from the bottom. If the laborer were the equal of the capitalist before the law, would he not rave in an orgy of unrestrained power as soon as he was able to comprehend what his opportunities really meant? In the earlier days of the United States the labor question had adjusted itself. There was land enough for all; work for every hand; the laborer of today became the millionaire of tomorrow. Capital was unorganized, and labor had felt no special need to band together for its own protection.

In the carnival of energy which had subdued half of a vast continent in a century, building teeming cities on virgin soil and establishing new Commonwealths in bewildering succession from the Atlantic to the Pacific, men had been too busily employed in constructive labor to debate the ethics of the problem. But the work had now advanced far, and there was time to pause. Railroads spanned the continent and radiated in every direction. Civilization had carried its banner up the Rocky Mountains and to the shores of the Golden Gate. The army of workingmen was still here, but there was not so much work to do. Nearly all the lands opened by the Government to free settlement had been taken up. The economic pendulum was beginning to swing, and times of scarcity succeeded eras of plenty.

American workingmen were not prepared for this. They were no more ready to meet a sudden economic change than were the rural colonists to face the mouths of British cannon in 1775. Anarchy, imported from Europe, had found here what its apostles believed to be fertile soil for the propagation of its ideas. Socialism swept across the ocean and began its preachments in the great cities. The genus tramp, in some respects peculiarly an American development, was spreading the cult of idleness and the industrial code of the leech. The tariff laws had built up vast industries, whose captains controlled politicians and legislatures. Before them dangled the gilded prize of monopoly, and in a short time a few men were beginning to aggregate to themselves the lion's share of the fruits of the earth.

It was now possible for the first time in the United States for one man to raise his hand and thousands would be without bread. Workingmen might crowd to the polls, intoxicated with the dreams of the Declaration of Independence, and find their ballots nullified by the insidious influences of corrupting wealth. At heart, the body politic was healthy; these were merely sores that did not reach the organism, though they grievously affected the surface. In time, their poison might penetrate to the heart. None could tell. It might be that once again men would take arms in their hands to work out the problems of a free government amid the crash of battle.

The growth of labor organizations in America in the decade preceding the election of President Cleveland had surpassed anything of the kind which the world had known. Wrongs needed a remedy; half uncertain, the toilers banded together to act, if they could find a way. Chief among these organizations was the Knights of Labor, a secret order which, from a small beginning, had suddenly increased its membership by tens of thousands, and, like a great storm-cloud, overspread the political as well as industrial structure of the country. Its head, Terence V. Powderly, seemed to the toiling masses a Peter the Hermit called to lead them on a new crusade. Bearing the modest title of "general master workman," he wielded greater power than the Governor of a State. He possessed many of the traits of successful leadership, and was inspired by a fervent belief in the justice of his cause. Men thronged from the workshops to hail him when he went from city to city, proclaiming his evangel. In 1886 the order had a membership of 500,000, "although," as Mr. Powderly said to a committee of Congress, "we have been credited with 5,000,000."*

Simultaneously with this movement, Henry George's economic theories were fast winning converts, particularly in New York, his home, where the influence of his powerful personality was naturally strongest.

---

* Carroll D. Wright, Industrial Evolution of the United States, p. 248.

In Canada the ecclesiastical authorities adjudged the Knights a forbidden organization, and the Holy Office sustained the condemnation.   They were classed with secret societies working against religion.   Under the decrees of the Third Plenary Council of Baltimore, they could be condemned in the United States only by unanimous action of the archbishops; and, in case the archbishops disagreed, the question was to be referred to Rome.   The critical aspect of the problem made action imperative; Mr. Powderly, himself a Catholic, came to Baltimore several times and conferred with Cardinal Gibbons; on one occasion he appeared before a committee of the archbishops at a meeting at the Cardinal's house and pleaded the cause of the Knights.   He offered to amend any order or rule of the organization to which the ecclesiastical authorities might object. The obligation of secrecy, he pointed out, was a simple pledge and not an oath.   Its purpose was to keep the knowledge of the organization's business from enemies or strangers, and it was not such as to hinder Catholics from manifesting everything to competent ecclesiastical authority, even outside of confession.   When the archbishops came to consider the question, only two out of twelve—Kenrick, of St. Louis, and Salpointe, of Santa Fe—voted for condemnation.

In his consideration of this grave question, Cardinal Gibbons conferred with President Cleveland, and was in active correspondence with Cardinal Manning, his close friend, the Church's apostle of labor in England.   He found both in full sympathy with his own views, and Cardinal Manning was ready to assist actively in the program to which he had resolved to commit himself—to urge the Holy Office not to forbid the organization of the Knights.   By not a few who were unable to see in advance of the moment, his views were considered too far-reaching.   The Knights were even regarded as socialistic; and, in truth, they might have become such had a program of repression been adopted against them.

Rome heard the echoes of these doubts and fears, and the delicate susceptibilities of conservatives were jarred by the assertion that Cardinal Gibbons had turned radical and was attempting to engraft his views on the Church. This cloud of misunderstanding made his task all the more difficult. He explained his views fully in several interesting letters to Cardinal Manning,* who fully concurred with him and rejoiced to find his own ideas on the relations between capital and labor shared by one occupying such a distinguished position in the Church in the United States. Manning considered that Cardinal Gibbons was doing a great and needed work in America in advancing the position of the laboring classes, and wished ardently that he might have as much success in England.

Several bishops in France, and not a small number of Catholic writers, expressed alarm at the advanced and liberal views of these two eminent men. The element in England which was unable to understand thoroughly the great purposes of Cardinal Manning was also willing to cry, "Beware!"; but in America, as the task of Cardinal Gibbons developed and the real significance of what he was doing came to be more clearly seen, the general tone of comment, in and out of the Church, was one of praise and enthusiastic support.

When Cardinal Gibbons sailed for Europe in January, 1887, to receive the red hat, a part of his mission was to present the plea of organized labor. The atmosphere which he was about to enter was hostile to his views on this question. One of his companions on the voyage was Cardinal Taschereau, on whom also the red hat was to be bestowed and who was going to urge adherence to the judgment condemning the order in Canada; while to Cardinal Gibbons fell the far more difficult task of appealing to Rome to recognize the order as one not to be forbidden.

He presented his views vigorously in the Eternal City, with the active assistance of Archbishop Ireland, Bishop Keane and

---

* Purcell, Life of Cardinal Manning, Vol. II, pp. 650-51.

Monsignor O'Connell. Under date of February 20, 1887, he addressed to Cardinal Simeoni, Prefect of the Propaganda, for presentation to the Holy Office a report on the whole subject, which was marked by broad statesmanship, searching logic and enlightened foresight—perhaps the strongest document he ever wrote.

This letter, a milestone in the Church's journey toward the hearts of the American people, is of sufficient importance to be quoted in full. Following is the translation of it as published in the *Moniteur de Rome,* the official organ of the Vatican.*

"To His Eminence Cardinal Simeoni, Prefect of the Sacred Congregation of the Propaganda:

"Your Eminence—In submitting to the Holy See the conclusions which, after several months of attentive observation and reflection, seem to me to sum up the truth concerning the association of the Knights of Labor, I feel profoundly convinced of the vast importance of the consequences attaching to this question, which is but a link in the great chain of the social problems of our day, and especially of our country.

"In treating this question I have been very careful to follow as my constant guide the spirit of the encyclical letters, in which our Holy Father Leo XIII has so admirably set forth the dangers of our times and their remedies, as well as the principles by which we are to recognize associations condemned by the Holy See. Such was also the guide of the Third Plenary Council of Baltimore in its teachings concerning the principles to be followed and the dangers to be shunned by the faithful either in the choice or in the establishment of those various forms of association toward which the spirit of our popular institutions so strongly impels them. And, considering the evil consequences that might result from a mistake in the treatment of organizations which often count their members by thousands and hundreds of thousands, the council wisely ordained (n. 225) that, when an association is spread over several dioceses, not even the bishop of one of these dioceses shall condemn it, but shall refer the case to a standing committee consisting of all the archbishops of the United States; and even these are not authorized to condemn, unless their sentence be unanimous; and in case they fail to agree unanimously, then only the supreme tribunal of the Holy See can impose a condemnation; all this in order to avoid error and confusion of discipline.

---

* A copy of the letter in French is in the Cathedral Archives, Baltimore.

"This committee of archbishops held a meeting towards the end of last October, at which the association of the Knights of Labor was specially considered. To this we were not impelled by the request of any of our bishops, for none of them had asked it; and I must add that among all the bishops we know of but two or three who desire the condemnation. But our reason was the importance attached to the question by the Holy See itself, and this led us to examine it with all possible care. After our deliberations, the result of which has already been communicated to the Sacred Congregation of the Propaganda, only two out of the twelve archbishops voted for condemnation; and their reasons were powerless to convince the others of either the justice or the prudence of such a condemnation.

"In the following considerations I wish to state in detail the reasons which determined the vote of the great majority of the committee—reasons whose truth and force seem to me all the more evident after this lapse of time; nor will I fail to do justice to the arguments advanced on the other side:

"1. In the first place, though there may be found in the constitution, laws and official declarations of the Knights of Labor things that we would not approve, still, we have failed to find in them those elements so clearly pointed out by the Holy See, which would class them among condemned associations:

"(a) In their form of initiation there is no oath.

"(b) The obligation to secrecy by which they keep the knowledge of their business from enemies or strangers is not such as to hinder Catholics from manifesting everything to competent ecclesiastical authority, even outside of confession. This has been positively declared to us by their chief officers.

"(c) They make no promise of blind obedience. The object and laws of the association are distinctly declared, and the obligation of obedience does not go beyond them.

"(d) They not only profess no hostility against religion or the Church, but their declarations are quite to the contrary. The third Plenary Council commands (n. 254) that condemnation shall not be passed on any association without the previous hearing of its officers or representatives. Now, their president, when sending me a copy of their constitution, declared that he is a devoted Catholic; that he practices his religion faithfully and receives the sacraments regularly; that he belongs to no Masonic society or other association condemned by the Church; that he knows nothing in the organization of the Knights of Labor contrary to the laws of the Church; that, with filial submission, he begs the pastors of the Church to examine their constitution and laws, and to point out anything they may find objectionable, promising to see to its correction. Assuredly, there is in all this no hostility to the authority of the Church, but, on the contrary, a disposition in every way praiseworthy. After their convention, held last year in Richmond, he and several of the principal members, devout Catholics, made similar declarations concerning the action of that convention, the documents of which we expect to receive shortly.

"(e) Nor do we find in this organization any hostility to the authority and laws of our country. Not only does nothing of the kind appear in their constitution and laws, but the heads of our civil government treat with respect the cause which such associations represent. The President of the United States told me personally, a few weeks ago, that he then had under consideration a proposed law for the amelioration of certain social grievances, and that he had had a long conversation on these topics with Mr. Powderly, the President of the Knights of Labor. The Congress of the United States, in compliance with the views presented by President Cleveland in his annual message, is at present engaged in framing measures for the improvement of the condition of the laboring classes, in whose complaints they acknowledge that there is a great deal of truth. And our political parties, far from considering them the enemies of the country, vie with each other in championing the evident rights of the workingmen, who seek not to resist or overthrow the laws, but only to obtain just legislation by constitutional and legitimate means.

"These considerations, which show that in these associations those elements are not to be found which the Holy See has condemned, lead us to study, in the second place, the evils which the association contends against and the nature of the conflict.

"2. That there exist among us, as in all other countries of the world, grave and threatening social evils, public injustices which call for strong resistance and legal remedy, is a fact which no one dares to deny—a fact already acknowledged by the Congress and the President of the United States. Without entering into the sad details of these evils, whose full discussion is not necessary, I will only mention that monoplies, on the part of both individuals and of corporations, have everywhere called forth not only the complaints of our working classes, but also the opposition of our public men and legislators; that the efforts of monopolists, not always without success, to control legislation to their own profit, cause serious apprehensions among the disinterested friends of liberty; that the heartless avarice which, through greed of gain, pitilessly grinds not only the men, but even the women and children in various employments, makes it clear to all who love humanity and justice that it is not only the right of the laboring classes to protect themselves, but the duty of the whole people to aid them in finding a remedy against the dangers with which both civilization and social order are menaced by avarice, oppression and corruption.

"It would be vain to dispute either the existence of the evils, or the right of legitimate resistance, or the necessity of a remedy. At most, a doubt might be raised about the legitimacy of the form of resistance andeof the remedy employed by the Knights of Labor. This, then, is the next point to be examined.

"3. It can hardly be doubted that, for the attainment of any public end, association—the organization of all interested—is the most efficacious means—a means altogether natural and just. This is so evident, and besides, so comfortable to the genius of our country, of our essentially popular social conditions, that it is unnecessary to insist upon it. It is almost the only means to public attention, to give force to the most legitimate resistance, to add weight to the most just demands.

"Now, there already exists an organization which presents innumerable attractions and advantages, but with which our Catholic workingmen, filially obedient to the Holy See, refuse to unite themselves; this is the Masonic Order, which exists everywhere in our country and which, as Mr. Powderly has expressly pointed out to us, unites employers and employed in a brotherhood very advantageous to the latter, but which numbers in its ranks hardly a single Catholic. Nobly renouncing advantages which the Church and conscience forbid, our workingmen join associations in no way in conflict with religion, seeking nothing but mutual protection and help, and the legitimate assertion of their rights. Must they here also find themselves threatened with condemnation, hindered from their only means of self-defense?

"4. Let us now consider the objections made against this sort of organization:

"(a) It is objected that in such organization, Catholics are mixed with Protestants, to the peril of their faith. Naturally, yes; they are mixed with Protestants at their work; for, in a mixed people like ours, the separation of religious creeds in civil affairs is an impossibility. But to suppose that the faith of our Catholics suffers thereby is not to know the Catholic working men of America, who are not like the working men of so many European countries—misguided children, estranged from their Mother, the Church, and regarding her with suspicion and dread—but intelligent, well-instructed, and devoted Catholics, ready to give their blood, if necessary, as they continually give their hard-earned means, for her support and protection. And, in fact, it is not here a question of Catholics mixed with Protestants, but rather that Protestants are admitted to share in the advantages of an association, many of whose members and officers are Catholics; and, in a country like ours, their exclusion would be simply impossible.

"(b) But it is asked, instead of such an organization, could there not be confraternities, in which the working men would be united under the direction of the clergy and the influence of religion? I answer frankly that I do not consider this either possible or necessary in our country. I sincerely admire the efforts of this sort which are made in countries where the working people are led astray by the enemies of religion; but, thanks be to God, that is not our condition. We find that in our country the presence and direct influence of the clergy would not be advisable where our citizens, without distinction of religious belief, come together in regard to their industrial interests alone. Short of that, we have abundant means for making our working people faithful Catholics; and simple good sense advises us not to go to extremes.

"(c) Again, it is objected that, in such organizations, Catholics are exposed to the evil influences of the most dangerous associates, even of atheists, communists and anarchists. That is true; but it is one of those trials of faith which our brave American Catholics are accustomed to meet almost daily, and which they know how to face with good sense and firmness. The press of our country tells us, and the president of the Knights of Labor has related to us, how these violent, aggressive elements have endeavored to control the association, or to inject poison into its principles; but they also inform us with what determination these machinators have been repulsed and beaten.

"The presence among our citizens of those dangerous social elements, which have mostly come from certain countries of Europe, is assuredly for us an occasion of great regret and of vigilant precautions; it is a fact, however, which we have to accept, but which the close union between the Church and her children which exists in our country renders comparatively free from danger. In truth, the only thing from which we would fear serious danger would be a cooling of this relationship between the Church and her children; and I know nothing that would be more likely to occasion it than imprudent condemnations.

"(d) A specially weighty charge is drawn from the outbursts of violence, even to bloodshed, which have accompanied several of the strikes inaugurated by labor organizations. Concerning this, three things are to be remarked—first, strikes are not an invention of the Knights of Labor, but a means almost everywhere and always resorted to by the working classes to protect themselves against what they consider injustice, and in assertion of what they believe to be their just rights; secondly, in such a struggle of the poor and indignant multitudes against hard and obstinate monopoly, outbursts of anger are almost as inevitable as they are greatly to be regretted; thirdly, the laws and the chief authorities of the Knights of Labor, far from encouraging violence or the occasions of it, exercise a powerful influence to hinder it, and to retain strikes within the limits of good order and of legitimate action.

"A careful examination of the acts of violence accompanying the struggle between capital and labor last year leaves us convinced that it would be unjust to attribute them to the association of the Knights of Labor; for this association was but one among the numerous labor organizations that took part in the strikes, and their chief officers used every possible effort, as disinterested witnesses testify, to appease the anger of the multitudes, and to hinder the excesses which, therefore, in my judgment, could not justly be attributed to them. Doubtless. among the Knights of Labor, as among the thousands of other working men, there are to be found passionate or even wicked men who have committed inexcusable deeds of violence, and have instigated their associates to the same; but to attribute this to the association would, it seems to me, be as unreasonable as to attribute to the Church the follies or the crimes of her children against which she strives and protests.

"I repeat that, in such a struggle of the great masses of the people against the mail-clad power which, as it is acknowledged, often refuses them the simple rights of humanity and justice, it is vain to expect that every error and every act of violence can be avoided; and to dream that this struggle can be hindered, or that we can deter the multitudes from organizing, which is their only hope of success, would be to ignore the nature and forces of human society in times like ours. Christian prudence evidently counsels us to hold the hearts of the multitudes by the bonds of love, in order to control their actions by the principles of faith, justice and charity; to acknowledge frankly what is true and just in their cause, in order to deter them from what is false and criminal, and thus to turn into a legitimate, peaceable and beneficent contest what might easily, by a course of repulsive severity, become for the masses of our people a dread volcanic force like unto that which society fears and the Church deplores in Europe.

"Upon this point I insist strongly, because, from an intimate acquaintance with the social conditions of our country, I am profoundly convinced that here we are touching upon a subject which not only concerns the rights of the working classes, who ought to be especially dear to the Church which our Lord sent forth to preach His Gospel to the poor, but with which are intimately bound up the fundamental interests of the

Church and of human society for the future. This is a point which I desire, in a few additional words, to develop more clearly.

"5. Whoever meditates upon the ways in which divine Providence is guiding mankind in our days can not fail to remark how important is the part which the power of the people takes in shaping the events of the present, and which it is evidently destined to take in molding the destinies of the future. We behold, with profound regret, the efforts of the prince of darkness to make this power dangerous to the social weal by withdrawing the masses of the people from the influence of religion, and impelling them towards the ruinous paths of license and anarchy. Hitherto our country has presented a spectacle of a most consolingly different character—that of a popular power regulated by love of good order, respect for religion, by obedience to the authority of the laws; not a democracy of license and violence, but that true democracy which aims at the general prosperity through the means of sound principles and good social order.

"In order to preserve so desirable a state of things it is absolutely necessary that religion should continue to possess the affections and thus rule the conduct of the multitudes. As Cardinal Manning has well written, 'A new task is before us. The Church has no longer to deal with Parliaments and princes, but with the masses and with the people. Whether we will or no, this is our work; we need a new spirit and a new law of life.' To lose influence over the people would be to lose the future altogether; and it is by the heart, far more than by the understanding, that we must hold and guide this immense power, so mighty either for good or for evil.

"Among all the glorious titles which the Church's history has deserved for her there is not one which at present gives her so great influence as that of 'Friend of the People.' Assuredly, in our democratic country, it is this title which wins for the Catholic Church not only the enthusiastic devotedness of the millions of her children, but also the respect and admiration of all our citizens, whatever be their religious belief. It is the power of this title which renders persecution almost an impossibility, and which draws towards our Holy Church the great heart of the American people.

"And since it is acknowledged by all that the great questions of the future are not those of war, of commerce or of finance, but the social questions—the questions which concern the improvement of the condition of the great popular masses, and especially of the working people—it is evidently of supreme importance that the Church should always be found on the side of humanity—of justice towards the multitudes who compose the body of the human family. As the same Cardinal Manning has wisely written, 'I know I am treading on a very difficult subject, but I feel confident of this, that we must face it, and that we must face it calmly, justly, and with a willingness to put labor and the profits of labor second—the moral state and domestic life of the whole working population first. I will not venture to draw up such an act of Parliament further than to lay down this principle. * * * These things (the present condition of the poor in England) can not go on; these things ought not to go on. The accumulation of wealth in the land, the piling up of wealth like mountains, in the possession of classes or individuals, can not go on. No Commonwealth can rest on such foundations.' (Miscellanies, Vol. 2, p. 81.)

"In our country, above all, this social amelioration is the inevitable programme of the future, and the position which the Church should hold towards it is surely obvious. She can certainly not favor the extremes to which the poor multitudes are naturally inclined; but, I repeat, she must withhold them from these extremes by the bonds of affection, by the maternal desire which she will manifest for the concession of all that is just and reasonable in their demands, and by the maternal blessing which she will bestow upon every legitimate means for improving the condition of the people.

"6. Now let us consider for a moment the consequences which would inevitably follow from a contrary course—from a course of want of sympathy for the working class, of suspicion for their aims, of ready condemnation for their methods.

"(a) First, there would be the evident danger of the Church's losing, in popular estimation, her right to be considered the friend of the people. The logic of the popular heart goes swiftly to its conclusions, and this conclusion would be most pernicious both for the people and for the Church. To lose the heart of the people would be a misfortune for which the friendship of the few rich and powerful would be no compensation.

"(b) There would be a great danger of rendering hostile to the Church the political power of our country, which has openly taken sides with the millions who are demanding justice and the improvement of their condition. The accusation of being un-American—that is to say, alien to our national spirit—is the most powerful weapon which the enemies of the Church can employ against her. It was this cry which aroused the Know-Nothing persecution thirty years ago, and the same would be used again if the opportunity offered. To appreciate the gravity of this danger it is well to remark that not only are the rights of the working classes loudly proclaimed by each of our two great political parties, but it is not improbable that, in our approaching national elections, there will be a candidate for the office of President of the United States as the special representative of the popular complaints and demands.

"Now, to seek to crush by an ecclesiastical condemnation an organization which represents more than 500,000 votes, and which has already so respectable and so universally recognized a place in the political arena, would, to speak frankly, be considered by the American people as not less ridiculous than rash. To alienate from ourselves the friendship of the people would be to run great risk of losing the respect which the Church has won in the estimation of the American nation, and of forfeiting the peace and prosperity which form so admirable a contrast with her condition in some so-called Catholic countries. Angry utterances have not been wanting of late, and it is well that we should act prudently.

"(c) A third danger—and the one which most keenly touches our hearts—is the risk of losing the love of the children of the Church, and of pushing them into an attitude of resistance against their Mother. The world presents no more beautiful spectacle than that of their filial devotion and obedience; but it is well to recognize that, in our age and in our country, obedience can not be blind. We would greatly deceive ourselves if we expected it. Our Catholic working men sincerely believe that they are only seeking justice, and seeking it by legitimate means. A condemnation would be considered both false and unjust, and, therefore, not binding. We might preach to them submission and confidence in the Church's judgment; but these good dispositions could hardly go so far. They love the Church, and they wish to save their souls; but they must also earn their living, and labor is now so organized that without belonging to the organization, it is almost impossible to earn one's living.

"Behold, then, the consequences to be feared. Thousands of the Church's most devoted children, whose affection is her greatest comfort, and whose free offerings are her chief support, would consider themselves repulsed by their Mother and would live without practicing their religion. Catholics who have hitherto shunned the secret societies would be sorely tempted to join their ranks. The Holy See, which has constantly received from the Catholics of America proofs of almost unparalleled devotedness, would be considered not as a paternal authority, but as a harsh and unjust power. Surely these are consequences which wisdom and prudence counsel us to avoid.

"7. But, besides the dangers that would result from such a condemnation, and the impracticability of putting it into effect, it is also very important that we should carefully consider another reason against condemnation, arising from the unstable and transient character of the organization in question. It is frequently remarked by the press and by attentive observers that this special form of association has in it so little permanence that, in its present shape, it is not likely to last many years. Whence it follows that it is not necessary, even if it were just and prudent, to level the sole condemnations of the Church against so evanescent an object. The social agitation itself will, indeed, last as long as there are social evils to be remedied; but the forms of organization meant for the attainment of this end are naturally provisional and short-lived. They are also very numerous, for I have already remarked that the Knights of Labor is only one among many labor organizations.

"To strike, then, at one of these forms, would be to commence a war without system and without end; it would be to exhaust the forces of the Church in chasing a crowd of changing and uncertain spectres. The American people behold with perfect composure and confidence the progress of our social contest, and have not the least fear of not being able to protect themselves against any excesses or dangers that may occasionally arise. Hence, to speak with the most profound respect, but also with the frankness which duty requires of me, it seems to me that prudence suggests, and that even the dignity of the Church demands, that we should not offer to America an ecclesiastical protection for which she does not ask, and of which she believes she has no need.

"8. In all this discussion, I have not at all spoken of Canada, nor of the condemnation concerning the Knights of Labor in Canada; for we would consider it an impertinence on our part to meddle with the ecclesiastical affairs of another country which has an hierarchy of its own, and with whose social conditions we do not pretend to be acquainted. We believe, however, that the circumstances of a people almost entirely Catholic, as in lower Canada, must be very different from those of a mixed population like ours; moreover, that the documents submitted to the Holy Office are not the present constitution of the organization in our country, and that we, therefore, ask nothing involving an inconsistency on the part of the Holy See, which passed sentence *'localiter et juxta exposita.'*

"It is of the United States that we speak, and we trust that we are not presumptuous in believing that we are competent to judge about the state of things in our own country. Now, as I have already indicated, out of the seventy-five archbishops and bishops of the United States, there are about five who desire the condemnation of the Knights of Labor, such as they are in our own country; so that our hierarchy are almost unanimous in protesting against such a condemnation. Such a fact ought to have great weight in deciding the question. If there are difficulties in the case, it seems to me that the prudence and experience of our bishops and the wise rules of the Third Plenary Council ought to suffice for their solution.

"Finally, to sum up all, it seems to me that the Holy See could not decide to condemn an association under the following circumstances:

"1. When the condemnation does not seem to be *justified* either by the letter or the spirit of its constitution, its law and the declaration of its chiefs.

"2. When the condemnation does not seem *necessary*, in view of the transient form of the organization and the social condition of the United States.

"3. When it does not seem to be *prudent*, because of the reality of the grievances complained of by the working classes, and their acknowledgment by the American people.

"4. When it would be *dangerous* for the reputation of the Church in our democratic country, and might even lead to persecution.

"5. When it would probably be *ine,, cacious*, owing to the general conviction that it would be unjust.

"6. When it would be *destructive* instead of beneficial in its effects, impelling the children of the Church to disobey their Mother, and even to enter condemned societies, which they have thus far shunned.

"7. When it would turn into suspicion and hostility the singular devotedness of our Catholic people towards the Holy See.

"8. When it would be regarded as a cruel blow to the authority of bishops in the United States, who, it is well known, protest against such a condemnation.

"Now, I hope that the considerations here presented have sufficiently shown that such would be the effect of condemnation of the Knights of Labor in the United States.

"Therefore, I leave the decision of the case, with fullest confidence, to the wisdom and prudence of your Eminence and the Holy See.

"J. CARD. GIBBONS,
"*Archbishop of Baltimore.*"

Rome, February 20, 1887.

The report, as will be observed from its perusal, was a complete exposition of the labor question involved in the organization of the Knights and an analysis of the relation between the Church and the social and economic situation in the United States. The principles and methods of the order were the same in the United States as in Canada; but with an adroitness which he knew well how to use when occasion warranted it, the Cardinal gave the Holy Office an opening for reversing itself by pointing out differences in the general conditions of the two countries. In person, as well as by formal appeals, he carried his case to the other members of the Curia. In the face of what seemed like a stone wall of opposition, his aggressiveness was aroused. He made an energetic appeal to the commissary of the Holy Office, declaring vehemently that he would hold him responsible for the loss of souls in America through his attitude; at the end of this interview, that important official promised to consider the question. Only those hostile to the Knights had previously been heard at Rome. Opinion, fixed and deliberate, had to be assailed in its powerful citadel. Cardinal Gibbons boldly declared that if the condemnation were allowed to stand, it would be ruinous to the financial support of the church in the United States; that it would turn into doubt and hostility the marked devotion of the people to the Holy See, and would lessen the contribution of Peter's pence.

The Cardinal's letter to the Propaganda had not been intended for the public eye; but a newspaper correspondent having contrived to get possession of a copy, it was published in America and Europe. The Cardinal was surprised one day to receive cablegrams of congratulation from home, and in a short time learned that the argument he had framed for the Curia alone was a theme of discussion throughout the world.

The case was won. Not only did Rome decide not to forbid the organization of the Knights in the United States, but the ban was lifted in Canada. Labor rejoiced that it had gained a signal victory; the Church was still the champion of the poor. Said the *Moniteur de Rome:*

"His Eminence's document has been widely commented upon by the newspapers throughout the United States. They have unanimously recognized in it not only a great benefit conferred upon the millions of workingmen who compose the great mass of people in America and in every other country, but also a victory for the Catholic Church, which, in showing itself the friend of the people, naturally secures their affections. * * * As a matter of course, a few journals—organs of the monopolies—have uttered their protests; but their voice has scarcely been heard amid the general applause."

England echoed the acclamation. "I have read with great assent," Cardinal Manning wrote, "Cardinal Gibbons' document in relation to the Knights of Labor. The Holy See will, I am sure, be convinced by his exposition of the state of the new world. I hope it will open a new field of thought and action. * * * The Church is the mother, friend and protector of the people. As the Lord walked among them, so his Church lives among them."*

In the acuteness of the labor question at the time, Cardinal Gibbons' declaration was criticised and lampooned in some quarters. *Puck* caricatured him as imparting a blessing, with uplifted hands, to a body of riotous working people pursuing a non-union man. He faced denunciation and received praise with equal calmness. The tumult was soon stilled and the adjustment of the relations of labor and capital proceeded, for the most part, on natural and orderly lines.

Throughout the remainder of his pontificate Leo retained vividly the views of the labor question which Cardinal Gibbons had helped to impress upon him. He rejoiced at the opportunity to put the Church in touch with the times on this problem of vast and fundamental importance to the spread of religion among the working people of America and Europe. His mature thought was embodied in an encyclical on "The Condition of Labor," which he addressed to the bishops of the Catholic world a few years later. Considering the subject from its elements, he warmly defended the dignity of labor, as Cardinal Gibbons had done before him; dwelt upon the Christian interdependence of capital and labor, and argued

---

* Taylor, The Cardinal Democrat. p. 180.

that no perfect solution of this question would ever be found without the assistance of religion and of the Church.

Dealing with the cult of the Socialists, who were beginning to carry local elections in Europe, and who even threatened to gain control of several governments by alliance with wings of other political parties, he declared that they were working on the poor man's envy of the rich and were endeavoring to destroy private property. He pronounced their proposals clearly futile for all practical purposes, and held that if they were carried out, the workingman himself would be among the first to suffer. More than that, he found them emphatically unjust, because they would rob the lawful possessor, bring the state into a sphere not its own and cause complete confusion in the community.

The Church, he set forth, was not so occupied with the spiritual concerns of her children as to neglect their temporal interests. Her desire was that the poor should rise above poverty and wretchedness. Christian morality was the key to the situation; if practiced by employer and employee, it would always find part of its expression in the attitude of the state toward social questions. While the state should safeguard private property, it should also protect the rights of the laborer, and special consideration was due to the poor as the weaker members of every community. He warned against the employment of child labor, and emphasized the moral obligation resting on employers to pay fair wages. Both employers and employees, he held, had a right to combine, and it was highly important that workingmen should multiply their associations. In lawful combinations for their own betterment, he found not only justice, but an imperative necessity, if workingmen were to improve their condition. As far as practicable, he desired these organizations founded on the principles of religion. He instructed the bishops to take into their purview the condition of labor in their dioceses, and, without interfering with the state, to aid the workingmen in every lawful way to promote their own just interests without resorting to violence and without recourse to revolutionary doctrines, which, by upsetting the foundations of the world's economic system, would bring suffering upon themselves.*

---

* Encyclical Letter of Leo XIII., May 15, 1891 (Cathedral Archives).

CHAPTER XII.

EARLY YEARS OF CARDINALATE.

After the almost fierce conflict of the winter in Rome, Cardinal Gibbons found relaxation in a leisurely trip homeward, studying the religious, social, economic and political condition of the countries through which he passed. In Paris he was the guest of the Sulpicians, who had founded in Baltimore the first seminary for the training of American priests and thus laid the foundation of a native priesthood. Another stop was made at the University of Louvain, and in May he was the guest of Cardinal Manning in London. In Manning's study, the workshop of a marvelous mind, he found the floor characteristically piled high with books and strewn with papers; and these two eminent champions of human rights passed delightful hours together. The English Cardinal often spoke, even in ordinary conversation, with a precision of logic that was almost resistless, and his conclusions struck with the force of a battle axe. For this compressed and formal habit of thought, the easy graces and ready versatility of Cardinal Gibbons were an admirable foil.

Manning again congratulated him, as he had done in writing, on the victory in the Knights of Labor question. They found common ground in the belief that the time had come when the dynasty of the masses, and not of the classes, was ruling, and ought to rule; that public opinion was the dominating force of the enlightened world, and that in the atmosphere of freedom the great results of the future were to be worked out. They talked of the dignity and rights of labor; agreed that social betterment must come from the bottom, rather than the top; and that the Church, as the friend of the helpless, the champion of the poor, must be in touch with the spirit of the age and continue to prove the universality of her mission.   Naturally akin in sympathy and view, these two had been drawn closer by the struggles through which they had passed, and each was an inspiration to the other.

Cardinal Gibbons had long been interested in missionary work among the negroes, and he took advantage of his visit to England by studying the methods of the Josephite Fathers, at Mill Hill College, near London, where students are trained for this field.   He spent part of two days at Mill Hill, carefully observing the work of the college, and made an address to the students, expressing great gratification at what was being done.   Cardinal Manning entertained him at dinner with a company which included Canon Benoit, rector of Mill Hill, and other persons deeply interested in the conversion of the negroes.

Cardinal Gibbons had particularly good opportunities for studying the condition of the colored race in the United States. Most of his life had been spent in the South; and his experience in North Carolina during Reconstruction times had given him additional light on this momentous problem.   While always regretting that the slavery question, or any other question, should be worked out by the Bismarckian treatment of blood and iron, he felt and frequently expressed a deep and benevolent sympathy for the negro race in its unfortunate position of contiguity with the superior whites.   Like almost all Americans, he was glad to see slavery abolished in the end; but he viewed with alarm the consequences of thrusting the ballot into the hands of millions of black men, unfitted by history or training to comprehend its meaning.   The best solution of the negro question, he felt, was in diffusing among the race the gentle and uplifting influence of Christianity, training the character as a groundwork and building upon this as much of the superstructure of education as it might be found possible to add with benefit.   He felt that the whole problem in its aspects at that time was social rather than political; that the negro must be trained to habits of industry and thrift, to understand the sacred relations of family life and of duty as a member of the community, however humble.

He had shared at no time the expectations of extremists, who had believed the negro capable of developing in a few years what the white race had obtained by centuries of sacrifice, toil and evolution. But, since the blacks were here, and since as far as men of his generation could foresee, they would remain in the United States indefinitely, they must be considered as a weak and helpless people to whom the ministrations of religion were more necessary than to the stronger race. He did not know how far it would be wise to extend the plan of ordaining negro priests for work among their own kind; but he felt that the special character of the negro's needs required a priesthood particularly trained for supplying them.

The fathers of Mill Hill welcomed with enthusiasm the deep and discriminating interest which he showed in their work and its possible extension to America. Soon after his return* his investigations bore fruit in the opening of Epiphany Apostolic College, an institution of the Josephites in Baltimore, founded as an offshoot of Mill Hill, and since the nucleus of a successful work.

The Cardinal sailed from Queenstown, arriving in New York June 4, 1887. A Baltimore committee, including the venerable Monsignor McManus and other friends from among the clergy, gave him a warm welcome at the steamer. He tarried a few days in New York, where he celebrated pontifical mass in St. Patrick's Cathedral, and was greeted by a host of visitors; and then proceeded, on June 7, to Baltimore, whose committees were in a fever of final preparation for a public reception.

As the train arrived at Union Station, the streets were thronged with an acclaiming crowd, as if it were a municipal

* November, 1889.

festival.* Mayor Hodges, Charles J. Bonaparte, a grand-nephew of Napoleon I, and a guard of honor greeted him in behalf of the city.

The Mayor could not permit the opportunity to pass without eulogizing one who had conferred so much honor upon Baltimore abroad. "Your gradual rise from the ranks of the people," he said, "to scholarship, usefulness and popularity, and then to eminence, and now to pre-eminence, although achieved within the ecclesiastical division of life, is so thoroughly an American experience that every self-made man, and others who admire meritorious advancement, must regard your promotion as well earned and well deserved. Those of your fellow-townsmen whose religious faith is in harmony with your own, and who are justly proud of the successful administration of this ancient see for nearly one hundred years, are doubtless gratified to know that you are so worthy a successor of the eight illustrious primates, from Carroll to Bayley, who preceded you as archbishops of Baltimore. They are also gratified to know that you are qualified by learning, good works and religious zeal to be a member of the Sacred College of Rome. * * * Few American citizens during their visits to Europe have been welcomed with more sincere cordiality or made more agreeable impressions on the people they met than you have; and as this effect was produced by the exercise of a rare congenial intelligence, Christian piety, moral worth and gentleness of manner and speech, it is reasonable to surmise that it will be lasting."

Mr. Bonaparte, a leader of the laity, expressed the joy of Catholics.

The Cardinal was, naturally, full of emotion at such an earnest and overwhelming tribute. His warmth of heart and the closeness of his ties with the people among whom his lot had been cast made neighborliness one of the most pronounced traits of his disposition. No matter how great might

* *Catholic Mirror*, June 11, 1887.

be the problems engrossing his mind and occupying his labors, he could turn from these to the purely personal side of his life with a simplicity that was no less charming than rare among men whose work is mingled with so much of the formalism of the world. As he gazed out upon the great crowd he could see men of his own faith, who had often knelt when he celebrated the mass; men of other faiths, who greeted him on the street, in public halls where they met for a common purpose, in the pleasant diversions of social gatherings, and all of whom were proud to call him friend as well as leader.

He began his response to the addresses by saying that he was overcome by a sense of gratitude for this "splendid ovation and this great outpouring of the clergy and people of Baltimore, who have come to bid me welcome on my return to the city which I love so well." It had always been his disposition to shrink from public demonstrations, and on several previous occasions of his return from Rome he had uniformly declined them; "but," he added, "there are times and circumstances—and the present is one of them—when the individual is sunk in his representative capacity, and personal preferences should yield to the wishes of others.

"I thank you most cordially, Mr. Bonaparte, for the beautiful and chaste address you have delivered in the name of the Catholics of Baltimore, and I have to thank you also, honored Mayor, for your excellent remarks, which I appreciate the more as you stand before me as the highest representative of the city and speak for the entire community, without reference to religion or nationality. I beg to assure you both, and the citizens of Baltimore, that the beautiful sentiments of kindness and fraternity you have so well expressed are most heartily reciprocated on my part.

"While traveling in Italy and on the Continent it was always a source of pleasure to me to meet someone who spoke our mother tongue; still more gratifying to me was it when I saw one who hailed from America; but how great was my delight when I had the pleasure of meeting one who could claim Baltimore as his home! Your kindness will bind me still more strongly, if that is possible, to my fellow-citizens, and to this city, where I was born, where Providence has cast my lot, and where I hope to die."

Greetings being over, the Cardinal took his place in a procession which stretched from the station to the archiepiscopal residence, a mile distant. With this long escort he proceeded, in a handsome carriage, surrounded by a guard of honor selected from the members of Catholic societies. Companies of religious knights in handsome uniforms, city officers in carriages and divisions of organizations from all parts of the city took part in the parade. Red badges were everywhere; and, as the guest of honor passed, bowing and smiling, like a President of the United States at his inauguration, the crowds on the streets, in characteristic fashion, raised their hats in respectful salute.

Arriving at the archiepiscopal residence, there was a brief interval, and then the Cardinal entered the Cathedral, where, after prayer, the Vicar-General, Mgr. McColgan, made an address on behalf of the clergy. He spoke of the services which the Cardinal, their bishop, had performed for religion while in Rome, and of their gratitude for the honors which had come to him. "You have exposed to the view of European nations," said the Monsignor, "the blessings which civil and religious liberty bestow on the citizens of America, where the rights of all are guaranteed, where political and social distinctions are open to all, where freedom reigns for all without license, and authority is recognized and maintained without despotism. Your patriotic love for your native country has obtained for you a national character. Your memory, like that of the illustrious Carroll, first Archbishop of Baltimore, will be treasured and enshrined in the hearts of your people."

Again the Cardinal felt the touch of personal association, for no bishop was ever closer to his clergy than he.

"Since my departure from Baltimore," he said in reply, "I have, indeed, received marked favors in the countries through which I have passed. In Rome and throughout Italy, in France, Belgium, Holland, Scotland and Ireland, many kind attentions have been shown me, which I shall never forget; but, while fully appreciating the courtesies which have been paid me in foreign lands, I value immeasurably more than all the words of greeting which have fallen from your lips. For what would a father care for all the honors that might be lavished upon him abroad, were he not revered and loved by his own children and in his own household?"

On the Sunday following, at the services in the Cathedral, the Cardinal spoke in detail of his European trip.* Fresh from contact with Leo XIII, he naturally thought first of that pontiff, who had inspired and upheld him in the trying circumstances through which he had passed.

"Though he is deprived of his temporal possessions," said the Cardinal, "it can be safely said that today he exercises more power over the civilized world than any king or potentate; and, although he has no military force to back him, his words are more conducive to peace than the actions of all the standing armies of Europe. In his case it can be truly said that his voice is mightier than the sword. He enjoys the love of two hundred and fifty million of Catholics, scattered throughout the length and breadth of the world; and he has the respect and esteem of our separated brethren, who have not failed to recognize his many personal virtues, his benevolent character, and his broad, statesmanlike views. He has a special regard for this republic of ours and the citizens of the United States, which was amply demonstrated during my sojourn in Rome. At the time there was a large number of Americans in the city, all of whom very naturally wished to see the Holy Father. I mentioned the fact to him at the first opportunity, and in reply he said he would, indeed, be much

---

* *Catholic Mirror*, June 18, 1887.

pleased to see them.   When the visitors were afterward presented, they were charmed by his presence and went away favorably impressed with all that he had said and strengthened with God's benediction upon them.   Another illustration of his love for Americans was shown on Easter Tuesday, when all the cardinals then in Rome paid their respects to his Holiness.   He took that occasion to again speak of his great love for this country."

The Cardinal proceeded to describe in colloquial fashion to his congregation his experiences in some of the countries of Europe which he visited.   At Louvain he had been impressed with the strength of its ancient university, and within him had been born the wish that the new university at Washington would some day be its equal.   Speaking at a time when the skies of labor in the United States were full of clouds, when men accustomed to think calmly and speak judiciously were predicting that those clouds might break into a terrible storm, he expressed without hesitation his own clear faith that the people would be equal to the responsibilities thrust upon them.

"Whatever may be the grievances of the laboring classes here," he said, "I believe our men are better paid, better clothed, better housed and have fairer prospects than those of any other nation I have visited.   *   *   *   As we all have a share in the blessings of the republic, so should we all take an active and loyal part in upholding the Commonwealth, which gives liberty without license and wields authority without despotism.   The man who would endeavor to undermine the laws and institutions of this country deserves the fate of those who laid profane hands on the Ark of the Lord.   There are some misguided men in our country—thank God, they are very few—who are appropriately called anarchists and nihilists.   They are so infatuated, not to say ungrateful to their country, that, like Samson, they would fain pull down the constitutional temple which shelters them, even though they should perish in the ruins.   May Almighty God, by whom rulers reign and lawgivers decree just things, preserve our country for the peace and prosperity of our generation and for the happiness of countless peoples yet unborn!"

Seeing not the slightest conflict between allegiance to church and allegiance to country, he alluded to a sight he had recently witnessed in the parade held in his honor—the flags of the United States and of the papacy carried by marching Americans. "I always wish to see those two flags lovingly entwined," he said, "for no one can be faithful to God without being faithful to his country. 'Render unto Cæsar the things that are Cæsar's, and to God, the things that are God's.' "

It had not been customary for Catholic prelates to take part in civic events in America. During the first century of the nation's existence this would have been misunderstood, and at times would have been positively dangerous. But when Philadelphia decided to celebrate in 1887 the centennial of the American Constitution, it was felt that the occasion would be incomplete without Cardinal Gibbons, so strong a place had he won in the affections of the nation. He was invited to offer the closing prayer on September 17, the anniversary of the signing.

President Cleveland, his Cabinet and a host of distinguished men were there. Many of these the Cardinal knew personally, and others were eager to meet the churchman who had done so much for his country at home and abroad. His red robe, an unfamiliar sight in America, invested his presence among the crowds with a half-mystic interest; and they found that it covered a man as typically American as any, alert, active, patriotic to the core, sharing keenly the enthusiasm and pride in the institutions of the country.

His prayer was based on one written by Archbishop Carroll, and was modified to suit the occasion. It was as follows:[*]

"We pray Thee, O God of might, wisdom and justice, through whom authority is rightly administered, laws are enacted and judgment de-

_____

[*] *Catholic Mirror*, September 24, 1887.

creed, to assist with Thy holy spirit of counsel and fortitude the President of these United States, that his administration may be conducted in righteousness, and be eminently useful to Thy people over whom he presides, by encouraging due respect for virtue and religion, by a faithful execution of the laws in justice and mercy, and by restraining vice and immorality.

"Let the light of Thy divine wisdom direct the deliberations of Congress and shine forth in all their proceedings and laws framed for our rule and government, so that they may tend to the preservation of peace, the promotion of national happiness, the increase of industry, sobriety and useful knowledge, and may perpetuate to us the blessings of equal liberty.

"We pray Thee for all judges, magistrates and other officers who are appointed to guard our political welfare, that they may be enabled by Thy powerful protection to discharge the duties of their respective stations with honesty and ability.

"We pray Thee especially for the judges of our Supreme Court, that they may interpret the laws with even-handed justice. May they ever be the faithful guardians of the temple of the constitution, whose construction and solemn dedication to our country's liberties we commemorate today. May they stand as watchful and incorruptible sentinels at the portals of this temple, shielding it from profanation and hostile invasion.

"May this glorious charter of our civil rights be deeply imprinted on the hearts and memories of our people. May it foster in them a spirit of patriotism; may it weld together and assimilate in national brotherhood the diverse races that come to seek a home amongst us. May the reverence paid to it conduce to the promotion of social stability and order, and may it hold the ægis of its protection over us and generations yet unborn, so that the temporal blessings which we enjoy may be perpetuated.

"Grant, O Lord, that our republic, unexampled in the history of the world in material prosperity and growth of population, may be also, under Thy over-ruling providence, a model to all nations in upholding liberty without license, and in wielding authority without despotism.

"Finally, we recommend to Thy unbounded mercy all our brethren and fellow-citizens throughout the United States, that they may be blessed in the knowledge and sanctified in the observance of Thy most holy law, that they may be preserved in union and in that peace which the world can not give, and after enjoying the blessings of this life, be admitted to those which are eternal.

"Our Father, who art in Heaven, hallowed be Thy name; Thy kingdom come; Thy will be done, on earth, as it is in heaven; give us this day our daily bread, and forgive us our trespasses, as we forgive those who trespass against us; and lead us not into temptation, but deliver us from evil. Amen."

At the conclusion of the prayer the Cardinal invoked a benediction in the following words:

"May the blessings of Almighty God, Father, Son and Holy Ghost, descend upon our beloved country and upon all her people, and abide with them forever. Amen."

He had never visited the fast-developing West, which, according to the signs of the times, was about to take on far greater importance in the outlook of the United States and the Church. With something akin to eagerness, he accepted the invitation to confer the pallium at Portland, Ore., on Archbishop Gross, his long-time friend, "born nearly in the same street," as he said, and a brother of that faithful priest, Rev. Mark S. Gross, with whom he had shared privations and labors in North Carolina. As a student of history, he felt that such a large portion of his country, in whose beginnings adventurous missionary priests had performed such heroic service, should share in eminent degree the benefits of Catholic effort in its fuller development along the pathways of civilization and material progress. Was not a cardinal of the Roman Church at home in the country watered by the great river which De Soto had discovered and named in honor of the Holy Ghost; which Marquette and Joliet, boldly trusting themselves to an Indian canoe, had explored for thousands of miles and dedicated to the Immaculate Conception; which Hennepin had ascended to the falls he had named in honor of St. Anthony of Padua? Was he not at home in the new States created from the vast region which Coronado had penetrated with his adventurous Spaniards, carrying the cross and celebrating the mass on prairie and desert and by the sides of great rivers which flowed into the still greater "Father of Waters?"

In the whole region won from Mexico, the Catholic Church retained the affections of the people. Germans, Irishmen and Italians, and the peoples of other European countries who had been children of the Church in the land of their birth, were helping to make the prairies blossom with their industry, and mine and factory rang with the sound of their labor.

The Church would follow them, as, centuries before, she had gone in advance of them. She would try to train them to build American homes to take the places of those which they had had left in Europe. Some day a thousand men would dwell where one now cultivated a township farm or ranged his cattle over half a county. A city would grow where a house now stood; and men with a mission to the whole nation would arise from among the sons of these pioneers, who as yet toiled only at the foundations of what, as far as human foresight went, would one day be a magnificent structure.

Above all, the Cardinal desired that these new peoples, taking root in new soil, should one day be homogeneous with their brothers in the forests of Maine and the cotton fields of Louisiana. If America were to integrate instead of disintegrate, these people must be one—not one in individuality, but sharing a common respect for the rights of others, a common faith in the perpetuity of their institutions, in the liberty which gave every man a chance, a common aspiration for a greater America, that would be an example and a blessing to the remainder of the world. Whatever their origin, all were now brothers in the citizenship of the same great republic. While treasuring the memory of the brave stocks from which they sprang; while never forgetting the good that was behind them, yet, their future would be in the United States; and no trace of antagonism, of racial differences, of political ideals born in diverse surroundings must prevent the consummation of their proper destiny.

In the Cardinal's view, the foreigner who was populating the West must be brought as rapidly as possible into intimate touch with his new environment; must be made to feel that his children would look to the men of '76 as the authors of the political system under which they lived, a system of free Commonwealths, retaining local self-government in a large sense, and yet bound by unity of purpose and a common aim for the realization of a grand destiny. Assimilation was, after all, one of the most vital problems to be solved by Americans of the last half of the nineteenth century and the beginning of the twentieth. It would never do for the people of European nationalities that were pouring over here in thousands to cling together longer than might be necessary to enable them to adapt themselves to new conditions. They might be Germans by ancestry, as were thousands of the first citizens of the growing West; they might be Italians, Swedes or Poles; but the work of the Church, no less than of the political authorities, must be to make them, as soon as possible, Americans.

All Americans were foreigners by descent, except the Indians reduced to the helpless condition of wards of the nation; but had all retained the spirit born in other lands, had there been a clash of systems instead of a union of thought, America would never have gotten far in the realization of the possibilities opened by the devoted men who had explored it, pointing the way to the peoples who were to come in the future generations. The Catholic Church, which had been the guide of most of the new-comers, in which they had been baptized and taught, in which they had found the means of access to Divine truth—this Church could perform a great service to the nation by leading them forward to that community of language, social custom and political idealism which were essential to their own welfare and the nation's safety.

Leaving Baltimore late in September, Cardinal Gibbons went to Chicago, where he was the guest of Archbishop Feehan; then to Milwaukee, a center of German Catholicism, where he was entertained by Archbishop Heiss. The city of St. Paul, the see of Archbishop Ireland, his ardent champion, was busy with preparations to receive him. A great reception was given there September 20, and a banquet was held, at which the Archbishop spoke in eulogy of his distinguished guest.* The tone of all the speeches was one of pride in the new Cardinal as an American citizen and a prince of the Catholic Church. Judge William L. Kelly, speaking for the laity, recalled what had happened only recently at Philadelphia.

"But yesterday," he said, "at the invitation of your fellow-citizens, irrespective of religious faith or political association, you, priest, archbishop, cardinal, raised your hand above the assembled multitudes and, in the name of your sacred office, invoked the blessing of Almighty God upon the Constitution of these United States. In that particular, illustrious sir, your voice, it seems to me, was not merely that of the priest, but of the prophet of God as well. * * * The old lines that have long kept us apart from our brethren without the fold are, thank God, well nigh obliterated here. On all great questions, social and political, we stand in St. Paul side by side. We are staunch in our religious faith, and they in theirs, and the honesty of neither is questioned; and no one has done more to bring about that cordial catholic condition of things than the man who sits at your side. To name him is to do him honor—John Ireland."

Responding to the addresses, the Cardinal could not forbear to refer to his colleague in so many struggles. "For many years," he said, "I have been closely watching Archbishop Ireland's career. It was my pleasure to be associated with him at the last Plenary Council of Baltimore. For three weeks I studied him, and the more I studied him, the more I admired and loved him. Archbishop Ireland came to you as a Providential mes-

---

* *Catholic Mirror*, October 8, 1887. Subsequent issues contain further details of the Cardinal's Western trip.

senger sent to you by Almighty God. He has done untold good through the temporal blessings which he has helped to bestow upon society.

"You were pleased," he added, "to mention my pride in being an American citizen; it is the proudest earthly title I possess."

Referring to the movement, then much discussed, to incorporate the name of God in the national Constitution, he remarked: "For my part, I have not desired to see that venerated name used in this respect, so long as it remains inscribed on the tablets of the hearts of the people and the rulers of the nation. I would rather speak with the living captain than with the figure on the prow of the ship."

Helena, Montana, the seat of Bishop Brondel, was another city which greeted him with an outpouring. With a touch of the spirit of the West, he ventured to predict that the time was likely to come when the city would be a community of a hundred thousand souls. Again, he spoke of his pride in being an American citizen, saying that it was as great a title as the one of which the ancient Romans were fond of boasting. His travels abroad had enhanced his love for his own country, and he declared that he felt a pride and a faith in its destiny which upheld him in the trials through which he passed.

On Sunday, October 9, he officiated in Portland at the investiture of Archbishop Gross, a splendid ceremony, attended by all the prelates of the Northwest. The next day there was a public reception, at which H. E. McGinn, in an address to the Cardinal in behalf of the citizens of Portland, took occasion to pay this tribute:

"As long as men are compelled to labor; as long as they feel called upon to unite for their own protection; as long as the Divine mandate remains true, that 'In the sweat of thy face shalt thou eat bread,' so long shall the name of Cardinal Gibbons be venerated among men."

The earnestness of the speaker was in part due to the fact that the labor question was then acute on the Pacific Coast, and the Cardinal took occasion in his own address at the reception to refer to it.   He pleaded, as he had so often done before, for peace between capital and labor.

He continued his travels to San Francisco, where he was hospitably entertained by Archbishop Riordan, and to Los Angeles, where a public address of welcome was made to him by Lieut.-Gov. Stephen M. White, afterward United States Senator. At Fort Vancouver Gen. John Gibbon, the commander, entertained him. When he arrived there by boat Lieutenant Anderson, who commanded the squad sent to meet him, said:

"Your Eminence, it was customary in ancient times, when a prince of the realm traveled, for the governors of cities to release some prisoners in honor of his visit. As you are a prince of the Church, I propose to release some men confined here."

He then summoned six private soldiers from the prison in the fort and said to them: "Soldiers, consider yourselves free in honor of Cardinal Gibbons."

Everywhere the Cardinal was received as an eminent citizen, no less than as a prince of the Church; and through the welcoming speeches ran the thread of his bold and patriotic attitude in Rome but a few months before.

Proceeding homeward by way of New Orleans, where he had spent part of his youth and where his family still resided, that city hailed him as its own.   In behalf of the Catholics there, he was presented, at a public reception, a gold ring and chain and a diamond cross.   An address of welcome was made to him by Edward Douglas White, afterward Chief Justice of the United States Supreme Court.   The Cardinal returned from his transcontinental tour with new vigor and inspiration.

The year 1887 marked the close of half a century's labors in the priesthood by Leo XIII, the friend of America and of America's Cardinal. The rulers of European nations, and even the Sultan, were sending to Rome gifts expressive of their felicitations, not only to the earthly head of a Church of 250,000,000 people, but to a man who had been the balance-wheel of Europe. What would be America's part in such an occasion? The Holy See had intimated to Cardinal Gibbons that an expression from the United States would be welcome. One day after his return from his Western tour he was considering how to bring this to President Cleveland's attention, when the following letter arrived, in the handwriting of the President:

"EXECUTIVE MANSION.

"Washington, Nov. 17, 1887.
"His Eminence Cardinal Gibbons:

"My Dear Sir—I have thought that you would send to the Pope your congratulations on the occasion of the approaching Jubilee.

"Remembering with much gratitude and satisfaction the kind words you brought from the Holy Father upon your recent return from Rome, I should be very much pleased if you could, without impropriety on your part, convey to him my congratulations and felicitations.

"Hoping that you are quite well after your extended travel, I am,

"Yours very sincerely,
"GROVER CLEVELAND."*

The Cardinal paid another of his visits to the White House, now growing frequent, and thanked Mr. Cleveland for the letter. He expressed at the same time his hope that the President would not be content with a formal communication, but would send some memento to the Pontiff indicative of his sentiments. As the centennial of the Constitution had just been commemorated, he suggested that a copy of that instrument would be one of the most appropriate of gifts.

---

* Cathedral Archives.

"None can question the fitness of such a present," said the Cardinal, "for the dissemination of the principles of our government abroad would be above criticism."

Mr. Cleveland assented with eagerness. The Cardinal offered to have a copy of the Constitution bound if the President would furnish one unbound.

"I will do nothing of the kind," rejoined the President, "but will insist on having a copy bound in a costly and beautiful manner, if you will tell me how to do it."

The Cardinal suggested white silk or satin as appropriate. Mr. Cleveland then asked what should be the form of presentation, and the Cardinal dictated these words:

"Presented through his Eminence Cardinal Gibbons to the Holy Father, Pope Leo XIII, on the occasion of the golden jubilee of his Holiness, with the profound regard of Grover Cleveland, President of the United States."

"How much time is there to have the book prepared?" asked the President.

"Ten days," said the Cardinal.

On the tenth day afterward there arrived by express at the archiepiscopal residence, in Baltimore, from a noted New York jeweler, a superb volume of the Constitution printed in old English characters on vellum, bound in white and red, and bearing the presentation inscription from President to Pope. Col. John T. Morris, of Baltimore, was selected to carry it to Rome, for presentation at the jubilee festivities.

The presentation, in the throne room of the Vatican, was marked by an exchange of warm sentiments. Archbishop Ryan made an appropriate address, and Mgr. O'Connell read a letter to the Pope from the Cardinal, conveying the President's personal congratulations.

"As an archbishop," said the Pontiff in reply, "you enjoy in America perfect freedom. That freedom, we admit, is highly beneficial to the spread of religion. * * * Toward America I bear especial love. * * * Your government is free, your future full of hope. Your President commands my highest admiration."

Leo was so much delighted that for a long time he exhibited the gift in his private apartment, with the presentation page open, that favoured visitors might see. That the pleasure was mutual is indicated by the fact that when the cardinal called on the president to show him the letter from the pontiff acknowledging the receipt of the gift, the president, after hearing the translation read, was so much pleased with it that he asked the cardinal to give him the original, a favor which was readily granted.

The letter of the Pope, which Mr. Cleveland retained, was addressed to Cardinal Gibbons, and charged him with the duty of conveying his warm thanks to the President. "In fulfilling this duty," Leo wrote, "we desire that you should assure the President of our admiration for the Constitution of the United States, not only because it enables industrious and enterprising citizens to attain so high a degree of prosperity, but also because, under its protection, your Catholic countrymen have enjoyed a liberty which has so confessedly promoted the astonishing growth of their religion in the past and will, we trust, enable it in the future to be of the highest advantage to the civil order as well."*

All the churches of the diocese of Baltimore observed the papal jubilee January 1, 1888, the Cardinal delivering the sermon in the Cathedral. His heart must have been full to overflowing as he arose to speak on the career of this illustrious Pontiff, to whose enlightened comprehension of modern conditions he owed so much of what he had been able to accomplish;

---

* A copy of the letter is in the Cathedral Archives.

and whose fatherly interest in himself had so often overcome him with gratitude. At the outset he dwelt on the perpetuity of the papacy, and the mission it had worked out, under God, for mankind. While a great conservative force, it had turned progress and invention into the service of Christianity, and at great crises in the world's history had guided events in the direction of civilization.

"What means," he asked, "can be employed to overthrow an institution which for nineteen centuries has successfully overcome every opposition waged against it? Is it by the power of kings and emperors and prime ministers that the papacy can be destroyed? They have tried, and tried in vain, from the days of the Roman Cæsars to our own times. Many persons labor under the false impression that in former times the Church was leagued with the princes of this world for the purpose of overthrowing the liberties of the people; that the altars were sustained by the thrones, and that they would crumble if this protection were withdrawn. The truth is. that, with some honorable exceptions, the most unrelenting enemies of the Church and the papacy have often been the princes of this world, and so-called Christian princes, too. They chafed under the salutary discipline of the Church and wished to be rid of her yoke, because she was the only power on earth that could stand between the princes and the people and tell the former that, if the people have their obligations, they have their rights, too.

"But can the Church cope with modern inventions and the great discoveries of the nineteenth century? Rest assured the Church will not hide her head, like the ostrich in the sand, at the approach of these modern inventions and discoveries. For, if Christianity was propagated to the uttermost bounds of the earth at a time when we had no other ships but frail canoes, no other compass but the naked eye, no other roads but eternal snows and virgin forests and desert wastes, how much more now can we effect by means of railroads and steamships? Yes, we bless you, O men of genius. We bless your inventions and discoveries, and will press you into the service of the Gospel, and we will say: 'Lightning and clouds, bless the Lord; fire and heat, bless the Lord; all ye works of the Lord, bless the Lord, praise and exalt Him above all forever.'

"But may not the light of Christianity grow pale and be utterly extinguished before the intellectual blaze of the nineteenth century? Have we not much to fear from the arts and sciences and literature? We have nothing to fear, but everything to gain, from intellectual development. The Church has always been the patroness of literature and the fostering mother of arts and sciences. At no period of the history of Christianity did the popes wield a greater power than from the twelfth to the sixteenth century. They exercised not only spiritual power, but also temporal jurisdiction, and had great influence with the civil rulers of those days. Now, at no period did the human intellect revel in greater freedom in the pursuit of speculative knowledge of every kind than in those days. It was emphatically the age of universities. Forty-one universities sprang up during those four centuries—in France, Germany, Belgium, Ireland, Italy, Spain, England and Scotland. There can be no conflict between science and Christianity, for the same God is the author of all revealed truth and all scientific truth. Science and religion, like Mary and Martha, are sisters, because they are the daughters of the same Father—only they serve the Lord in a different manner; science, like Martha, is laboring among the things of material creation; religion, like Mary, is kneeling at the feet of the Lord.

"But has not the papacy much to fear from the progress of liberty? Give us liberty, this is all we ask—a fair field and no favor. The Church is always hampered in her operations wherever despotism casts its dark shadow. She always blooms and expands in the genial air of liberty. Amid the changes in human institutions the papacy is one institution that never changes. It has seen the birth of every existing government in Europe, and it is not improbable that it may witness the death of some of them and chant their requiem. It was 1,400 years old when Columbus discovered America, and our own Government is but of yesterday as compared with it.

"The present illustrious Pontiff, Leo XIII, is a worthy successor of the Gregories, the Innocents, the Piuses, and of the long line of Leos that have preceded him. For ten years he has occupied the chair of Peter, a spectacle to the world, to angels and to men; and during all that time he has excited the admiration of the civilized world by his luminous intellect, his broad statesmanship, his strong judgment, his keen appreciation of things; by his conciliatory disposition, his personal integrity and purity of life, and by his great benevolence of character.

"Leo XIII is today, perhaps, the most popular man in Europe, if not in the world, and this is the secret of his popularity: He understands the times in which we live; he appreciates the fact that we are living in the nineteenth century, and not in the ninth; he understands the wants of the people, and sympathizes with their legitimate aspirations, while at the same time he is always the promoter and vindicator of law and order and legitimate government everywhere. He has found the key to the hearts of the people, and has entered there. Let us hope and pray that this great luminary, whom the Lord has set over His Church, may long linger above the horizon to enlighten us by his wisdom and to cheer us by his example; and when his course is run and his light on earth is extinguished, may he shine for all eternity in the kingdom of our common Father, the source of all light and the author of all justice."*

In November, 1888, the Cardinal issued a Thanksgiving circular, in which he drew a lesson from the Presidential election

---

* *Catholic Mirror,* Jan. 7, 1888.

a few weeks before at which General Harrison had been chosen to succeed Mr. Cleveland.

"In other lands," he wrote, "the times for choosing the rulers of the nation are often occasions of political convulsion, of the interruption of all peaceful pursuits, and sometimes even of strife and bloodshed. The recent contest between ten millions of voters of this republic, representing sixty millions of people, has been settled peaceably and constitutionally, without the loss of a single life or even any interruption in men's ordinary avocations."*

During 1888 and part of 1889 he was much engaged in writing his second book, "Our Christian Heritage." Authorship naturally had a powerful appeal for a devourer of literature like himself, and the success of "The Faith of Our Fathers" had led to many offers from publishers. From early manhood reading had been a large part of his recreation—theology, philosophy, history and civics, with now and then a novel at night in the quiet of his study to draw his mind away from the absorbing events of the day. In his first book he had been the priest preaching to the people; but from the pages of "Our Christian Heritage" shines the character of citizen as well as priest. It may be described, in brief, as an argument in behalf of Christianity addressed to the average busy man of the time, accustomed to be guided by material considerations in his daily work and doubting, from force of habit, conclusions whose premises he cannot clearly comprehend. The Cardinal aimed to demonstrate the fundamental truths underlying Christianity by the unaided reason, which, he declared, was sufficient, though "they are made still more luminous by the light of Christian revelation."

The book is not sectarian. The author stated positively that he was glad to acknowledge that "most of the topics discussed have often found, and still find, able and zealous advo-

---

* Cathedral Archives.

We have grown up not as distinct,
independent, & conflicting communities, but as one corporate body, breathing the same atmosphere of freedom,
governed by the same laws, enjoying
the same political rights. I see
in all this a wonderful manifestation of the humanising &
elevating influence of christian
civilisation. We receive from
abroad people of various nations,
races & tongues, habits & tempera-
ments who speedily become assimilated to the native mass, & who
form one homogeneous society.
What is the secret of our stability
& order? It results from wise laws
based on christian principles, & which
are the echo of God's eternal law. What is
the cohesive power that makes us one body
politic out of so many alien elements?
It is the religion of Christ.

cates in Protestant writers. * * * I would gladly hold
out to them the right hand of fellowship, so long as they unite
with us in striking the common foe."

Having concluded a searching and logical examination of
the elements of Christian truth, he proceeded to argue that
religion is the essential basis of civil society.   He showed how
it has been interwoven in the thread of events throughout the
history of the United States, and sought to apply it as a remedy
for the "dangers that threaten our American civilization."
These he enumerated as five—

"Mormonism and divorce, which strike at the root of the
family and society;"

An "imperfect and vicious system of education, which undermines the religion of our youth;"

"Desecration of the Christian Sabbath;"

"Gross and systematic election frauds;"

The "unreasonable delay in carrying into effect the sentences
of our criminal courts."

A chapter was devoted to the "dignity, rights and duties of
the laboring classes," which, he argued, found their best guide
in the wholesome influence of religion.

In and out of the pulpit he was fond of quoting lessons
from the life of Washington, whom he considered the greatest
American.   At the hundredth anniversary of the first President's inauguration—April 30, 1889—he issued a pastoral
letter directing the ringing of all the church bells half an
hour and a special service in every Catholic house of worship
in the Diocese of Baltimore.   In this letter he expressed "profound satisfaction that the citizens of the United States, without regard to race or creed or previous allegiance to any flag
whatsoever," were about to recognize the life and achievements
of Washington, "a gift of Almighty God to his own age, and
an exemplar to all the ages to be."   The Cardinal himself was
present at the mass celebrated in the Baltimore Cathedral in
honor of the event.

CHAPTER XIII.

Centennial of the American Hierarchy.

In an era of centennials, the Catholic Church in America could not forget the origin of her own hierarchy. John Carroll, a cousin of that signer of the Declaration of Independence who survived last to receive the grateful plaudits of his fellow-countrymen, had been appointed November 6, 1789, first Bishop of Baltimore and head of the Church in the then infant republic. The total population of the United States was then less than 4,000,000, including 40,000 Catholics; in 1889 the population had grown to 65,000,000, of whom 9,000,000 were of the Catholic faith. From Carroll as a corner-stone, the hierarchy had risen in a hundred years to the proportions of 13 archbishops and 71 bishops, the spiritual overseers of 8,000 priests, 10,500 churches and chapels, 27 seminaries for training the clergy, 650 colleges and academies for the higher education of youth, 3,100 parish schools and 520 hospitals and asylums.

The nation had marshalled its strength with pride in the unexampled rapidity of its achievements; might not the Catholic Church do the same, exhibiting not only her own greatness, but her thorough identification with the spirit of the people and the Government?

Cardinal Gibbons had been accustomed to works of organization, and when it was decided to hold a great celebration in Baltimore to mark the hierarchy's centennial, he began the undertaking with characteristic energy and skill. Aided by the staff of priests attached to his household and to the Cathedral, he soon had under way the beginnings of a project of far-reaching scope. Surrounding him at the time were Rev. P. J.

Donahue, an undergraduate of his "School of Bishops," afterward head of the Wheeling Diocese; Rev. John T. Whelan, his secretary, a man of rare energy, tact and capacity for detail; Rev. Thomas S. Lee, rector of the Cathedral, and Rev. William A. Reardon, assistant. They called to their aid Rev. J. A. McCallen, of St. Mary's Seminary, who had long been recognized as a master of Church ceremonial, and who had managed some of the most imposing events that had taken place in the Cathedral and elsewhere.

The celebration included five days crowded with ambitious events. For the opening, on Sunday, November 10, there was a solemn pontifical mass, at which, as far as possible, the American hierarchy were assembled, as well as representatives of the Church in other countries on both sides of the Atlantic. After this was a dinner at St. Mary's Seminary, at which the principal foreign delegates spoke. On Monday and Tuesday a congress of laymen was held, and on Tuesday night a torchlight procession. On Wednesday the School of Sacred Sciences at the new university was dedicated. On Thursday the visiting prelates were escorted in carriages to the principal places of interest in or near Baltimore, and there was a reception at the City Hall.

Cardinal Gibbons had written to the Pope, outlining the plans for the celebration. The Pontiff encouraged it with lively interest.

"That great love for country and for religion," wrote Leo, "which you and our brethren the bishops of the United States, have so often and so nobly manifested, is again strikingly illustrated in the letter which you have recently addressed to us. From it we learn that pastors and people are about to assemble in Baltimore to celebrate the one hundredth anniversary of the establishment of the hierarchy of the United States. On the same occasion you propose to dedicate the Catholic University, which, with the generous help of the faithful, you have founded in Washington as a happy presage of future greatness for the new era upon which you are about to enter.

"It is truly worthy of your faith and hope thus gratefully to recall the blessings bestowed upon your country by Divine Providence, and at the same time to raise up in memory of them a monument which will be an honor to yourselves and a lasting benefit to your fellow-citizens and to the country at large. We gladly unite with you in returning thanks to God, the author of all gifts. At the same time, we cordially congratulate you on the zeal with which you emulate the example of your glorious predecessors, faithfully treading in their footsteps, whilst ever widening the field opened by their apostolic labors.

"Most joyfully have we welcomed the expression which you and the other bishops convey to us of your loyalty and devotion to the Apostolic See. We desire, in return, to assure you that, like our predecessors of blessed memory, we, too, bear an especial love toward you, our brethren, and the faithful committed to your care, and that we pray frequently for your prosperity and welfare, gathering comfort meanwhile, no less from the readiness of your people to co-operate in all manner of good works than from the examples of sacerdotal virtue which are daily set before them.

"In regard to your wish that some representative from this city should, in our name, be present at your celebration, we readily assent to it, the more willingly because his presence will be an especial mark of our esteem and benevolence, and of that bond of affection and charity which unites pastors and people to the supreme head of the Church.

"In conclusion, we earnestly pray to God, protector and guardian of the Catholic cause, that under the excellent and favored public institutions by which you are able to exercise with freedom your sacred ministry, your labors may redound to the benefit of Church and country; and as a pledge of our especial affection we lovingly impart apostolic benediction to you, to our venerable brethren, the bishops of the United States, and to the clergy and faithful committed to your charge."*

Mgr. O'Connell brought this letter from Rome to Cardinal Gibbons. He was soon followed by the representative whom the Pope had promised to send, Francesco di Paola Satolli, Archbishop of Lepanto, an Italian theologian of deep learning and wonderful eloquence, who was destined to play a great part in the relations between the Holy See and the Catholics of the United States. Satolli's first impression of the people was amazement at the proportions of the celebration; and, though he could speak no English, he soon showed, after the manner of De Toqueville and Bryce, a faculty for understanding the true spirit of American institutions beyond the capacity of most men born here.

Cardinal Manning was invited with a special warmth, and, had he come to Baltimore, would have shared with his friend, Cardinal Gibbons, the honors of the occasion; but age had at last interposed its relentless barrier against that iron will, and he was forced to decline, sending Bishop Virtue, of Portsmouth, and Mgr. Gadd in his place.

From Canada came Cardinal Taschereau and six archbishops; from Mexico, Bishops Gillow and Montez D'Oca; and Archbishop Croke sent a fervent letter from the prelates of Ireland. Nearly all the bishops and archbishops of the United States gathered in Baltimore for the event.

A prelude to the main celebration was the observance, February 20, 21 and 22, 1889, of the one hundredth anniversary of Georgetown University, the first Catholic collegiate institution in the United States. This, too, was one of the

---

* Letter of Leo XIII to Cardinal Gibbons, Sept. 7, 1889 (Cathedral Archives).

fruits of the ministry of John Carroll, who had founded it to meet a great need then existing, and who would have been its first president had he not been raised to the episcopate in the same year.   At the celebration the two most conspicuous figures were Cardinal Gibbons and President Cleveland, who, following the example of nearly all his predecessors, from Washington down, visited this widely known Jesuit institution.

In the presence of an assemblage more largely representative of the true spirit of the Church in America than any other which had gone before, the splendid ceremonies of the hierarchy's centennial began November 10 with the pontifical high mass at the Cathedral.*   Every American prelate was there, except the aged Archbishop Kenrick, of St. Louis, who was too feeble to make the trip halfway across the continent. Besides these, four hundred priests, the same number of seminarians and several organizations of laymen took part in the procession.   Archbishop Ryan, then in the prime of his powers as an orator and celebrated far and near for the eloquence and force of his pulpit utterances, preached a masterly sermon. While they were celebrating the first centennial of the Church in the United States, he pointed out, the beginnings of Catholicity in America reached back to a much earlier period.   He recalled that a Catholic discoverer, representing a Catholic nation, "had first planted the all-civilizing Cross on these shores" in 1492.   He rejoiced to welcome the Mexicans, representatives of "that older Catholicity."

"The fathers of this republic," he said, "had to form a constitution and government for a people of every race, language, color and nationality, who, they foresaw, would inhabit this land.   They had to combine a political Catholicity with a political unity, and to hold the most discordant elements together

---

* Souvenir Volume, Centennial Celebration and Catholic Congress, published by Wm. H. Hughes, Detroit, 1889. (This book and Reily's Collections in the Life and Times of Cardinal Gibbons, Vol. I, the files of the *Catholic Mirror* and the Baltimore newspapers are the authorities for most of the facts cited in the present chapter.)

by force of law.   So also before the establishment of the Catholic Church in this world, religions were national in their organization, though universal in their fundamental principles, and were adapted to particular peoples of the same race and language.   But the Church was destined to embrace within her government the peoples of every nation under heaven, to combine the most diverse elements and firmly to unite them and hold them for all time; and in no one country of the world had we to exercise this power so much as here, for nowhere else were they found together."

Sketching the labors of Carroll, Archbishop Ryan pronounced him an American patriot as well as a Christian bishop. "Love of country and race," he remarked, "is a feeling planted by God in the human heart, and, when properly directed, becomes a wall of virtue."

Outlining the history of the Church in the century that had just passed, Archbishop Ryan pointed out that "since the Civil War there is a great change in popular sentiment in relation to the Catholic Church.   In addition to this, it must be remembered that Catholics and Protestants now associate more freely and intimately and understand each other better.   Intelligent Protestants are gradually being dispossessed of the old notion that Catholics exalt the Blessed Virgin to a position equal to that of the Son, that priests can forgive sins according to their own wish, that images may be adored after the fashion of the pagans, that the Bible should not be read, and other absurd supposed doctrines and practices of the Church.   Because of this enlightenment, and because of the high character of American converts in the past—men like Dr. Brownson, Dr. Ives, Father Hecker and many others—it is possible that some of the ablest defenders of the Church in this coming century may be men who are at present in the ranks of her opponents. * * *

"A wonderful future is before the Church in this country, if we are only true to her, to the country and to ourselves. She has demonstrated that she can live and move and widen without state influence, that the atmosphere of liberty is most congenial to her constitution and most conducive to her progress.   Let us be cordially American in our feelings and sentiments, and, above all, let each individual act in his personal life and character the spirit of his Catholic faith."

At pontifical vespers the same day Archbishop Ireland preached in his characteristic vein on "The New Century: Responsibilities, Hopes and Duties."   He boldly voiced his own aspirations and those of others who thought the same way, men to whom progress was the breath of life, development the countersign of duty.

"The past," he said, "our fathers wrought; the future will be wrought by us.   The next century in the life of the Church in America will be what we make it.   Our work is to make America Catholic.   If we love America, if we love the Church, to mention the work suffices.   Our cry shall be 'God wills it,' and our hearts shall leap with Crusader enthusiasm.   *   *   *

"The Catholic Church will confirm and preserve as no human power or human church can, the liberties of the republic. The importance of the position of America to the cause of religion can not well be overestimated.   It is a Providential nation.   How youthful, and yet how great!   How bright in glorious promise!   *   *   *

"The movements of the modern world have their highest tension in the United States.   The natural order is here seen at its best, and here it displays its fullest symmetry.   Here should the Church, unhampered by the government or by despotic custom, come with the freedom of the son of Issai, choose its arms, and, marching straight for the opposing foe, bring the contest to a speedy close.

"Of inestimable value to us is the liberty the Church enjoys under the Constitution of the republic.   No tyrant here casts chains around her.   No concordat limits her action or cramps her energies.   She is as free as the eagle upon Alpine hills—

free to spread out in unrestricted flight her pinions, to soar to
vast altitudes, to put into action all her native energies. The
law of the land protects her in her rights, and asks in return
no sacrifices for those rights; for her rights are those of
American citizenship.   *   *   *

"There is needed a thorough sympathy with the country.
The Church of America must be, of course, as Catholic as in
Jerusalem or Rome; but, so far as her garments assume color
from the local atmosphere, she must be American. Let no
one dare paint her brow with foreign tint or pin to her mantle
foreign linings! There is danger; she receives large accessions of natives from foreign countries. God witnesseth it,
they are welcome! I will not enter upon their personal affections and tastes; yet, should those be foreign, they shall not
encrust upon the Church. Americans have no longings for a
church of foreign aspect. It would acquire no influence over
them. In no manner could it prosper; exotics have but sickly
forms. I would have Catholics be the first patriots in the
land.

"This is an intellectual age; it worships intellect. All things
are treated by the touchstone of intellect, and the ruling power,
public opinion, is formed by it. The Church will be judged
by the standard of intellect.   *   *   *

"We have a dreadful lesson to learn from certain European countries in which, from the weight of tradition, the
Church clings to thrones and classes and loses her grasp upon
the people. Let us not make this mistake. We have here no
princes, no hereditary classes; still, there is the danger that
there may be in religion a favorite aristocracy upon which we
lavish so much care that none remains for others. What, I
ask, for the multitude who peep at us from gallery and vesti-
bule? What of the thousands and tens of thousands of nominal Catholics or non-Catholics who seldom or never open a
church door? What of the uncouth and unkempt, I ask, of

the cellar and the areaway, the mendicant and the outcast? It is time to bring back the primitive Gospel spirit, to go out into the highways and byways, to preach on housetops and in market places. * * * Save the masses! Cease not planning and working for their salvation. * * *

"Seek out social grievances; lead in movements to heal them. Speak of vested rights, for this is necessary; but speak, too, of vested wrongs, and strive by precept, word and example, by the enactment and enforcement of good laws to correct them. Breathe fresh air into the crowded quarters of the poor."

Cardinal Gibbons presided at the dinner held at St. Mary's Seminary. A cablegram from the Pope, expressing his joy at the triumphs of faith which the occasion commemorated, was read; and Archbishop Satolli, whose Latin eloquence was then heard for the first time in America, predicted that Leo or some future pontiff would visit this country. Greetings to the American Church were conveyed by Cardinal Taschereau for Canada; by the Mexican bishops, for their country, and letters were read from English and Irish prelates.

The congress of laymen had been proposed by Archbishop Ireland. It was a plan which had been tried to some extent in Europe, but never before in America. Had such a gathering been suggested in one of the periods of religious storm to which the country had been subject before the Civil War, it would have been rejected at once as impracticable; but in the altered temper of the times it was at least worth considering, and Cardinal Gibbons finally adopted it.

For centuries the followers of the Catholic religion in the United States had been the victims of groundless distrust. In Virginia, the oldest colony, which shared the religious prejudices of England, they were regarded with suspicion; and in Massachusetts, during the earlier days, they were considered to be only a little less dangerous than the witches of Salem. Even in Maryland, founded by a Catholic Lord Proprietor and dedicated by him to religious liberty, the later Calverts, turned Protestants, had assented to the imposition of double taxes on Catholics and to depriving them of the suffrage. A petition to Governor Sharpe, in which they pathetically recited the origin of the province and the full freedom which they formerly enjoyed, bears eloquent testimony to the patience with which they bore their burdens.* No Americans were more sincerely loyal in the preliminary days of the Revolution and, during the progress of that intense struggle, in forum and on battlefield. It was even said that "every Catholic was a Whig." Debarred before the war from holding even a commission in the militia, a number of them speedily rose to high rank in the army led by Washington. Of the members of the Continental Congress, a considerable number were Catholics. John Carroll went to Canada with Franklin on the vain mission designed to win that country to the cause of independence.

Catholics had shared with their Protestant brethren, knowing no discrimination in public life, the burdens of citizenship in the formative days of the republic. In the War of 1812 they had again proved the mettle of their patriotism. Andrew Jackson, victorious over Packenham, was welcomed to New Orleans by the Catholics of that city, headed by Bishop Dubourg, who celebrated in the Cathedral a solemn service of thanksgiving for the triumph of American arms. Catholics were active in Congress and in State Legislatures, accepting prejudice with equanimity and losing no fraction of their public spirit under the sting of calumny. In Know-Nothing times they had conducted themselves with singular moderation; and in the Civil War they had divided in sympathy like their brethren of other faiths.

Still, there was a lingering remnant of prejudice that came down from other days. How could it be met? Perhaps the time had come for them to follow collectively where Cardinal Gibbons had led. None doubted his patriotism. No Protest-

---

* Maryland Historical Society Manuscripts.

ant cleric was half so conspicuous in the eyes of his country and of the world as an advanced and liberal champion of the American idea.

Nevertheless, there was danger of immature discussion at the congress of laymen, which the Cardinal had prudently considered. In the atmosphere of American freedom, unrepresentative men are prone to utterances which may be misinterpreted. It was decided that the bishops should appoint the delegates to the congress, and that the program should be submitted to episcopal authority beforehand, so that, as far as possible, tendencies to individual extremism might be checked.

The congress met in the Concordia Opera House, and was presided over by John Lee Carroll, a former Governor of Maryland, and a great-grandson of Charles Carroll of Carrollton. The range of discussion included the opportunities of the laity, state and religious education, temperance, Sunday observance, social questions, church music, the Catholic press, and the independence of the Holy See. In the main, the atmosphere of the congress proved to be one of sound ideas and patriotic spirit. When a false chord was struck by Daniel Dougherty, of Philadelphia, the opinion of his associates revolted and gave a more effective demonstration of the healthy tone of the congress than would have been possible had complete unanimity prevailed. Dougherty, whose gifts of oratory had won for him the name of "silver-tongued," made an address concerning the colonial persecutions of Catholics, long forgotten by nearly everybody else. He went so far as to declare that there was even yet a disposition to exclude them from public office. "The highest honors of the republic are denied us," he exclaimed, "by a prejudice which has all the force of a constitutional enactment."

The offices held by many of the delegates, in state and nation, formed the most effective answer to his criticism. Dougherty himself had been selected to make the nominating speeches for Hancock in 1880, and Cleveland in 1888, in the national conventions of the Democratic party; surely, there was no great discrimination in his case. It was true that there had been no Catholic President; but no man of sufficient political prominence to be eligible to that exalted office had been rejected because he was of the Catholic faith.

In contrast to Dougherty's pessimism, the general spirit of the congress was one of buoyant hope, and his gloomy retrospection found no echo in any other part of the proceedings. Resolutions which were adopted on the closing day expressed the views and aspirations of the laity. They set forth that there was no conflict between the Church and the institutions of the country; denounced Mormonism, the tendency to divorce, nihilism, socialism, communism, and declared that "we equally condemn the greed of capital." As was to be expected, a school system which included a course of religious training was advocated. An outgrowth of the current agitation for a "Continental Sunday" was found in a clause favoring the Sunday closing of saloons. The absolute freedom of the Holy See was held to be necessary for the peace of the Church and the welfare of mankind.

The Cardinal addressed the congress, expressing the view that it had not been convoked in vain. "It will form an admirable school," he said, "for enlightening and instructing the members and preparing them for holding a more elaborate convention at some future day. This congress, by the mere fact of being called together, emphasizes and vindicates the important truth that it is the privilege as well as the duty of our laity to co-operate with the clergy in discussing those great economic, educational and social questions which affect the interests and well-being of the Church, the country and society at large. I confess that the desire of my heart for a long time has been to see the clergy and the laity drawn more closely. They have, perhaps, in some respects been much and too long apart; for, if the clergy are the Divinely constituted channels for instructing the laity in faith and morals, the clergy, on their part, have much to learn from the wisdom and discretion, the experience and worldly sense of the laity.

"And in no other country on the face of the earth should the clergy and the laity be more united than in our own. The laity build our churches; they erect our schools; they voluntarily and generously support our clergy; the salaries of our clergy are not ceremoniously handed to them by Government officials on a silver salver, but come from the warm hands and warm hearts of the people."

Archbishop Ireland inspired the delegates with one of his short and vigorous addresses.

The congress ended with a torchlight parade, in which 30,000 men and boys took part. The streets were brilliant with illumination as this great procession passed. Cardinal Gibbons reviewed it from his residence, and enthusiastically joined in the applause. It was nearly midnight when the last men in line passed his bay-window. The utmost good humor prevailed, and in the dense throngs on the streets there was not the slightest disorder. The parade, in which nearly all who took part were Marylanders, was as much a tribute to the Cardinal as to the visiting prelates and laymen. It took the form of a popular demonstration in his honor as it wound along picturesque Charles street and thousands gazed upward for a word of approval from the head of the Church in America.

The dedication of the School of Sacred Sciences at the new university on the fourth day of the celebration marked the triumph of an idea. The project was close to the Cardinal's heart, and, he said in later years, it had given him greater concern than anything else he had undertaken. It had been born in hopes at the Second Plenary Council of Baltimore; clothed with reality at the Third Council, where Bishop Spalding's zeal and Miss Mary Gwendoline Caldwell's gift of $300,000 led the prelates to authorize it as a practical undertaking; and now, with the Pope's blessing and with the prayers of the clergy, the university was about to begin its mission of instruction. Miss Caldwell's gift had been increased by $50,000 from her sister, Lina; and through the energetic efforts of Bishop Keane and others the amount had been gradually swelled to $800,000. Bishop Keane, the first rector, traveled throughout the country with the zeal of an apostle, pleading as few men could plead for the substantial help of the laity. His saintly life, his winning personality, the fervor of his mission and the direct vigor of his appeals opened the way readily. He seemed never to tire; and, when the results of his labors were summed up, it was found that progress had been made beyond the dreams of the project's most sanguine promoters.

The question of a site for the university was much discussed; but all finally agreed on Washington as the best place for the capstone of the Catholic educational system. The wisdom of this choice was confirmed in a few years by the Methodists, who laid the beginnings of the American Methodist University in the same city; and the Protestant Episcopal Church a little later raised Washington to the dignity of an independent bishopric. When Carroll decided to found his academy at Georgetown, in 1789, he had no idea that the capital of the country would be established there. In this, as in other things, he "builded wiser than he knew."

It had been projected to start the university with a Divinity course, and gradually develop it as means were obtained. With American buoyancy, some of the bishops dared to hope that it would spring, like Minerva, full armed from the brow of Jove. Others, more cautious, pointed to the history of the European universities, which had gradually developed for centuries from small nuclei; but the great majority were united in the desire to go ahead with the work.

The cornerstone of the School of Sacred Sciences, the first of the group, had been laid May 24, 1888, in the presence of President Cleveland, members of his Cabinet, Cardinal Gib-

bons and other distinguished persons. Early the next year
the Pope addressed a brief to the American bishops, declaring
that, "as the See of Baltimore is the chief among the apostolic
sees of the United States of North America, to the Archbishop of Baltimore and to his successors we grant the privilege of discharging the office of supreme moderator or chancellor of the university."

Nearly all the great assemblage of prelates went over from
Baltimore to attend the dedication, in the midst of a pouring
rain, which soaked the spongy soil of the suburban estate on
which the university had been planted, as yet unresponsive to
the magic touch of the landscape gardener. Archbishop Satolli
celebrated mass, and Bishop Gilmour, of Cleveland, preached.
He pointed out that it was fitting to begin with a Divinity
course, for, from the Catholic point of view, "all true education must begin in God, and find its truth and direction in
God. * * *

"There is a widespread mistake," he continued, "a rapidly
growing political and social heresy, which assumes and asserts
that the state is all temporal and religion all spiritual. This is
not only a doctrinal heresy; but, if acted upon, would ruin
both spiritual and temporal. No more can the state exist
without religion than the body without the soul; and no more
can religion exist without the state, and on earth carry on its
work, than can the soul on earth, without the body, do its
work. The state, it is true, is for the temporal, but has its
substantial strength in the spiritual; while religion, it is true,
is for the spiritual, but in much must find its working strength
in the temporal. In this sense it is a mistake to assume that
religion is independent of the state, or the state independent of
religion. As a matter of fact, religion must depend upon the
state in temporalities; and, vice versa, the state must depend
upon religion in morals; and both should so act that their
conjoint work will be for the temporal and moral welfare of
society."

But, the Bishop proceeded to show, he did not mean that any form of direct or legalized partnership between church and state was necessary or desirable. "In this country," he said, "we have agreed that religion and the state shall exist as distinct and separate departments, each with its separate rights and duties; but this does not mean that the state is independent of religion or religion independent of the state."

The Bishop remarked that it was perhaps the first great university of the world "begun without state or princely aid, but originating in an outpouring of public thought, and founded and provided for by the gifts of the many, rather than by the offerings of the few. It bespeaks the widening character of American ideas and the existing conviction of the public mind that higher studies are clearly needed."

A brilliant banquet in one of the halls of the university was made notable by the attendance of President Harrison, Vice-President Morton, and nearly all the members of the Cabinet. Archbishop Satolli's Latin eloquence flowed again. "God loves America," he said. "It is Leo's feeling that this is true; and he believes, therefore, that in America nothing is impossible."

A cablegram from the Pontiff, conveying his blessing and sending congratulations, was read.

Secretary of State Blaine, in a speech, said he had come to the banquet to represent the United States, "not in a political sense, much less a partisan one, and not in a sense in any way in conflict with any church or sect or principle of religion. Freedom of religion is guaranteed in the United States, and this is one of our greatest blessings. I have spoken thus often in Protestant assemblages, and it gives me pleasure to repeat it to a Catholic audience. * * * Every college in the United States increases the culture of the United States. We have the criticism of an English professor, who admired America as the most intelligent land in the world and the least cultivated. Universities will, in time, give us a greater excellence in learning."

Cardinal Taschereau spoke in French, saying that the time was a troublous one for the Church abroad, because of the "intense opposition of the potentates of Europe." "In the United States," he pointed out, "there is full freedom; and there is great comfort in the universal confidence placed in Cardinal Gibbons as the glorious representative of the Church in America. The Pope has always had unbounded faith in him, and he has often been spoken of by the Holy Father as the first priest in America."

After President Harrison had briefly expressed his thanks for the reception accorded him, Cardinal Gibbons spoke of the "Hierarchy of the United States." "We have all been more than anxious," he said, "for the visit of the President, the Vice-President and members of the Cabinet, who have honored the university by their presence. They assure us of their sympathy for every cause to promote the religion and morality of the people in the United States. Though there is no union of church and state, in any sense, the people have always upheld religion. * * * In olden times the Church admonished obedience to rulers when they were even obnoxious. How much more can she do so now, when salutary laws are made to foster the home and better society? A government is pleasing to God when it is in harmony, and how good it is when both clergymen and laymen, working in an individual capacity, bring about harmony."

Vicompte de Montalembert made a lengthy address in French in behalf of the universities of Paris and Lyons. There were many other speeches; and after the banquet the university course was formally opened by an oration in English by Bishop O'Farrell, of Trenton, and a Latin address by Mgr. Schroeder, the new professor of dogmatic theology. The ceremonies were elaborate and prolonged. Surely no university was founded under more notable auspices.

The reception at the City Hall of Baltimore on Thursday given by Mayor Latrobe to the visiting prelates and laymen was a revelation to many of them. These men, shut off in many cases from direct contact with the world in the solitude of ecclesiastical life, were amazed to see Cardinal Gibbons apparently on terms of familiar acquaintance with nearly everybody present, from the Mayor down to the little children who came with their parents. What surprised them almost as much was the fact that the crowd, with singular unanimity, seemed to look upon him as the foremost citizen of Maryland, rather than as a churchman, and appeared to take this view as if from the force of long habit. For not a few of the distinguished prelates this was a sermon in itself more powerful than any to which they had listened during the week. If an archbishop were in the community, of the community, and a leader of the community, what need to fear a misunderstanding, a lack of common purpose? The foreigners found an especial lesson in this. The formality, the diplomatic restraint between the churchmen and public men in Europe was lost in the fusing of American life within the crucible of freedom and co-operation. Neither had favors to ask, but both felt the impulse of a united object. Delicate forms of ceremony, designed, perhaps, as much to uphold prerogative as to promote cordiality, were notably lacking. The Mayor and the crowd met on terms of simple friendship, greater in its potency than documents stamped with official seals or precedent brought down from mediæval days.

When the great gathering broke up, what had been accomplished? The Church, through her laity as well as her bishops, had set her face against socialism, and the other transplanted political organisms which had threatened to grow in the virgin soil of America; had condemned the prevalent hostility between labor and capital; had entered a militant conflict against social evils, like divorce; had sent forth champions in pulpit and pew with new inspiration, with co-ordinated ideas, to begin aggressively the work of a new century of Catholic effort.

Simultaneously with the congress, "Our Christian Heritage" appeared in print. The delegates found a guide for their own labors in the Cardinal's vigorous declarations on current evils.

Leo XIII turned again to the American hierarchy for consolation in the European difficulties which were accumulating around him. Cardinal Rampolla, writing to Cardinal Gibbons, conveyed the "liveliest satisfaction" which the Pontiff had felt in the events of the centennial. "His Holiness also," he wrote, "spoke of yourself in terms of the highest praise for all you did on that occasion, and said at the same time that he approves most fully the prudent line of conduct you pursue in your management of every work undertaken to promote the greater development of your young and illustrious Church."*

With characteristic readiness to turn everything to practical use, Cardinal Gibbons presided over a mass-meeting held in the Baltimore Academy of Music on the Sunday following the celebration, which resulted in the adoption of a high-license law regulating liquor selling in Maryland. This meeting had been hastily arranged by his secretary, Rev. John T. Whelan, who wished to take advantage of a golden opportunity to strike a blow for temperance; and the Cardinal willingly acquiesced in the plan when it was presented to him a short time before the meeting was to be held. It was at a moment when Archbishop Ireland's temperance crusade was reaching the zenith of its activity, and the ardor of the prelate from St. Paul was also aroused by the opportunity. One of the conspicuous visitors to the centennial exercises had been Rev. James Nugent, of Liverpool, called "the Father Mathew of England," a lion in the cause of temperance in his own country. Some of the most prominent laymen in Maryland, Protestant as well as Catholic, sat on the stage to lend the encouragement

* Cathedral Archives.

of their presence to this new movement for the social betterment of the community.

"The blow we strike tonight," the Cardinal said, "is for the
benefit of the laborer, and as such it must and shall be successful."

The enactment of the proposed law by the Legislature soon
afterward could not have been accomplished without this
demonstration, which marshalled public opinion in an irresistible phalanx. The Cardinal, while not so radical as the
Archbishop of St. Paul in his views on the liquor question,
was thoroughly committed to a reduction of the evils arising
from drink. He had been a moderate user of light wines at dinner, in which he found partial relief from the pangs of indiges-
tion. Had he believed prohibition practicable of enforcement,
he himself would have been the first to exemplify total abstinence; but, in his view, statutory abolition of the use of liquor
would defeat its own object. It would lead, he believed, to
wholesale violations of the law, and, therefore, to a growing
disrespect for the law. He had not been able to find encouragement from the object-lessons in communities which had attacked the problem by this means. Example and judicious
restriction, it seemed to him, were the best means of contending with the situation.

Violent methods in the solution of the temperance question
always excited his disapproval. When Mrs. Carrie Nation, of
Kansas, began a campaign of open destruction of saloon property, which for a time was a sort of national sensation, he
remarked:

"Nothing, in my opinion, can warrant Mrs. Nation and her
followers in taking the law in their own hands and wrecking
the property of saloonkeepers."

For many years he has made a practice, when he confirms at
the altar, to obtain a pledge of abstinence from intoxicating
liquors by the young until they reach the age of twenty-one
years; and the addresses on temperance which he has made on

such occasions would fill volumes. His steady adherence to this plan must have had a tremendous effect; and, whether due in part to his example and precept or not, there has been a steady and pronounced decrease in the evidences of intoxication in Baltimore. Scarcely ever is a drunken man seen on the streets, and the good order which prevails in the city is a common subject of surprise to strangers.

Not only in this direction, but in many others, he has exercised a continuous and powerful influence for the social welfare of the city in which he lives; but he is not prone by nature to radicalism in such questions, and is always inclined to allow for the rebound of human nature from the strain of extreme restriction.

CHAPTER XIV.

APOSTOLIC DELEGATE: THE SCHOOL QUESTION.

By the year 1890 the Catholic Church had assumed a new aspect in the eyes of the American people as a result of the liberalizing policy of Cardinal Gibbons, powerfully supported, as it was, by the far-sighted Pontiff who sat in the chair of Peter. A Pentecostal wave of accessions to the Church was the natural result. Not only was she able to retain within her fold a host of the immigrants who were arriving from Catholic countries in Europe, but conversions were numerous, and dioceses were springing up everywhere. To be a Catholic was no longer to be an object of suspicion in an ultra-Protestant neighborhood. Protestant ministers were inclined to welcome a Catholic Church in their vicinity in the same spirit in which they would welcome one of a non-Catholic denomination. It was amazing how the old lines of religious prejudice were disappearing. Catholic and Protestant pastors worked together in movements for the moral and social betterment of the communities in which they were thrown.

A militant evangelism was building new edifices where the mass might be celebrated in areas to which population was flocking. With the increased wealth of the country, it was easier to erect churches, parish halls and schools, and to support the clergy in their ministrations.

This awakening of Catholic activity had the effect of accentuating differences of view that had been gradually arising and of thrusting upon the hierarchy the necessity for a solution of problems which had not hitherto reached a climax. Chief among these were the school question and the so-called question of Americanism—the nationalization of the diverse foreign elements introduced by immigration; but around them clustered a multitude of lesser problems upon which opinion was dividing with increasing definiteness of demarcation. It was difficult, under the circumstances, to get these great questions settled promptly at Rome. The United States, being still a missionary country in the organization of the Church, was under the jurisdiction of the Propaganda, already overcrowded with the tremendous undertaking of managing Catholic mission movements throughout the world. There was a feeling among some American bishops and priests that a method should be provided for a prompter determination of ecclesiastical questions arising in this country.

Archbishop Satolli had gone back to Leo with glowing accounts of what he had seen in America. The strength and freedom of the Church had powerfully impressed him. In Washington he had been cordially received by President Harrison; and had become amazed no less by the vast possibilities for the advancement of the Church than by the material resources of the nation.

The advisibility of more direct relations between the Vatican and the Government at Washington had long been considered at Rome. As early as 1885 Cardinal Gibbons received a letter from Cardinal Simeoni, asking his opinion about the expediency of the Holy See entering into diplomatic relations with the United States. In his answer he deprecated the idea, giving many reasons why, in his judgment, such an undertaking would be imprudent and might compromise the pontiff as well as the Catholics of America. The only circumstance, he wrote, under which such a communication should be made would be on an occasion of sympathy or congratulation regarding a public calamity or a signal blessing to the nation.

Later inquiries of the same character were made of the American archbishops, but all except Mgr. Ireland replied that such a step would be inadvisable. Cardinal Gibbons' reason

for doubting the wisdom of appointing an apostolic delegate
was based on his well-known views of the respective functions of church and state. It had so long been one of his
favorite themes that the Church prospers most when wholly
divorced from political entanglements, that he conceived the
result of the experiment to be at least doubtful. Misinterpre-
tation would be apt to arise; it might be held in some quarters
that the appointment of an apostolic delegate, though his functions might be confined to an adjustment of purely ecclesiastical questions, would be an entering wedge for the opening of
full diplomatic relations between the Vatican and the White
House. He knew that this last was impossible and not in accord with the spirit of American institutions. It would harm,
not help, the Church, and the justification of great need was
lacking. The Church had no difficulty with the Government
of the United States. The national administrations had not
only not been repressive, but had shown no disposition to interfere with Catholic interests in any place over which the
American flag floated. Ecclesiastical authorities were generally sustained in their legal property rights before the courts,
and the Cardinal felt that they could always obtain justice.
There was no discrimination in chaplaincies in the army and
navy, nor in anything else that the Government had to take
within its purview. The Vatican, even when it controlled the
states of the Church, before the spoliation by Victor Emanuel,
had never had a minister at Washington, though it is interesting to note that the United States was long represented at its
court by an accredited member of the diplomatic corps, appointed by the President. The first of these ministers was
James L. Martin, of North Carolina, appointed in 1848; his
successor was no less a personage than Lewis Cass; and the
position was abolished in 1868, when Rufus King was minister.

Leo was so far moved by the objections that he decided to
take no final step at that time; but an opportunity presented by

the approach of the World's Fair, soon to be held at Chicago, prompted him to make a test of the situation.

Secretary of State Foster, in September, 1892, requested Cardinal Gibbons to confer with him regarding a letter to be addressed to the Pope, through Cardinal Rampolla, asking for the loan of maps and other relics relating to the discovery of America, which were in possession of the Vatican.*   The Cardinal went to Washington, where Mr. Foster gave him a letter, which he promptly transmitted.

The letter of Mr. Foster began with a request for the loan of the relics.   "I need not assure you," he wrote, "that the greatest care will be taken of them from the moment of their delivery into the hands of the agent of this Government who may be authorized to receive them; or, should his Holiness see fit to entrust them in the care of a personal representative who will bring them to the United States, I am authorized by the President to assure his Holiness that such representative shall receive all possible courtesy upon his arrival and during his sojourn in this country.

"The intimate association of the Holy See with the Columbian enterprise and its results has so linked the memory of Rome and her pontiffs with the vast achievement of Columbus and his competitors in the work of discovery and colonization, that an exhibit such as by the President's direction I have the honor to suggest could not fail to be among the most noteworthy contributions to this international celebration.   By co-operating to this end, his Holiness will manifest for our country a regard which will be highly appreciated, not only by the managers of the exposition, but by the American people.

"His Eminence Cardinal Gibbons, with whom I have conferred on the subject, has very kindly agreed to convey this letter to your Eminence."†

---

* Cathedral Archives.
† Letter of Secretary Foster to Cardinal Rampolla, Sept. 18, 1892.

Cardinal Rampolla responded promptly, acknowledging the transmission of Secretary Foster's letter through the Cardinal, and stating that it had been presented to the Pope.

"His Holiness has learned," wrote Mgr. Rampolla, "how great was the gratification felt by the President of this great republic at the prospect of receiving the Columbus records, which will be sent by the Holy See to the exposition which is to be held next year at Chicago in honor of the immortal discoverer of America. The august Pontiff felt certain that the United States Government would spare no pains to preserve the various objects that are to be intrusted to it from any mishap, and he returns his thanks for the kind offer that has been made for their transportation.

"In the meantime, his Holiness, who has so many reasons to entertain special regard for the United States Government on account of the liberty which is enjoyed in those States by the Catholic Church, and who justly admires the enterprise and progress of that country, has decided to be represented at the public demonstrations which are to be held there in honor of the Genoese hero on the fourth centenary of his memorable discovery, by a person who is no less distinguished by his personal qualities than by his grade in the ecclesiastical hierarchy. This person is Mgr. Francesco Satolli, Archbishop of Lepanto, a prelate who is as highly to be esteemed on account of his virtues as for his profound scholarship, of which he has given many evidences in his writings.

"His Holiness does not doubt that this decision of his will be received with pleasure by the Government, and feels sure that your Excellency will welcome the prelate with your accustomed courtesy."*

In the following November, the Pope commissioned Archbishop Satolli as temporary apostolic delegate to the American Church with plenary power. In addition to this, he was the

---

* Letter of Cardinal Rampolla to Secretary Foster, Sept. 28, 1892.

representative of the Pontiff at the public demonstrations of the World's Fair; but he was not accredited to the Government of the United States, and had no diplomatic status. Before leaving Rome as the custodian of the relics, he conferred at length with the Pope regarding the ecclesiastical problems with which he was to deal on this side of the Atlantic; and, full of the spirit and purposes of the head of the Church, sailed for America. Leo said to him at parting that he looked with flowing tears on the steadily failing Orient, but his heart and soul were filled with great joy in seeing the progress of liberty in the great Republic of the West.

His first conference in this country was with Cardinal Gibbons, with whom he spent some time at the archiepiscopal residence in Baltimore, absorbing from the Cardinal views of the situation which would aid him in the successful transaction of his mission. Perhaps it was fortunate that the first apostolic delegate had not been trained in the diplomatic school of the Vatican. Although a man of remarkable breadth of view and sympathies, he was essentially a theologian, and had no impulse to concern himself with political questions. A native of the Diocese of Perugia, he had studied in the seminary of that city, which was presided over at the time by Joachim Pecci, archbishop of the diocese, destined to be elevated to the pontifical chair as Leo XIII. When Cardinal Pecci became Pontiff, he called Satolli to Rome, in whose atmosphere he broadened. He filled with success important professorships in the College of the Propaganda and the Academy of Noble Ecclesiastics. In his early studies he had been fascinated by the Thomistic philosophy. His commentary on the Summa of St. Thomas, in five volumes, established clearly the profundity of his intellect, and other works of his pen procured the honor of a special brief of commendation from the Pontiff.

In appearance, he suggested the thinker. Slight and of medium height, his brilliant dark eyes were capable of great expression. Surmounting them was a broad and intellectual forehead. Mingling with the expression of the scholar were strong traces of strength and self-repression, which indicated that he was cast in a mold adapted to great affairs.

Foremost of the problems with which Satolli was to concern himself was the school question. It was by no means new. From the beginnings of the public school system in the United States, Catholics who were taxed for its support and yet who sent their children, from conscientious conviction, to the parochial schools, had felt the desire to be rid of the double burden. The special interest of Cardinal Gibbons in education from the days when he was a parish priest in Baltimore had brought him in intimate touch with the situation. He could not bring himself to believe in any form of intellectual training of youth in which there was no religious teaching. He feared that a secularized childhood would mean an atheistic manhood. Abroad, he had noted the spirit of agnosticism and other forms of denial of the supernatural in religion. His hope was in the American home; if religion and morality did not enter there, what of the future of his country? Was it safe to trust the children to a form of daily instruction in which they would not be taught the elementary religious and moral precepts which lie at the foundation of character?

He had no wish to use the funds of the state for forcing the Catholic religion on non-Catholics; but wherever youth was to be trained, much as he valued the development of the mind, much as he desired a cultured citizenship, his belief was that religion was the foundation of true culture, and that without it at the base, the superstructure would topple of its own weight.

In his view, it was desirable that the state should contribute to the support of Catholic schools only to the extent to which the parents of the children in those schools were citizens. State supervision commended itself to his judgment, if it were properly applied. His idea of a public school for Catholic children was one under the supervision of the local examiner, no matter what his religious faith, subject to regulation in the use of text-books the same as other schools; in discipline, class work, sanitary regulation, and other points conforming to the standard set by the public authorities; the teachers to be appointed on certificate, subject to the tests provided for instructors in the public schools. But, apart from all this, he desired that the teachers should be Catholics, and that for a portion of the day, perhaps before or after the regular school hours, they should instruct the children in the principles and practice of religion. An American of Americans, he could see nothing un-American in this.

His interest in education had led him to issue a pastoral letter on the subject to the clergy and laity of the Archdiocese of Baltimore in 1883.* In this he had pointed out how the Catholic Church has been the "fostering mother and munificent patroness" of secular education. He admonished parents to develop the "minds and hearts" of their children. "Then can they go forth into the world," he wrote, "gifted with a well-furnished mind and great confidence in God." He advised that the history of the United States, with the origin and principles of the government, and the lives of the eminent men who had helped to found and preserve it, should be an especial object of study, in order that the children might grow up "enlightened citizens and devoted patriots."

"But it is not enough," he insisted, "for your children to have a secular education; they must also acquire a religious training. Indeed, religious knowledge is as far above human sciences as the soul is above the body; as Heaven is above earth; as eternity is above time. The little child who is familiar with his catechism is really more enlightened on truths that should come home to every rational mind than the most profound philosophers of pagan antiquity, or even than many so-called philosophers of our own time. He has mastered the great problems of life; he knows his origin, his sublime des-

---

* Cathedral Archives.

CARDINAL GIBBONS' RESIDENCE, BALTIMORE

tiny, and the means of attaining it—a knowledge which no human science can impart without the light of revelation."

While a knowledge of bookkeeping was valuable for elementary pupils, he showed, it was not enough, unless the child were taught how to balance his accounts daily between his conscience and his God. "What profit," he asked, "would it be to understand the diurnal and annual motions of the earth, if the pupil did not know and feel that his future home is beyond the stars in heaven?" While it was important to be acquainted with the lives of heroes who had founded empires, of men of genius who had enlightened the world, it was still more necessary to learn something of the King of Kings, who created all those kingdoms and by Whom kings reign. If the soul were to die with the body, then, secular education would be enough; but was it wise to train the young for the comparatively brief time to be spent in earthly existence and leave them without training for the infinite future beyond this life?

"Our youth," he wrote, "cherish the hope of becoming one day citizens of heaven as well as of this land; and, as they can not be good citizens of this country without studying and observing its laws, neither can they become citizens of heaven, unless they know and practice the laws of God."

He declared as a fundamental principle that the religious and secular education of children can not be divorced from each other "without inflicting a fatal wound upon the soul." A high development of the intellectual without a corresponding expansion of the religious nature, he believed, would often prove a curse instead of a blessing. His idea of religion was to make it an every-day affair, not something to be put on, like a holiday dress, on Sunday. The religious and moral training of the young should be interwoven with the thread of daily life. At every step, as far as possible, their feet should be guided in the paths that would lead to the higher life, which he considered the most precious position they could attain. Church and Sunday-school were not enough. "They should, as far as possible," he wrote, "breathe every day a healthful religious atmosphere in these schools, where not only their minds are enlightened, but where faith, piety and sound morality are nourished and invigorated."

He also feared that the children of Catholic parents, if they did not lose all religion in purely secular schools, might lose their own distinctive faith. To him, this was a jewel which should be preserved. With all his remarkable liberality, it would have been absurd to say that he considered "one church as good as another," any more than a minister of the Methodist, or some other Protestant faith, would have considered the Catholic faith "as good as" his own. To his mind, the Catholic Church was the divinely appointed agent for the spread of the Gospel on earth, and the custodian of the deposit of heavenly truth. None ever heard him say a word in reproach of any religious denomination or of its members, individually or collectively. He could recognize as truly good men who differed from him in religious conviction, acknowledging their entire sincerity and the common brotherhood of all as the children of God. But he considered that it was desirable to exercise the utmost efforts, without encroaching upon the rights of others, to retain within the fold of his Church all children born of Catholic parents.

The same privilege and duty he freely conceded to Protestant denominations. They, as far as they desired, might impart religious instruction to children of their own faith in connection with the branches of profane learning. The greatest danger of all, in his view, was the rearing of the young without the guidance of any church, without moral instruction, without character-building apart from the cultivation of the intellect. Without parochial schools, he saw danger that the parishes would languish in the midst of the corrupting tendencies of modern life. He did not, for a moment, question the sincerity or underrate the zeal of those who believed in secular education in the schools; as far as their view extended, he sympathized with it. But his contention was, that the system did not go far enough and embrace religious training also.

Some priests and laymen in Baltimore set on foot a movement, in 1893, to obtain from the public authorities an appropriation for Catholic schools.* A circular embodying their views was distributed, and preparations were made to introduce in the Maryland Legislature a bill in conformity with them. This proposed bill provided that denominational schools be incorporated by the State; that the trustees of such schools should have the right of selecting their own teachers; that the teachers should be required to pass the regular examinations provided by the public authorities as tests for competency; that the schools should be subject to inspection and regulation by those authorities; that the denominational school buildings should be rented to the city or State at the nominal sum of one dollar a year each, which, it was urged, would save the State from an expense of some hundreds of thousands of dollars; and that the teachers be paid from the public funds.

The preamble to the bill declared with emphasis that its adoption meant no form of union of church with state. "As the state is not united to any particular religious denomination," it declared, "the state is not expected to teach religion; but it can be supplied by public denominational schools."

If the support of Cardinal Gibbons to this program could be enlisted, it was intended to launch the project. But he firmly refused to countenance it, and his influence was sufficient to crush the movement before it had been directly brought to the attention of the Legislature. He was persuaded that the time was not yet ripe for an annual concession by the Legislature of an appropriation for the support of Catholic schools. He made it clear that the circular which had been prepared did not

---

* Reily, Collections in the Life of Cardinal Gibbons, Vol. III, p. 200 *et seq.*

emanate from him, and was not drafted or published with his authorization, and the movement in Maryland soon subsided.

He approved the reading of the Bible in the public schools, if no other form of religious instruction could be provided. A year later, addressing the president of the Chicago Women's Educational Union, he wrote:

"The men and women of our day who are educated in our public schools will, I am sure, be much better themselves, and will also be able to transmit to their children an inheritance of truth, virtue and deep morality, if at school they are brought to a knowledge of Biblical facts and teachings. A judicious selection of Scripture readings; appropriate presentation of the various Scripture incidents, born of reflection on the passages read and scenes presented—can not but contribute, in my opinion, to the better education of the children in our public schools, and thus exercise a healthy influence on society at large, since the principles of morality and religion will be silently instilled while instruction is imparted in branches of human knowledge."[*]

He clung to the hope that the problem would be worked out without excitement or injustice. Speaking at the dedication of a handsome building for St. Joseph's school of the Baltimore Cathedral, in September, 1892, he said:

"I trust that the Catholic schools will one day become in some way connected with the public school system."

Throughout the United States, Catholics held about the same views regarding the proper method of public education. The decrees of the Third Plenary Council of Baltimore, over which Cardinal Gibbons had presided, plainly and forcibly urged the development of the parochial schools, but refused to impose any penalty upon parents who thought it best for their children to attend the public schools.

An experiment which Archbishop Ireland undertook at the towns of Faribault and Stillwater, Minnesota, served as a

---

* Reily. Collections in the Life of Cardinal Gibbons, Vol. III, p. 173.

storm center for a great controversy which sprang up because of the personality of the St. Paul prelate himself rather than from the novelty of his methods. To such an extent was attention focused upon him that when the question became suddenly inflamed in the early nineties, the designation "Faribault Plan" was often bestowed upon the whole problem. As far as general questions were concerned, the Plenary Council had settled them; but as the temper of the times seemed to make a test case necessary, the controversy in the Diocese of St. Paul was carried to Rome itself.

The hostility directed at Archbishop Ireland was not alone founded upon the school system which he introduced, but was interwoven with other questions that were beginning to force themselves upon the consideration of the Church in America. It seemed to be his fate to draw fire wherever he went. A crusader by nature, nothing would have pleased him better than to die fighting on the sands of the desert, in full armor, stricken down by the blow of a Mameluke scimitar. His powerful convictions could hardly be repressed on any occasion. He never acted hastily; but once his conclusion was formed, and fortified by the verdict of his conscience, merely temporal considerations had no weight with him. According to his view, the American people were fair, and would in time see that justice was done, no matter how fierce might be the storm of popular misunderstanding.

The situation at Faribault and Stillwater, where Archbishop Ireland made an arrangement with the public authorities, was buried under a cloud of misunderstanding. So many exaggerated accounts were given of its nature and purposes, that an impartial consideration of it in the public mind was, for a time, impossible. When the archbishops assembled in St. Louis, in 1891, at the celebration of Mgr. Kenrick's episcopal jubilee, this was among the topics which they considered in council. Cardinal Gibbons, in virtue of his primacy, presided, and asked Archbishop Ireland to explain in detail what had been done.

Mgr. Ireland made an explanation with simplicity and frankness. He went so far as to say that he was happy to submit his action to the cognizance of his colleagues, and ready to retrace his steps if they thought he had passed the limits of right and prudence. The agreement between himself and the School Commissioners of Faribault and Stillwater he stated as follows:

"1. The school buildings remain the property of the parish. They are leased to the school commissioners during the school hours only—that is, from 9 A. M. to 3.45 P. M. Outside these hours they are at the sole disposal of the parish; the pastor and the Sisters who teach can hold in them such exercises as they deem proper. The lease is for one year only; at the end of the year, the archbishop may renew the lease or resume the exclusive control of the buildings.

"2. The teachers must hold diplomas from the State, and the progress of the pupils is determined, as to the various branches of profane learning, by parochial examinations held in conformity with official requirements. The class rooms have been furnished and are kept by the school commission, and the Sisters receive the same salaries as are paid to the ordinary teachers.

"3. During school hours, the Sisters give no religious instruction; but as they are not only Catholics, but also members of a religious order, they wear their religious habits, and do not alter their teachings in any respect. The schools, although under the control of the State, are, in respect to instruction, precisely what they were before the arrangement was made. The Sisters teach the catechism after school hours, in such a way that the pupils notice merely a change from one lesson to another. Besides, at 8.30 A. M., that is, before the regular school hour, the children attend mass; and on Sundays, the school buildings are at the exclusive disposition of the parish.

"4. The public schools are scattered in various parts of Minnesota cities, and children are required to attend the school in the district wherein they live. Faribault and Stillwater are excepted from this rule. Catholic children can attend the schools in question from all parts of the cities; the Protestant children living in the districts where our schools are situated may do so, but are not obliged. The result is that almost all the Catholic children of the two cities attend these schools, whereas there are very few Protestants, and the influence is almost wholly Catholic."

After Mgr. Ireland's explanation and his answers, not one of the archbishops offered a word of blame; many were explicit in approval.   Archbishop Williams, of Boston, did not hesitate to say that he congratulated his colleague on the result obtained; that his own wish would be to submit the schools of his diocese to a similar arrangement, and that he hoped to succeed, at least as to some.   It was pointed out in the discussion that the teachers were paid more highly than the parish could afford to pay them; Catholics had no longer to pay the double tax to the public school and the parochial school, and the pastor no longer had to worry to find the necessary money to carry on the school—money often impossible to procure without recourse to means inconvenient for more than one reason, and sometimes gravely so.   Almost all the Catholic children of these two cities were under religious influence.

In placing these two schools under the school boards, which were only local or municipal organizations, Mgr. Ireland did not intend to invalidate the principle of the parochial school, though he had been accused of so intending.   His plan was to save two schools which were perishing, and to procure for the large number of children in Faribault and Stillwater the religious influence of which they were deprived in the public schools.

It was also true that Archbishop Ireland had not even made an innovation; that many schools were under similar rule in different dioceses; for example, in New York, Milwaukee, Albany, Buffalo, Erie, Harrisburg, Peoria, Rochester and Savannah.

"No one," Cardinal Gibbons remarked, "had dreamed of raising objections and of accusing the bishops and priests of these dioceses of unfaithfulness to their mission and of treason to the·Church; but the passions were stirred up the instant Mgr. Ireland had acted."

Archbishop Ireland, with characteristic boldness, carried his own case to Rome, leaving St. Paul early in January, 1892, on that mission. He won at every point. At a special congregation of the Propaganda held April 21, a decision was reached that—"Without derogating from the decrees of the Councils of Baltimore on parochial schools, the arrangement entered into by Archbishop Ireland concerning the schools at Faribault and Stillwater, taking into consideration all the circumstances, can be tolerated."

In an audience held the same day, the Pope approved this action; and in July Cardinal Ledochowski, Prefect of the Propaganda, addressed letters* to Cardinal Gibbons advising that the archbishops at their next reunion search with care for a means of supplying the religious needs of Catholic children who, outside the system of the parochial schools, frequented in great numbers the public schools.

The archbishops met in New York November 17, 1892. Archbishop Satolli, who had recently arrived in this country, was present, and spoke with authority as Papal Delegate regarding the general lines for working out the school question. He outlined fourteen propositions, basing them upon the decrees of the Third Plenary Council of Baltimore, which were still in force. He quoted from these decrees the declaration that all care must be taken to erect Catholic schools, to enlarge and improve those already established, and to make them equal to the public schools in teaching and discipline. When there was no Catholic school, or when the one that was available was little fitted for giving the children an education in keeping with their condition, he pointed out that the Council had decreed that the public schools might be attended with a safe conscience. In cases where it was necessary for Catholic children to attend the public schools, measures to provide for their religious instruction were to be taken by the parish priest.

---

* Cathedral Archives.

The Papal Delegate called attention to the decree strictly forbidding anyone, whether bishop or priest, either by act or by threat, to exclude from the sacraments, as unworthy, persons who chose to send their children to the public schools, or the children themselves.

"The Catholic Church in general," he continued, "and especially the Holy See, far from condemning or treating with indifference the public schools, desires rather that by the joint action of civil and ecclesiastical authorities there should be public schools in every state, as the circumstances of the people require, for the cultivation of the useful arts and the natural sciences; but the Catholic Church shrinks from those features of public schools which are opposed to the truths of Christianity and to morality; and since in the interest of society itself, these objectionable features are removable, therefore, not only the bishops, but the citizens at large, should labor to remove them, in virtue of their own right and in the cause of morality."

The Archbishop went on to say that public schools bore within themselves approximate danger to faith and morals, because in them a purely secular education was given, and also because teachers were chosen indiscriminately from every sect, "and no law prevents them from working the ruin of youth, in tender minds." He also considered it a serious objection that in many of such schools children of both sexes were brought together for their lessons in the same room.

But the Archbishop proceeded to say that "if it be clear that in a given locality, owing to the wise dispositions of public authorities, or to the watchful prudence of school boards, teachers and parents, the above dangers to faith and morals disappear, then, it is lawful for Catholic parents to send their children to these schools to acquire the elements of letters and arts, providing the parents themselves do not neglect their most serious duty, and the pastors of souls put forth every effort to instruct the children and train them in all that pertains to Catholic worship and life."

The Archbishop touched on the Faribault plan by saying that it was greatly to be desired and would be a most happy arrangement, if the bishops should agree with the civil authorities or with the members of school boards to conduct the schools with mutual attention and due consideration for their respective rights. He urgently advised that steps be taken to raise the standard of instruction in Catholic schools, and that normal schools should be established for the preparation of teachers.*

The declaration of Archbishop Satolli was an official one as a representative of the Pope; and the archbishops closed their sessions with an expression of gratitude and satisfaction with the way he had fulfilled his commission. After the meeting Leo took the additional precaution to secure from each of them a private letter fully opening his mind on the subject. From these, he gathered that there was still a doubt on the part of some as to whether the decrees of the Council of Baltimore had not been abrogated, in part, by the Archbishop's interpretation. He took the opportunity to settle the whole question by a letter, which he addressed to Cardinal Gibbons, and which decided the controversy by final authority.

The Pontiff began by announcing his intention to establish permanently an apostolic delegation at Washington. He expressed his satisfaction with what Satolli had done, declaring: "The principal propositions offered by him were drawn from the decrees of the Third Plenary Council of Baltimore; and especially declare that Catholic schools are to be most sedulously promoted, and that it has been left to the judgment and conscience of the Ordinary to decide according to the circumstances when it is lawful and when unlawful to attend the public schools."

---

* Satolli, Loyalty to Church and State, p. 27 *et seq.*

These decrees, the Pontiff stated, were to be faithfully observed, so far as they contained a general rule of action. Although the public schools were not to be entirely condemned, since cases might occur, as the council itself had foreseen, in which it was lawful to attend them; still, every endeavor should be made to multiply the Catholic schools and to bring them to perfect equipment. "Wherefore," concluded the Pontiff, "we confidently hope (and your devotedness to us and to the Apostolic See increases our confidence) that, having put away every cause of error and all anxiety, you will work together, with hearts united and with perfect charity, for the wider and wider spread of the Kingdom of God in your immense country. But, while industriously laboring for the glory of God and the salvation of the souls entrusted to your care, strive also to promote the welfare of your fellow-citizens and to prove the earnestness of your love for your country, so that they who are entrusted with the administration of the government may clearly recognize how strong an influence for the support of public order and for the advancement of public prosperity is to be found in the Catholic Church.

"And as to yourself, beloved son, we know for certain that you will not only communicate to our other venerable brethren in the United States this our mind, which it hath seemed good to us to make known to you, but that you will also strive with all your power that, the controversy being not only calmed, but totally ended, as is so greatly to be desired, the minds which have been excited by it may peacefully be united in mutual good-will."*

Along these lines the settlement of the school question was worked out. In time, the flames of controversy which had sprung up around the personality of Archbishop Ireland and his experiments in Minnesota subsided. His enemies had made use of the situation for a twofold purpose: some, to

---

* Letter of Leo XIII to Cardinal Gibbons, May 31, 1893 (Cathedral Archives).

make it appear that he was compromising Catholic principles of education by submerging them in his own diocese, and accepting the principle of purely secular schools; others, that he was making war upon the public schools by insidiously attempting to undermine them by the introduction of sectarian influences.

Archbishop Satolli, the warm friend of Cardinal Gibbons and of Archbishop Ireland, lost no opportunity of defending the motives and prudence of both; and, in time, the questions which were agitating the Church found new foci.

The controversy regarding religious influences in education spread far beyond the cities and towns of the United States, and out over the great prairies, where stood the isolated mission schools erected by the Church for the instruction of the Indians.   Cardinal Gibbons had been deeply interested in these outposts of Catholic missionary endeavor, and when a general assault upon them was begun, he girded himself for the defense.   The Bureau of Catholic Indian Missions had been originated in 1874 by his predecessor, Archbishop Bayley, for the purpose of carrying on a work begun by the zealous priests of Spain and France who followed in the wake of Columbus and Champlain.   When President Grant, deciding that it was "better to Christianize than to kill," inaugurated his "Peace Policy," the Catholic and Protestant denominations were urged to maintain schools on the reservations, the teachers and other employees, though in effect appointed by the various denominations, being put on the Government payroll.   Later, the practice was adopted of making formal contracts with religious bodies conducting schools for the tuition and support of Indian pupils who could be induced to attend them.   This was called the "contract system," and under it the Government appropriations to Catholic Indian mission schools reached a maximum of $397,756 in 1892.   These schools multiplied greatly in numbers and efficiency.   The heirs of Francis A. Drexel, of Philadelphia, gave largely from their great wealth to the cause, and one of them—Mother M. Katharine Drexel—consecrated her life to the welfare of the Indians and negroes, founding for their special benefit the missionary congregation of the Sisters of the Blessed Sacrament.*

Simultaneously with the development of the school controversy elsewhere, hostile public sentiment was aroused, chiefly through the efforts of the "American Protective Association," and strong pressure was exerted on Congress to abolish all aid to sectarian schools. In time this had its effect. Congress began in 1895 to curtail the appropriations for the contract schools, and two years later† declared it to be the settled policy of the Government "to make hereafter no appropriation whatever for education in any sectarian school." In 1900 it made what it termed the "final appropriation" for this purpose; but the Catholic Bureau, though staggering under its burden, kept up the work by means of funds obtained largely through Lenten collections in the churches and the generosity of Mother Drexel.

The bureau was incorporated in 1894, and two years later Cardinal Gibbons was elected its president, which office he continues to hold. So strongly did he feel on the question, that he addressed a petition to Congress December 5, 1898, in behalf of himself and the other archbishops of the United States, urging a reopening of the contract school question, and an inquiry concerning the whole subject of Indian education.‡ He took the ground that an impartial investigation by a committee of Congress would show the great benefits of Catholic Indian education, and that only harm could come to the Indians by abandoning it. He declared the system "an essential element in the solution of the Indian problem—a system which could not be called sectarian, and yet did actually put the

---

* "Our Catholic Indian Missions," a paper read before the Catholic Missionary Congress in Chicago, November 16, 1898, by Rev. Wm. H. Ketcham, director of the Bureau of Catholic Indian Missions.
† Act of June 7, 1897.
‡ Records of the Bureau of Catholic Indian Missions.

spirit of Christianity into the educational work of the Government and enabled the Government to use the indispensable factor of Christianity in the effort to elevate a race below us in civilization." From the beginning of the work he traced the labors which had been undertaken, the obstacles met, the successes obtained.

"Certainly we are justified," he wrote," in saying that the well-informed on the subject cannot escape the conclusion that the mission school is better adapted to the civilization of the Indian than any other. In the mission school are engaged men and women set apart for its special work; men and women who, through noble inspiration, have chosen this field in which to do lifework in the cause of humanity and to the glory of God. They are selected for the work by the several denominations employing them, not only because of their scholastic attainments, but also because their devotion to the Christian religion has been evidenced by the purity of their lives."

Even after Congress had ceased its appropriations, the bureau did not accept defeat. It took the ground, with the Cardinal's hearty support, that appropriations for the contract schools could still be made out of the tribal funds of the Indians, which were their own property and not public moneys of the people of the United States. President Roosevelt, after obtaining from the Attorney-General an opinion that this view was legally correct, sanctioned new contracts in cases where the Indians expressed the wish, by petition, to have a portion of their funds so used. Although a determined effort was made to secure the enactment of legislation prohibiting the use of tribal funds for the support of religious schools, the influence of the "A. P. A." had waned, and Congress refused to do so. By a decision of the United States Supreme Court, the course of President Roosevelt was fully sustained.* Congress also ordered a resumption of the distribution of rations to the

---

* May 18, 1908.

children in mission schools, which had been withheld by the Indian Office for five years.

Cardinal Gibbons' sympathy with the dependent races inhabiting his country was so strong that it took the form of a personal characteristic; and none felt greater anxiety than he during the period of grave trial through which the Bureau of Indian missions passed. He adhered to the Catholic view that when the Indian's faith in his own pagan creed is shattered by education, it will not do to turn him adrift without any creed, but that something must be put in the place of what has been taken away. To all denominations he conceded equal rights in the field of missionary labor, but to him it seemed indefensible that the light of Christianity should be shut out from the eyes of the young Indian in the schoolroom where his steps were to be guided up the steep path that led from the darkness of aboriginal savagery.

CHAPTER XV.

AMERICANISM: THE CAHENSLY QUESTION.

Simultaneous in its development with the school controversy was the question of "Americanism," which embraced within itself, to a greater or lesser degree, all the other problems of the Church in America in the last two decades of the nineteenth century. It directly involved the nationalization of the foreign elements which were crowding into the population of the country; and, indirectly, the broader consideration of whether the Church in the United States should retain the distinctive character in which she had been clothed by Cardinal Gibbons and other apostles of progressive thought, or whether she should become responsive to the reactionary influences developing in Europe. The latter was in conflict with all that Cardinal Gibbons had done or hoped to do. His steady purpose had been to bring the Catholic Church out into the brilliant sunlight of public opinion and display her as a tremendous and benevolent power, closely in touch with the political and economic institutions of every country, but entangled with none.

His plans would fail if the Church were to mingle in foreign politics. He had asked no favors from the Government, and desired no discrimination. In his view, the Government existed for the purposes decreed in the Constitution which he admired so much, and it was not one of those purposes to concern itself about questions directly concerning religion. All forms of religious belief had the same opportunities under the

American flag.*   Catholics in their faith adhered, without fraction of modification, to the universal Church as founded by the apostles and transmitted through ages of struggle by the fathers from generation to generation.   This concerned only their religious belief; it had nothing to do with questions of language or race or politics.   Catholics were citizens or subjects of the country in which they lived.   Upon the basis of their spiritual and moral natures as developed by the ministrations of the Church might be found fruitful soil for the flower of patriotism.   An American was no more and no less an American because he was a Catholic; no more and no less a man because his supreme spiritual shepherd on earth was the Pope.

In America, separated by 3,000 miles of ocean from Europe, the Church could lend herself to nothing of a political or social nature which might be at variance with the ideals of the nation.   There could be no divided allegiance; the Catholic was either an American or a foreigner.   If an American, he must be an American in every sense, and cast in his lot without reservation among the people who were his fellow-citizens. Apart from the public policy of this, apart from the broad-minded wisdom which inspired it, it comported with the cardinal's own aspirations as a man and a citizen.   He regarded the institutions of his country as the best in the world.   With sorrow he saw them sometimes perverted to base uses; and when occasion presented itself, he never failed to raise his voice against abuses that crept into the body politic.   He knew the dangers of popular government; but he also knew the perils of less liberal systems.   In the atmosphere of freedom he found the best final solution for all merely material questions which af-

---

* Dr. Philip Schaff, in Church and State in the United States, p. 9, defines the American system as "a free church in a free state, or a self-supporting and self-governing Christianity in independent but friendly relation to the civil government."

fected mankind. His political ideals clustered around the fathers of the republic, in whom he found exemplars for the men of his own generation. He maintained that the duty of the Catholic, which was nothing more nor less than the duty of the citizen, was to identify himself, without thought of religious discrimination, with all that concerned the best that was in American institutions, setting his face firmly against corruption, the evils of partisan politics, economic wrong and social disorder.

Foreigners who came to these shores he welcomed as Catholics, if they happened to be such; but, at all events, as Americans of the future; men of the same origin, either directly or remotely, as all who had peopled the country; men who would, in time, share in the responsibilities, the burdens, the honors of citizenship, and become as thorough upholders of the American idea as were those whose ancestors had come earlier from the Old World to seek better opportunities in the New.

He deeply realized that the most effective argument, however absurd, which had been used against the Church in periods of religious intolerance, from Colonial days down through the first century of American independence, had been that she possessed, in some measure, a foreign tinge. He had thrown the whole fervor of his being into a battle of years to dissipate this view. His success had been amazing; and it would have crushed him, had the results been snatched away at the last moment.

He had the sympathy, the approval and the ready support of Leo XIII; a large majority of the archbishops of the United States were one with him in spirit and purpose; the American laity hailed him as the pattern of citizenship; and non-Catholics, without distinction of creed, regarded him as an American of Americans. No wonder, then, that when an assault was contemplated upon the corner-stone of his characteristic policies, he should throw himself into the struggle with all his energy.

The widespread agitation about "Americanism," which began in the late eighties, was attributed in part to Herr Peter Cahensly, secretary of the Archangel Raphael Society for the Protection of German Emigrants, and was often referred to as "Cahenslyism." This society had been formed for the laudable purpose of promoting the spiritual welfare of settlers in foreign countries. It had done a notable work, when its aims suddenly widened so as to include within its scope the preservation of the nationality and language of those who emigrated from Europe. It had caught a breath from the gust of militant Pan-Germanism, which, starting on the banks of the Elbe and the Weser, swept through the Teutonic realms and the diverse peoples embraced within the Austrian empire, spread into Russia, thence to the United States, Brazil, Argentina, and wherever a German might go from his native town or farm to begin life anew.

Pan-Germanism was a vivid dream, springing from natural causes that took their root in the unification of the Empire by Bismarck and its closer welding by Wilhelm II. From the time of the Napoleonic wars, when the German principalities, divided against themselves, lay crushed and humbled at the feet of the conqueror, the national spirit of Germania had slept until awakened by the magic touch of the man of blood and iron. Now rising from its slumber, it shook itself like a lion, and, half uncertain of its real destiny, wrestled with its own fierce energy. Pan-Germanism had its prototype in the Pan-Hellenism of the ancient world. It was an aspiration which any race might justly cherish. The hope was not so much to promote a political object, as to spread and consolidate throughout the world Teutonic ideals of character and culture; but, in time, this might be made to serve political and commercial ends. If the German emigrants who were pouring at the rate of 400,000 a year into America, Africa, and even into Asia, could be made to retain their national spirit and customs, their race solidarity, some day there might be a greater Germany, which, like a very Colossus, would bestride the world. German influence might predominate throughout the hemispheres. Should the Fatherland be threatened by another Napoleon, or should Russia and France carry an alliance to the extent of closing in with their united power upon the new empire, an army might spring up across the seas that would defy the power of any who might seek to despoil the temple of their ancestors.

It was felt that Germany was losing all the time by the withdrawal of some of its best and strongest elements to seek a new start in life under conditions more propitious to material prosperity. When they left they were none the less Germans, and they cherished the ideals of their ancestors, as Teutons have done since the days of the great Hermann; but they were soon absorbed across the seas by the peoples among whom they settled, and in a few generations all trace of their origin was lost.

Though the Germans were the backbone of the Cahensly movement, Italians, French, Poles, and others became involved in it to some extent.   In Italy, the Marchese Volpi Landi, and in France, the Abbe Villaneuve, championed the same cause. After years of agitation, the Archangel Raphael Society carried the case to Rome itself.   At an international congress held at Lucerne in December, 1890, it decided to address a memorial to the Holy See, setting forth its petition.

This memorial began by declaring that the losses which the Church had sustained in the United States amounted to more than ten millions, caused by immigrants and their descendants falling away from the faith. As a remedy, it proposed the formation of immigrants into separate parishes, congregations or missions, according to nationality, and that the direction of these parishes should be confined to priests of the same nationality. "In this wise," the memorial set forth, "the sweetest and most cherished relations of the fatherland would be constantly brought to the immigrants, who would love the Church all the more for procuring them these benefits."

In parts of the country where immigrants of different nationalities had settled in too limited numbers to form a separate parish for each, the memorial asked that a priest should be selected for the care of each group who would be conversant with the respective languages spoken, and use in his ministrations to each the distinctive tongue to which the parishioner had been accustomed. It was recommended that parochial schools be provided, in which instruction should be given in the native language of the parents. The organization of Catholic societies founded on nationality was also advised.

The core of the question was summed up in this wise:

"It would be most desirable that as often as might be judged feasible, the Catholics of every nationality should have in the episcopate of the country to which they have emigrated some bishops of their own race. It seems that such an organization of the Church would be perfect. Every different nationality of immigrants would be represented, and their respective interests and needs protected or cared for at the meeting of bishops in council."

The real object of those in America, as well as in Europe, who advocated the Cahensly movement, was to have the bishops appointed by nationality, according to population; if, for instance, the Germans formed one-sixth of the Catholic population, it was desired that one-sixth of the bishops should be chosen from those who spoke that language and would use it in the transaction of their official duties.

In conclusion, the memorial begged special protection for the seminaries and other schools instituted in Europe for the education of missionaries to work among the emigrants, and help for the Archangel Raphael societies was invoked. The Pope was urged to appoint a cardinal protector as a guardian for these societies.*

---

* Reily, Collections in the Life of Cardinal Gibbons, Vol. III, part 3, pp. 7, 8, 9.

In a subsequent memorial, from the same source, presented to Leo in June, 1891, the demands of the Cahensly element were presented with even more vigor, and with considerable amplification of argument. It was set forth that "the current which is carrying away to America populations of different nationalities is already formidable. In the future, it is likely to become irresistible." Statistics were appended, stating that 439,400 Catholics had left Europe for the American continent during the year 1889; of these, 178,900 came to the United States. It was declared that calculations based on authoritative statistics showed that Catholic immigrants and their children ought to constitute in the United States a population of 26,000,000, though the number of Catholics in the country did not much exceed 10,000,000. "Catholicity, therefore," asserts the memorial, "has sustained, up to the present date, a loss of 16,000,000 in the great American republic."

Causes for desertion of their faith by Catholics were enumerated. These included lack of sufficient protection for the immigrants at the time of their departure from home, during the voyage, and on their arrival in America; insufficiency of priests and parishes of their own nationalities; pecuniary sacrifices—"often exorbitant"—that were exacted of the faithful; the public schools; insufficiency of Catholic societies based on nationality and language, and lack of representation for different nationalites of immigrants in the episcopate. It was vehemently argued that immigrants and their descendants who forgot their language also forgot their religion. Regarding the all-important question of bishops, the memorial declared:

"Bishops who are strangers to the spirit, character, habits and customs of other nations can not, in the required measure, despite their virtues, knowledge and zeal, appreciate and effectually attend to the wants of these nations. Again, the harmony and concord between the different nationalities are affected. If the episcopate be handed over almost exclusively to one nationality to the detriment of others, a feeling of uneasiness, of general discontent, is created among these last—a feeling which assumes the proportion of disastrous international rivalries. It is desired that concord and harmony should reign among the different nations that go to make up the Church of the United States. Nothing is more desirable; nothing more esential. The only way to attain this end is to give to every one of these nations bishops of their own, who will represent their respective nations in the episcopal body, just as those nations are represented among the parochial clergy and among the faithful."*

From the viewpoint of Germans in America who sympathized with the Cahensly agitation, the question had been embodied in a pamphlet prepared by Rev. P. M. Abbelen, Vicar-General of the Diocese of Milwaukee, which was submitted to the Propaganda in November, 1886. Archbishop Ireland and Bishop Keane were in Rome at the time, having gone there to discuss with the Propaganda plans for the establishment of the Catholic university; and they availed themselves of the opportunity to make a vigorous reply. They repudiated the idea that there was any question between German and Irish Catholics, and insisted that the only question which could be considered was that "between the English language, which is the language of the United States, and the German language, which emigrants from Germany have brought to the United States." They insisted that there was not even a sign of a conflict of races in America. They pointed out that there were no Irish parishes, and no efforts had been made to establish them; that the Irish readily assimilated with the rest of the population, and were second to none in their devotion to American ideals.

Proceeding with their argument, they showed that there were many diverse nationalities in addition to the Germans, and that if bishops were allowed to each in proportion to pop-

* Reily, Collections in the Life of Cardinal Gibbons, Vol. III, part 3, pp. 9 to 13.

ulation, unity of Church government would be at an end. They pronounced as reprehensible the complaint which had been made at a reunion of Bohemian societies in a previous year, that up to that time there had been no Bohemian in the American episcopate.

Regarding the Germans, they declared that the people of that nationality were not, by any means, a unit in support of the Cahensly point of view. There existed "what we may call the active party, whose object seems to be to preserve intact the German spirit among immigrants and their descendants, and to prevent them from changing their language for the English language, and to give a preponderating position to German influence in the Church in America." This was the party for which Father Abbelen spoke, and in behalf of which he was even then in Rome. They denied that he had in any way a representative character. The project of establishing a permanent Germany in America, it was shown, was approved only by a comparatively small proportion of immigrants, the great majority of whom desired complete and early identification with the institutions and language of their adopted country.

It was conceded that the German immigrants should have facilities for themselves and for their children to practice their religion in the language most familiar to them. To this end, the American bishops had been multiplying churches for the benefit of different nationalities. Yet, it was the tendency of the immigrant to get away from such a church as soon as possible, and to identify himself with the great mass of the people. German children who were taught their native language in the school spoke English by preference when they entered the recreation yard. The churches established for foreigners, and in which foreign languages were spoken from the pulpit and in the confessional, were constantly losing by the departure of parishioners to English-speaking parishes, though gaining, naturally, through the arrivals from Europe.

"The Church will never be strong in America," they continued; "she will never be sure of keeping within her fold the descendants of immigrants, Irish as well as others, until she has gained a decided ascendency among the Americans themselves. Thank God, the time seems favorable for their conversion; prejudices are disappearing; there is a distinct movement toward the Church. To accelerate it, the Church naturally must, as far as it can be done without danger to other interests, be presented in a form attractive to Americans. The great objection which they have until now urged against her—an objection which at certain periods of their history they entertained so strongly as even to raise persecution—is that the Catholic Church is composed of foreigners; that it exists in America as a foreign institution, and that it is, consequently, a menace to the existence of the nation."

They insisted that there was no desire to exclude Germans from the American episcopate; but that only those should be bishops who knew the language of the country well, who understood the needs of the Church, and who could eradicate from themselves foreign nationalism.*

Cardinal Gibbons wrote to the Pontiff, fully stating his own views on the question. These were subsequently adopted at a meeting of the archbishops in Philadelphia, by whom a strong protest against Cahenslyism was drawn up and sent to the Propaganda. They urged three basic principles:

First, there should exist among all the parishes of the United States, without distinction of nationality, a perfect equality, and each should be independent of the other.

Second, it is not necessary that any privilege be accorded to any nationality in the administration of dioceses and parishes.

---

* Letter of Archbishop Ireland and Bishop Keane to Cardinal Simeoni, Prefect of the Propaganda, Dec. 6, 1886.

Third, it is the plain duty of every bishop to do his utmost that all the faithful of all languages who may be in his diocese be taken care of with the same charity.

Cardinal Gibbons felt that there was great danger that the harmony and fraternal affection which had existed among the prelates of the United States would be broken. He insisted that the only way to arrest the evil was to refuse to recognize any distinction in the government of the Church; for, if one nationality were accorded special privileges, others would demand them also.

The Germans would have been glad to obtain the assistance of Cardinal Gibbons in behalf of the Cahensly movement. Throughout their agitation, most of them spoke of him with respect and even filial affection, because his conduct in the Diocese of Baltimore had been such as to remove any ground for charges of discrimination on account of nationality. The largest congregation in the city—St. Michael's—was German, presided over by Redemptorist Fathers, who conducted their ministrations in their own language. There were admirable church facilities for all German immigrants to be instructed in their own tongue. Poles, Bohemians, and other nationalities were similarly provided for. The Cardinal frequently visited these churches and co-operated with the pastors in the care of their flocks. The religious and material welfare of the immigrants was a subject close to his heart; and in his case as a bishop, criticism was disarmed before the fight began.

But, in the country at large, he saw great danger from Cahenslyism. He lost no suitable opportunity of openly declaring his own sentiments.

One of the characteristically bold acts of his life was the delivery of a strong sermon on this subject in Milwaukee, when he conferred the pallium on Archbishop Katzer in St. John's Cathedral, August 20, 1891. This ceremony was marked by the presence of more than 700 prelates and priests, coming from almost every State in the Union and embracing every nationality represented among the American people. The Cardinal began his address by saying, after contemplation of the remarkable scene before him, that the Catholic Church in America was a family derived from many nations. He compared it to the heterogeneous multitude which assembled on the day of Pentecost, each person of whom heard in his own tongue the works of God proclaimed by the Apostles. He pointed out that a large proportion of the American bishops were natives of different countries in Europe; yet he ventured to say that in no country in Christendom were the members of the hierarchy more united and compact. "Woe to him, my brethren," he said, "who would destroy or impair this blessed harmony that reigns among us! Woe to him who would sow tares of discord in the fair field of the Church of America! Woe to him who would breed dissension among the leaders of Israel by introducing a spirit of nationalism into the camps of the Lord! Brothers we are, and brothers we shall remain. * * * 'God and our country!' this be our watchword. Next to love of God, should be love of our country. * * * Let us glory in the title of American citizen. To one country we owe allegiance, and that country is America. We must be in harmony with our political institutions. It matters not whether this is the land of our birth or our adoption. It is the land of our destiny."*

The training of a native clergy thoroughly in touch with the institutions of their country was one of his great objects. While the subject was at white heat, he made an address at the centennial celebration of St. Mary's Seminary, Baltimore, in October, 1891, in which he used these significant words:

"We can never, indeed, be sufficiently grateful for the apostolic labors of the clergy who have come to us from Europe in the past century. Without them, tens of thousands would

---

* Reily, Collections in the Life of Cardinal Gibbons, Vol. II, p. 145 *et seq.*

have died of spiritual starvation. But if the Church is to take deep roots in the country and to flourish, it must be sustained by men racy of the soil, educated at home, breathing the spirit of the country, growing with its growth, and in harmony with its civil and political institutions."

Leo XIII took formal note of the agitation for the selection of bishops according to nationality, and on July 4, 1891, addressed to Cardinal Gibbons, through Mgr. Rampolla, Papal Secretary of State, a letter setting forth the views of the Apostolic See on this question. The Pontiff declared that the existing laws for the selection of bishops were to be observed without modification, and that no toleration could be accorded to certain practices which had arisen in opposition to it. He announced his determination not to grant the petition of Herr Cahensly asking that national bishops be appointed for the United States. The cardinal sent copies of the letter to all the archbishops.

President Harrison was walking at Cape May a few days later with his little grandchild, "Baby McKee," when he met the cardinal. He invited the prelate into his cottage, and there they talked at length about the Cahensly question. The president showed a rather broad comprehension of questions affecting the Church in the United States, remarking that it seemed to him to have grown sufficiently strong to be regarded no longer as a missionary jurisdiction. The attempt to introduce the question of nationality in selections for the episcopate appeared to him to have great potency for harm, and he expressed his unbounded satisfaction that the movement had been checked. He said he had sometimes thought of writing to the Cardinal on the subject, but hesitated lest he might be interfering.

The Cardinal told the President that he was much pleased to hear his views, and suggested that, as he had contemplated writing a letter on the subject, it might not be too late even yet to express his views in that form. General Harrison replied that, while he feared "burning his fingers" by meddling in ecclesiastical questions, he had no objection to the Cardinal stating his views in a letter to the authorities in Rome. The Cardinal transmitted to Mgr. Rampolla a full account of the conversation, and received a prompt reply, expressive of the satisfaction which these facts created at the Vatican.

As the agitation continued, Cardinal Ledochowski, Prefect of the Propaganda, addressed a letter to the American primate in May, 1892, in which he used this language:

"You are certainly well aware that on the occasion of vacancies in episcopal sees in the United States divers commotions very often arise among both clergy and people, which the event shows are growing more serious and frequent as time goes on. The effects which usually result in such cases are neither trivial nor hidden, nor are they of such a nature that this Sacred Congregation can pass them over in silence. For we have now and again seen clergy and people active beyond their legitimate rights in the nominations of candidates for the episcopal office; contentions are diffused and are fomented through the press. But what particularly fosters these contentions is the violent zeal with which each faction endeavors to secure bishops of its own nationality, as if private utility and not the Church's interest were the end to be looked to in the selection of a suitable pastor.

"Moreover, while the Apostolic See has the interest of the Church alone in view in appointing bishops for the Christian flock in the world at large, it is more especially influenced by this consideration in naming bishops for the United States of America, where immigrants from the different nations of Europe, by adopting that country as their own, are blended together into one people, and form consequently but one nation. Since, therefore, the manner of electing bishops in the Church of the United States, accurately and wisely defined, is laid down in the decrees of its National Councils, and particularly in those of the Third Plenary Council of Baltimore, strenuous efforts should be made to do away with all action that is contrary to it.   For these decrees, which are above all in harmony with the requirements of time and place, and which have been enacted by the unanimous voice of the bishops and confirmed by the authority of the Apostolic See, are not such as can in any wise be set aside in favor of private individuals without serious injury to discipline.

"I consider it my duty to communicate these matters to you, so that this evil may be opposed at its birth, before it has grown strong with time.   It is desirable, therefore, that in every diocese both clergy and people be warned, in the first place, of the deplorable results which come from contests of this kind; that they not only rend asunder the bond of harmony which should exist among souls and relax the vigor of ecclesiastical discipline, but become a stumbling-block and scandal to non-Catholics as well.   Furthermore, let the bishops, in the name of the Sacred Congregation, publicly make it known that whatever is done beyond the prescriptions of the Councils will be of no avail, since the Apostolic See esteems nothing of greater importance than to uphold the vigor of the ecclesiastical law, which is at once the defense of order and the bulwark of peace.*

A correspondent of the Frankfurter Zeitung interviewed the Cardinal in Baltimore about this time on the pending question, and to him the American prelate spoke firmly and clearly: "People in Germany and elsewhere," he said, "seem not to understand that the Americans are striving for development into one great nationality; just as Germany has developed into one national union by a struggle of many years' duration, so we are striving in the States for a certain homogeneity whose outward expression consists in the possession of one common

---

* Reily, Collections in the Life of Cardinal Gibbons, Vol. III, pp. 1 to 3.

language, the English.   This explains the propaganda for one language, the English tongue, in the Catholic Church of North America.   There is no thought of violating the love of the old fatherland—a sacred feeling.   The Germans in America are handicapped; without the knowledge of English, they are socially at a disadvantage; only in agricultural centers the German is preserved pure.   The Germans are shining examples of industry, energy, love of home, conservatism, and attachment to their religion.   They are beginning to comprehend that it is impossible to stem the course of natural evolution.   For some time I have been in possession of petitions from German clergymen desiring the introduction of the English language. The transition from German to English will necessarily be gradual, and in accordance with the wishes and needs of the people concerned.   What Germany herself does in this respect to solidify her union by a common language, no German will think wrong when applied in advancing the homogeneity of the people of the United States."

The controversy was not without its effect in stirring up popular prejudice, too ready at all times to thrust itself into questions concerning religion.   The so-called American Protective Association, a weak recrudescence of the Know-Nothing movement, began to develop more actively about this time, and aimed a large part of its thunders at the participation of Cardinal Gibbons and other Catholics in the affairs of the United States.   It was pointed out that the Cardinal had been present, by invitation of Speaker Crisp, in the United States House of Representatives when the final vote on the Wilson tariff bill was taken; and the bold declarations of Archbishop Ireland on many political questions formed fuel for the flame of the incendiaries who promoted this organization.   They professed to see particular peril in the Pope's action in appointing Satolli apostolic delegate.   The great wave of immigration was pointed out as a menace, and furnished arguments for men who worked unseen, by methods made familiar in the fifties, to influence elections. While the movement never attained sufficient influence to stamp itself as more than sporadic, it served to call attention to the danger of departing from the straight path in the consideration of questions affecting American nationality.

In the national political campaign of 1892 anti-Catholic agitators were active, and found a theme in Mr. Cleveland's friendship for Cardinal Gibbons. William Black, of Chelsea, Mass., wrote to Mr. Cleveland regarding the following extract from a report of a speech in the *British American:*

"When Cleveland became president he had a wire run from the White House to the Cardinal's palace, and placed a Roman Catholic at the head of every division of the 15,000 employees in the public departments, and permitted nuns, without authority and against the printed instructions hung up in every public building in Washington, to go twice each month through them and command every clerk to contribute to the support of the Roman Catholic Church," etc.

Mr. Cleveland made this characteristic reply:

"GRAY GABLES,
"BUZZARD'S BAY, MASS,
"July 11, 1892.

"*Wm. Black, Esq.:*

"Dear Sir—I am almost ashamed to yield to your request to deny a statement so silly and absurd on its face as the one you send me. However, as this is the second application I have received on the same subject, I think it best to end the matter so far as it is possible to do so by branding the statement in all its details as unqualifiedly and absolutely false.

"I know Cardinal Gibbons and know him to be a good citizen and first-rate American, and that his kindness of heart and toleration are in striking contrast to the fierce intolerance and vicious malignity which disgrace some who claim to be Protestants. I know a number of members of the Catholic Church who were employed in the public service during my administration, and I suppose there were many so employed.

"I should be ashamed of my Presbyterianism if these declarations gave ground for offense.

"Yours very truly,
"GROVER CLEVELAND."

In January, 1896, the American Catholic League was organized as an offset to the "A. P. A." This society wished to obtain the Cardinal's endorsement; but he expressed his views clearly, as follows, in a statement issued through Rev. C. F. Thomas, of the Cathedral:

"The Cardinal wishes to be understood as in no way approving any secret organization, political or non-political, within the Church or without. He believes that it is the duty of all to regard, in electing to office, the best men, irrespective of their religious convictions; and that no man should be debarred from offices of public trust or private confidence because of his religious professions."*

In the campaign of that year the agitation of the American Protective Association was particularly aggressive. It fought by its peculiar methods the nomination and support of Catholics by any party. So pronounced was the movement that the Cardinal felt impelled to write a letter, in which he further stated his own attitude, as follows:

"It is the duty of the leaders of political parties to express themselves without any equivocation on the principles of religious freedom which underlie our Constitution. Catholics are devoted to both the great political parties of the country, and each individual is left entirely to his own conscience. We are proud to say that in the United States the great Catholic Church has never used or perverted its acknowledged power by seeking to make politics subservient to its own advancement. Moreover, it is our proud boast that we have never interfered with the civil or political rights of any who may have differed from us in religion. We demand the same rights for ourselves and nothing more, and will be content with nothing less. Not only is it the duty of all parties distinctly to set their faces against the false and un-American principles thrust forward of late; but, much as I would regret the entire iden-

---

* Reily, Collections in the Life of Cardinal Gibbons, Vol. IV, p. 587.

tification of any religious body, as such, with any particular party, I am convinced that the members of any religious body whose rights, civil and religious, are attacked, will naturally and unanimously espouse the cause of the party which has the courage to avow openly the principles of civil and religious liberty according to the Constitution. Patience is a virtue, but is not the only virtue; when pushed too far, it may degenerate into pusillanimity."

Another influence which sprang up about this time was an organization called the "National League for the Protection of American Institutions." It was formed at Saratoga Springs, N. Y., in August, 1889, and included in the membership of its board of managers a number of men prominent in the affairs of New York city and State. Its first president was John Jay, who was succeeded by William H. Parsons.* The principal object which it sought was a sixteenth amendment to the Constitution of the United States, prohibiting the use of money raised by taxation in aid of any church or religious society, or any institution under "sectarian or ecclesiastical control." While this part of its plan never progressed further than the stage of agitation, the influence of the league was strongly exercised in bringing about abolition of Government appropriations for Catholic Indian schools, and in inserting clauses in a number of State constitutions in conformity with its principles.

Cardinal Gibbons made a significant address at the installation in January, 1897, of Rev. Dr. Thomas J. Conaty as rector of the Catholic University in place of Bishop Keane, who had resigned. The Cardinal laid down as the watchword of the university, "Revelation and Science, Religion and Patriotism, God and Our Country." He declared that if he had the privilege of modifying the Constitution of the United States, he would not expunge or alter a single word of that instrument.

---

* King, Facing the Twentieth Century, p. 520 *et seq.*

The Constitution was admirably adapted to the growth and expansion of the Catholic religion, and the Catholic religion was admirably adapted to the genius of the Constitution. He contrasted the conditions at the university, with which the Government never thought of interfering, and where the only obstacle to further development was lack of money, with a situation he had found in the course of one of his European trips. In company with Archbishop Spalding, he had visited a bishop of Europe, whose tolerant policies and eloquent sermons he greatly admired. Congratulating the bishop on his favored condition, he was surprised to receive the reply: "Monsignor, 'all is not gold that glitters;' I can not build so much as a sacristy without first obtaining permission of the government."*

In his inaugural address, Dr. Conaty emphasized that the university was Catholic, and knew no nationality but that which intelligent faith enjoined. He declared that the university was for the Church in America and was American in the fullest sense, having as the circle of its beneficiaries the American Catholic people.

A question which began to be much debated was that of the religious orders. In some quarters it was held that they were not in accordance with the spirit of modern life; that men of God were needed to go out into the world and spread their influence rather than to retire within the walls of religious institutions, where their discipline might benefit only themselves. While the Cardinal consistently exemplified the idea of an aggressive Christianity carried into every-day life, he warmly defended the piety and usefulness of the life of religious retirement, both for its example and for the benefits it conferred in special cases.

The whole question regarding Americanism came finally to center around the "Life of Father Hecker," a biography by

---

* *Catholic Mirror*, Jan. 23, 1897.

Rev. Walter Elliott, of the Paulist Order, of his famous leader. Hecker, as we have seen, had been instrumental in turning the thoughts of Cardinal Gibbons, when a youth in New Orleans, to the mission of the priesthood. He died in 1888, having firmly established his order as the leading American association for the conversion of Protestants, and for the evangelization of the people already in the fold of the Church. Its preachers traveled from the Atlantic to the Pacific, stirring up the flames of religious ardor upon the dying embers of indifferentism and the thousand and one influences constantly at work to undermine the spirituality of the Church.

Father Hecker took the ground that since the Vatican Council had formally defined the doctrine of papal infallibility, and had fixed the constitution of the Church in final form, the time had come for a wide development of individual action within the limits laid down. He always insisted upon "absolute and unswerving loyalty to the authority of the Church, wherever and however expressed, as God's authority upon earth and for all time;" but he believed, at the same time, that men, as the children of God, must receive the direct inspiration of the Holy Spirit.* He held that the Holy Spirit acts directly upon the inner life of man, and, in that light, is his superior and director. That its guidance may become more and more immediate in the interior life, and the soul's obedience more and more instinctive, was the object, in his opinion, of the whole external order of the Church, including the sacramental system. He taught that the sum of spiritual life consisted in observing and yielding to the movements of the spirit of God in the soul. He saw no conflict between the external authority of the Church as a guide of the soul, and the direct action of the Holy Spirit without human intervention.

---

*Sedgwick, Life of Father Hecker, p. 97 *et seq*.

"The action of the Holy Spirit," he wrote, "embodied visibly in the authority of the Church, and the action of the Holy Spirit dealing invisibly in the soul, form one inseparable synthesis; and he who has not a clear conception of this twofold action of the Holy Spirit is in danger of running into one or the other, and some times into both of these extremes, either of which is destructive of the end of the Church.   The Holy Spirit in the external authority of the Church acts as the infallible interpreter and criterion of Divine revelation.   The Holy Spirit in the soul acts as the Divine life-giver and sanctifier."

Hecker also taught that the individuality of each nation should be used as the instrument by which its people might be brought to God.   He held that it was not without the will of God that this individuality had been developed; why, then, not take advantage of it?   In America, the people had worked out a political system which had brought them liberty and power, making the country a refuge for the oppressed and the unfortunate.   This, he felt, had been due to the blessing of God, working in secular affairs through the freedom and independent character of Americans.   These qualities could be utilized in a special manner by the Church to bring the people within her fold.   He desired the cultivation of the natural and active virtues as being more in accordance with the age than the passive ones.

After Father Hecker's death, his biography, by Father Elliott, was issued with the *imprimatur* of Archbishop Corrigan, and with a eulogistic introduction by Archbishop Ireland.   It attracted marked attention in Europe as well as in America.   In 1897 an anonymous translation of it into French was made, which was compressed and not exact, and therefore, perhaps, did not convey with complete accuracy the spirit of the English version.   The preface of the translation was written by Abbe Klein, a professor in the Catholic Institute of Paris, who expressed his ardent admiration for Father Hecker.   In the same

year Mgr. D. J. O'Connell, in an address before a Catholic
scientific congress at Fribourg, outlined what were beginning to
be known as American ideas in the Church, and expressed his
earnest approval of them.   On the other hand, the conservative party among French Catholics raised a chorus of objections.

Abbe Maignen, of the Congregation of St. Vincent de Paul,
wrote a book entitled *"Le Pere Hecker, Est-il Un Saint?"* and
afterward an English version of it, with some changes, entitled, "Father Hecker: Is He a Saint?"   Cardinal Richard,
Archbishop of Paris, to whom jurisdiction properly belonged,
refused his *imprimatur* for this work.   Abbe Maignen then
applied to Father Lepidi, a Dominican monk, master of the
Sacred Palace in Rome, who gave the *imprimatur* of the Vatican, and thus brought the subject directly to the attention of
Rome.   The book was a commentary upon Father Elliott's
"Life of Hecker," and a vigorous reply to some of Hecker's
ideas, as interpreted by Maignen, with which he could not
agree.

The discussion was soon agitating Europe to an extraordinary degree.   Among Americans it attracted less attention.
If Abbe Maignen correctly stated the subject, they admitted
that there would be room for doubt as to whether it was desirable to accept Hecker's views; but they held that it was a false
Hecker who was being debated, and not the real missionary,
whose saintly life and ardent labors had won so many souls to
the Church.

Only the Pope could speak with final authority.   Leo set
himself to the task, and on January 22, 1899, addressed to
Cardinal Gibbons a long letter, which had the effect of closing
the discussion.*   He began by stating that the publication of
the life of Father Hecker, "especially as interpreted and translated into a foreign language," had excited not a little contro-

---
* Cathedral Archives.

versy, because it had voiced certain opinions concerning the way of leading a Christian life.

"The underlying principle of these new opinions," he continued, "is that, in order more easily to attract those who differ from her, the Church should shape her teachings more in accord with the spirit of the age and relax some of her ancient severity and make some concessions to new opinions. Many think that these concessions should be made not only in regard to ways of living, but even in regard to doctrines which belong to the deposit of the faith. They contend that it would be opportune, in order to gain those who differ from us, to omit certain points of her teaching which are of lesser importance, and so to tone down the meaning which the Church has always attached to them. It does not need many words, beloved son, to prove the falsity of these ideas if the nature and origin of the doctrines which the Church proposes are recalled to mind.
* * *

"Let it be far from any one's mind to suppress for any reason any doctrine that has been handed down. Such a policy would tend rather to separate Catholics from the Church than to bring in those who differ. There is nothing closer to our heart than to have those who are separated from the fold of Christ return to her, but in no other way than the way pointed out by Christ.

"The rule of life laid down for Catholics is not of such a nature that it can not accommodate itself to the exigencies of various times and places. The Church has, guided by her Divine Master, a kind and merciful spirit, for which reason from the very beginning she has been what St. Paul said of himself: 'I became all things to all men that I might save all.'"

"History proves clearly that the Apostolic See, to which has been entrusted the mission not only of teaching, but of governing the whole Church, has continued 'in one and the same doctrine, one and the same sense, and one and the same judgment.'

"But in regard to ways of living, she has been accustomed so to moderate her discipline that, the Divine principle of morals being kept intact, she has never neglected to accommodate herself to the character and genius of the nations which she embraces.

"Who can doubt that she will act in the same spirit again if the salvation of souls requires it? In this matter the Church must be the judge, not private men, who are often deceived by the appearance of right. In this, all who wish to escape the blame of our predecessor, Pius the Sixth, must concur. He condemned as injurious to the Church and the Spirit of God who guides her, the doctrine contained in proposition lxxviii of the Synod of Pistoia, 'that the discipline made and approved by the Church should be submitted to examination,' as if the Church could frame a code of laws useless or heavier than human liberty can bear.

"It is alleged that now the Vatican decree concerning the infallible teaching authority of the Roman Pontiff having been proclaimed, nothing further on that score can give any solicitude, and accordingly, since that has been safeguarded and put beyond question, a wider and freer field both for thought and action lies open to each one. But such reasoning is evidently faulty, since if we are to come to any conclusion from the infallible teaching authority of the Church, it should rather be that no one should wish to depart from it, and, moreover, that the minds of all being leavened and directed thereby, greater security from private error would be enjoyed by all. And further, those who avail themselves of such a way of reasoning seem to depart seriously from the overruling wisdom of the Most High—which wisdom, since it was pleased to set forth by most solemn decision the authority and supreme teaching rights of this Apostolic See, willed that decision precisely in order to safeguard the minds of the Church's children from the dangers of these present times.

"These dangers, viz., the confounding of license with liberty, the passion for discussing and pouring contempt upon any possible subject, the assumed right to hold whatever opinions one pleases upon any subject and to set them forth in print to the world, have so wrapped minds in darkness that there is now a greater need of the Church's teaching office than ever before, lest people become unmindful both of conscience and of duty.

"We, indeed, have no thought of rejecting everything that modern industry and study have produced; so far from it, that we welcome to the patrimony of truth and to an ever-widening scope of public well-being whatsoever helps toward the progress of learning and virtue. Yet all this, to be of any solid benefit, nay, to have a real existence and growth, can only be on the condition of recognizing the wisdom and authority of the Church. * * *

"Nor can we leave out of consideration the truth that those who are striving after perfection, since by that fact they walk in no beaten or well-known path, are the most liable to stray, and hence have greater need than others of a teacher and guide. Such guidance has ever obtained in the Church; it has been the universal teaching of those who throughout the ages have been eminent for wisdom and sanctity—and hence to reject it would be to commit one's self to a belief at once rash and dangerous. * * *

"This overesteem of natural virtue finds a method of expression in assuming to divide all virtues into active and passive, and it is alleged that whereas passive virtues found better place in past times, our age is to be characterized by the active. That such a division and distinction can not be maintained is patent—for there is not, nor can there be, merely passive virtue. 'Virtue,' says St. Thomas Aquinas, 'designates the perfection of some faculty, but the end of such faculty is an act, and an act of virtue is naught else than the good use of free will,' acting, that is to say, under the grace of God if the act be one of supernatural virtue. * * *

"From the foregoing it is manifest, beloved son, that we are not able to give approval to those views which, in their collective sense, are called by some 'Americanism.' But if by this name are to be understood certain endowments of mind which belong to the American people, just as other characteristics belong to various other nations; and if, moreover, by it are designated your political conditions and the laws and customs by which you are governed, there is no reason to take exception to the name. But if this is to be so understood that the doctrines which have been adverted to above are not only indicated, but exalted, there can be no manner of doubt that our venerable brethren, the bishops of America, would be the first to repudiate and condemn them as being most injurious to themselves and to their country. For it would give rise to the suspicion that there are among you some who conceive and would have the Church in America different from what she is in the rest of the world.

"But the true Church is one, as by unity of doctrine, so by unity of government, and she is Catholic also. Since God has placed the center and foundation of unity in the chair of Blessed Peter, she is rightly called the Roman Church, for 'where Peter is, there is the Church.' Wherefore, if anybody wishes to be considered a real Catholic, he ought to be able to say from his heart the self-same words which Jerome addressed to Pope Damasus: 'I, acknowledging no other leader than Christ, am bound in fellowship with your Holiness; that is, with the Chair of Peter. I know that the Church was built upon him as its rock, and that whosoever gathereth not with you, scattereth.' "

There seems to have been no doubt that the Pontiff saw in the aspect which Heckerism took before the eyes of Europe a real danger to Catholic truth, whose correction he deemed necessary. His letter, therefore, was a warning against current evils, rather than against the teachings of Hecker. He expressly assented to the primary proposal of Hecker when he declared that the "rule of life laid down for Catholics is not of such a nature that it can not accommodate itself to the exigencies of various times and places." He also declared that the Church had never neglected to accommodate herself to the character and genius of the nations. This, in the view of Americans, embraced all of real importance that Hecker had maintained. None would have subscribed more readily than the founder of the Paulists to the words of Jerome, laid down as a test at the end of the Pope's letter.

As the letter was sifted and its real meaning became clear, it began to be accepted that, while Leo XIII had directed his pious admonitions at real evils, they were not such as were characteristic of America; that they were merely abnormal views nurtured abroad, and, in correcting them, the Pontiff had performed a necessary service. Cardinal Gibbons wrote to the Pontiff, thanking him for dispelling the cloud of misunderstanding and assuring him that the false conceptions of Americanism emanating from Europe "have no existence among the prelates, priests and Catholic laity of our country."

The Paulist Fathers, who had idolized their leader, sent a letter fully embracing the doctrines of Leo, from which they had never thought of departing.

Archbishop Ireland wrote: "Scarcely have I finished reading the letter which your Holiness has addressed to his Eminence, Cardinal Gibbons, and to the other members of the American episcopate, when I hasten to thank you for this act of esteem and of love for the Catholics of the United States, as for our whole American nation. Today light has come; misunderstandings cease. Today we are in a condition to define the fault which some have wished to cover with the name of Americanism, and define the truth, which alone Americans call Americanism. * * * Seeing the astonishing confusion of ideas and the virulent controversies stirred up, especially in France, about the book, 'The Life of Father Hecker,' the extent of which can be measured by the apostolic letter, I can no longer be blind to the fact that it was a necessity for the chief pastor to raise his voice to enlighten and pacify men's minds."

The Archbishop went on to say that the things condemned were those which, as the papal letter said, "are called by some Americanism." Champion of Father Hecker himself, he emphasized the fact that he had never for a single instant opened his soul to such extravagances.

The effect of the Pope's letter was to calm the waves; Americanism stood as it did before. The expression of the policy of Leo himself was accepted as an enlightened and liberal view of modern conditions, based upon thorough obedience to the discipline and doctrine of the Church.

In America, the serene course of the Church's progress was unchecked. She continued in her high position in the favor of the people. Her numbers multiplied with rapidity; new dioceses sprang up; churches, chapels and schools were built without number. "Onward!" was the countersign of the hierarchy, priesthood and laity.

Cahenslyism was, perhaps, the most serious danger which has ever threatened the progress of the Catholic Church in this country. The most powerful force in checking it was undoubtedly Cardinal Gibbons, with the active assistance of his warm friends and able coworkers, such as Archbishop Ireland, Bishop Keane and Mgr. O'Connell. If the United States is a unit, unbroken by divergences and jealousies of race and language, the country owes a debt to him more than to any other single force for arresting the progress of a propaganda perhaps more ominous to the future of the nation than was the anti-slavery agitation in its beginnings. A Gibbons with the will, the power, the fertility of resource, the clear vision of the future, the tact and firmness, the rare traits of statesmanship which he showed in extinguishing the flame of Cahenslyism, might have nullified the violent forces unloosed by Garrison and Phillips, and brought about a solution of the slavery problem with the same substantial results, but without the interposition of a tremendous and fratricidal war.

CHAPTER XVI.

THE WORLD'S FAIR: PARLIAMENT OF RELIGIONS.

The project of the World's Fair at Chicago, in 1893, commemorating the four hundredth anniversary of the discovery of America by Columbus, appealed strongly to Cardinal Gibbons. Not only did he see in it another opportunity to make America better understood by foreigners; but he could not forget that Isabella the Catholic was the patron of the discoverer, who had matured his great project in the sympathetic atmosphere of the Convent of La Rabida. While economic causes had given birth to the movement which led to the discovery of the hitherto unknown continents, zeal for the propagation of the Christian religion undoubtedly played a great part in its immediate inspiration; nor could it be forgotten that had Columbus sailed due westward, as he desired, instead of yielding to the advice of Pinzon and following the flight of birds, he would have touched the mainland of Florida on his first voyage, and all North America might have been Catholic instead of predominantly Protestant.*

Not only Cardinal Gibbons, but the Catholic Church as a whole, took the deepest interest in the ambitious plans for the commemoration. We have seen how the request for the Columbian relics at the Vatican by the United States had led to the designation of Archbishop Satolli as their custodian, and also as papal delegate to the Church in America. Leo XIII was so much moved by the event that in July, 1892, he issued a letter to the archbishops and bishops of Spain, Italy and the two Americas upon Columbus, in which he took the

---

* Justin Winsor, Christopher Columbus, p. 206.

view that the voyages of the discoverer were prompted by zeal for the extension of the Catholic faith. He declared that Columbus was superlatively inspired by this motive, and, therefore, his undertaking was on a far higher plane than that of those who before him had explored the unknown seas.

"This does not say," wrote the Pontiff, "that he was not in any way influenced by the very praiseworthy desire to be master of science, to deserve the approval of society, or that he despised the glory whose stimulant is ordinarily sensitive to elevated minds, or that he was not at all looking to his personal interests. But, above all these human reasons, that of religion was uppermost, by a great deal, in him, and it was this, without any doubt, which sustained his spirit and his will, and which frequently in the midst of extreme difficulties filled him with consolation."*

He argued that Columbus discovered America at a time when a great tempest was about to be unchained against the Church, and that it seemed he was designed by a special plan of God to compensate Catholicism for the injury it was destined to suffer in Europe. The Pontiff ordered that on October 12, or the following Sunday, the mass of the Holy Trinity should be celebrated in the cathedrals.

Cardinal Gibbons promptly followed this with a pastoral letter to the clergy and laity of the Archdiocese of Baltimore. He repeated his favorite thesis, that America was the congenial home of liberty, "and the truest democracy allied with a stable government." He held that peace and happiness, as far, perhaps, as they are attainable on earth, result from these favored conditions.

"Climate, soil, vegetation and mineral products, found almost in endless variety and confusion," he continued, "conspire to make our country the most desirable in the world. Nor can we forget to note that, with a love for our religion as strong

* *Catholic Mirror,* August 6, 1897.

and as true as that for our country, the magnificent expansion God has given to the Church, and how sturdily and fruitfully this flower of Christian faith has grown, untrammeled, under the benign influence of our republican institutions."*

A month before this, Cardinal Gibbons had called a meeting in Baltimore to arrange a local celebration. This rapidly took shape. On October 12, the Italians of the city unveiled a monument to Columbus, at which the Cardinal made an address. He declared that Americans were, above all, indebted to two men—Columbus and Washington—and accepted the Pope's view in declaring that the great mariner had been inspired by the lofty ambition of carrying the light of the Gospel to people buried in the darkness of idolatry. The following Sunday, splendid services were held in the Cathedral, at which the Cardinal pontificated. Archbishops Satolli and Ireland lent their presence to the occasion. Catholic laity and pupils of the parochial schools to the number of 30,000 took part in a procession through the streets on the 21st, when the celebration was general throughout the United States, in accordance with the proclamation of the President designating as a national holiday that day—the real anniversary, in accordance with the correction of the Julian Calendar by Gregory XIII.

Cardinal Gibbons was invited to offer a prayer at the dedication exercises of the fair on the 21st. This prayer was, as usual on such occasions, inspired by lofty patriotism as well as by deep piety.

"Not only for this earthly inheritance do we thank Thee," he said, "but still more for the precious boon of constitutional freedom which we possess; for even this favored land of ours would be to us a dry and barren waste, if it were not moistened by the dew of liberty. We humbly implore Thee to continue to bless our country and her cherished institutions; and we solemnly promise today, in this vast assembly

---

* *Catholic Mirror*, Sept. 8, 1892.

and in the name of our fellow-citizens, to exert all our energies in preserving this legacy unimpaired and in transmitting it as a priceless heirloom to succeeding generations. * * * Grant, O Lord, that this pacific reunion of the world's representatives may be instrumental in binding together in closer ties of friendship and brotherly love all the empires and commonwealths of the globe. May it help to break down the wall of dissension and jealousy that divides race from race, nation from nation, and people from people, by proclaiming the sublime lesson of the fatherhood of God and the brotherhood of Christ. * * * Arise, O God, in Thy might and hasten the day when the reign of the Prince of Peace will be firmly established on the earth, when the spirit of the Gospel will so far sway the minds and hearts of rulers that the crash of war will be silenced forever by the cheerful hum of industry, when standing armies will surrender to permanent courts of arbitration, when contests will be carried on in the cabinet instead of on the battlefield, and decided by the pen instead of the sword."*

In the discussion which arose concerning the question of opening the fair on Sundays, Cardinal Gibbons took a pronounced stand. In a letter in November, 1892, he wrote that "the Sunday closing of this spectacle would be very unfortunate for thousands of our countrymen, who would be tempted to spend the day in dissipation. In their name, I would favor the opening of the fair Sunday afternoon to evening, with the provision that all the machinery should be stopped and all mechanical and laboring work that will not be urgently necessary cease."

Catholics generally were in favor of opening the fair during a part of Sunday, and this was the course at length adopted. The Cardinal took the view that the Lord's Day was not only a time for rest and religious observance, but also for innocent recreation. He held that Catholics having performed the re-

---

* Reily, Collections in the Life of Cardinal Gibbons, Vol. II, p. 854 *et seq.*

ligious duties required of them in the morning were free to spend the day in such relaxation as was becoming to Sunday. In particular, he was anxious that the fair should be open on that day, in order that the workingmen might have a good opportunity to see it. He was by no means in sympathy with the spirit of the old Puritan Sabbath, and he regarded the observance of the day in America, outside of a few large cities, as being eminently satisfactory.

Another example of his tolerance was indicated by the pronounced stand which he took regarding participation in the Parliament of Religions, one of the characteristic features of the fair. This project was considered at the meeting of the archbishops in New York, in the autumn of 1892. Some objections were made, but in the end the prelates decided to accept the invitation to take part. The Cardinal was heartily in favor of this. He recalled that St. Paul had preached before the Areopagus; and in the Parliament of Religions he hoped to reach a peculiar audience with which it would be difficult to get in touch again. The Church was too often presented to the world in apparel that made her repulsive to the people. His hope was to discard these garments and, as he remarked, "Let all see the Church in her true beauty—a beauty sure to endear her to all lovers of the truth. The more the Church is known, the better she is liked." He could not see that the part which Catholics would take in the parliament would involve any recognition or approval of the multitudinous sects represented.

The Anglicans, under the inspiration of Archbishop Benson, declined; but Cardinal Gibbons accepted the personal invitation which was sent to him. He wrote:

"I deem the movement you are engaged in promoting worthy of all encouragement and praise. * * * I rejoice to learn that the project for a religious congress has already won the sympathies and enlisted the active co-operation of those in the front rank of human thought and progress, even in other

lands than ours. If conducted with moderation and good-
will, such a congress may result, by the blessing of Divine
Providence, in benefits more far-reaching than the most san-
guine could dare to hope for."

The name of the Cardinal was among the first on the list of
speakers, closely followed by that of Ameer Ali, a Mussulman
of Calcutta. Archbishop Feehan was on a committee of which
a Presbyterian minister was chairman. In the speeches welcoming the Parliament to Chicago, in September, Archbishop
Feehan spoke in behalf of the Catholic Church. Cardinal
Gibbons had suffered an attack of illness, but insisted on being
present.

"If I were to consult the interest of my health," he said, "I
should be in bed; but as I was anxious to say a word in response to the kind speeches that have been offered, I can not
fail to present myself, at least, to show my interest in the great
undertaking. I would be wanting in my duty as a minister
of the Catholic Church if I did not say it is our desire to
present the claims of the Church to the observation, and, if
possible, to the acceptance of every right-minded man who will
listen to us; but we appeal only to the tribunal of conscience
and of intellect. I feel that in possessing the faith, I possess
treasures compared with which all the treasures of this world
are but dross; instead of having these treasures in my coffers,
I would like to share them with others; especially, as I am
none the poorer in making others richer. But, though we do
not agree in matters of faith, there is one platform on which
we all stand united; it is the platform of charity, of humanity,
of benevolence. * * * We know that the Good Samaritan
rendered assistance to his strange brother, who was of a different name, a different religion, a strange nationality, and
with a wide difference in social life. That is the model we all
should follow. * * * Let no man say, 'Am I my brother's keeper?' That was the language of Cain. I say to you

here today, no matter what may be your faith, that you are and ought to be your brother's keeper."

On the fourth day of the parliament, an address by the Cardinal on the "Needs of Humanity Supplied by the Catholic Church," was read by Bishop Keane, the Cardinal being prevented by illness from being present. He began by a general defense of Christianity, addressed to Mohammedans, Brahmins and other sects assembled from the corners of the earth. If he were not drawn to the Church, he said, by her unity of faith, which binds together in a common worship 250,000,000 souls, by her sublime moral code, by her world-wide Catholicity, and "by that unbroken chain of succession which connects her indissolubly with apostolic times," he would be drawn still more forcibly by her wonderful system of organized benevolence for the elevation and comfort of suffering humanity. He proceeded to state some points in this system. He showed that the Church had purified society at its fountain head, the marriage bond; that she had proclaimed the sanctity of human life as soon as the body is animated by the vital spark; that she had established asylums for infants, orphans, the aged, the sick; that she had labored not only to assuage the physical distempers of humanity, but also to reclaim the victims of moral disease; that she had been the unvarying friend and advocate of the slave; that she had ennobled manual labor.

But he did not hold that activity in these fields was restricted to Catholics. "I will not deny," he said, "on the contrary, I am happy to avow, that the various Christian bodies outside the Catholic Church have been and are today zealous promoters of most of these works of Christian benevolence which I have enumerated. * * * But will not our separated brethren have the candor to acknowledge that we had first possession of the field; that these beneficent movements have been inaugurated by us; and that the other Christian communities in their noble efforts for the moral and social regeneration of mankind have been stimulated in no small measure by the example and emulation of the ancient Church?" He concluded with the doctrine that there is no way by which men approach nearer to God than by contributing to the welfare of their fellow-men.

Another phase of the fair was the Columbian Catholic Congress, a continuation of the gathering of laymen instituted in Baltimore at the time of the centennial of the hierarchy. The Cardinal made the opening address before it, in which he advised moderation in the discussions, and presented a letter from the Pope, bestowing his blessing upon the laity there assembled.

As the foremost Marylander, he was naturally invited to take part in the observance of Maryland Day at the fair. He offered the opening prayer, and pronounced the benediction, giving thanks for the blessing of religious liberty which the fathers had brought to St. Mary's, and which had since spread over all the United States.

After the close of the fair, the Columbian relics were returned to Rome on the United States cruiser Detroit. In receiving them, Leo expressed his lively satisfaction that he had been able to contribute to the success of the great American celebration. He also announced that he was preparing to issue an encyclical to the American bishops, conveying the sentiments of his especial affection for their country. This letter, issued in January, 1895, pointed out what the ministry of the Church had done in opening the American Continent to civilization, and the warm friendship between Washington, the first President, and Carroll, the first bishop. The Pontiff found the greatest satisfaction in the lofty spirit of the Church in the last portion of the century about to close. While this was in part due to the wisdom and zealous labors of bishops and priests, he was moved to write:

"But, moreover (a fact which it gives us pleasure to acknowledge), thanks are due to the equity of the laws which obtain in America, and to the customs of the well-ordered republic; for the Church among you, unopposed by the Constitution and

Government of your nation, fettered by no hostile legislation, protected against violence by the common laws and the impartiality of the tribunals, is free to live and act without hindrance." He could not so far depart from the ancient policy of the Vatican as to assent that this condition was the most desirable one for the Church; but held that she would bring forth more abundant fruits if, in addition to liberty, she enjoyed the "favor of the laws and the patronage of public authority."

Rehearsing the reasons for the establishment of the apostolic legation, the Pope pointed out that it was intended to bring the Church in America in more direct touch with the pontificate; but that it was by no means desired to weaken the authority of the bishops. The great aim, he said, was the extension of the Catholic faith in America. "All intelligent men are agreed," he continued, "and we ourselves have intimated it with pleasure, that America seems destined for greater things. Now, it is our wish that the Catholic Church should not only share in, but help to bring about, this prospective greatness. We deem it right and proper that she should, by availing herself of the opportunities daily presented to her, keep equal step with the republic in the march of improvement, at the same time striving to the utmost by her virtue and her institutions to aid in the rapid growth of the States."*

Following the Parliament of Religions, the subject of Christian unity was much discussed. It enlisted the earnest attention of men of many different faiths. New impetus was given the movement for reuniting the branches of American Protestantism, which has been separated by differences of opinion growing out of the slavery question and the Civil War. Substantial hope began to be entertained that the numerous branches of Methodism would find a common ground for organic union. The same impulse spread to Presbyterianism. It became a common theme for pulpit discussion.

---

* *Catholic Mirror*, Feb. 2, 1895.

A Methodist pastor at Taunton, Mass., addressed several letters to the Cardinal on this subject, to which he replied.* He agreed that aspirations for the reunion of Christendom were worthy of all praise; but proceeded to show that such reunion would be only fragmentary if the Catholic Church were excluded. No reunion would be possible without a solid Scriptural basis, and he held that this was to be found only in the recognition of the successor of Peter as the visible head of the Church. If the churches of the world look for a head, where would one be found with the standard of authority except the Bishop of Rome? The terms of union, he said, were easier of solution than was commonly imagined. The Catholic Church, in his view, held to all the positive doctrines of all the Protestant churches, and the acknowledgment of the Pope's supremacy would make the way easy for accepting her other doctrines. He pointed out that many doctrines are ascribed to the Church which she repudiates, and that Protestants were nearer to her than some of them imagined.

He preached at the Cathedral on the reunion of Christendom, November 4, 1894. He began by recognizing the yearning desire for such a reunion, particularly in the English-speaking world; and declared that gladly would he give his life to bring about this devout consummation; but he saw no hope for reunion except within the fold of the Catholic Church. "On faith and morals," he said, "there can be no compromise; what Christ has left us must remain unchangeable. We can not improve on the work of Christ; but the Church can modify her discipline to suit the circumstances of the times. I would affectionately say to all who desire to share in the inestimable blessings of this reunion, that you surrender nothing worth possessing—not your liberty or independence, or moral freedom. The only restraint placed upon you is the restraint of the Gospel. In coming back to the Church, you are not entering a strange place, but are returning

* Letter of Cardinal Gibbons to Rev. Geo. W. King, July 28, 1894.

to your Father's house. The furniture may seem odd to you, but it is just the same as your fathers left three hundred and fifty years ago."*

Pope Leo summoned him to Rome in the autumn of 1894, for his first visit to the Eternal City since 1887, when he had received the red hat. In the following May, shortly after attending the golden jubilee of his warm friend, Archbishop Williams, he sailed from New York, arriving in Rome May 31. Conferences with the Pope ensued. Though Leo was then eighty-five years old, the Cardinal found his memory surprisingly fresh, recalling even the small details of questions which had arisen in the United States, and especially the Diocese of Baltimore. The Pope, as on previous occasions, received him with particular cordiality, and he spent more than a month in Rome.

When he went to pay his parting visit to Leo, the Pontiff commanded him to defer his departure, so that he might call at the Vatican again. The Cardinal attended a meeting of the Propaganda, the new prefect of which, Cardinal Ledochowski, showed him marked attention. In the course of his interviews, he presented to the Pontiff a program for the philosophical department which it was hoped soon to inaugurate at the university at Washington. He also asked a pontifical brief in behalf of a eucharistic congress similar to those previously held in Europe, which it was proposed to convoke in America. June 29, the Pontiff addressed a brief to him, bestowing his hearty approval upon the plans for the university, and he entered earnestly into the project of the congress. The Cardinal in his interviews with the Pope warmly praised the work of Satolli, whose faithful friend and defender he had been.

He returned to Baltimore in August, and found a great crowd at the railroad station, which, as usual, welcomed him with enthusiasm and escorted him to his residence. A reception was given in his honor by the Catholic Club, at which

---

* *Catholic Mirror.* Nov. 10. 1894.

tributes were paid to him for the continuance of his efforts to break down the impression that the Church was in any way alien to American institutions. Edgar H. Gans, a distinguished lawyer, delivered the address of welcome, saying:

"Not many years ago the view was prevalent that the Catholic Church was a foreign growth, was not adapted to modern American life and, indeed, that its teachings and tendencies were hostile to our free institutions. This prejudice became powerful and widespread. It would not yield to the ordinary weapons of logic and reason. There was needed a living illustration of its absurdity. That illustration was found in your Eminence. In you the American people see the highest spiritual authority absolutely consistent with the civic allegiance of the patriotic citizen."

With that simple neighborly feeling which characterized the Cardinal, he bespoke his delight in returning to his home city, which he preferred to any other he had seen.

"Would that I could deserve one-half the praise showered upon me," he remarked, simply; "I often ask the good Lord what I have done that I should receive so much praise?"*

In September, he preached at the Cathedral on his visit to Rome. He pictured the Pope as an emaciated old man, with the pallor almost of death upon him, intensified by his white cassock and zuchetta. His body was bent; but his eye was bright and penetrating; his voice strong; his intellect amazingly clear. One thing which particularly astonished the Cardinal was Leo's power of physical endurance, which enabled him to hold audiences for several consecutive hours with cardinals and foreign representatives, as well as with private individuals, changing with ease and elasticity of mind from one subject to another.

Passing to impressions of his trip, the Cardinal spoke of the sadness with which he observed the civil authorities of France

---

* *Catholic Mirror*, Aug. 31, 1895.

and some other Catholic nations of Europe drifting away from religious ties.   He compared the burdensome taxation of Europe with conditions in America; but he found one thing abroad which might well be copied at home.   The people of the agricultural districts were not yet infected with the fever to flock to the cities; all seemed happy and contented in their rural surroundings.   While he would by no means discourage ambition, he regarded discontent with an honorable though humble situation in life as a serious fault of his fellow-countrymen.*

Following the Cardinal's return, the eucharistic congress for which he had received the pontifical approbation was held in Washington, in October.   In the same month the new course of philosophy at the university was instituted by the dedication of McMahon Hall, erected with a gift of $400,000 from Rev. James M. McMahon, an aged priest of the Diocese of New York.   The Cardinal made an address at the dedication, urging the laity, no less than the clergy, to lend their earnest support to the university in the program of expansion which would be inseparable from its healthful activity.

A movement was started by Methodist ministers of Chicago in 1894 to obtain a modification of laws regarding public worship and marriage in Peru, Bolivia and Ecuador.   They decided to appeal direct to the Pope to secure for Protestants in those countries "the same liberty of conscience that is enjoyed by Roman Catholic citizens of this country."   A letter was sent to Cardinal Gibbons in Rome asking his co-operation, and he promptly took up the matter with Cardinal Rampolla.   In a reply to the chairman of the Chicago Methodist Committee,† he incorporated a communication to himself from the Papal Secretary of State, setting forth that the complaint "has reference to a state of things solely dependent upon the civil laws in force in the republics of Peru, Ecuador and Bolivia.

---

* *Catholic Mirror,* Sept. 14, 1895.
† Letter of Cardinal Gibbons to Rev. John Lee, of Chicago, June 14, 1895.

McMahon Hall—Catholic University Washington

Nevertheless, as your Eminence has been pleased to communicate to me the said letter, I have written to the apostolic delegate in the above-named republics to obtain precise information concerning the laws which affect the condition of the Protestants there as regards both the exercise of their religion and the celebration of marriage." The Secretary of State gave the assurance that he would "call the attention of the Holy See to the information which the aforesaid delegate would send."

After the completion of these inquiries, Cardinal Rampolla wrote to Cardinal Gibbons,* stating that "the Protestants in Peru, far from being restricted in the free exercise of their worship, are rather accorded a larger degree of toleration than is compatible with a strict construction of the political constitution of that country. This is evidenced by the fact that in Peru, especially in the cities of Lima and Callao, there are several Anglican and Methodist chapels where weekly conferences are held. As to the solemnization of marriages, the delegate informs me that, while the constitution of Peru recognizes no other form than that prescribed by the Council of Trent, Protestants do, as a matter of fact, wed with religious ceremony in the presence of their ministers, and civilly before the consuls and ambassadors of their respective countries. The same condition of things relative to marriage exists in Bolivia and Ecuador, where the exercise of religious worship is regulated by special constitutional enactments, with which the Holy See cannot interfere."

---

* Letter of Nov. 30, 1895.

CHAPTER XVII.

SPANISH-AMERICAN WAR.

When the United States and England came perilously near an open clash over the Venezuelan boundary dispute, in 1895, Cardinal Gibbons saw with misgivings how easy it would be for the nation to plunge suddenly into a war that might have the most momentous results to the world. As a parish priest in Baltimore, he had been a witness of the horrors of armed conflict—the broken homes, prostrate communities, the ravings of animosity instead of the sober conclusions of reason. In the South, as a young bishop, he had labored in the track of Sherman's march, where great rows of chimneys stood like melancholy sentinels on what had been the sites of peaceful dwellings. He had heard the tales of ruin by the people, how soldiers had swept like a great plague through village and countryside, laying a wide region bare, and plunging the helpless into keen suffering and abject want. In reconstruction times he had seen the vials of misery poured upon the striken South, and the pathetic struggle of the people to work upward from the havoc.

In the sometimes too expressive colloquialism of America he had much of the "fighter" in him. Possessing strong convictions, he did not hesitate to declare them when occasion seemed to call for it. But he regarded war as the last resort. In his own country, his wish was to see all vital questions decided by the ballot; and among nations, he was an earnest advocate of arbitration.

When the movement for an arbitration treaty between the United States and England was started, following the peaceable adjustment of the Venezuelan question, he lent it his heartiest support. On Easter Sunday, 1896, he joined Cardinals Vaughan, of England, and Logue, of Ireland, the representatives of the English-speaking peoples in the Sacred College, in an appeal in behalf of a permanent tribunal of arbitration. Although the United States Government was not then ready to take as pronounced a position in favor of a permanent international court as was afterward the case, the appeal of the three cardinals had a tremendous effect in arraying the Catholics of their countries on the side of this great and humane reform. The appeal is here quoted in full:

"An appeal by the American, Irish and English cardinals in behalf of a permanent tribunal of arbitration.

"We, the undersigned cardinals, representatives of the Catholic Church in our respective countries, invite all who hear our voices to co-operate in the formation of a public opinion which shall demand the establishment of a permanent tribunal of arbitration as a rational substitute among the English-speaking races for a resort to the bloody arbitrament of war.

"We are well aware that such a project is beset with practical difficulties. We believe that they will not prove to be insuperable if the desire to overcome them be genuine and general. Such a court existed for centuries when the nations of Christendom were united in one faith. And have we not seen nations appeal to that same court for its judgment in our own day?

"The establishment of a permanent tribunal, composed, may be, of trusted representatives of each sovereign nation, with power to nominate judges and umpires, according to the nature of the differences that arise and a common acceptance of general principles defining and limiting the jurisdiction and subject-matter of such a tribunal, would create new guarantees of peace that could not fail to influence the whole of Christendom.

"Such an international court of arbitration would form a second line of defence, to be called into requisition only after the ordinary resources of diplomacy had been exhausted. It would, at least, postpone the outbreak of hostilities until reason and common sense had formally pronounced their last word.

"This is a matter of which the constitution and procedure must be settled by governments. But as governments are becoming more and more identified with the aspirations and moulded by the desires of the people, an appeal in the first instance must be addressed to the people.

"We do not hesitate on our part to lift up our united voices and proclaim to all who are accustomed to hearken to our counsels that it is a sign of a divine influence at work in their midst when nation shall not lift up sword against nation, neither shall they be exercised any more in war, (Isaiah, ii, 4,) for it was written for a future time: 'Come ye and behold the work of the Lord, what wonders He hath done upon the earth, making wars to cease even to the end of the earth.' (Psalms, xvi. 9.)

"Others may base their appeal upon motives which touch your worldly interests, your prosperity, your world-wide influence and authority in the affairs of men. The Catholic Church recognizes the legitimate force of such motives in the natural order and blesses whatever tends to the real progress and elevation of the race.

"But our main ground of appeal rests upon the known character and will of the Prince of Peace, the Living Founder, the Divine Head of Christendom. It was He who declared that love for the brotherhood is a second commandment to the people. 'Blessed,' said He, 'are the peace-makers, for they shall be called the children of God.' (Matt. v, 9.)

"We therefore earnestly invite all to unite with us in pressing their convictions and desires upon the respective governments by means of petitions and such other measures as are constitutional.

"JAMES CARDINAL GIBBONS,
    "Archbishop of Baltimore.

"MICHAEL CARDINAL LOGUE,
    "Archbishop of Armagh,
        "Primate of All Ireland.

"HERBERT CARDINAL·VAUGHAN,
    "Archbishop of Westminster."

In common with his fellow-countrymen, Cardinal Gibbons felt the shock when the battleship Maine was blown up in Havana harbor, February 15, 1898. It was a time when all Americans whose opinions were apt to guide others found it necessary to exercise the utmost moderation. At the outset he took positive ground against war except as a last resort from which there could be no honorable escape. He said he hoped and believed, for the honor of humanity, that the explosion was caused by an accident, and, in that case, Spain could not be held responsible. Neither was Spain to blame if some fiendish Cuban had occasioned the fearful loss of life in order to embroil the United States in a war with Spain. Even if some fanatical Spaniard had perpetrated the crime, he could see no necessity for war. The only circumstance, he held, which would warrant active hostilities would be evidence that the Spanish Government had connived at the explosion; but he refused to believe, and held that no sane man could believe, that a chivalric Christian nation would be guilty of such inhumanity. When the United States appointed a commission to investigate the cause of the disaster, he publicly advised that the people should await the verdict calmly and dispassionately and should not anticipate the judgment.

He knew his country's power, and did not doubt what the result would be if war should come; but he felt that this very power, this immense superiority of resources over Spain, was, in itself, a strong reason why the magnanimous people of America should be more than ordinarily careful to be guided by the light of justice and humanity.

A solemn requiem mass for the repose of the souls of the officers and sailors of the Maine who lost their lives was offered in the Baltimore Cathedral, February 28. The Cardinal preached, and expressed the opinion that it was out of the question to believe Spain was responsible for the disaster.

"We do not realize," he said, "how ardently we love our country until some crisis occurs which awakens our devotion to her and arouses our admiration and gratitude for those who have died in her service. Such a crisis has quite recently occurred; for we have assembled to assist at the holy sacrifice offered up for the souls of the brave officers and men who have lost their lives at the post of duty. Too much praise can not be bestowed on the President, his Cabinet, and particularly on the Secretary of the Navy and his able assistants, as well as on the Houses of Congress, for the calmness and tranquillity, the self-control and the self-possession which they have exhibited during the fearful ordeal through which the country has been passing in the last few days. It needed only a spark to kindle a great conflagration, and the patient and dignified bearing of the Executive and Legislative bodies is all the more commendable in view of the mischievous and intemperate utterances of some sensational papers. This nation is too brave, too strong and too just to engage in an unrighteous or precipitate war. Let us remember that the eyes of the world are upon us, whose judgment we can not despise, and that we will gain more applause and credit for ourselves by calm deliberation than by recourse to arms. 'Thrice is he armed who hath his quarrel just.' "*

The Cardinal earnestly expressed the hope that the day was not far distant when a grateful nation would show its appreciation by erecting a monument to the memory of those who died on the Maine. When a meeting was held at the City Hall in Baltimore to arrange a public performance in aid of the monument fund, he accepted an invitation to act as a member of the committee.

He continued to entertain the strongest hopes that war would be avoided. On Palm Sunday, April 3, when sermons were preached throughout the country by ministers of all denominations, urging the people to be calm, the Cardinal again occupied the pulpit at the Cathedral. "On this day," he said, "when we commemorate the entrance of the Lord of Peace into Jerusalem, let us implore Him that He will so guide the minds and hearts of the President and members of Congress; that He will so direct the counsels of Spain; that He may inspire both nations with a happy solution of the problem which confronts us, a solution honorable to both nations, so that the clouds of war may be dispelled and the blessings of peace may be preserved."

---

* Baltimore *Sun*, March 1, 1898.

The Cardinal and Archbishop Ireland ventured to entertain hopes that war might be averted by the mediation of the Holy See. Cardinal Rampolla, acting in behalf of the Pope, formally offered mediation April 2.* Spain met this offer in the spirit in which it was presented, replying to Rampolla as follows:

"The moment the United States Government is disposed to accept the aid of the Pope, the Queen of Spain and her Government will gladly accept his mediation; and in order to facilitate the high mission of peace and concord which his Holiness is attempting, promise further to accept the proposal that the Holy Father shall formulate a suspension of hostilities; informing his Holiness that, for the honor of Spain, it is proper that a truce should be accompanied by the retirement of the American squadron from the waters of the Antilles, in order that the North American Republic may also show its purpose not to support, voluntarily or involuntarily, the insurrection in Cuba."

In the United States, the offer seemed only to increase the war feeling. The purpose of the papal action was regarded, in some quarters, as an attempt at foreign interference. The Spanish Minister of Foreign Affairs made the unfortunate statement that papal mediation came at the suggestion of President McKinley, and this further ruffled the waves of popular excitement. Mediation, of course, was not to be confounded with intervention, and the Pope never went further than to convey to the two powers, in an informal manner, his earnest hope that war might be averted, placing his help and influence at the service of the two governments impartially.

Archbishop Ireland, with the full sympathy of Cardinal Gibbons, went to Washington and used his efforts to induce the American Government to take steps for persuading the Cuban insurgents to agree to an armistice. All this was

* Spanish Diplomatic Correspondence and Documents, 1896-1900.

preliminary to formal mediation, which did not take place, and could not be set in motion until both powers were ready to accept it.*

The representatives at Washington of Germany, France, Austria, Great Britain and Russia made a united appeal for peace to President McKinley, April 6. Through the influence of Great Britain, this was moderate in tone, and was neither a threat nor a protest. Two days afterward representatives of the same powers supported at Madrid the papal suggestion of an immediate armistice in Cuba. Spain was so desirous of averting war that in its reply to these powers, April 9, it announced a suspension of hostilities against the insurgents; but nothing which could be done at Washington served to lessen the force of the constantly increasing sentiment in America for war.

Cardinal Gibbons shared the disappointment of Archbishop Ireland, and of many other peace-loving Americans, at the failure of these well-meant efforts. Had the United States agreed to mediation, there would have been little doubt that peace could have been secured on the basis of Cuban independence. The passions roused by the destruction of the Maine created a popular feeling in the United States for which there was no corresponding influence in Spain; and, although Minister Woodford subsequently declared that the desire of President McKinley's heart was to avert war,† the tide appeared too strong to be stemmed at Washington.

The Cardinal believed that the conservative and thoughtful people of the nation did not desire war, and that the inflammable state of public opinion was chiefly due to the young and adventurous, who knew nothing of the miseries of hostilities between two nations, and were eager to enjoy the excitement of battle. It soon became evident to him, as to all other ob-

---

* Benton, International Law and Diplomacy of the Spanish-American War, pp. 86-89.
† Address to the Hebrew Young People's Societies, New York, March 8, 1904.

servers, that war was bound to come; and when hostilities broke out he threw in his lot with his country.   In an address, June 13, at the commencement of Loyola College, in Baltimore, he said:

"We must love our country next to God, and be ready to die for it if necessary.   We must loyally and firmly sustain our laws and our governing powers.   There was a time, before the war began, when every citizen had the right to express his views upon the policy of the nation; but after Congress has spoken the words that bring us to war, it is our duty now to work with and for our country, and by prayer for and full sympathy with those in authority to help bring the conflict to a speedy and s^uccessful conclusion."

As the United States army and navy expanded and large forces were assembled for the invasion of Spanish territory, the appointment of chaplains for the soldiers became a matter of importance.   Early in July the Cardinal called upon President McKinley, at Washington, and urged that additional Catholic chaplains be assigned to duty, so that they might be more nearly in proportion to the number of Catholics in the service.   He pointed out to the President the great number of Catholics who were wearing the uniform of their country and that few chaplains of their own faith were available to look after their religious welfare.   President McKinley, whom he knew well and greatly esteemed, received him with the utmost cordiality, and readily agreed to appoint additional chaplains upon proper recommendation.

He was engaged in diocesan work in Western Maryland when the battle of July 3 resulted in the utter overthrow of Cervera's fleet.   He cherished a genuine respect for the courage and high character of Cervera.   Soon after the Spanish Admiral was carried as a prisoner to the Naval Academy at Annapolis, the Cardinal called upon him there.   The Admiral expressed to him his great satisfaction with his treatment by his American captors.   Upon his release, before starting for his home in Spain, he called upon the Cardinal in Baltimore to bid him farewell, and was shown through the Cathedral and St. Mary's Seminary.

When more than 100 members of the Fifth Maryland Regiment were brought back from the front to the City Hospital, in Baltimore, the Cardinal visited them, shaking hands with each and saying a kindly word. By chance he met Captain Eulate, commander of the Spanish cruiser Vizcaya, at a railroad station, and they had a pleasant conversation.

President McKinley, in July, 1898, issued a proclamation inviting the people of the nation to offer thanks for the American victories, and the Cardinal promptly responded. A circular letter issued by him was read in all the churches of the archdiocese Sunday, July 17, from which the following extract may be quoted:

"While the President naturally rejoices in the extraordinary achievements of our naval forces, he is far from indulging in a tone of vain complacency and passionate exultation. Filled with a profound sense of his responsibilities as the chief magistrate of a great nation, and in solemn language worthy of the occasion, he depicts the horrors of war with its long train of suffering, disease and death, and he asks us to implore the Lord of Hosts, who holds in His hand the destinies of nations and of men, to restore to our beloved country the blessings of peace. In compliance with the President's proclamation, you will request your congregation to unite with you in thanking Almighty God for the victories He has vouchsafed to us; in beseeching Him to protect our brave soldiers and sailors from the dangers of disease and death which surround them; to lead the conflict in which they are engaged to a speedy and happy issue and bring back to us once more the inestimable blessings of enduring peace at home and abroad. You will also exhort your congregation to pray for those brave men who have sacrificed their lives in their country's cause."

The Cardinal looked with misgivings upon the growing sentiment in favor of the permanent acquisition from Spain of the islands occupied by the United States forces. President McKinley requested him to come to Washington for consultation, and, upon his arrival, suddenly asked him whether it would be best for the United States to retain the Philippines. The Cardinal had not expected to express an opinion under such circumstances, but he replied briefly and to the point. "Mr. President," he said, "it would be a good thing for the Catholic Church, but, I fear, a bad one for the United States." He saw that the acquisition of the islands would add immensely to the Catholic population under the American flag. In the Philippines, Cuba and Porto Rico the Protestant religion was hardly known. Their people, as Mr. Taft afterward reported to Congress, were sincerely attached to the Church, and for solid reasons. The friar question in the Philippines was a political one, and was not complicated with any desire to throw off allegiance to the Church, which had been the nursing mother of the Philippine people for so many centuries. Catholics proudly pointed to the fact that the Filipinos were the only Christian people in all Eastern Asia and the territories adjacent. Their conversion had been accomplished by incredible sacrifices on the part of Spanish ministers of religion, who had gradually introduced the habits of civilization among the previously barbarous natives, and had developed a high degree of culture in Manila and not a few other centers.

In the Island of Luzon, and to some extent in other parts of the archipelago, the friars were ardent Spaniards, as well as ardent priests. In time, by natural process, they had come to absorb many of the functions of government.* They became inspectors of the primary schools and presidents of the boards of health, prisons and charities; were in charge of the collection of taxes; acted as recruiting officers for the Spanish army; attended municipal elections and council meetings, audited municipal accounts, and passed upon budgets. They resided permanently in the country, identifying themselves completely

---

* Atkinson, The Philippine Islands, p. 320 *et seq.*

with the people; while the Spanish officials were few in number and continually changed. As was reported by the Taft Commission:

"The truth is that the whole government of Spain in these islands rested on the friars. * * * Once settled in a territory, a priest usually continued there until superannuation. He was, therefore, a constant political factor for a generation. The same was true of the archbishops and the bishops. * * * The friars were exempt from trial for offenses, except the most heinous, in the ordinary civil courts of the islands, under the Spanish rule."

As the owners of a great proportion of the best agricultural lands in the Philippines, the friars were firmly entrenched by property rights. Many of them were driven from the islands by the Aguinaldo revolution; but, with the restoration of peace and the complete triumph of American authority, they began to return. Although deprived of their civil functions, it was incumbent upon the United States to protect them in the ownership of their land, and the problem seemed only a little nearer solution than before. There was but one thing to do, in the judgment of the Government; and Mr. Taft was sent to Rome to confer with Leo XIII for the purchase of the friar lands. On his way to the Eternal City, he met Cardinal Gibbons at a dinner party in Baltimore, and they exchanged views. His negotiations in Rome formed a precedent for the American Government, which had not for a long time previous found it necessary to deal direct with the papacy. They opened a way for a complete settlement, and in a short time the United States acquired the greater part of the agricultural lands of the friars for $7,239,000, to be resold to other purchasers.

With the process of years, the intensity of feeling gradually calmed. Arrangements were made for purchasing the property rights of the Church in Cuba and Porto Rico as a means of abolishing the public support of the clergy. With these adaptations to new conditions, Pope Leo expressed himself thoroughly satisfied. "The American Government," he said to Archbishop Ireland in 1900, "gives proof of good-will, and expresses in these acts a spirit of justice and of respect for the liberty and rights of the Church. The reports we receive from bishops and others indicate this. Differences of detail occur as a consequence of war and the newness of complexions. We have confidence in the intelligence and the spirit of justice of the American Government, and believe that the future will not lead us to a change of sentiment toward it. Under the American Government there will be due respect for rights of property and of conscience. You will thank, in my name, the President of the Republic for what is being done."

While the settlement of the difficult Church problems in the Philippines, Cuba and Porto Rico was in process of adjustment, the Cardinal paid another visit to Rome. He had intended to make the journey in the year 1900, which, as the closing one of the century, Leo XIII had decreed to be a holy year, offering special privileges to those who would make the pilgrimage to the Eternal City. The Cardinal issued a circular letter to the clergy of his archdiocese, urging the faithful to avail themselves of this privilege; but circumstances caused him to postpone his own visit to the spring of the following year. He bade farewell to his congregation at the Cathedral May 5, after a conference with Archbishops Ireland, Williams and Kain, who journeyed to Baltimore for the purpose.

Sailing from New York for Naples, he arrived in Rome May 22. On the steamship he said mass and delivered a brief discourse, as he often did when taking ocean voyages. Archbishop Chapelle, Papal Delegate to the Philippines, and Mgr. Nozaleda, Archbishop of Manila, had arrived a few days before him. He took up his residence at the Procura of St. Sulpice, in the Via delle Quattro Fontane, and was soon engrossed in audiences with the highest authorities of the Church. His first reception by the Pontiff was on May 25. He found

Leo in wonderful health at 92, though seeming as frail as a child, but young in his thoughts as most men of 70. The aged head of Catholic Christendom talked of the people of the United States, and referred again to the special love for them which he consistently bore. There was no weakening in the marvelous memory, which seemed as universal as the exalted office which he held. He showed great knowledge of events in the United States, not only ecclesiastical, but political, social and economic. The spiritual needs of the Filipinos he believed to be reasonable, and he relied on the sense of justice of President McKinley and his advisers in working out the difficult problems which were constantly arising. The Pontiff agreed with Cardinal Gibbons on the great need of American priests in the islands, who would understand the American system as applied to church and state better than the Spanish priests and the friars, who were beginning to return after their exodus a few years before.

June 18, Leo received the Cardinal in farewell audience, expressing the belief that it was the last time he would see him; but so vigorous did he appear that the American primate was led to believe he might reach his hundredth birthday.

While in Rome, the Cardinal gave a dinner, at which seven nationalities were represented in the group of fourteen persons, including two members of the Sacred College, three archbishops, three bishops, four priests and two laymen. He commented on this as exemplifying in a striking manner the unity of faith. He assisted at his titular Church of Santa Maria in Trastevere on two occasions.

Leaving Rome June 21, he spent a few days in Florence, and then proceeded homeward by way of France, Belgium, Holland, England and Ireland. A stop in Paris brought him in intimate touch with the church legislation by the French Chambers, the threatening character of which was already beginning to cause great concern. On this trip his health was not of the best at times, and the heat of the Roman summer oppressed him. Paul Bourget was moved to write of him in *Figaro:* "Cardinal Gibbons is of the race of those ascetics in whom it seems that mortifications may have left only as much flesh as suffices for the labors of the soul."

In London he was much sought by English Catholics, and was hospitably entertained by Cardinal Vaughan.

In Ireland, while the guest of the Bishop of Cloyne, he was presented addresses from Catholic societies and the town council. These commented in glowing terms on the advance of Catholicism in America during his primacy. The Cardinal was glad to testify to the great share which Irish immigrants had borne in building up America's prosperity, and to the devoted efforts of the hundreds of Irish priests who labored among the American people. He went on to say, however, that the time had come for the Irish to remain at home, where, by the exercise of as much industry and initiative as they would show in America, they might obtain prosperity which would satisfy their desires.

He sailed from Queenstown August 18, and, as usual, was enthusiastically welcomed on his arrival at New York. Summing up his observations abroad, he found that Americans were now regarded in a different light by Europeans.

"As 'nothing succeeds like success,'" he said, "the vigor with which we carried on the Spanish-American War and the ease with which we gained possession of the Philippines and Porto Rico, have caused Europeans to regard the United States as a world power. Certainly we are more feared than formerly, and there is not a movement made in Europe now without consideration of what effect it will have on the United States. I will not say that our successes will contribute to our happiness as a nation; but certainly they have increased our power and prestige abroad. But a few years ago, the United States was hardly taken into account at all; now, we are regarded as rivals with the powers of Europe, and are feared by them, politically and commercially."*

Baltimore had not neglected to provide one of the characteristic receptions for its chief citizen. When he arrived in his home city, August 25, an immense crowd was waiting in the vicinity of the railroad station, where he was formally received by Acting Mayor Henry Williams and Charles J. Bonaparte. To their welcoming speeches he briefly responded, saying there was no country as dear to him as America, and no place like Baltimore. He was escorted to the Cathedral by a long parade of uniformed knights and others, and in that noble edifice spoke again of his pleasure in returning, and bestowed the apostolic benediction. Standing on the front steps of his residence, he reviewed the parade. It was characteristic of his intense piety, and a notable example to his priests, that on the same evening, putting aside the exactions of business which had accumulated in his absence, he went into retreat with the clergy of his diocese for five days at St. Mary's Seminary.

---

* Baltimore *Sun,* August 26, 1901.

CHAPTER XVIII.

THE STRENUOUS LIFE: LABORS AND REFORMS.

One of the most notable reforms which Cardinal Gibbons has been instrumental in bringing about was the abolition of the Louisiana Lottery, a gigantic scheme of licensed gambling which had long been an offense to the nation. Its power, derived from the laws of the State in which it was entrenched, was fortified by organized corruption, and, for a long time, seemed impregnable. Able and devoted men undertook to overthrow it, but for years their efforts were futile. It appeased hostile opinion by giving large sums to charities, and secured no less personages than Generals Beauregard and Early to supervise its drawings.

The Cardinal, at length, determined to throw his whole weight into the struggle. By a letter addressed January 11, 1892, to Gen. George D. Johnston, of the Anti-Lottery Committee, which was opposing a renewal of the charter by the State of Louisiana, he turned the tide. He took the ground that the question of permitting the lottery to continue was pre-eminently one of morality and virtue. Its practical working, he showed, tended to enrich the few at the expense and misery of the many, to tempt the poor to squander their earnings "in the vain, delusive, Tantalus-like hope of one day becoming the possessor of a winning number." This fever impelled many to theft and dishonesty. He pronounced a lottery an enemy to the honor and peace of any community, to the happiness of home, to individual thrift and enterprise, and vigorously called on every public-spirited citizen and earnest Christian to aid in its suppression.

"Christian charity and natural philanthropy," he wrote, "alike dictate that we remove from the unwary pitfalls of destruction and withdraw the innocent and weak from temptation. Those bent on suicide should be restrained. The burning fagot should be snatched from the child's hand. That the Louisiana Lottery, as it is presented to us, proves a snare and a delusion to thousands, and is destructive to the peace of mind and energy of action so necessary to pursue honorable careers and properly to acquit one's self of life's duties, we can not doubt. The daily operations of the scheme make the point clear. Worthy, then, of praise and commendation are they who strive to quicken the public conscience and to array public sentiment against the continuance of the evil, who speak and labor in behalf of their fellow-men, by seeking to remove from their midst a dire enemy of their manhood, their homes and their prosperity. Were the evil confined only to the State of Louisiana, I should refrain from giving expression to my sentiments; but since, like a giant tree, it has extended its branches over the entire land, embracing in the area of its operations Maryland and the District of Columbia, with which I am connected, I could not but raise my voice in protest, and in particular that our faithful people may help forward the good work of putting an end to its ravages."*

The words of the Cardinal had tremendous influence, not only in the country at large, but in Louisiana itself, the home of his youth and where his family still resided. He was venerated there as much as in Baltimore; and an aroused public opinion was sufficient to crush the lottery out of existence.

Throughout the nation there was a powerful chorus of praise that a contest so long and unceasingly waged had become victorious through the timely and effective help of the Cardinal. Rev. Lyman Abbott, preaching in Plymouth Church, Brooklyn, in the following month, expressed the view of Prot-

---

* *Catholic Mirror*, Jan. 23, 1892.

estant crusaders, who, like himself, had so long been grappling with the monster.   He exclaimed:

"I can not understand the folly of men who would blot out the Roman Catholic Church from this country.   Thank God for Cardinal Gibbons!   Long may he wear his red cloak and his red cap; and if there should be an election now, and you and I could vote, I would vote to make him Pope!   His word, flung out with courage and with strong significance, has done more than any other word in this country, by press, by politician, or by preacher, to make the leaders of that Louisiana abomination call a halt, and, at least, pretend a retreat.   God give us courage to turn it into a rout."

When the lottery took refuge in Honduras and illicitly carried on its operations in the United States, though in a much modified form, the Cardinal wrote another letter, severely condemning it, and expressing the hope that public opinion would stamp it out everywhere.

Again he raised his voice against current evils, in an article on "Patriotism and Politics," in the *North American Review* for April, 1892, in which he actively ranged himself on the side of those who were trying to stop the ballot frauds which prevailed in many States.   He pointed out that when the fountains of legislation were polluted by lobbying and other corrupt means, when the hand of bribery was extended to municipal, State and national legislatures, when lawmakers became the pliant tools of selfish and greedy capitalists, then, indeed, patriotic citizens had reason to be alarmed about the future of the country.   "Let the buyers and sellers of votes be declared infamous," he declared, "for they are trading in our American birthright.   Let them be cast forth from the pale of American citizenship and be treated as outlaws.   I hold that the man who undermines our elective system is only less criminal than the traitor who fights against his country with a foreign invader; the one compasses his end by fraud; the other, by force."

If the purchase of votes were permitted or condoned, he showed, sovereignty would be no longer vested in the people, but in corrupt politicians and wealthy corporations. Another lamentable result would be that the better class of citizens would lose heart and absent themselves from the polls, leaving elections to be decided by irresponsible political managers. For the correction of these evils he suggested:

First, the enactment of stricter laws against bribery and corruption of the ballot, providing adequate punishment.

Second, consistent efforts to improve the standard of the judiciary, which interprets and enforces the laws.

Third, a vigilant and fearless press, creating a healthy public opinion.

Fourth, greater attention to American history and civics in the schools.

Fifth, a more hearty celebration of the national holidays.

Sixth, the maintenance of party lines as an indispensable means for preserving political purity. One party, he argued, watches the other, takes note of its shortcomings, its blunders and defects; and has at its disposal the means for rebuking any abuse of power by the dominant side.

The death of Cardinal Manning, January 12, 1892, profoundly moved him. In the labors of his episcopate he had found his principal support and sympathy in Leo XIII, and next to that Pontiff, in Manning. It would be difficult to contemplate what might have been the story of the Catholic Church in the last few decades of the nineteenth century had the inspiration of these three men been removed. It was fortunate that the influence of Gibbons and Manning was exercised in English-speaking countries, which are naturally readier to respond to liberal ideas. Sustained as they were by Rome, the zone of their work extended, in some measure, over the whole of the civilized world.

From the year 800 to 1870 the Church had a twofold part to play, temporal and spiritual. Since the latter year her mission has been almost wholly confined to the characteristic spiritual field in which she was born; and it was fortunate that in adapting herself to this sudden change from the view-point of centuries, Leo, Gibbons and Manning were able to read the signs of the times aright and interpret them with a vision that stretched far into the future.   Manning was an admirer of Gibbons, and the American Cardinal neglected no opportunity to express his high estimate of his English col-league.   He believed that, had Manning remained in the es-tablished Church, he would have been elevated to the See of Canterbury; or, had his activities been exercised in secular fields, he might have been a chancellor of the exchequer as distinguished as Gladstone, a philanthropist as great as Wil-berforce, a temperance apostle as successful as Father Mathew. Both these cardinals were in thorough sympathy with the wants and legitimate aspirations of the race.   They felt that the Catholic Church was the greatest force toward realizing these aspirations.   They went outside the arena of theology to grapple with social questions; and the welfare of the laboring classes powerfully enlisted their zeal.

Cardinal Simeoni, Prefect of the Propaganda, with whom Cardinal Gibbons had been thrown in close contact in the settlement of many important questions, died the same day as Manning.   His loss was keenly felt by the American prelate, who had learned to find in his judgment and sympathy a strong prop on trying occasions.

President Cleveland was warmly interested in the golden jubilee of the episcopate of Leo XIII.   Through Cardinal Gib-bons, he sent to the Pontiff as a present one of an edition of twenty copies containing the official papers and documents written by him during his first term in the Presidency.   He sent his congratulations in the following letter, addressed to Cardinal Gibbons :*

---

* Letter of President Cleveland to Cardinal Gibbons, June 9, 1893 (Cathedral Archives).

"Please permit me to transmit, through you, to his Holiness, Leo XIII, my sincere congratulations on the occasion of the golden jubilee of his episcopate. The pleasure attending this expression of my felicitations is much enhanced by the remembrance that his Holiness has always manifested a lively interest in the prosperity of the United States, and great admiration for our political institutions. I am glad to believe that these sentiments are the natural outgrowth of the Holy Father's solicitude for the welfare and happiness of the masses of humanity, and his especial sympathy for every effort made to dignify simple manhood and to promote the moral and social elevation of those who toil. The kindness with which his Holiness lately accepted a copy of the Constitution of the United States leads me to suggest that, if it does not seem presumption, it would please me exceedingly to place in his hands a book containing the official papers and documents written by me during my previous term of office."

The Cardinal was at the full of his popularity, abroad as well as at home, when the silver jubilee of his own episcopacy was celebrated, at the Baltimore Cathedral, October 18, 1893. The actual anniversary was August 16; but the celebration was held later, in compliance with the wishes of a number of prelates living at a distance, who desired to attend. In June, a committee of the clergy took the arrangements in charge, and issued a circular letter, announcing that a testimonial of their devotion would be presented to him. His relations with his priests were particularly cordial; and nowhere in the country had the clergy a higher standard than in his own diocese.

"By his wise and progressive principles," the circular read, "he has raised the Church before the American public to a position of which we may be justly proud. In the administration of the archdiocese he has displayed all the characteristics of the Good Shepherd; and he has ever been united to the clergy and his people by the closest bonds of devotion and love. To his priests he has been, indeed, the amiable and sympathetic elder brother, always ready to receive, to counsel, and to assist them in the great responsibilities of their vocation."

Archbishop Satolli and a remarkable gathering of the hierarchy assembled. The Cardinal himself celebrated mass, and Archbishop Corrigan preached. At the conclusion of the sermon, Rev. Frederick Z. Rooker, vice-rector of the American College, who had arrived from Rome, presented to the Cardinal, as a gift from the Pope, a massive design of gold and precious stones, bearing a profile miniature of the great bronze statue of St. Peter in Rome, representing him as seated upon a throne, blessing the whole world. The jewels were sardonyxes, emeralds, and pearls, set in gold. Accompanying the gift was a letter from the Pontiff, conveying his heartiest congratulations. In the same year, Leo had enjoyed the extraordinary distinction of celebrating the golden jubilee of his own episcopate, and he expressed the fervent wish that the Cardinal might be granted the same privilege.* In making the presentation, Father Rooker took the opportunity to offer the congratulations of the rector and students of the American College, of the executive committee of which Cardinal Gibbons was chairman.

The sermon of Archbishop Corrigan was eloquent. He pointed out that the Cardinal's labors had been crowned with the pontifical approval in his elevation to the Sacred College.

In the afternoon, the priests of the archdiocese presented an address to him, in the large hall of St. Mary's Seminary. The venerable Mgr. McColgan, his vicar-general, took occasion to recall that a Protestant who had watched the future Cardinal as a young pastor going from house to house, visiting the poor and ministering to their wants, remarked to him that this priest would some day become a great man. The Cardinal

---

* Letter of Leo XIII to Cardinal Gibbons, August 30, 1893, (Cathedral Archives).

replied in terms of warm affection, attributing the unexampled growth of the Church in the diocese to the work of the clergy, and saying that in the years of his episcopate he had known not a single case of insubordination.

Following, came a dinner, at which a number of the Baltimore clergy pleased the Cardinal greatly by singing the stirring strains of "Maryland, My Maryland!" The phonograph was then a comparatively new invention, and a message from Leo XIII, bestowing his blessing on the Cardinal and on the American people, reproduced by this means, created great interest. Mgr. Nugent, of Liverpool, who had been sent to convey the felicitations of Cardinal Vaughan, and Father Ring, who came as the representative of Cardinal Logue, made happy addresses.

In the evening, vespers were celebrated in the Cathedral by Archbishop Redwood, who had traveled half of the earth's circumference from his home in New Zealand. Archbishop Ireland preached one of the most notable sermons of his life, on "The Church and the Age."* He began by saying that every walk of life was full of men who performed the common duties, but few rose above mediocrity. "This evening," he said, "be it my coveted privilege to honor a man among men. The record of the Cardinal Archbishop of Baltimore! I speak of it with pride and exultation; it is the record I should have traced for my ideal bishop and leader of men in these solemn times through which the Church is passing."

Launching into his theme, the Archbishop boldly declared:

"There is discord between the age and the Church. We recall the fact with sorrow. The interests of society and religion suffer where misunderstanding and separation exist. The fault lies with the age and with the Church, or rather, with statesmen of the age and statesmen of the Church. Age and Church, rightly apprehended, are in no manner at war. * * * I indicate the opportunity for the great and singular church-

* *Catholic Mirror,* Oct. 21, 1893.

man; his work is to bridge the deep valley separating the age
from the Church.   *   *   *   What the Church at any time
was, certain people hold she ever must be; they do her much
harm, making her rigid and unbending, incapable of adapting
herself to new and changing surroundings. The Church,
created by Christ for all ages, lives in every age and puts on
the dress of every one."

The Archbishop turned to note the characteristics of the
age. It was ambitious for knowledge. It was an age of
liberty, civil and political, and of democracy. It was an era
of social cravings for justice to all men. He found in this
the best opportunity for Catholic sympathy and effort. Leo
he hailed as the "Providential Pope," and Cardinal Gibbons
as the "Providential Archbishop."

"How oft in past years," he said, "have I thanked God that
in this latter quarter of the nineteenth century Cardinal Gibbons has been given to us as a primate, a leader, a Catholic
of Catholics, an American of Americans, a bishop of his age
and of his country; he is to America what Leo is to all Christendom. Aye, far beyond America does his influence go.
Men are not confined by frontier lines, and Gibbons is European as Manning was American. A particular mission is reserved to the American Cardinal. The Church and the age
fight their battles with especial intensity in America. America
is watched. The prelate who in America is the representative
of the union of Church and age is watched. His leadership
guides the combatants the world over. The name of Cardinal
Gibbons lights up the pages of nearly every European book
which treats of modern social and political questions. The
ripplings of his influence cross the threshold of the Vatican.
The work of Cardinal Gibbons forms an epoch in the history
of the Church in America. He has made known as no one before him did, the Church to the people of America. He has
demonstrated the fitness of the Church for America, the natural alliance existing between the Church and the freedom-

giving democratic institutions of this country. Through his action the scales have fallen from the eyes of non-Catholics—prejudices have vanished. He, the great churchman, is the great citizen; Church and country unite in him, and the magnetism of the union pervades the whole land, teaching laggard Catholics to love America, teaching well-disposed non-Catholics to trust the Church.

"How noble the mission which Heaven has assigned to him; how well it has been followed out! * * * He is large-minded. His vision can not be narrowed to a one-sided consideration of men or things. He is large-hearted. His sympathies are limited by the frontiers of humanity; careless of self, he gives his best activities to the good of others. He is ready for every noble work—patriotic, intellectual, social, philanthropic, as well as religious; and in the prosecution of these he joins hands with the laborer and the capitalist, with the white man and the black man, with the Catholic, the Protestant and the Jew. He is brave. He has the courage to speak and to act in accordance with his convictions. * * * Cardinal Gibbons, the most outspoken of Catholics, the most loyal co-laborer of the Pope of Rome, is the American of Americans!"

The next day there was a banquet of the Catholic Club of Baltimore, attended by Vice-President Stevenson, Senator Gorman, Mayor Latrobe, and other men of note. A letter from President Cleveland was read, and a number of addresses from organizations in the diocese were presented. The Cardinal, when called upon, said he was thankful for two things—that he had Christ for his instructor and guide, and that he had the privilege of being born in and raised a citizen of the United States, a citizen of Maryland, of Baltimore. In no country on the face of the earth had a difficult problem been better solved—that of maintaining harmonious relations between church and state. Here the church and state ran in parallel lines, and did not conflict with one another. The church upheld the state; religion educated the state and proclaimed the divinity of the laws.   Religion sanctified the virtue of obedience and respect for civil laws, by teaching that obedience to civil authority is not a servile homage, but the homage of freedom to God Himself.

"For my part," he added, "I would be sorry to see the relations of church and state any closer than they are at present; for, if the civil authorities built our churches or subsidized our clergy, they might want to have something to say as to the doctrines we teach, and we believe that the Gospel should be free. I thank God that we have religious liberty.   Foreign governments, while recognizing the liberties we enjoy, do not recognize our strength.   The first thing that strikes a foreigner on reaching our shores is the absence of soldiers such as he is accustomed to see abroad; but we are strong in the intelligence of the people; we are strong in the patriotism that in a few hours would transform every citizen into a brave and valiant soldier.

"Another mistake is made in supposing that, because there is no union here between church and state, we are not a religious people.   I maintain that no country in the world has a stronger religious basis than the United States.   Our common law is taken from the common law of England, which is thoroughly permeated with the spirit of Christianity.   Where is the Christian Sabbath better observed than here?   The proceedings of the National and State legislatures are opened with prayer; and still another evidence of our respect and regard for religion is the fact of our setting apart a day in each year for special thanksgiving, the President of the United States and the Governors of States calling upon the people, by proclamation, to return thanks for the blessings they have enjoyed."

He closed by expressing the fervent hope that religion and patriotism might ever characterize the American people.*

* *Catholic Mirror,* October 21, 1893.

For several weeks the Cardinal was besieged with delegations presenting gifts and addresses. Almost every institution in the Diocese of Baltimore sought to present some striking token of the affection in which he was held. It was a combined tribute, which would have overwhelmed almost any man. In November a series of public celebrations was held in Washington.

Preaching at the Cathedral, Sunday morning, November 5, the cardinal expressed his deep gratitude to those who had taken part in his jubilee.

Archbishop Satolli performed his duties as apostolic delegate with satisfaction to the Pontiff. The archbishops decided at their meeting in Chicago, in 1893, to issue an appeal for funds to establish a legation at Washington, and this was done soon afterward. Leo held the view that it would not be well to retain any delegate in the United States long. It had seemed to him that one of the special advantages of such an emissary from abroad would be that he would arrive in this country free from the local associations which might beset an American. After a few years he decided to elevate Satolli to the cardinalate, and to nominate a successor. Satolli had served three years, when Cardinal Gibbons received a cablegram from Rome, announcing the pontifical decision to confer the red hat upon the delegate. The ceremonies of his elevation took place January 5, 1896, in the Baltimore Cathedral. Archbishop Kain, who had succeeded the venerable Kenrick as Archbishop of St. Louis, preached, reviewing the perplexities which had confronted the delegate, and the success with which he had overcome them. Cardinal Satolli, responding to the address of Cardinal Gibbons, spoke from the fullness of his heart.

"It was you," he said, "who received me at my coming, and who immediately became my friend and most zealous protector. It was with the aid of your wise counsels and unfailing encouragement, not without the continual assistance of all the prelates of this great American hierarchy, that my labors progressed and were crowned with success."

In a short time, Satolli was succeeded by Archbishop Sebastiano Martinelli as "Delegate Apostolic in the United States of North America." Nearly all the questions with which he had dealt so well were permanently settled.

In the midst of his engrossing labors, in the most strenuous part of his life, the Cardinal found time to write his third book, "The Ambassador of Christ," issued late in 1896. The title is taken from the twentieth verse of the Fifth Chapter of II Corinthians: "For Christ we are ambassadors; God, as it were, exhorting by us." It is a book for priests, embodying the experiences and views of a man who had achieved remarkable success in developing other men for the active ministry.

He pointed out in its pages that it was doubtful if any age or country ever presented a more inviting field for missionary labor than the United States. Catholic pastors had here free opportunity for their spiritual effort. "No military satrap or state functionary is permitted to enter our churches in the capacity of an official censor to arrest, fine or imprison a minister of the Gospel for his conscientious utterances in vindication of social morals and in denunciation of official corruption." Americans, he thought, were fundamentally a religious people. He differed emphatically from the view of those who characterized them as a nation so absorbed in trade and commerce, in agriculture and politics, as to give scarcely a thought to eternal truths. A people having slight regard for Christianity would not have spent millions annually in the erection of churches and in the maintenance of home and foreign missions. He held that the American people possessed, in a marked degree, the natural virtues that were the indispensable basis of supernatural life. They were gifted and intelligent, self-poised and deliberate, of industrious and temperate habits, frank, moral, and ingenuous. They had a deep sense of justice and fair play; were brave and generous, usually having the courage of their convictions; and, with all this, were a law-abiding people.

He maintained that while the Catholic Church accommodated herself to every form of government, she had a special adaptability to the American political system, and to the genius of the people. As the great conservative element of society the world over, he took the ground that the Church was particularly necessary in a government of constitutional freedom, where there would naturally be at times a tendency to extremes.

In the "Ambassador of Christ," he discussed the Divine vocation of the ministry; the duties of teachers to scholars, and of scholars to teachers; the traits which make a successful priest, and the virtues and accomplishments he ought to exemplify. A reflection of his own deep and constant study of the Scriptures is found in a chapter on that subject, in which he urged, with particular forcefulness, the necessity of intimate communion with the Book of Books. He took strong ground in favor of congregational singing, expressing the belief that Charles Wesley had accomplished as much in the cause of Methodism by his hymns as John Wesley effected by his preaching. He urged that priests should get out among their people, declaring that the visitation of the sick and distressed was the touchstone of apostolic zeal and charity. In particular, he advised attention to the young; and paid a beautiful tribute to the Christian mother.

Learning he pronounced essential for a priest. Piety, though indispensable, could never be an adequate substitute for learning. Regarding the argument sometimes cited, that the Apostles, except St. Paul, were illiterate men, he answered that, apart from their spiritual inspirations, they were far from being deficient in theological knowledge. They exhibited a marked familiarity with the ancient prophecies; and did they not study divinity for three years at its very source? Since their day, he pointed out, knowledge had become far more generally diffused; and the priest should keep pace with the trend of modern thought in order to make himself an effective unit in the world around him. He insisted upon the poverty of the priesthood, citing Christ as the model.

In the parish schools he advised the clergy to see that, next to God, their country should hold the strongest place in the affections of the children. Familiar lessons should be incorporated in the text-books, inculcating reverence for American political institutions, and embodying a knowledge of the duties and rights of the citizen. The public reading in the school room, at intervals, of the Declaration of Independence and the Constitution he recommended as a profitable and instructive task. "The Ambassador of Christ," since its publication, has been used as a guide for the clergy throughout the English-speaking world.

The Cardinal warmly sympathized with the sufferers from the terrible Armenian massacres which were perpetrated in the closing decade of the nineteenth century. At a mass-meeting held in Baltimore, February 12, 1896, to protest against the outrages, he sat on the platform with a number of prominent Protestants, and spoke earnestly in favor of providing means for relief.

He was not insensible to the characteristic American sin of worry; and in a sermon at the Baltimore Cathedral, December 4, 1898, he preached on "Solicitude in Worldly Affairs." He ventured to say that there was scarcely a member of his congregation who was not agitated by some vain hope or fear. He warned them against deranging the order of Divine Providence by superadding to the cares of today the solicitudes of tomorrow, which are often imaginary, or magnified by the imagination.

The splendid ceremonies which marked the return of Admiral Dewey as a victor from the Philippines, in the autumn of 1899, took the form of a national ovation. The Cardinal pronounced the benediction at the presentation of a sword to

Dewey by President McKinley in behalf of Congress. This event took place in Washington, October 3, 1899, a few days after the triumphal reception of Dewey in New York.

The Cardinal did not fail to take note of the development of the woman suffrage movement in America, but could find in it nothing to commend. He uniformly insisted that the Christian home was the corner-stone of the nation, and in numerous addresses exalted the Christian mother. His ideas on this, like many other topics, were clear cut. In a sermon in the Cathedral, February 4, 1900, he said:

"I regard 'woman's rights' women as the worst enemies of the female sex. They rob woman of all that is amiable and gentle, tender and attractive; they rob her of her innate grace of character, and give her nothing in return but masculine boldness and brazen effrontery. They are habitually preaching about woman's rights and prerogatives, and have not a word to say about her duties and responsibilities. They withdraw her from those obligations which properly belong to her sex and fill her with ambition to usurp positions for which neither God nor nature ever intended her.

"Under the influence of such teachers, we find woman, especially in higher circles, neglecting her household duties, never at peace unless she is in perpetual motion or unless she is in a state of morbid excitement. She never feels at home unless she is abroad. When she is at home, the home is irksome to her. She chafes and frets under the restraints and responsibilities of domestic life. Her heart is abroad; it is exulting in imagination, in some social triumph or reveling in some scene of gayety and dissipation. Her afflicted husband comes home to find it empty or occupied by a woman whose heart is empty of affection for him. She is ill at ease. Hence arise disputes, quarrels, recriminations, estrangements, or the last act of the drama is often divorce! I speak with sober truth when I affirm that for the wrecks of families in our country woman has a large share of the responsibility.

CARDINAL GIBBONS, PRESIDENT McKINLEY AND ADMIRAL DEWEY AT PRESENTATION OF SWORD TO ADMIRAL

"Where will woman find the charter of her rights and dignity? In the Gospel. The Catholic Church, following the teachings of the Gospel and the Epistles of St. Paul, proclaims woman as the peer of man.

"Christian women, when your husbands and sons return to you in the evening after buffeting with the waves of the world, let them find in your homes a haven of rest. Do not pour into the bleeding wounds of the heart the gall of bitter words, but rather the oil of gladness and consolation."*

The Cardinal remained firmly opposed to confounding the Christian Sunday with the Jewish, or even the Puritan Sabbath. When a movement for stricter Sunday observance was started in Baltimore, early in 1900, he expressed his views vigorously. The Christian Sabbath, he said, prescribes the golden mean between rigid Sabbatarianism on the one hand, and lax indulgence on the other. Rigorously enforced laws would cause a revulsion of public feeling, "and the pendulum would oscillate to excessive laxity." Sunday he defined as a day for joy, and by no means of gloom.

"It is a day," he remarked, "when we are exhorted to be cheerful without dissipation, grave and religious without sadness or melancholy. We should remember that 'the Sabbath was made for man, and not man for the Sabbath;' that it is a day consecrated not only to religion, but also to relaxation of mind and body. My idea of the Lord's Day is expressed in these words of the Psalmist, 'This is the day which the Lord hath made; let us rejoice and be glad.' "

At the dedication of the Louisiana Purchase Exposition at St. Louis, April 30, 1903, he was invited to deliver the invocation, which he pronounced as follows, in the presence of a vast assemblage:

"We pray Thee, O God of might, wisdom and justice, through whom authority is rightly administered, laws are

---

* *Catholic Mirror*, Feb. 10, 1900.

enacted and judgment decreed, assist with Thy Holy Spirit of counsel and fortitude the President of these United States, that his administration may be conducted in righteousness and be eminently useful to thy people over whom he presides, by encouraging due respect for virtue and religion, by a faithful execution of the laws in justice and mercy and by restricting vice and immorality.

"We pray for the president and directors of the Louisiana Purchase Exposition, that their arduous labors may be crowned with success and may redound to the greater growth and development of this flourishing city on the banks of the Father of Waters.

"May this vast territory which was peacefully acquired a hundred years ago, be for all time to come the tranquil and happy abode of millions of enlightened, God-fearing, and industrious people, engaged in the various pursuits and avocations of life.

"As this new domain was added to our possessions without sanguinary strife, so may its soil never be stained by bloodshed in any foreign or domestic warfare.

"May this commemorative exposition, to which the family of nations are generously contributing their treasures of art and industry, bind together the governments of the earth in closer ties of fellowship and good-will, and of social and commercial intercourse.

"May it hasten the dawn of the reign of the Prince of Peace, when national conflicts will be adjusted, not by hostile armies, but by permanent courts of arbitration.

"May this international exhibition inaugurated in the interests of peace and commerce, help to break down the wall of dissension, of jealousy and prejudice that divides race from race, nation from nation, and people from people, by proclaiming aloud the sublime Gospel truth that we are all children of the same God, brothers and sisters of the same Lord Jesus

Christ, and that we are all aspiring to a glorious inheritance in the everlasting Kingdom of our common Father."*

On the day before the dedication he presided at a public debate on questions of theology at the Catholic University of St. Louis, which is directed by the Jesuit fathers. President Roosevelt sat beside him, and listened to the discourse.

The "sweatshop" evil having developed to extensive proportions in Baltimore, where the manufacture of clothing had become one of the principal industries, he took a prominent part in an agitation which resulted in laws that greatly restricted the evil. Preaching in the Cathedral December 6, 1903, he sharply condemned those who were responsible for the unsanitary conditions under which thousands of men and women were compelled to labor, and demanded remedial measures.

* Baltimore *Sun,* May 1, 1903.

CHAPTER XIX.

The Papal Conclave of 1903.

The prophecy of the flickering taper borne before Leo XIII when he was carried into St. Peter's for the first time in the *sedia gestatoria* must be fulfilled.* That soul which had aspired to link heaven and earth was immortal; but the mind which had glowed so long like a brilliant torch could not burn forever, and the worn body, almost transparent in its frailty, must yield in time to the weakness of the flesh. His eyes had beheld the rising sun of a new century; and it was beginning to set when, as often before, a whisper that the Pope had been taken ill passed around the Vatican.† This time it was pneumonia, "the friend of the aged." There was little hope from the first; but the world had become so accustomed to the marvels of Leo's vitality that it was prepared for anything.

Four months before, he had passed the twenty-fifth anniversary of his pontificate. When he was elected to succeed Pius IX, his age—68 years—had been the only argument used against him; but, though his predecessor's reign was the longest in the history of the papacy, he had not fallen far short of equaling it.‡

With the approach of the silver jubilee, Cardinal Gibbons wrote a letter in the name of himself and all the American bishops, congratulating the Pontiff upon the memorable anniversary.§ He enumerated three things as special proofs of Leo's interest in the Church in America. These were:

---

* When a pope is crowned, a priest bears in front of him a waxen taper, which is alternately lit and snuffed out, to indicate the temporary nature of life and earthly greatness.

† July 3, 1903.

‡ Pius IX reigned 32 years.

§ Letter of Cardinal Gibbons to Leo XIII, March 3, 1902.

The convoking of the Third Plenary Council.

His cordial commendation of the Catholic University, and continuous assistance in the development of that great project.

His special letter of congratulation on the centennial of the American hierarchy.

The Pope's reply reflected his joy at the growth of the Catholic faith in the United States. "After long experience of the fact," he wrote, "we are impelled to declare that, thanks to your influence, we have always found among your people that submissiveness of mind and responsiveness of will which become true children of the Church, and so, while the tendencies of nearly every nation that has for centuries professed the Catholic religion are a source of sorrow, the flourishing condition of your churches in the strength of their youth uplifts the soul and fills it with joy."

The Cardinal ordered a triduum, April 3, in honor of the jubilee.

Leo had reached the age of ninety-three years when his last illness fell on him. It was not long before his physicians and household saw that recovery was hopeless, and their efforts were directed toward prolonging his life by the artificial use of oxygen and other devices of medical science. When it appeared that death was inevitable, Cardinal Gibbons was promptly advised from Rome. No American up to that time had taken part in the election of a Pope. Cardinal McCloskey was a member of the Sacred College at the death of Pius IX, in 1878, and sailed for Rome to take part in the conclave; but he had proceeded only as far as Paris, when notified that a new pontiff had already been elected. Travel to Europe was quicker now, and Cardinal Gibbons was resolved that physical obstacles should not prevent his participation in this exalted function of his office.

For several days before the final message from Rome caused him to resolve to start, accommodations were secured for him provisionally on every steamship that sailed from New York. He was kept informed of the movements of vessels and other details regarding the prospects for his trip, until midnight on each of those days; and when he set foot on La Savoie, July 9, he found his apartments ready, despite the fact that the tide of European travel was then at its heaviest, and accommodations on fast ocean ships could usually be obtained only by waiting for months. So hurried was his departure from Baltimore that when he entered the room of Rev. P. C. Gavan, chancellor of the diocese, who was to accompany him as conclavist, to summon him to start, Father Gavan was compelled to leave a letter half-written on his desk. When he returned it was still there, but he had met abroad the one for whom it was intended.

Weeks passed, but still Leo lived. At last, all human resources failed, and on July 20 he expired.

Cardinal Gibbons was then in Paris. His presence in Rome was not immediately necessary, as custom prescribes that the conclave shall assemble on the tenth day after the death of the Pope. He spent several days in Lucerne, where United States Senator Elkins, of West Virginia, gave a dinner in his honor, and where he also met Senator Depew, of New York and the man who was to be Depew's successor, Justice O'Gorman. He arrived in Rome Sunday morning, July 26, and took up his quarters at the Procura of St. Sulpice, where there were also four French cardinals—Richard, of Paris; Perraud, of Autun; Lecot, of Bordeaux, and Coullie, of Lyons.

The conclave did not assemble until the following Friday evening. In the interim there were different services in the Sistine Chapel every morning, after which the cardinals gathered in the hall of the Vatican and attended to the business of the Church, as is their custom when the papacy is vacant. For the time being, they were all sovereigns, sharing equally in the decision of questions which came before them. The Camerlengo, Cardinal Oreglia, the only member of the conclave who had not been created by Leo, presided. The business to be transacted was read by Mgr. Merry del Val, secretary of the conclave, who was not then a cardinal, but was destined soon to succeed to that dignity and to the papal secretaryship of state.

About six o'clock Friday evening the electors entered the conclave and drew lots for the apartments in the Vatican which they were to occupy. The American Cardinal drew No. 5, and was given two rooms near the entrance to the beautiful staircase leading to the apartments lately occupied by Leo. These rooms had been used by a lay official of the Vatican. They were small and scantily furnished, each containing a desk, one chair, a bed and a washstand. One room was for the Cardinal himself; the other for his conclavist. Their meals were served by a domestic, who occupied quarters in another part of the building.

Leo himself had been camerlengo at the death of Pius IX. He had revised, to some extent, the elaborate regulations for the election of a pope, and had written the prescriptions carefully in a book, which was used for the first time in the choice of his own successor. These formalities are a historic inheritance, and have developed from the necessity of safeguarding the secrecy and fairness of an election. The cardinals are practically prisoners while in conclave. In some respects, they are in the position of an English or American jury locked up to deliberate upon a verdict, though infinitely more dignity and solemnity surround them and far greater precautions are taken to bring about the best decision.

It may be mentioned that after an interregnum of two years and nine months had followed the death of Clement IV, in 1269, the seventeen cardinals who were voting at Viterbo were shut up in the papal palace, with nothing to eat and drink but bread and water. In order to hasten the decision, Charles of Anjou went further and took off part of the palace roof;

but even after this, six months elapsed before they united in electing Gregory X.* The pontiff whose election had been thus protracted drew a lesson from experience, and decreed by an ordinance of 1274 that the electing cardinals should be subjected to a rigorous seclusion. Time has somewhat modified the severe discipline imposed by him and succeeding pontiffs in the Middle Ages; but the principles of seclusion and secrecy have been carefully preserved. At Rome, in 1903, a ballot was taken every morning. The master of ceremonies passed along the corridors where the electors were lodged, summoning them with the formula: *"In capellam, Domini"* (to the chapel, my lords). They proceeded to the beautiful Sistine Chapel, where they took the seats allotted to them, over each of which was a canopy, indicating the sovereign dignity which they possessed for the time being. The sub-dean celebrated low mass, and then the voting began.

Three cardinals (*scrutatores*) were chosen by lot each time to preside over the voting; three (*revisores*) to verify the count, and three (*infirmarii*) to collect the ballots of the sick. Each elector received a *schedula,* or voting paper. The ballots were folded thrice. On the top of the form were printed the words, *"Ego cardinalis,"* and there the elector wrote his name. On the middle were the words, *"Eligo in summum Pontificem Rm. Dm. meum D. Card."* (I elect for sovereign pontiff my most Reverend Lord Cardinal . . . .). The name of the candidate for whom the elector wished to vote was written here. At the bottom of the ballot, which was left empty, the elector inscribed a device, which was not infrequently a text of Scripture or a prayer. The top and bottom of the ballot were then folded together, the bottom being over the top, and were secured by a seal, which did not betray the elector's identity. Two designs were engraved on the reverse

---

* Slayden, The Secrets (Private Apartments) of the Vatican, p. 49 *et seq.* This book, the title of which is not meant to convey any invidious meaning, gives an accurate and sympathetic, as well as recent, account of the method of electing a pope.

side. The word "Nomen" was printed on the top one, meaning that under it on the obverse side would be found the name of the voter. The word "Signa" was on the lower, indicating that on the obverse would be found the voter's device. These designs prevented the paper from being read through.

On the altar stood a chalice, in which the cardinals, advancing, deposited their ballots, one by one, in due order. Each kneeling, pronounced in Latin these words: "I call Christ our Lord, Who will judge me, to witness that I elect the person who, before God, I think should be elected, and which I shall make good in the vote of accession."*

After a vote has been completed, the ballots are burned. If there has been no election, a little damp straw is strewn on the flames, which causes a thick column of smoke (*sfumata*) to arise from the chimney. By this means, the waiting crowd in the piazza of St. Peter's knows that the papacy is still vacant. After a pope is elected the ballots are burned without the straw.

At the outset of the balloting for the successor of Leo, Cardinal Rampolla developed the greatest strength; but an unexpected event on Sunday morning, August 2, after the third scrutiny, was the communication of the veto of Austria, by the Archbishop of Cracovia. The three great Catholic powers— Austria, France and Spain—had been allowed this right by custom rather than law, and had not infrequently sought to exercise it. Austria feared that the gifted Rampolla was too friendly to France. The difficulty which an aggressive papal secretary of state must find in obtaining the equal good-will of

---

* The vote of accession represents a second step, but by vote of the cardinals it was dispensed with in 1903. It is seldom that a candidate receives the required two-thirds majority on the first ballot. If no candidate has received two-thirds, and the vote of accession is to be taken, a second ballot begins immediately. Each of the electors now marks his vote with the same device and number as before; but in the middle part of the voting paper the words are altered to read, "*Accedo Reverendissimo D. meo D. Card.*" (I transfer my vote to my Lord Cardinal ————————.) If an elector wishes to vote as on the first ballot, he writes "*Nemini*" after this, meaning: "I do not wish to transfer my vote to anyone." If the votes of accession combined with those of the first ballot give any cardinal the requisite majority, a minute verification begins.

all the powers is apparent; and from the first it had been suspected that the career of Rampolla had been so prominent that his election as pontiff would be impossible.

On this scrutiny Rampolla received 29 votes; Sarto, 21, and Gotti, 9. The admirable attitude taken by the former secretary of state increased his vote to 30 on the next scrutiny, Sunday evening, while Sarto received 24 and Gotti received but 3. It seemed that the tide was turning to Sarto, the pious and simple-hearted patriarch of Venice, who beheld with anxiety—almost terror—the unexpected turn of affairs. So little had it entered into his thoughts that he might be chosen to the pontificate, that when he left his see to take part in the conclave, he had bought a return ticket. Seeing that the votes for him were increasing, he arose and, in earnest and pathetic manner, besought his colleagues not to consider him, insisting that the burden was too heavy for his shoulders, and that he wished to return to Venice. With tears in his eyes, he exclaimed: *"Electio mea esset ruina ecclesiæ"* (my election will be the ruin of the Church). His great humility deeply impressed all, but more votes were cast for him, and on Monday morning he received 27, while Rampolla fell to 24. Again he seemed positively frightened, and begged the cardinals not to think of him. With tears, he exclaimed: *"Obtestor vos ut nominis mei obliviscamini"* (I beseech you to forget my name). Cardinal Lecot having addressed a remark to him in French, he replied that he did not understand that language. With Gallic pride, Lecot responded: "You will never be pope if you do not speak French." *"Deo gratias"* (thanks be to God!), murmured Sarto fervently.

Such appeals could not be disregarded, and all the cardinals seemed to consider his election as out of the question. When Cardinal Gibbons questioned several of them, they took the view that Sarto could no longer be a candidate. Rampolla's election seemed impossible, and this threw the situation back to where it was before they entered the conclave.

After the meeting on Monday morning, Cardinal Satolli called on Cardinal Gibbons in his room, and they discussed the situation with grave concern. Satolli could see no available candidate. Cardinal Gibbons suggested to him that he talk with Sarto, his fellow-countryman, and implore him to lay aside his objections, urging upon him, as a duty, to submit to the will of Providence and sacrifice himself in the interest of religion. Satolli promised to undertake this mission. So well did he execute it that at their next meeting Satolli informed the American Cardinal that Cardinal Sarto had yielded to the plea and withdrawn his declination. Cardinal Gibbons requested Satolli to announce this to the conclave, when a joyful *"Annuit"* (he has consented) passed among the electors. Cardinal Satolli declared to the conclave that Sarto, yielding to the pressure of his colleagues, had resigned himself to Providence. On the ballot he received 35 votes, 7 less than the required number. His election soon followed.

Thus was the voice of an American, heard for the first time in a papal conclave, potent in bringing about its decision. It was in other respects a repetition, in part, of the conclave of 1878, when Cardinal Pecci, the future Leo XIII, had been on the point of pleading with the Sacred College not to elect him. O'Reilly relates that just before the voting began Pecci went to one of the most revered members of the Sacred College and said:

"I can not control myself. I must address the Sacred College. I fear that they are about to commit a sad mistake. People think I am a learned man. They credit me with possessing wisdom; but I am neither learned nor wise. They suppose I have the necessary qualifications for a pope; I have nothing of the kind. That is what I want to say to the cardinals."

The other cardinal replied: "As to your learning, we, not you, can best judge of that. As to your qualifications for the pontifical office, God knows what they are. Leave it all to Him." Cardinal Pecci obeyed.*

On Monday, when the election of Cardinal Sarto was assured, Cardinal Gibbons visited him in his room. They spoke of the heavy trials and responsibilities which the papacy would bring; but Cardinal Gibbons hastened to say that he thought the American Church would be a source of consolation in the midst of these burdens. Afterward the new Pope wrote to him that he had verified the truth of this prediction.

Again Cardinal Gibbons met the new Pope on the evening of the day of election, and obtained for some Americans the first public audience which Pius X gave. These pilgrims had started to Rome to see Leo XIII, and were obliged to leave the next day. When the Cardinal presented his request for an audience, the new Pontiff replied that he would grant it with pleasure "at any time you suggest." Cardinal Gibbons replied:

"I shall be glad if you will receive them, your Holiness, at any time which *you* may suggest."

"I will receive them tomorrow afternoon," replied Pius, and he kept his word.

The American Cardinal accompanied the pilgrims. When he went forward to kiss the Pope's hand, as is customary, Pius would not permit it; but, opening his arms, embraced him with warm affection and kissed him on both cheeks.

In another audience before his departure, Pius expressed deep interest in the United States. He lacked the almost encyclopædic knowledge of America which Leo had acquired, and asked many questions. He had met but few Americans; but those with whom he had come in contact impressed him favorably. For the American Cardinal he expressed his admiration and love. The Cardinal took advantage of the opportunity to interest Pius in the Catholic University, and to obtain from him a promise that he would issue a brief in aid

---

* O'Reilly, "Life of Leo XIII," p. 310.

of that project, so dear to the hearts of the American hierarchy. One of his first pontifical acts was to direct an exhibit of the Vatican treasures at the St. Louis Exposition.

After spending several days at Castle Gandolfo, the summer home of the American College, Cardinal Gibbons left Rome for Switzerland, where he remained ten days at Territet, on the Lake of Geneva, as the guest of Francis de Sales Jenkins, a member of a noted Catholic family of Maryland, identified with the State since the days of the Calverts. This beautiful home, which was called the "Villa Maryland," was near the Castle of Chillon, made famous by Byron; and there, amid congenial surroundings, the Cardinal was able to recuperate after the memorable experience through which he had passed. From Territet, he proceeded to Houlgate, Normandy, where he was the guest of Leopold Huffer for ten days, at the "Villa Columbia."

Sailing from Cherbourg, the Cardinal returned to Baltimore September 24, and found, as before, a great city full of people eager to acclaim him.* This time they regarded him with additional pride because of his participation in the conclave, and enthusiasm overflowed. In the waiting-room of the railroad station to receive him were Mayor McLane and other representatives of the civic authorities, while, outside, the crowds cheered a large delegation which had come from Washington, and otherwise vented their feelings in perfect good humor. Applause almost shook the building when the Cardinal stepped from his car. The Mayor greeted him in the following words:

"Your Eminence has already received a most hearty welcome, most properly extended to you on your arrival in this country by the members of the society in which you have shown so much interest, and to whose success you have contributed so much. It becomes my pleasant duty to extend to you a wider welcome, which embraces the citizens of Baltimore generally, of all creeds and conditions, who, one and all, cher-

---

* Baltimore *Sun*, Sept. 25, 1903.

ish the deepest reverence and respect for your great and noble character.

"When the news of the death of the late Pope reached us, it was received with a feeling of apprehension by us on account of the arduous strain of your great responsibilities in a trying climate, and we feared its influence upon your health, and the sympathies of the entire community went out to you. To see you return in good health is a great pleasure, and, in behalf of my fellow-citizens of Baltimore, I extend to you a most hearty welcome and the best wishes of the entire community for a long life of perfect happiness."

Judge Heuisler, a Catholic, spoke in the name of the members of his faith, when he said:

"It is true, your Eminence, and happy am I to say it, that all the people of America appreciate you, revere you, and love you for the work that you have done; and this greeting, while with us but local, will be heard with pleasure and with sympathy in all sections of our common country. In the presence of profound emotions, all hearts must speak from out the windows of the soul; the eye must flash the welcome and the lips be dumb; and I will say no more. A thousand million welcomes."

The Cardinal replied briefly and simply, saying that he would defer his response until he arrived at the Cathedral.

A great parade of societies, not a few of them in uniform, escorted him to that noble edifice. Every window along the route was crowded with people, who joined in the applause of the dense throngs on the streets. He was, in truth, a popular hero; and, after the American fashion, bowed continuously, smiling and acknowledging the numerous salutes from personal friends. In front of the Cathedral a group of young ladies, in white, fluttering little American flags, greeted him, and one of them presented him a bouquet of 69 roses, one for each year of his life. Seated on the portico of the Cathedral, with the Mayor beside him, he spent an hour reviewing the parade.

After the procession was over, the Cardinal entered the church, and spoke simply to his friends and neighbors. He told them of his travels; of some of his experiences in Rome; and did not fail to mention that the American pilgrims had been the first to be received by the new Pontiff.

"And now," he remarked simply, "I am most happy to be home again."

He commended Pius X to the prayers of all, and bestowed his blessing on the multitude.   Solemn benediction followed. Proceeding to his residence, he found another cheering crowd, and was obliged to appear at his window repeatedly and express his thanks.

Following what had long been his custom after returning from a trip abroad, he preached at the Cathedral Sunday, October 4, on his experiences.   A great congregation, including many Protestants, was present, and the service was conducted with the air of piety and majesty characteristic of those held within its walls.   The Cardinal spoke of the nations represented by the 62 electors who had taken part in the conclave, and added:

"I should not be surprised if in the next conclave the Catholic Church of the United States were to be represented by several members of the Sacred College, so that the number of cardinals from our country may be commensurate with the population, the grandeur and the commanding influence of the nation, and may be in keeping also with the numerical strength of our hierarchy and laity and the splendor and progress of our religious and charitable institutions.   Without revealing its secrets, I can most positively assure you and the American people that the election of the Pope was conducted with absolute freedom, with the utmost fairness and impartiality, and with a dignity and solemnity becoming the august assemblage of the Sacred College and the momentous consequences of their suffrages. * * * On leaving the Sistine Chapel at the conclusion of the conclave, and contemplating the overruling action of the Holy Ghost in those heterogeneous elements, I exclaimed: 'The finger of God is here.'

"Two ballots were cast each day in the conclave, one in the forenoon and another in the afternoon. The votes for Cardinal Sarto steadily increased from the first to the seventh ballot, on which he was elected. When the Cardinal observed that the suffrages for him were augmenting, he was visibly disturbed, and in a fervent speech he implored his colleagues not to regard him as a candidate. Contrary to his wishes, the votes for him increased. He then became alarmed, and in a second speech, in most pathetic language, he again besought the cardinals to forget his name, as he would not accept a burden too heavy for him to bear. All were moved by the modesty and the transparent sincerity of the man. When he resumed his seat, his cheeks were suffused with blushes, tears were gushing from his eyes, and his body trembled with emotion. It was only after some of the leading cardinals entreated him to withdraw his opposition, that he finally and reluctantly consented to abide by the will of God and accept the sacrifice. Never did a prisoner make greater efforts to escape from his confinement than did Cardinal Sarto to escape from the yoke of the papacy. With his Divine Master, he exclaimed: 'Father, if it be possible, let this chalice pass from me. Nevertheless, not my will, but Thine be done!' When his election was officially announced, his florid countenance assumed a deathly pallor and restoratives were applied to save him from fainting."*

The Cardinal characterized the new Pontiff as "a man of God and a man of the people."

The promised brief on the Catholic University, in the support of which all elements in the Church in America were again united, was dated September 9, 1903. It was addressed

---

* Baltimore *Sun*, Oct. 5, 1903.

to Cardinal Gibbons as chancellor of the institution. The Pontiff gave his hearty sanction to the proposal that a collection be taken up in all the churches throughout the United States annually for ten years, on the first Sunday in Advent, or the first convenient Sunday thereafter, "with a view of enhancing the dignity and enlarging the influence of this noble seat of learning." He declared it to be his earnest wish that the bishops and laity should "labor strenuously for the good of the university."

The Cardinal paid another visit to Rome in 1908, when he went to London to attend the International Eucharistic Congress there, at which he was invited to preach. Sailing from New York July 18, he arrived in the Eternal City on the 30th, and took up his quarters at the Procura of St. Sulpice. He was greeted later by 200 Americans, who happened to be there on a pilgrimage.

Pius X received him in audience August 1, and for a while they discussed the general conditions of the American Church. He found the viewpoint of Pius was still that of the ecclesiastic rather than the diplomat, in contrast to Leo, with whom he had weathered so many storms. The Pontiff sighed for Venice, which he felt that he was never more to see. He had not been unmindful of the progress of the Church in America, and he conveyed to Cardinal Gibbons his compliments and warm appreciation.

The Cardinal visited a number of the high dignitaries of the Church, and received many callers. He was a guest for a short time at the summer home of the American College, where he was taken ill with a serious ailment incident to the climate, and it was necessary to remove him to Rome for treatment. The Pope sent his sympathy, and asked to be constantly informed of his condition. In a short time he fully recovered; and after a rest in Switzerland, where he was the guest of Benziger, the artist, at Brunnen, on Lake Lucerne, he was able to proceed to London, where he preached in Westminster Cathedral on the last day of the congress, September 13, 1908.

His sermon sounded a note of unity between English and American Catholics. "We across the Atlantic claim, as well as you," he said, "to be the spiritual children of Gregory, of Augustine, Patrick, Alban, the venerable Bede, of Anselm and Thomas of Canterbury, of Peter and Pius." He recalled that his own State of Maryland had been founded by English Catholics, and that Carroll had been consecrated in Lulworth Castle.

In the procession on that day it had been intended to carry the Host in the streets; but, fearing disturbances, Premier Asquith interposed, and the program was changed. In the main, the congress was a notable success; but the Cardinal could not help noting the difference between the attitude toward the Church in his own country and that taken even in so enlightened a nation as England. He was among the guests of honor at a garden party given by the Duke of Norfolk, the principal Catholic nobleman of England.

When he heard that Baltimore was planning another reception on his return, he hoped to prevent it, and wrote home an earnest request that the plans be abandoned; but so great was the popular desire to testify the almost unique esteem in which he was held by his neighbors of all religious faiths that, despite his own desires, preparations moved forward with redoubled energy. He arrived in Baltimore Saturday, October 10, and at the depot found himself face to face with a reception committee, which included Governor Crothers and his staff, Mayor Mahool and the City Councilmen, Charles J. Bonaparte, then Attorney-General of the United States, and other prominent persons.

The Governor, a Methodist, and the Mayor, an active layman of the Presbyterian Church, welcomed him with laudatory speeches. "I am profoundly moved by this expression of kindness," he replied; "I have no words to convey the deep gratitude that fills my heart. When I learned for the first time of this, I wrote back to Baltimore, requesting and directing that it be abandoned, as I saw no occasion for it; but when I learned that it came from all the people, and that the Governor of this liberty-loving State was to take part in it, and the Mayor of this city, which I love so dearly, I waived all personal feelings."*

He was escorted to the Cathedral by a parade in which 15,000 persons took part, including 500 from Washington. On the portico of the beautiful old building, he stood with the executive officers of the State and city and reviewed this notable procession, which required nearly an hour to pass. Within the edifice, he gave solemn benediction and the papal blessing.

Though a national figure, he had so endeared himself to the people of the localities where his labors had been chiefly performed that they could not restrain their desire to testify to the honor in which they held him. The North Carolina Society of Baltimore, composed of former residents of the State in which he had worked so faithfully as vicar apostolic, presented him an engrossed address, conveying warm compliments and grateful praise.

---

* Baltimore *Sun*, Oct. 11, 1908.

CHAPTER XX.

CENTENARY OF THE BALTIMORE CATHEDRAL.

A great demonstration might have been held in the Cardinal's honor, October 3, 1902, the twenty-fifth anniversary of his accession to the archbishopric; but, at his desire, observance of the event was postponed to the spring of 1906, in order that the centenary of the laying of the Cathedral corner-stone might be celebrated at the same time. When this date drew near, it was found that he had carefully eliminated his own personality from the program.

Although he had reached the age of 71, he entered with characteristic intensity of energy and fertility of ideas into the organization of a new demonstration of Catholic progress. He contrived that the event should assume a wider scope than a purely ecclesiastical ceremony, and one of the forms it took was a condemnation of the rising cult of socialism by the Church in America. While he lost few opportunities to praise the institutions of his country and to express faith in its people, he was constantly warring against some national evil or denouncing some wrong which might threaten the political or social structure of the United States. Socialism was now arising as a stronger force in America. It had made great progress in Germany, where the Emperor and most of the confederated states of the Empire had enacted into law not a few of its principles. It had won converts by the tens of thousands in France, where it had a strong and aggressive representation in the Cabinet and the Chamber of Deputies. Wherever men were discontented, its adherents multiplied.

When labor had struggled for the right of combination, and for legislation protecting its just interests, Cardinal Gibbons had been its friend and champion; but in socialism he could see only danger to those who were most allured by the remedies it proposed.   In the United States, the party had presented a few Presidential candidates, whose support had been relatively insignificant.   Among the Germans of the Northwest, it was growing rapidly, and in Milwaukee, where the German population was large, it was soon afterward* able to elect a Mayor.

Preaching in the Baltimore Cathedral, February 4, 1906, the Cardinal declared his own position and that of the Church with clearness and force.   He began by saying that he had been deeply impressed in studying the material world to observe that all the works of God were marked with the stamp of variety and inequality.   The Almighty never casts any two creatures in the same mold.   "Ascending from the natural to the spiritual world, from the order of nature to the order of grace," he said, "we know there is not only variety, but that there are also grades of distinction among the angels in heaven. The angelic hierarchy is composed of nine distinct choirs. There are angels and archangels, thrones and dominations, principalities and powers, virtues, cherubim and seraphim. These angelic hosts ascend in rank, one above the other.   One order of angels excels in sublimity of intelligence, or in intensity of love, or in the dignity of the mission assigned to them.

"And, in like manner, God is unequal in the distribution of his graces to mankind.   He gives in large measure to one and in less measure to another.   To one He grants five talents, to another He grants two, and to another He gives one talent. When the Divine Husbandman hires his laborers to work in His vineyard, He recompenses those who labored but one hour as much as He does those 'who have borne the burden of the day and the heat.'   The reward is altogether dis-

* 1910.

proportioned to the toil.   If you complain of God's discrimination, Christ will answer you: 'My friend, I do thee no wrong.   Take what is thine and go thy way.   Is it not lawful for me to do what I will?   Is thine eye evil because I am good?   What claim have you on my justice?   Is not all that you possess of nature or of grace the gratuitous gift of my bounty?'   *   *   *   Nevertheless, among God's elect there is no jealousy or discontent.   Those who enjoy a high grade of bliss, do not look with disdain on their inferiors; and those who are in a lower grade of felicity do not envy those above them. All are happy and contented, and praise the God of bounty for his gratuitous mercies."

The Cardinal went on to say that it was inevitable there should be inequality of rank and station and wealth.   The much-discussed statement in the Declaration of Independence— "All men are created equal"—he interpreted to mean that all men are subject to the same political and moral laws; that all enjoy the same air and rain and sunshine of heaven, and that all are equal before the law.   He added:

"The most mischievous and dangerous individual to be met with in the community is the demagogue, who is habitually sowing broadcast the seeds of discontent among the people. He is disseminating the baneful doctrine of socialism, which would bring all men down to a dead level, would paralyze industry and destroy all healthy competition.   *   *   *   He has not the capacity to discern that, after all due allowance is made for human energy, this varied condition of society must result from a law of life established by an overruling Providence."*

The heart of every American Catholic swells when he thinks of the old Cathedral, where the services in honor of the centenary were held.   How much more did it mean to Cardinal Gibbons, who was almost as much a part of it as its beautiful altar rail and its majestic pillars!   "What Mecca is to the Mohammedan," he once said, "what the temple of Jerusalem

---

* Baltimore *Sun*, February 5, 1906.

is to the Jew, what St. Peter's basilica in Rome is to the faithful of the Church universal, this Cathedral is to the American Catholic."

Pius X shared the pride in the coming event, and addressed the following letter to the cardinal :*

"To our Beloved Son, James Gibbons,

"*Archbishop of Baltimore, Cardinal Priest of the Title of St. Mary,*

"*across the Tiber. Pius P. P. X.*

"Beloved son, health and apostolic benediction.

"When the first archbishop of Baltimore, 100 years ago, laid the corner-stone of the Cathedral, he laid, we may truly say, the foundation upon which the Church of America was to rise to its full and glorious height. For, whether we consider the ever increasing number of priests ordained within its walls, the bishops there consecrated, the national councils there celebrated or the various magnificent solemnities or ecclesiastical functions which it has witnessed, all have happily found, as it were, their home in the Cathedral of Baltimore.

"Happily, we say, and ever with the promise of better things, as is proven by the extension of the hierarchy; by the growth of the Catholic population; by the peaceful state of religion, your steadfast union with the See of Rome and by the manifold consolations which our heart has gathered from your achievements. Hence, we deem it worthy of our highest approval that you propose to commemorate with general rejoicing so signal an event. We need not tell you with what sentiments of good will and of heartfelt interest we share in this celebration. You are all aware that we have always most ardently adopted and are now equally eager to adopt whatsoever may avail to enhance the honor of our religion among the American people.

"Our eagerness herein is the greater because we are sure that you will respond, with common accord and endeavor, to the invitations which we, prompted by the memory of what you have accomplished for religion, extend to you on this timely and joyous occasion in urging the American people to still greater efforts in behalf of our Catholic faith. This exhortation we repeat in all earnestness, knowing full well that our words must aim not only at advancing the cause of religion, but also at furthering the public weal. Intent, therefore, as you now are, upon extolling the sacred memories of your forefathers, and setting forth the glories of your faith, we offer you our sincere congratulations and bestow upon you the praise that you fully deserve, both by your zeal in organizing this public celebration and by the habitual attitude

---

* Cathedral Archives.

of mind therein displayed. You manifest, indeed, a temper that we ardently desire to see cultivated by all Catholics—a temper, namely, which holds within itself strong and full of promise the hope of the future.

"Right joyously, then, we express our wishes for the prosperity of your churches and the success of this centenary observance. At the same time, as a pledge of heavenly graces and a token of our deep affection, we impart most lovingly our apostolic benediction to you, the bishops, the clergy and the whole American people.

"Given at St. Peter's, Rome, on the second day of March, 1906, in the third year of our pontificate.

"Pius P. P. X."

The main celebration took place Sunday, April 29, and was marked by one of the most remarkable assemblages of Catholic prelates that had taken place in modern times, outside of Rome itself. Archbishop Falconio, who had succeeded Martinelli as Papal Delegate; nine other archbishops, fifty-six bishops, four abbots and about eight hundred priests assembled at the fountain head of the mother see. Pontifical mass was celebrated by Archbishop Farley, of New York, and Archbishop Ryan preached, as he had done at so many ecclesiastical ceremonies of the first rank in America.

Only a short time before, President Roosevelt had made his "muck-rake" speech, in which, while denouncing excessive criticism of public or semi-public men, he had suggested an inheritance tax as a means of restricting the piling up of enormous fortunes by private individuals. A few days later Mr. Taft, then Secretary of War, had spoken in the same strain, and a similar note sounded in the sermon of Mgr. Ryan. The eloquent preacher pointed out that there were great evils to be corrected. "We justly laud," he said, "the institutions and spirit of our country, but indiscriminate praise is no evidence of genuine rational patriotism. On the contrary, it is often dangerous and holds out false security. * * * Marvelous as has been our progress in a single century, there is the greater need to preserve what we have gained and to correct where we have been deficient. Some have stated, and with a show of reason, that our leading, radical fault has been, and is, love of money, amounting to national avarice, and our eagerness in both the natural and religious order should be directed to neutralize or, at least, to moderate this tendency.

"But I can not believe that love of money is the predominant fault of the American people. They are too noble and generous a people to be a nation of misers. They freely give what they freely get, and are often prodigal in their generosity. No, I believe that ambition, pride and inordinate independence and self-reliance are our most dangerous foes. Humility is becoming a name for pious weakness, and ambition is no longer a sin. The desire to be unknown is considered foolishness. * * *

"There are three great and increasing evils in our day— one affecting the individual; the second, the family, and the third, the state. I mean suicide, divorce and communism, leading to anarchy."

After the mass, the Cardinal made a brief address on the significance of the growth and progress of the Catholic faith. He thanked the prelates for their attendance, and expressed the joy they felt at the position the Church had attained after more than a century of struggle.

Archbishop Messmer, of Milwaukee, celebrated pontifical vespers, and Archbishop Glennon, the gifted head of the Archdiocese of St. Louis, preached. He dwelt even more strongly upon the Church's attitude toward socialism, which he had a better opportunity to observe in his Western province.

"The social fabric," he said, "appears today to be in imminent danger, because old principles are ignored and old foundations are attacked. What was held as law, is regarded now as injustice; what was held as government, is now deemed tyranny. It were folly to deny that the shadow of socialism is hanging over the land, and, while learned men are busy pointing out its unreasonableness, its injustice, its lack of feasibility, the shadow deepens. And yet we fear not. The Church has a message for these coming years. Standing by that cross, the

Church would teach an equality that mere forms of poverty and wealth could not affect."

The usual dinner at St. Mary's, characteristic of ecclesiastical ceremonies in Baltimore, followed. Cardinal Gibbons, as toastmaster, called first on the Papal Delegate, who spoke of the Pontiff's gratification at the extraordinary progress of the Church in America, where there were now 105 archbishops and bishops, 92 dioceses, and a Catholic population of more than 12,000,000, although a century before there was but one bishop. The Papal Delegate said he felt proud in offering best wishes and congratulations to Cardinal Gibbons, and expressed the hope that he might long be spared to carry on his work.

The next evening, Monday, there was a reception to the hierarchy by Cardinal Gibbons and the clergy of the archdiocese at the Lyric, one of the largest public halls in the State. Governor Warfield and Mayor Timanus were there, and joined heartily in the exercises. The principal address was made by Bishop Donahue, of Wheeling, who had spent years in the Cardinal's household, and who spoke from intimate acquaintance when he said:

"His life and achievements have shed undying luster on the Church for all time. He is a prince of the Church; he is also one of the plainest and most democratic citizens of the land. His mind can rise to and grasp momentous questions of Church and state, yet with children he can be a child in playfulness and glee. With the wise, he is wise; with the simple, simple; simple in his tastes and habits of life, simple in demeanor, and a friend to the poor and helpless. I doubt if ever churchman trod the soil of America who has endeared himself to more hearts."

CHAPTER XXI.

SYMPATHY WITH FRENCH CATHOLICS.

While the American Catholics were aggressively pursuing their mission, pausing now and then to take note of the Church's advancement, upholding the institutions of the country in one breath and condemning in another influences antagonistic to religion and social peace, the "eldest daughter of the Church" was passing through a period of bitter trial. They could not, as churchmen, forget the ardent and fruitful help of France any more than, as citizens, they could forget Lafayette and Rochambeau. In the early days the Jesuits from the banks of the Seine and the Loire had carried the cross up and down the New World, and as civilization followed savagery, and the cross, no longer a wanderer, pointed to heaven from the tops of thousands of churches, Cheverus and Flaget and Dubois and Dubourg, and many others, as bishops or clergy, had helped to lay the foundations of religion in the youthful nation. Now the Church of France was in tears—spurned by the Government of which she had been a partner, and despoiled at the point of the bayonet. The passage of the "Law of Associations" and subsequent agitation and legislation, ending in the rupture of the Concordat, had excited deep feelings on the part of Catholics in the United States.

At the spring meeting of the archbishops, held at the Catholic University a short time before the celebration of the centenary, they had decided to address a letter to the French Catholics, and requested Cardinal Gibbons to prepare it. He drew it up while the great assemblage of prelates was in Baltimore, and sent it to Cardinal Richard, Archbishop of Paris, as the principal representative of the Church in France.

"We would profit," he wrote, "by the presence of so many distinguished prelates to offer to our brethren in France, not so happily circumstanced as we, an unequivocal testimony of our sympathy and our sincere wishes for the welfare of the Church of France. * * * We are compelled to assure you of the keen regret which we feel at sight of the bitter persecution to which the Church of France is subjected—a persecution which, particularly during the last quarter of a century, has been marked by exceptional and vexatious legislation. To crown these irritating enactments, the agreement which for a century bound the eldest daughter of the Church to Rome, has been, contrary to all the requirements of justice and honor, ruthlessly dissolved. The bloody conflicts immediately consequent upon the first application of this notorious law sanctioning the separation of Church and state, so recently and peremptorily condemned by Pius X, do but forecast disturbances of a more serious character. However, such misfortunes are bound to enlist in your behalf the sympathy and prayers of all true children of the Church. * * *

"It is difficult for minds accustomed to the complete liberty which we enjoy in this country to understand how a civilized government can, in the name of liberty, subject an entire Christian people to the yoke of official atheism. Here, on the contrary, our rulers recognize that religion is necessary for the prosperity of the nation. While they arrogate to themselves no authority in religious matters, thanks to the kindly feeling which animates them, vexed questions are amicably settled. To illustrate by a single example, far from enacting legislation hostile to the Church, disputes involving ecclesiastical property are decided by the civil courts, in conformity with her recognized laws. If the Church has the right of protection because she is the truth, her progress requires only liberty worthy of the name. This we have fully and completely. We sincerely hope the Church of France may soon enjoy the same advantage."*

Cardinal Richard expressed his gratitude in a formal reply, bewailing the woes of his country and expressing his reliance on God for a happy issue from their afflictions.

The struggle proceeded. The elements in control of the French Government were bent on the execution of their program, and the wishes of American Catholics were of no more avail than of those in Europe. In a public statement,† Cardinal Gibbons called attention forcibly to some of the excesses which were being committed. He declared that hatred of religion, rather than love of the republic, actuated the French Anti-Clericals.

"In France," he said, "the Jacobin party is not dead. Its spirit is as live today as it was in the last decade of the eighteenth century. Its adherents hate God; they hate Christ; they hate His religion as much as ever their fathers hated them."

He quoted M. Briand, Minister of Public Worship and afterward Premier, who said in an address to teachers:

"The time has come to root up from the minds of French children the ancient faith, which has served its purpose, and replace it with the light of free thought. It is time to get rid of the Christian idea. We have hunted Jesus Christ out of the army, the navy, the schools, the hospitals, the asylums for the insane and orphans, and the law courts, and now we must hunt Him out of the state altogether."

"What," asked the Cardinal, "would we Americans say if a Cabinet officer were to propose this as the great aim of his administration?"

He pointed out the contrast between the attitude of the French Government toward Church property rights and that of the courts of the United States in the Philippines, where the

---

* Cathedral Archives.
† Baltimore *Sun,* Dec. 14, 1906.

legal claims of the Church had been fully respected and a settlement effected to the satisfaction of both parties.

The Pope sent to the Cardinal an expression of his great satisfaction with the strong presentation of the case. The ardor of even the French Cabinet was somewhat cooled by this dignified declaration. Premier Clemenceau felt its vigor to such an extent that he took occasion to declare that M. Briand had not delivered the statement attributed to him "as minister," although not denying that the statement had been made. Cardinal Gibbons promptly cited his authority in the London *Saturday Review,** and saw no occasion to modify anything he had said. His declaration led to many public protests in this country, the effects of which were felt in Europe.

* *Review,* August 18 and 25, 1906.

CHAPTER XXII.

Events of Later Years.

On the morning of February 7, 1904, Cardinal Gibbons, before preaching his customary sermon in the Cathedral on the first Sunday in the month, had noticed dense smoke moving from southwest to northeast in the business district of Baltimore, but saw nothing to indicate that it proceeded from more than an ordinary fire. The topic he had chosen for his discourse was "The Uses of Adversity." He enumerated some of the reverses of fortune to which human beings are subject, such as a fall from opulence to poverty, and a sudden visitation of Providence.

As he left the church after service, he found the streets thronged with excited people and resounding with the clang of fire engines. A great blaze was rising in fury from some of the most costly warehouses in the city, and the fact flashed upon him that while he had been performing his ministrations in the temple, the fire he had observed several hours before must have been spreading with amazing violence. Large embers began to fall on the Cathedral grounds, and an ash tree in the yard, naked of foliage in the winter wind, caught fire.

All that day and the next the conflagration raged, causing a loss estimated at $125,000,000, and visiting upon the Cardinal's beloved Baltimore one of the most appalling blows which an American city ever sustained. It reached within two squares of his residence, and would have swept away both it and the Cathedral, had not the wind changed the pathway of destruction eastward instead of northward.

He had arranged to start for New Orleans on a visit to his brother Sunday evening, and his train was one of the last to leave before railroad communication was suspended by the calamity. The Cardinal did not realize the full extent of the disaster until he reached New Orleans, when he was informed of it by telegraph. The treasured archives of the diocese, from Carroll's time down, were stored in his residence, and would have been destroyed, had the flames reached the house. His predecessors had been content to leave them in loose heaps or in barrels, but he had taken pains to have them carefully sorted out and indexed in a manner worthy of their value. The lesson of the great fire was not forgotten; and, by his direction, the archives were removed to a space beneath the Cathedral, where they would be comparatively safe from a similar disaster in future.

With the struggle of his neighbors upward from the ruins of their prosperity, he sympathized keenly. Not a few members of the Cathedral congregation were among those most sorely stricken, and he warmly commended them for the courageous spirit in which they met their affliction. Prominent Catholics were among the leaders in averting panic, restoring the normal operations of business and starting the community on an ambitious program of civic improvement which was characteristic of American spirit.

In a sermon, February 5, 1905, when hundreds of churches in the city rang with thanksgiving for the marvelous progress made in the year following the fire, he praised the fortitude of the people. When fears were entertained for the passage of a municipal loan of $10,000,000 to begin the construction of a sewerage system, he wrote a letter of commendation to the committee which was conducting a popular campaign in its favor, and its adoption soon followed.

His life was not in danger at any time from the great fire; but it was seriously imperiled by a driving accident in Druid Hill Park, Baltimore, July 30, 1891. It was often said of him that he was the only archbishop in the world who kept no private livery. When he was elevated to the cardinalate, the clergy of the diocese presented to him a two-seated brougham, which he kept at the public stable of James Martin, near his residence. If occasion required a drive, he used horses hired from Martin. He much preferred walking in winter and in the bracing days of spring and autumn; but in summer he sometimes took the air in the park, with Martin on the box of his carriage. On this occasion Martin was driving homeward, when the pole of the brougham broke and the horses began a mad flight. The driver was able to keep them in the road, but could not check them. After they had gone fully three-quarters of a mile, they approached a large stone gateway, which then stood at the Mount Royal entrance to the park, and Martin ran them against it, stopping their flight and severely injuring them by the impact. The Cardinal, who had remained calm, though he fully realized how narrow was his escape, alighted unhurt, and was taken to his residence in a passing carriage.

As a mark of his gratitude, he presented to Martin one of two large gold medals which he had received from Leo XIII, bearing on one side a bas-relief portrait of the Pontiff, and on the other an interior view of the basilica of St. Peter's in Rome. He had these words engraved on the medal, in addition to the previous inscription: "Presented to James Martin, Jr., by his Eminence, Cardinal Gibbons, August 1, 1891, as a recognition of his courage and self-possession displayed July 30, 1891."

For many years Martin continued to drive him, and he always felt safe in the hands of this intrepid and devoted man.

A man whose labors were so incessant and arduous must have at least brief intervals of rest. The Sisters of Notre Dame College, in a suburb of Baltimore, kept a room always ready, to which the Cardinal used sometimes to retire for a day or two, to enjoy the refreshment of an invigorating atmosphere and a view of rolling lawns and lofty trees.

The ideal rural homes of T. Herbert Shriver and B. Frank Shriver, brothers, seven miles from Westminster, Md., also became favorite places of retreat for him. He is sometimes the guest of one of these a week or more at a time, obtaining complete relief from the burdens which weigh upon him so heavily in Baltimore. The life of these families is of a type which is seen in Maryland at its best—that of the American Catholic country gentlefolk. Its original was the rural gentry of England, unanimously Catholic until the time of Henry VIII, and in no small part adhering to the same faith through all the periods of persecution which followed. Of this stock were the Calverts, the founders of Maryland. Their charter, granted by Charles I, gave them power to create titles of nobility and to authorize baronial courts,* as in the English palatine county of Durham. They themselves were rural barons, and in the earlier stages of their project they looked to a reproduction of their own social life in the colony which they planted. The unexpectedly independent course of the early assemblies at St. Mary's interfered with a full realization of this project; but it was true that, despite the violence of the Cromwellian period and the grievous discriminations which followed the accession of William III, Maryland was the only colony in English-speaking America in which wealthy Catholics founded large estates.† These estates were most numerous in Southern Maryland, in the region adjacent to St. Mary's, where many of them still exist. The Catholic planter lived in the midst of his numerous acres, cultivated by negroes, and was no less a spiritual than a material mentor of his dependents. Not infrequently he had his own chapel, where mass was regularly celebrated.

The blacks were instructed and trained in the practices of the Catholic faith, whose ministrations contributed to securing good treatment for them and making them contented with their lot. It was a common saying that a "Catholic negro is a good negro." The confession and penances, as well as the

---

* Charter of Maryland, Clause 19, Scharf, Vol. I, pp. 58, 59.
† Burton, Life and Times of Bishop Challoner, Vol. II, pp. 128, 130.

sacred character which they willingly acknowledged in the priesthood, exercised a powerful and salutary restraining influence upon their elemental impulses.   While the Church in no sense sympathized with slavery as an institution, submission to constituted authority was taught to the negro, and the responsibility of exercising authority with mildness and justice was impressed on the master.

At the rural churches, where high mass was celebrated on certain Sundays, it was a picturesque sight to see the cavalcade of gentry assemble for the general interchange of social amenities, as well as public worship.   The emancipation of the slaves did not greatly change social conditions, though it reduced the affluence of the masters.   The home of the Catholic landowner continued to have for the dependents in the community much the same aspect as before.

The pious family life of the Shrivers has been an inspiration to the cardinal, and the attentions which they bestow on him make him always at ease when he is their guest.   Of simple and unostentatious habits himself, and possessing a pronounced social instinct, he likes to feel at home in such a circle.   There is a small chapel at the home of T. Herbert Shriver, where the cardinal says mass every morning when he is there.   He writes much, staying in his room a great deal, but takes walks and always his after-dinner nap, besides pitching quoits occasionally.   He excels at this latter sport, being considered one of the best players in Maryland.   Sometimes he goes to Westminster by train, but not infrequently his host carries him there in an automobile, of which he is undeniably fond, though his habit of rigidly restricting his personal expenses prevents him from owning one for his private use.

For a number of years one of his favorite resorts for a brief rest in summer was Southampton, Long Island, where he was the guest of clerical friends.   It is a beautiful seaside town, and his presence there usually attracted a number of visitors from New York and Brooklyn, who attended mass in the local church when the Cardinal was present. There were pleasant walks and drives near by, and the Cardinal found the air peculiarly conducive to rest and sleep.

Once a year, just before the beginning of Lent, he has been accustomed to spend a week in New Orleans with his family. When the centenary anniversary of that see, the second in the United States, was observed, in 1893, he took a prominent part in the exercises. The Archbishop of New Orleans at that time was Most Rev. Francis Jannsens, his former vicar-general in Richmond. These pleasant excursions to his former home serve to prepare him for the rigors which he habitually practices during the penitential season.

The exalted character of his office has caused him to be regarded with awe at not a few places which he has visited. A story is told of one of his episcopal trips, in the course of which he took breakfast at the home of one of the principal residents, who may be called Mr. Jones. Neither host nor hostess appeared at the table, and when he inquired where they were, the butler reluctantly acknowledged that they were too diffident to eat in the presence of a cardinal. The eminent guest sent his companion, who may be designated as Mr. Brown, to make inquiries.

"What," exclaimed the host, "take breakfast with the Cardinal? No, sir! I wouldn't know what to do nor what to say. No, sir! I couldn't eat a mouthful. I wouldn't know whether I was standing on my head or my heels. No, sir!"

The host was told that the Cardinal was one of the gentlest and most unassuming of men; that he had been complimenting the cooking, and that it was rude to refuse to eat with him. The only answer was, "No, sir!"

"You don't mind me," said Mr. Brown; "why would you be embarrassed by the Cardinal?"

"Well, Mr. Brown," he replied, "you're only an editor, and I'm used to editors; but there's only one cardinal in this country, and I wouldn't know how to act in his company. No, sir!"

"Well, perhaps Mrs. Jones might like to"——

"No, sir, Mrs. Jones wouldn't. She's just as upset as I am."

"What shall I tell his Eminence?"

"Make my excuses; tell him I feel honored at having him as my guest; beg him to make himself at home, and thank him for inviting me to sit at the table with him; but tell him I couldn't do it. No, sir!"

When Mr. Brown related what had happened, the Cardinal was distressed at his host's unnecessary agitation, but made the best of the situation.

After breakfast, a church was dedicated, and the Cardinal held an informal reception. The local pastor took him back to dinner at Mr. Jones'. The meal was on the table, smoking hot, but neither host nor hostess appeared. After the butler had served dinner, Mr. Brown remembered that the Cardinal was in the habit of taking a nap at that time of day, and went to hunt Mr. Jones. The host was found marching up and down on the far side of the garden. Mr. Brown thanked him for a very good dinner, and then said:

"Mr. Jones, the Cardinal would like to take a nap."

"Oh! I have no bed good enough for a cardinal, Mr. Brown."

"The bed I occupied last night would do tip-top."

"Would it, Mr. Brown? Well, how shall we get him up there?"

"You go up with him and show him the way."

"Me? No, sir! I wouldn't do that."

"Well, go and see if the bed has been made up; then come down and tell me, and I'll show him the way."

"Oh! yes, I'll do that gladly, Mr. Brown."

The host ascended to the bedroom and came down to report that the room was in perfect order. Then he darted out the back door and into the garden again, as if an ogre were after him.

The Cardinal had his nap. As he left the house in the afternoon, there was no one to bid him good-by, the whole family being evidently in hiding.

This was an extreme instance, but experiences not greatly different have been far from uncommon to the cardinal. On one occasion a husband and wife, the latter carrying a baby, applied at his residence for the privilege of making confession to a priest. The porter informed them that the priests were resting, but one of them would be downstairs in a short time. The man persisted, saying that he lived in the suburbs, must return home before it grew late, and could not delay. When the porter returned from another trip to the private apartments, he said that the Cardinal had volunteered and would hear the confessions. This plunged the couple in a panic.

"I'll not go to the Cardinal," said the husband.

'Neither will I," said the wife; "why did you get him?"

"The priests are all resting, and he offered to come down," answered the porter.

Before the couple could withdraw, the Cardinal appeared. Both of them were so overcome that their embarrassment was painful. The Cardinal simply bowed his head, and neither by word nor act added to the confusion of the penitents. At first they forgot what to say, but at length managed to make their confession and left.

"I'm so glad that I went to confession to the Cardinal," said the wife before departing. "It is a great honor, and he was so kind and gentle. Besides, I feel so comforted by the instruction and advice he gave me. He made me see so clearly, and is one of the best confessors I ever met. I just thought I couldn't go to him, but now I wouldn't take anything for the recollection of this day."*

---

* These anecdotes, by Mr. L. W. Reilly, appeared in the *Catholic Union and Times*, of Buffalo, May 13, 1897.

The exalted piety of the Cardinal's own life finds a favorite mode of expression in Newman's wonderful hymn, "Lead, Kindly Light," and many are the times when he directs his choir leader at the Cathedral to render its beautiful words and music. He never seems to hear it often enough, and has frequently said that he regards it as an almost perfect expression of real piety, an epitome of the story of the soul from the cradle to the grave. A life-like engraving of Newman stands on an easel in his parlor, and he is fond of recounting the inspiring circumstances under which the hymn was written.

His familiarity with the Bible is extraordinary, and is, perhaps, not surpassed by that of any active minister of any denomination the world over. He knows it so well that he can clothe his every-day thoughts in Scriptural language, and not infrequently does so. He is never without a copy of the New Testament in his pocket. On several occasion when a Bible has been needed in a company of priests or laymen, and no one else could produce it, he was able to supply it.

His habitual tact enables him to conduct himself admirably in an assemblage of Protestants. On one occasion he and Bishop Paret, of the Protestant Episcopal Diocese of Maryland, who remained good friends, despite the fact that they had publicly taken opposite attitudes on the school question, were invited together to a public ceremony in Baltimore. When the procession was about to start, Bishop Paret said:

"Your Eminence, it is the custom in our church for the inferior to precede the superior, and, if it meets your approval, I will go first."

The Cardinal responded: "My dear brother, we will walk together;" and in that manner they proceeded to the place where the exercises were to be held.

A striking instance of the Cardinal's liberality of view was given in January, 1906, when the Baltimore committee of the Prohibition party arranged a meeting to be addressed by W. H.

Berry, State Treasurer of Pennsylvania, who had recently been triumphantly elected after a struggle against political corruption in that State.   The Cardinal promptly accepted an invitation to serve as a vice-president of the meeting.   The committee had intended to hold the meeting in a public hall, but later changed the place to Eutaw Street Methodist Episcopal Church, one of the historic edifices of Methodism in America, identified with memories of Francis Asbury.   When it was decided to make this change, the committee sent a letter to the Cardinal, giving him notice of it, and asking if, under the circumstances, he wished to have his name withdrawn.

"The holding of a civic meeting in a Protestant church," he replied, "does not excite any religious scruples in me.   I gladly allow the use of my name as one of the vice-presidents of the meeting."

When the Cardinal appeared in the church, he was vigorously applauded.   He expressed to Mr. Berry his cordial approbation of the struggle against ring politics.

Any warfare against private and political corruption waged by an awakened public opinion appealed to him powerfully.   In a sermon at the Cathedral, November 5, 1905, he sounded an emphatic warning against "graft" in public office and dishonest methods in business, which he attributed, in part, to the American weakness for living beyond one's means.

The position which the Cardinal occupies in the hearts of his Protestant neighbors was further illustrated at a mass-meeting in Brown Memorial Church, Baltimore, December 14, 1906, called to express disapproval of the policy of Leopold, King of Belgium, in the Congo State.   The meeting was addressed by Rev. H. Grattan Guinness, a leader in the Congo reform movement in Great Britain, who was traveling in the United States for the purpose of inducing the Washington Government to join England in intervention in the Congo.   As a rule, Catholics defended the policy of King Leopold, reflecting the views of the large number of missionaries of their faith who were actively laboring among the natives. Cardinal Gibbons on several occasions had expressed similar opinions, though he was not active in the controversy, and on no occasion tried to interfere. In a letter to Rev. Edward Everett Hale, in October, 1904, expressing his regrets at inability to attend a peace conference in Boston, he wrote:

"Had I been able to be present, I would have made it my duty to say a word in vindication of the policy of Belgium in the Congo State. The representatives of the different powers at the Berlin Conference were compelled to express their admiration and praise of the noble ideals of the founder of the Congo State and the splendid results achieved through his humane policy."

Mr. Guinness devoted most of his address to a description of conditions in the Congo from his point of view; but at the close he said:

"The United States and Britain long ere this would have gotten together and put an end to the atrocities in the Congo, but for one man in this country. The one strong hand that has been keeping this thing going is none other than that of Cardinal Gibbons."

In some localities such a statement might have passed unnoticed; but in this Baltimore church there was commotion in an instant. Rev. John T. Stone, pastor of Brown Memorial, and Rev. Wilbur F. Sheridan, pastor of Mt. Vernon Place Methodist Episcopal Church, one of the leading congregations of that denomination in the city, were both on their feet at once. Mr. Sheridan spoke first, saying:

"Pardon me, but I entertain a profound regard for Cardinal Gibbons, whom I admire for his catholicity of view. I can not think that such can be the case."

Mr. Stone remarked earnestly that he greatly deplored the words of the speaker.

Mr. Guinness seemed dumfounded, but there was abundant evidence that the two Protestant ministers were expressing the emphatic view of practically all who were present. At the request of Mr. Stone, the English speaker modified his statement almost immediately from the platform, and left the church with a new opinion of the regard in which Cardinal Gibbons is held in his home city.

Perhaps the most striking manner in which the esteem of the Cardinal's neighbors is shown is in the receptions which he customarily holds after high mass on the first Sunday of each New Year. Not to have attended the Cardinal's reception is almost a mark of reproach in Baltimore. The Mayor and living ex-Mayors of the city are almost always there, and not infrequently the Governor. Protestants mingle with Catholics in the great crowd which stretches far along Charles street, all eager to shake the hand of Baltimore's foremost citizen and to receive the cheerful words and smile with which he invariably greets his callers. Mothers bring their children, whom he knows by name no less than the prominent men who throng his residence on such occasions.

His ready wit, flashing suddenly at intervals, keeps everyone in good humor; and even in later years he has been able to preserve the buoyancy of his spirits for hours while the long line of callers is passing. Now and then he pauses to tell a story or to exchange a reminiscence. The whole atmosphere is neighborly and democratic, though complete decorum prevails.

It would be impossible for him to shake hands with all who come, and hundreds, wishing to avoid fatiguing the distinguished host, are in the habit of leaving their cards and then retiring. Strangers who occasionally attend these affairs are amazed at the demonstration of complete respect and warm affection on the part of the people, without regard to religious belief, for one whom they esteem above all a man as much as a churchman, catholic in the broad sense of the term.

That part of Charles street where the Cardinal's residence stands has fallen on evil days.   Mansions once occupied by the scions of colonial aristocracy and by leaders in the gay world of wealth and fashion are now given over to trade, preserving only their quaint architecture as a reminder of the glory that was once theirs.   Almost alone of all its neighbors, the Cardinal's residence stands in the dignified elegance of other days. It is still a favorite object of interest to visitors; and to hundreds of Baltimoreans who walk past it from their uptown homes to the center of the city, it is a landmark.   In front of it are flower beds, which blaze with beauty every spring and summer, when the people of the city pause at the iron railing to stand a few moments watching what they have long since learned to call "the Cardinal's tulips."   The flowers are usually of different kinds and colors, but often there is a bed of brilliant scarlet tulips, which matches the color of the Cardinal's robes of state.

Here in dignity and simplicity, the Cardinal has lived since 1877.   It has been workshop as well as home, for he is always busy.   His accomplishments, when considered collectively, are extraordinary.   Surprise is often expressed by those who note the comparative frailty of his physique, that he has been able to endure such great labors; but to those who know him best, there is no secret about it.   His capacity for sustained effort is due to regularity and simplicity of life, to moderation and order.   He has never been robust, though organically sound. The permanent impairment of his digestion by privations and fatigues in early life left an heritage which constantly admonished him to be careful, and he did not fail to heed the warning. When a student at St. Mary's Seminary, the future Cardinal and Father Dissez, his professor of philosophy, were considered so weak that they could not hope for more than a few years of life.   Yet Father Dissez lived to celebrate his fiftieth anniversary as a teacher, and nearly all his companions, except the Cardinal, have long since died.

The Cardinal has understood almost perfectly how to adapt himself to a system which enables him to draw upon his physical strength at the maximum without impairing its capacity for the future. He exemplifies the Greek motto, "Nothing too much." Rising punctually at six o'clock, he celebrates mass, and eats a light breakfast, dietically adapted to what experience has shown him he can assimilate with benefit. After a morning of hard work, he takes dinner sparingly; and then comes his nap, which refreshes him for additional hours of activity. His walk in the afternoon is never neglected, except from necessity. Usually it is about two miles long, one of his favorite routes being out Charles street to North avenue, a former boundary line of the city, and back to his residence; but sometimes he goes much further. After supper, he reads, writes, and receives a few callers in his study, where, surrounded by books and with a cheerful fire burning in an open grate in winter, he seems most at ease. No matter what the circumstances, he stops everything and retires punctually at ten o'clock every night. He leaves banquets and social entertainments at an early hour, that nothing may disturb his regularity of habit. If not able to sleep, he derives benefit from reclining in complete mental repose. He knows how to avoid extreme solicitude for the morrow, and is able to throw off his many cares when the time comes to do so.

His digestion is a barometer of his general health; any weakness is noticeable there, and receives prompt attention. He takes little medicine, believing that the American people are in the habit of using too many drugs, and wishing to avoid that failing himself. He consults his doctor only when necessary; he is his own best physician.

His habit of cheerfulness undoubtedly contributes much to sustaining him through his labors. One of the best of conversationalists, he possesses a rare fund of anecdote, which he relates in a manner becoming the time and place. His skill as a story-teller, fortified by the great resources of his experience,

makes him one of the most interesting of companions.   His
sense of humor is keen, and his knowledge of human nature
wonderful.   He knows how to adapt himself to every person,
from the infant to the patriarch.   On a social occasion, he
shines.   He is fond of company, and not infrequently accepts
an invitation to dine and spend the evening with a personal
friend.

Although a moderate user of cigars in later life, he did not
smoke until after he had passed thirty, and he did not always
enjoy it even after he began.   He sometimes said that he used
tobacco in order to be sociable; because he was frequently
thrown in gatherings where everybody else smoked, and he
never wished to appear constrained in any assemblage.   As
conspicuously as any other American of modern times, he exemplifies the saying of St. Paul: "All things to all men."   He
is *"suaviter in modo, fortiter in re."*

He has never attended a theatrical performance, though not
infrequently actors and actresses of the Catholic faith visit him
at the archiepiscopal residence.   While he recognizes that some
plays may be good, in fact beneficial to the moral nature as
well as entertaining, yet he regards so many of them as evil
in their effects on the mind that he could never bring himself
to take the chance.

He was well acquainted with William J. Florence, Mary
Anderson, and a number of other leading stage folk, to whom
he showed the utmost kindness when opportunity permitted.
While he was Vicar of North Carolina, Edwin Forest played
in Wilmington, and sent a member of his company to invite
the Bishop to occupy a box at the performance.   The emissary was, perhaps, not well chosen, for this is the way he expressed himself:

"Bishop, it is a question mooted among moralists as to
whether the stage, the press or the pulpit is the greatest force
for the advancement of religious and moral ideas.   As a

member of the theatrical profession, I hesitate to express my opinion."

The Bishop declined, with thanks, the invitation which was presented.

He regarded Mary Anderson (Mrs. Navarro) as a model of what a woman on the stage should be, and she in turn was devoted to him. After she abandoned a theatrical career and took up her residence in England, she esteemed it an honor to visit him whenever his presence in that country made it possible.

Even after the establishment of the legation at Washington, the Cardinal's position as primate of the American Church and the presiding officer at meetings of the archbishops, made it necessary that much of the correspondence with Rome should continue to center in him. His mail is extensive and varied, embracing not only the affairs of the Church, but the multitude of subjects about which a man of prominence would naturally be addressed. Non-Catholic ministers write to him for advice. Reformers seek his approval and aid. His well-known generosity leads to many appeals for help of all sorts; and, like other Americans of eminence, he receives many "crank" letters.

Every Christmas he is accustomed to send to each of his fellow-cardinals and the Catholic sovereigns of Europe letters wishing them prosperity and offering prayers in their behalf. In later years, these letters have been addressed to the Emperor of Austria, the kings of Spain, Belgium and Saxony, and the Prince Regent of Bavaria.

He has been in frequent correspondence with all the later American Presidents, as well as with many bureau and Cabinet officers. Cleveland, Harrison, McKinley, Roosevelt and Taft have been, in turn, his warm friends, and have owed not a little to the sound advice which they sought from him.

He has had his share of afflictions, and some of these have weighed upon him grievously. One of his heaviest blows in later years was the failure in business of Thomas E. Waggaman, treasurer of the Catholic University, as a result of which $850,000 of its investments were temporarily lost and never fully regained. He was almost overwhelmed by this at first; but threw all his strength into a determined effort to recover for the university what it had lost. Large contributions were sent to him by Protestants as well as Catholics, including not a few from men prominent in public life, who had learned to admire him, and to whom the pathetic aspect of his loss strongly appealed. The Knights of Columbus gave $50,000 to found a chair of American history, which the cardinal accepted in 1904. He was able to see the university again in the full tide of progress, and he has not ceased to regard it as the favorite project of his life.

Another misfortune which almost crushed him was the discovery that one of his priests, the pastor of a small congregation in Baltimore, had overwhelmed himself in speculation with debts amounting to $130,000. This priest had felt an ambition to erect a new church for his people, and, realizing that in their poverty they would be unable to pay for it, he conceived the idea of embarking in financial ventures with a view of raising the money through what he vainly supposed to be his own skill in business. He paid one debt by creating another until, finally, the extent of his operations became known to the Cardinal.* He was at once removed from his pastorate and sent to a sanatorium, for the mania on the subject of speculation which he developed was pronounced by medical opinion to be a form of insanity. The Cardinal pledged himself to pay every dollar which the priest owed, although he was not legally bound to do so, and in less than six months was able to secure enough help to accomplish it. He admitted not an atom of excuse for anything which the priest had done, and denounced it unsparingly. The reproach which he feared would be brought upon the Church, he felt so keenly that it

* March, 1909.

made him ill. It was a source of great satisfaction to him that no one lost through the priest's unfortunate delusion.

The death of Very Rev. A. L. Magnien, superior of St. Mary's Seminary, in December, 1902, affected him greatly. Dr. Magnien was one of the best types of the French priest and professor. For more than a quarter of a century he exercised a deep influence on the Church in America; and was the Cardinal's constant companion and adviser. The Cardinal wrote the preface for a printed memorial volume, in which he thus expressed his estimate of Father Magnien's value:

"For five and twenty years I was associated with Dr. Magnien by the ties of unbroken friendship and of almost daily intercourse. * * * He had the happy faculty of grasping the salient points of a question with intuitive vision. His judgment of men and measures was rarely at fault. He was in the habit of giving me his estimate of the intellectual and moral standards and characteristic traits of the newly ordained priests; he would even foreshadow their future careers as developed in the labors of the ministry. The subsequent lives of these clergymen usually verified the forecast of the sagacious observer. * * * I had been so much accustomed to consult the venerable Abbe on important questions and to lean upon him in every emergency, that his death is a rude shock to me, and I feel as if I had lost a right arm. He was, indeed, the the half of my soul."†

Father Magnien was essentially a practical man, with a clear vision and sound judgment; unshaken on questions of principle, but still adapting himself to circumstances. With the Cardinal, he had often discussed the ideals of the priesthood and methods by which these might be realized through the training at St. Mary's, the mother of so many devoted "ambassadors of Christ." The settled purpose of both was to develop men of God, and at the same time, practical men, who

---

† Very Rev. A. L. Magnien, a Memorial, pp. 5. 6, 7, 8.

Presentation of Gift by the Knights of Columbus to the Catholic University

would know how to reach out with strong personal appeal in
the communities which they served.

The Catholic priest is brought so close to his Maker by the
intensity of the discipline which absorbs his daily life that
it is little wonder if he considers only the judgment of Heaven
as valuable and ignores the view with which he may be regarded by man.   From the moment of beginning his preparation for the sacred ministry, he is so engrossed in prayer, meditation, scripture reading and study, that there is scarcely
room for anything else to enter.   Starting with the time
when he is awakened in the morning at the seminary by the
call of the priest, *"Benedicamus Domino!"* (Let us bless the
Lord), and he replies, *"Deo gratias!"* (Thanks be to God), he
must accept everything thrust upon him with a *"Deo gratias!"*
The whole object of his training is to teach him to be like
Christ.   When, at last, his arduous preparation is over and
he has been ordained, his daily mass and meditation, the reading of his office (a long series of scriptural quotations and
other precepts designed to impress upon him indelibly the spiritual duties of his mission), his round of pastoral calls, visiting
the sick, working in his school, hearing confessions in a stifling
closet for hours—all this requires him to pass his life almost
constantly at prayer or in the active performance of duties that
weigh upon him like a staggering burden.   He gives up family
and friends, and everything which men hold dear, that every
moment of his time may be spent in the service of God.   What
wonder if in lifelong meditation on the Divine, he should forget the human; if he should develop the habit of regarding the
world and its institutions with distrust; or if, in reprehending
sin and standing as a bulwark against wrong in the comparatively narrow circle of his parish, he should, perhaps, lose the
savoir faire and be regarded by some as hard and intolerant?
The fervor of his religious life, reaching its climax in the sacrifice of the mass and the sacred mysteries of the Catholic
Church, which he may approach with an authority handed

down to him through the Apostles, tends to an intensity of conviction which may cause the priest to regard with scant consideration those differing from him concerning spiritual questions.   Is it strange, then, if he considers monstrous the view that his Church is but a form and a shadow, when he knows the loftiness of the religious fervor which is her whole aim and object?

He sees few Protestants.   He is so busy attending to the wants of his own spiritual children that he can not participate in secular affairs and feel all the currents of life that pulse through the arteries of society.   Only a man of the strongest character, the widest vision, can avoid being what the world might call narrow, if he meets with whole-hearted devotion the tremendous responsibilities and duties of the priesthood.

The Cardinal and Father Magnien knew that it was necessary for priests to get more in touch with the times, and that they must learn how to do this without in the least detracting from the sacred character of their calling, or the ideals and impulses which they derived from the fountain of the Church. They felt that priests must have a red-blooded interest in the temporal as well as in the spiritual affairs of their neighbors, and must be able to meet them out of Church as well as in the confessional and at the altar.   They would have them know the laws, the institutions, the spirit of their country; share in movements for social betterment, for economic progress. There is a great gap between this ideal which they laid down for American priests and the sensation-monger, who clutches at merely transient events as material for constructing something to draw a congregation, which might be repelled by his shallowness and bigotry if he trod the even path of the Gospel.

So fruitful has been the cardinal's interest in the training of priests, that he has lived to see a great change in many of them. In his own diocese, he has been quick to reward merit and promote men who showed that they had the breadth to occupy the higher positions of the Church. His desire was that they should not only be pastors, but men in touch with the community, and able to express and exemplify all its noblest aspirations. He is called "the Father of Priests," because he has ordained so many of them. Up to 1911 he had ordained nearly 1,400, secular and regular. He has consecrated 27 bishops, and conferred the pallium on 12 archbishops. As the officially appointed delegate of the Pope, he has invested two cardinals—Satolli and Martinelli—with the rank and insignia of princes of the Church.

A severe blow to the Cardinal was the destruction by fire, March 17, 1911, of St. Charles College, where he had pursued his early studies in preparation for the priesthood. He gave $10,000 to aid in rebuilding this institution, which was identified with so many memories of his own life.

Another loss which wrenched the Cardinal's heart was the death, on February 11, 1911, of Archbishop Ryan, of Philadelphia, a companion and prop of the most fruitful years of his career. The beloved archbishop was stricken with heart disease and lay for weeks in the shadow of certain death, his soul seeming to hover on the border of the material and spiritual worlds. That rich and powerful voice which had penetrated the remotest recess of the Baltimore Cathedral on occasions big with importance to the Church in America became at times a whisper; yet in periods when the sufferer was conscious, it breathed of faith in God, charity to all men and love of country.

A few days before his death the cardinal went to Philadelphia to visit him. Entering the sick room, he placed his hands on the archbishop's brow and said softly:

"Your Grace does not know me."

"After forty years." came the answer, "I know every tone of your Eminence's voice and now as ever I am convinced that you are the instrument of Providence for every good thing for our Church and country."

For some minutes they talked, the visit of the cardinal seeming to endow his sick friend with new strength. They spoke of men and things long gone, of mutual hopes that had blossomed or withered. Naturally their thoughts turned to the future of the nation which they loved so well and served so faithfully. "If we keep America conservative," remarked the archbishop, "no country will be as great as this."

Tears were in the cardinal's eyes as he departed from the house of the dying. Another sympathizer—a Protestant—who visited the archbishop shortly before his death, said that it seemed like entering a room filled with angels.

One of the cardinal's close friends was Joseph Friedenwald, a wealthy and charitable member of the Jewish faith, who had been instrumental, when President of the Board of Trustees of the Baltimore Almshouse, in permitting the establishment of a Catholic chapel there. Mr. Friedenwald was a frequent caller at the cardinal's residence and at his death in December, 1910, bequeathed $2,000 to the eminent prelate whose breadth of soul could appreciate true worth without distinction of creed.

The Cardinal has been a favorite subject for painters, and several sculptors have also essayed to reproduce his features in marble and bronze. The expression of his face is such that, once seen, it is never forgotten; but it has the remarkable faculty of exhibiting such great changes, amounting almost at times to transmutation of characteristic features, that he has been the despair of not a few artists, and their prolonged efforts to depict him sometimes tired him out. Perhaps the most accurate likeness of him ever made was one by Gagliardi, of Rome, which has hung for many years in the main parlor of his residence. Another good likeness, by Healy, is in the rear parlor. Chartran, Bonnat, Benziger, Klots, Miss Keller, Miss Mackubin and Ury Muller had fair success in painting him. Innumerable photographs of him have been made; and such is the mobility of his expression that scarcely two of them are alike.

When the perpetration of unnatural crimes or the development of race feeling led to the spread of the lynching evil in States both North and South, the Cardinal's attitude was one of the powerful influences which arrested it.   An article on this subject from his pen appeared in the *North American Review* for October, 1905, in which he pronounced lynching "a blot on our American civilization."   He traced the evil to its source by pointing out the difficulty and, at times, the impossibility of securing prompt trial and punishment of offenders under the criminal laws which prevailed in a number of States. Revision of these laws in the interest of speedy and effective justice and their impartial enforcement he considered a sovereign remedy for the trouble.

A few years previously he had commented on recent race troubles in the South as follows:

"In the history of mankind it has been observed that when two distinct races coexisted in the same territory, one race has always exercised a certain supremacy over the other.   While this principle is admitted, it is the manifest duty of every patriot, statesman and Christian to see that the relations between the races should be friendly, harmonious and mutually beneficial.   The race conflicts, antagonism and bloodshed which have recently occurred in several States of the Union can be largely traced to two great causes — the one-sided and ill-directed system of negro education and the consequent abuse of the ballot-box.

"The colored race is naturally kind and gentle, affectionate and grateful, with religious emotions easily aroused.   But the education which it is generally receiving is calculated to sharpen its mental faculties at the expense of its religious and moral sense.   It fosters ambition without supplying the means of gratifying it.   It feeds the head, while the heart is starved. No education is complete that does not teach the science of self-restraint, and that is found only in the decalogue and the Gospels.

"The abuse of the ballot-box is chargeable more to white demagogues than to the blacks themselves. The politicians use the negro vote for their own selfish purposes. I am persuaded that a restriction of suffrage by a property qualification would be a wise measure."*

His views on the race question were further exemplified by his opposition to a bill introduced in the Maryland Legislature in 1904, requiring the separation of the races on the street cars of Baltimore. He actively exerted his personal influence against this bill, which was defeated. The Cardinal held that separation as thus proposed would have been a constant source of ill-feeling by openly illustrating the discrimination between the races in a conspicuous way.

His earlier views developed in the Knights of Labor controversy were confirmed by the experiences of riper years. As late as 1905 he wrote to Rome, opposing the condemnation of the societies known as the "Knights of the Maccabees," "Modern Woodmen" and "Improved Order of Red Men," and they were not put on the forbidden list.

He never lost an opportunity to lend his assistance to movements in the interest of universal peace. When conferences on this subject were instituted at Lake Mohonk, N. Y., he warmly approved them; and at a gathering of this kind, May 31, 1906, he made the principal address on "The Triumphs of Peace." He reminded his hearers that Christ was called "the Prince of Peace," and that He came, above all, "to break down the wall of partition which divided nation from nation." Since the Revolution, he pointed out, there had been four wars. in the United States. He said that at least three of these might have been easily averted by peaceful arbitration, and that a

---

* Baltimore *Sun*, Nov. 26, 1898.

large share of the responsibility rested upon the shoulders of the American people. He showed forcibly how Christianity had reduced war and mitigated its horrors. While the Roman Republic and Empire were almost constantly engaged in bloody strife, the United States had passed through only about ten years of war in the one hundred and twenty years of its existence. He contrasted the conduct of Titus toward the defeated Jews with the magnanimity of Grant in the hour of his triumph over the brilliant and noble Lee. It was not impossible, he said, to put a stop to the settlement of disputes between nations by bloodshed, any more than it had been to abolish the practice of dueling.

About this time, suggestions were advanced that a Secretary of Peace be added to the Cabinet of the President of the United States. For this post, if it should be created, George T. Angell, of Boston, president of the American Harmony Society, strongly urged Cardinal Gibbons, holding that his influence would be powerful in preventing future conflicts between the United States and Catholic nations.

The Cardinal's interest in the cause of peace has continued keen. With President Taft, Secretary of State Knox, Andrew Carnegie and other noted men, he took part in the dedication of a great Peace Palace of the American Republics in Washington, April 25, 1910. His address at the Third National Peace Congress held in Baltimore in May, 1911, was a powerful appeal for an arbitration treaty between the United States and Great Britain as a forerunner of similar conventions binding all nations. The president of the congress, in introducing him, characterized him as one of the most potent forces in the world for the abolition of war and recalled the appeal issued by Cardinals Gibbons, Logue and Vaughan at Easter, 1896, as one of the great contributory causes of the Hague Conference of 1899.

After a famous prize-fight in 1910, there was a wave of protest throughout the country against the exhibition in theatres of motion pictures reproducing its brutal details. As usual,

Cardinal Gibbons spoke with emphasis and went to the root of the whole question.

"If the pictures of this contest were permitted," he said, I am sure hundreds of children would see them, and what would be the result? Their morals would not only be contaminated, but they would have the wrong ideal of a true hero. After seeing the pictures a boy would naturally infer that the real American hero was a man bespattered with blood and with a swollen eye given him by another in a fistic encounter. The boy would go and try to do likewise. This would be a sad state of affairs. There are true heroes whom the young can emulate in a way to improve their manhood and ideals."*

The subject of proper religious care of the great host of immigrants who flocked to the United States in times of prosperity was close to the cardinal's heart. He opposed restricting this tide by a broad educational requirement, holding that many of the most desirable immigrants would be excluded by such a process. He wrote to President Roosevelt in June, 1906, expressing a warning against the prevalent zeal to go too far in this respect.

Considering divorce one of the most serious dangers which threatened the American people, he often declared vigorously his views on that subject. Writing in the *Delineator,* a journal for women, in July, 1907, he expressed himself as follows:

"The reckless facility with which divorce is procured in this country is an evil scarcely less deplorable than Mormonism. Indeed, it is in some respects more dangerous, for divorce has the sanction of the civil law, which Mormonism has not. Is not the law of divorce a virtual toleration of Mormonism in a modified form? Mormonism consists in a simultaneous polygamy, while the law of divorce practically leads to successive polygamy. * * * It is plainly manifest that the cancer of

---

* Baltimore *Sun,* July 7, 1910.

CARDINAL GIBBONS, PRESIDENT TAFT AND ARCHBISHOP FALCONIO AT THE GOLDEN JUBILEE OF ST. ALOYSIUS CHURCH, WASHINGTON, NOVEMBER 13TH, 1909

divorce is rapidly spreading over the community and poisoning the fountains of the nation. Unless the evil is checked by some speedy and heroic remedy, the existence of family life is imperiled."

In a letter addressed to the "Congress of Mothers," in Washington, May 1, 1911, the Cardinal further expressed his views of woman and her duties in the world. He wrote:

"The home is the primeval school. It is the best, the most hallowed and the most potential of all academies, and the parent, especially the mother, is the first, the most influential and the most cherished of all teachers.

"For various reasons mothers should be the first instructors of their children.

"First—As nature ordains that mothers should be the first to feed their offspring with corporal nourishment of their own substance, so the God of nature ordains that mothers should be the first to impart to their little ones 'the rational, guileless milk of heavenly knowledge, whereby they may grow into salvation' (1 Peter 11. 1).

"Second—The children that are fed by their own mothers are usually more healthy and robust than those that are nourished by wet nurses. In like manner, the children that are instructed by their own mothers in the elements of Christian knowledge are commonly more sturdy in faith and are more responsive to the call of moral duty than those who are committed for instruction to strangers.

"Third—The progress of a pupil in knowledge is in a great measure proportioned to the confidence he has in his preceptor. Now, in whom does a child place so much belief as in his mother? She is his oracle and prophet. She is his guide, philosopher and friend. He never doubts what his mother tells him. The lesson he receives acquires additional force because it proceeds from one to whom he has given his first love, and whose image in after life is indelibly stamped on his heart or memory. Mothers, do not lose the golden opportunity you have of training your children in point of morals while their hearts are open to drink in your every word.

"Fourth—You share the same home with your children. You frequently occupy the same apartment. You eat at the same table with them. They are habitually before your eyes. You are, therefore, the best fitted to instruct them and you can avail yourself of every little incident that presents itself and draw from it some appropriate moral reflection."

His voice was raised earnestly against "race suicide," to which attention was also vigorously called by President Roosevelt in the opening years of the twentieth century. Both in public and private, he did not hesitate to speak with unsparing plainness of this evil, in which he saw a certain sign of national decay unless it were arrested. In a letter to the Baltimore *Sun,* October 18, 1907, he wrote:

"Marriage, according to the Christian dispensation, is not intended for self-indulgence, but for the rearing of children in the knowledge and fear of God, who will fulfill their every obligation as individuals and as members of the social body, and prepare themselves for the eternal society of their Divine Master and His faithful servants. Its duties, properly fulfilled, develop in the highest degree self-denying, unfailing, courageous devotedness in the individual; and, consequently, in the family, the strong and tender bonds that hold its members in undying fidelity and love. * * * It is a great mistake to suppose that the two or three children of the small family, who receive all the advantages and all the indulgences that their parents can bestow, are going to become the best men and women. There is a discipline and a training in the large family, where the feelings and rights of others have constantly to be reckoned with, which is much more effective in preparing the right sort of men and women to meet the conditions of real life. Those thus reared will not so easily be found among the hordes of lazy, self-centered do-nothings, who are of no

good to church, or to society, or to themselves.   The race has
not improved, but has suffered disaster in both nations and
communities, where the procreation of children has not been
looked upon as a matter far too sacred and momentous to be
left to the control of individual appreciation of its manifold
and perplexing problems.   The accidentally occurring case of
exceptional hardship for the mother, where physical health is
gravely compromised, has been made far too much of.   All
important general laws bear hard at times upon the individual."

His sympathies were warmly enlisted in the systematic fight
against the ravages of tuberculosis.   In October, 1907, he
addressed a letter to the secretary-general of the International Congress on Tuberculosis, which was held in Washington in the autumn of the following year, expressing the belief
that the disease would ultimately be brought under as complete control as smallpox and yellow fever.

The Cardinal took a prominent part in the celebration of the
centenary of the New York Diocese, in 1908.   At a grand Te
Deum in St. Patrick's Cathedral, April 29, he delivered the
sermon, on which occasion Cardinal Logue, Archbishop of
Armagh, Primate of Ireland, celebrated pontifical mass, and
Mgr. Falconio, the Apostolic Delegate, imparted the papal
benediction.

Cardinal Gibbons, in his sermon, dwelt upon the strong men
who had helped to build up the Diocese of New York since it
was separated from the mother see of Baltimore by brief of
Pius VII.   He regarded Archbishop Hughes as having been
providentially raised up to meet the exigencies of the times, as
Carroll had been.   Hughes he characterized as active, bold,
vigorous, aggressive, in contrast to McCloskey, the first prince
of the church in America, "meek, gentle, retiring from the
world."   He did not fail to speak in warm praise of the piety
and learning of Archbishop Corrigan, his opponent in the consideration of so many questions about which leaders of the

Church might naturally differ. To the whole assemblage, he addressed this admonition:

"Take an active, loyal, personal interest in all that concerns the temporal and spiritual welfare of our beloved country. No man should be a drone in the social beehive. No one should be an indifferent spectator of the social, economic and political events occurring around him. As you all enjoy the protection of a strong and enlightened government, so should each man have a share in sustaining the burden of the Commonwealth. Above all, take an abiding and a vital interest in all that affects your holy religion."*

Another International Eucharistic Congress was held in September, 1910, this time in Montreal, the heart of Catholic Quebec. Cardinal Vincent Vannutelli attended in the capacity of Papal Legate, as he had done two years before in London, but under far different auspices; for government and people, under the same flag that floated over the mother country, welcomed him with a fervor which was in striking contrast to his cold reception in the British metropolis. Accompanied by Cardinals Gibbons and Logue, he carried the Sacred Host through the streets in a procession which was five hours in passing. Non-Catholics as well as Catholics watched reverently in the throngs which turned out to witness so impressive a religious spectacle, and not an untoward incident marked the events of the day. Before the procession Cardinal Gibbons preached at pontifical high mass in the Cathedral of St. James, picturing, with that abundance of metaphor which he knew so well how to use, the spiritual significance of the occasion.

"Your Eminence will be able to recount to the Holy Father," he said to Cardinal Vannutelli in conclusion, "the success which has crowned this congress from beginning to end. * * * You will speak of the solemn and public processions through the streets of Montreal, not only without let

---

* McNally, "The Catholic Centennial," pp. 52 to 61.

or hindrance, but with the cordial approval and co-operation of the civic authorities, and the piety and enthusiasm of the devoted people."

The admiration felt by the world-wide representation of Catholics there assembled for the beloved American cardinal was strikingly shown at a fete given in his honor by Sir Thomas George Shaughnessy, whose guest he was in Montreal; and soon after the close of the inspiring celebration Cardinal Vannutelli visited him in Baltimore, where the Roman prelate was welcomed with a procession in which leading men of the city escorted him to the Cathedral. Cardinals Gibbons, Vannutelli and Logue also attended the consecration of St. Patrick's Cathedral, in New York, then just freed from debt.

The Cardinal's last book, "Discourses and Sermons," appeared in 1908. Nearly all of these related to subjects strictly religious. They were selected for their appropriateness to every Sunday of the year and the principal festivals. In one of them, on the "Growth of the Catholic Church in America," he discussed the losses which the faith has sustained in America, a subject upon which the opponents of liberalism in the Church have not failed at times to dwell with emphasis. The Cardinal ascribed these losses to three principal causes. The first was the scarcity of priests, especially in the early periods of America. He pointed out that many of the immigrants who came to this country were scattered over a large area, where they were rarely, if ever, visited by clergymen of their own faith. For them there was no rallying point, no church where they could meet and be a source of growth to each other. Their children, not having access to a chapel or Sunday-school of their own, were often led to unite with their companions in attending services at variance with the religion of their fathers. The difficulty caused by the scarcity of priests, the Cardinal believed, had been stopped or considerably lessened, except in some remote sections of the country.

The second cause he found in the effects of mixed marriages. "The frequent outcome of such unions," he wrote, "is a spirit of indifference to religion on the part of the Catholic spouse, and its total loss on the part of the children; or, where their faith is actually preserved, it is often more or less diluted." But the Cardinal was by no means extreme in his views on this subject. He added:

"I must avow, as the result of my personal observations, that in the Diocese of Baltimore, we have gained at least as many as we have lost by mixed marriages. Not a few of the most edifying and prominent members of the Church in Baltimore are the fruit of such wedlocks. * * * My personal experience, however, has little weight when counterbalanced by the overwhelming testimony of missionaries throughout the length and breadth of the land."

He found another cause of shrinkage in the public schools, "from which all positive Christian doctrine is excluded." A considerable proportion of Catholic children, he believed, received little or no religious instruction from their parents, and when they visited the public schools their associations and environment were usually unfriendly to their faith.

In the general progress of the Church under the American flag, the Cardinal found cause for abundant rejoicing. One century after Baltimore was raised to a metropolitan see, he showed, the Church in the United States comprised a hierarchy of nearly 100 bishops, 16,000 priests, and a Catholic population numbering 14,000,000. "If we include Porto Rico and the Philippines," he added, "the number of the faith under the ægis of the American flag will amount to fully 22,000,000."

In a sermon on "Christian Marriage," he dwelt strongly on the untoward consequences which result from hasty plunges into matrimony. He advised young men not to choose women distinguished only for beauty, wealth or fascinating manners.

His standard for persons contemplating matrimony was stated in these words:

"Seek a wife who is virtuous in her conduct, modest in her demeanor, discreet and temperate in speech, and who is trained in the school of domestic habits. She will create for you a quiet, contented and cheerful home."

Protestant ministers who habitually omit the word "obey" from the marriage service will be interested in this declaration:

"And let me exhort you young women who have embraced the married state to love, honor and obey your husbands. 'As the Church,' says St. Paul, 'is subject to Christ, so also let wives be to their husbands in all things.' This obedience, far from being irksome, will become easy and delightful when prompted by genuine affection."

To husbands, he addressed the following advice of St. Paul: " 'Love your wives. As Christ also loved the Church and delivered Himself up for it, so ought men to love their wives as their own bodies. He that loveth his wife, loveth himself; for no man ever hated his own flesh, but nourisheth and cherisheth it as also Christ does the Church.' "

In a sermon on obedience to lawful authority, he showed that in America, where the laws are made by authority of the whole body of citizenship, the necessity of obedience rested upon all. He held that a citizen had an undoubted right to criticise the official conduct of public functionaries; but that this should be done with calmness, temperance and dispassionate judgment. He admitted that abuses existed in the system of popular elections, and said that, owing to the imperfection of human nature, they would always be found; but the fact that some abuses of power existed did not destroy the principle of submitting with obedience to lawful authority.

The sermons embraced within the book cover a wide range of topics, in which everyone can find something of interest and profit. Their lucidity and grace of style make them particularly valuable for popular reading, and the soundness of their doctrine gives the collection a value which has afforded it a permanent place in Catholic literature.

The seventy-sixth birthday of Cardinal Gibbons was marked by many expressions of affection and congratulation from the great and small alike. In speaking of the reflections which it called up he said:

"I am contented; happy. It is much to be given to any mortal to be able to say that. If it were given to me to live all of these seventy-six years again I should not wish them different. I should be a priest. The calling of a priest is a difficult one, but there is sublime happiness in the dedication of one's self to service."

He saw no attraction in the work of a representative in civil government, a lawyer or a physician to equal that of an "Ambassador of Christ." In the church he could reach the great, fundamental issues without the obscurity which so often clouds them in the mind of the time-server. He considered divorce, then as before, the chief problem of the nation.

"Divorce," he remarked, "is a canker which is eating into the very vitals of our life. Society—our whole civilization—uprears itself upon the sanctity of the home and the unity of the family. When you attack the family you attack government itself. And government to protect and perpetuate itself must expunge from its statutes the criminal divorce laws, which the best of our life abhors."

He considered that another ever-present danger was that young men regarded with apathy their civic responsibility. On this point he said:

"Let more young men of education and virtuous ideals give themselves to the public service, and if they do so with clean hearts and hands, the pregnant evils of government must be eliminated. In serving your country you are serving God. I have preached this and written it again and again. The better class of our citizens so often stand aloof from practical politics and the conduct of campaigns. One result of universal suffrage is that elections very frequently turn upon the vote of that large class made up of the rougher and baser sort."*

Thomas A. Edison, the famous inventor, having denied the doctrine of immortality, Cardinal Gibbons was prompt to take up the discussion with him.* This debate, because of the representative character of the disputants, attracted marked attention in the Christian world. Edison reasoned as a material scientist, but without that broad foundation of philosophy and psychology which is necessary, if simple faith be rejected, to guide the considerations of the human mind from the finite to the infinite. He began with the assertion that man is not an individual but a collection of myriads of individuals, as a city is.

"The cell, minute and little known," he proceeded, "is the real and only individual. A man is made up of many million cells. Not being, in effect, an individual, how could he go to heaven or hell as an individual or be given a reward or punishment after death had caused the separation of his cells and the diffusion of their collective intelligence? * * * We are no more individuals than cities are. * * * If you cut your hand it bleeds. Then you lose cells, and that is quite as if a city lost inhabitants through some tremendous accident."

It is the mind, he argued, that is divine, if he should admit the word at all, and mind consisted of the collective intellect of all the cells which constitute a man. To punish or reward the combined soul of the great cell-collection would be as unjust as it would be impossible and 'Nature is as just as she is merciless.' " Edison was careful to say that this did not affect his firm belief in the "great moral law," which he summed up in the precepts of the Golden Rule.

---

* New York *World*, July 24, 1910.
† *Columbian Magazine*, January and March, 1911.

"Science proves its theories," he continued, "or it rejects them. I have never seen the slightest scientific proof of the religious theories of heaven and hell; of future life for individuals or of a personal God. * * * Proof! Proof! That is what I have always been after; that is what my mind requires before it can accept a theory as a fact. * * * I do not know the soul. I know the mind. If there really is any soul, I have found, in my investigations, no evidence of it."

Edison expressed no doubt of a Supreme Intelligence, but could not personify it. Life, it appeared to him, goes on endlessly, but no more in human beings than in other animals or even in vegetables. While life, collectively, must be immortal, human beings, individually, could not be, because they were not individuals but mere aggregate of cells. The core of the great scientist's premise, argument and conclusion was summed up in the declaration: "There is no supernatural."

Cardinal Gibbons, in his reply, went to the root of the question by pointing out that while Edison's general theme was a denial, it was a denial based on assertion.

"The most striking assertion," reasoned the Cardinal, "is his fundamental one that cells have intelligence. Mr. Edison does not try to prove it; he asserts it over and over again. And he claims to accept no scientific fact without the final proof. Now, who ever proved the existence of an intelligent cell? There is not a scintilla of proof, not the beginning of a proof for such an assertion."

The cardinal cited as an example the remark of Mr. Edison that when one cuts his hand and it bleeds, there is a loss of cells, as if a city lost some of its inhabitants.

"If my hand bleeds," the cardinal argued, "then, according to his theory, I lose part of my intelligence. If I lose my hand then I lose more intelligence; and, as one of my friends put it, an appalling loss of mind would go with the loss of a leg or when a stout man reduces in flesh."

It seemed to him that "what Edison really meant was that the mind is made up of the combined intelligence of the brain cells; but so far as science knows, there is no more proof of the existence of intelligence in a brain cell than in the cell of a potato. We do know that there is a connection between the brain and the mind, that the mind thinks through the aid of the brain, as it sees through the aid of the nerves of the eye; but that does not prove that the brain thinks any more than it proves that the nerves of the eyes see; no more even than it would prove that the strings of a violin enjoy their own music. If we do not know that cells have intelligence, how can we know that any combination of cells can produce intelligence? Yet Mr. Edison believes it. * * *

"We know nothing, then, about intelligent cells; but we do know that a man has an intelligent mind or soul. We do not distinguish between mind and soul in the way Mr. Edison does, in his unphilosophical terminology. The mind is the soul in its intellectual operations."

The cardinal pointed to revealed religion as proof that the soul endures after death.

"Christ," he declared, "brings to humanity the certainty of eternal life. He proved it by his own resurrection; and, if any one thinks that the evidence of Christ's resurrection is weak, I ask him to study and think deeply over the fifteenth chapter of First Corinthians. No sane scholar denies that we have here the testimony of St. Paul himself; nor that St. Paul is honestly setting down the testimony of those who claim to have seen our Lord after his death. If so many sane men, apostles and disciples of Christ are mistaken; if they can not believe the testimony of their own eyes, if delusion can keep such a firm hold on so many different characters for so many years and become the basis of all their beliefs and the transforming power of their lives, then no human testimony is of any value; then let us close our courts of justice, for no case is proven by so many trustworthy witnesses."

The cardinal showed that the human mind, apart from the evidences of revealed religion, is able to reason up to the immortality of the soul.

"But happily," he proceeded, "it did not please God to save the world by logic or philosophy, nor would it have pleased man. The world was never governed by philosophy; it has never wanted to be and it never will be. Christianity knows the nature of man; it has a far deeper wisdom than was ever dreamed of in the philosophies of the great thinkers."

Visitors from abroad, particularly those from Catholic countries, have written much of their trips to Baltimore and their observations of the Cardinal. One of the most interesting of these is Abbe Felix Klein, professor in the Catholic Institute of Paris, who thus records his impressions:

"At four o'clock we started for a drive. Usually the Cardinal walks, but today he takes a carriage in order that I may see more of the city. Almost everybody salutes him.

"During our trip we had time to talk of many persons and many things. A part of our conversation may perhaps be repeated without indiscretion. The Cardinal praised highly the devoted wisdom of Father Magnien, the former superior of the Baltimore Seminary, who was foremost in his confidence and friendship. He inquired about the Montalembert family, who have had some relations with him, and who bear a name that he esteems among the most honorable in the world. He asked news of Paul Bourget, whose visit, some years ago, deeply interested him; he was astonished at the accuracy with which the author of 'Outre-Mer' was able, without having taken notes, to reproduce their conversation. * * *

"Our talk drifted to some more general questions. When the Cardinal speaks of America, his words breathe the warmest admiration for her institutions; comparison of them with those of other countries is not able to chill his sentiments. He rejoices in the splendid possibilities which the common freedom opens to the Church and to all well-meaning persons. He is pleased to see Catholics play the part of good citizens in the affairs of the country; he himself sets the example whenever occasion arises. His countrymen like to invite him to the great public ceremonies, at which a place is reserved for him next to the President.

"How important the work of Cardinal Gibbons has been I had fresh opportunities of learning during this visit to Baltimore. His Eminence honored me with several interviews, and we were together for a long ride through the beautiful country that surrounds his episcopal city. From this intercourse with him, I carried away a deep impression of the wisdom, prudence and tact with which this true shepherd of souls has led his people into the ways of fidelity to Catholic teaching, respect for the convictions of others, loyalty to country, and generous sympathy for the noble aspirations of our age. At the beginning of my sojourn in America, I should doubtless have less readily appreciated the mental qualities of the Cardinal, which are solid and just, rather than conspicuous and daring; or his achievements, which are substantial, rather than ostentatious; or, again, his eloquence, which he prefers should be of practical use, rather than for literary display; or, finally, that combination of traits of character which makes a true and genuine man, rather than the mere appearance of one. I say, I should not have been prepared at first properly to estimate all this; but as I became more familiar with American conditions, and more permeated with the American spirit—a spirit which is simple, practical, frank, optimistic and tolerant—I understood how greatly favored the Church has been in having for leaders men like Cardinal Gibbons; men who know and love their country, and in their own character exhibit in a high degree the qualities most dear to Americans. * * *

"How favored a place Baltimore is for great ecclesiastical events, the opportunities it affords for picking up ecclesiastical information and meeting distinguished churchmen, I learned from many indications during the three days I spent there. Mgr. Kain, Archbishop of St. Louis, who had come to the city some months previously to seek medical care at a sanitarium of the Sisters of Charity, died the day after my arrival. He left behind him the memory of an apostle, of a man of faith, fortitude and wisdom. On the third day of my visit, I found at dinner with Cardinal Gibbons, Mgr. Falconio, Apostolic Delegate. I remember with what lively sympathy he expressed himself on the religious conditions of the United States. He had lived there long enough to understand those conditions, and to appreciate them correctly. Happening to discuss with him affairs in France, and anxious to learn his opinion of the separation of Church and state in France, I was surprised, and, to be frank, delighted, to find that the prospect of such a separation far from disquieted him. He saw in such an event the way of deliverance; a rough way, indeed, but the only one that could lead to a revival of the religious life of France."*

The rigidity of the cardinal's routine has undergone no change as his years advanced. It has been his custom to rise at six o'clock every morning. In twenty minutes he is dressed. The next thirty-five minutes he spends in morning prayers and meditations in his room, his favorite subjects for spiritual reflection in this period being the Epistles or Gospels of St. Paul. From seven to half-past seven he celebrates his daily mass and afterward spends twenty minutes in prayer before the Blessed Sacrament (thanksgiving after mass). For the first time he then turns his attention to secular things, devoting ten minutes to glancing over his morning's mail and news-papers. At eight o'clock he breakfasts abstemiously and following this takes up the correspondence of the day with his secretary—a clergyman of his household. In former years he wrote many letters with his own hand in smooth, clear penman-

---

* Klein, "The Land of the Strenuous Life," p. 233 *et seq.*

ship, but often, after reading a letter, he gives the instruction "Answer on these lines" and leaves it to the secretary to draft the ideas which he expresses.

The reading of his office consumes about an hour and a half a day. This spiritual exercise prescribed by the Church consists of matins and lauds, three-quarters of an hour; the "Little Hours," twenty minutes to half an hour and vespers and complin, fifteen minutes. In the United States it is customary to say the matins and lauds* last and the cardinal follows this method.

At nine o'clock punctually he begins with the "Little Hours," which many busy priests, who have far less exacting duties, are inclined to put off until later. When this is finished he is ready for callers, whose reception forms one of the characteristic features of the day. Priests come to consult him as their bishop, not only about the problems of their parishes, but concerning lesser things which many prelates would not feel justified in taking the time to consider. He lends a ready ear to all, and this is the means through which he shapes the character of his clergy. He knows how to throw out a suggestion, say a word of praise or hint at disapproval in a manner that will be effective in the right way. But his callers are by no means confined to the clergy. They include men and women in every by-path of life; millionaire and mendicant; Catholic and Protestant, Jew and Gentile; men of light and leading in the nation, state or city, who call on him for advice; persons interested in reforms, seekers after guidance in projects great and small—and all are received to the utmost extent that time permits.

At half-past twelve the cardinal takes his cane and goes out for a call or on business. Sometimes he is accompanied, but often he is alone. Even in Baltimore, a city of multitudinous acquaintances, he is one of the best known of all its citizens. In the more frequented streets, which he not uncommonly tra-

---

* Of the next day.

verses in the busiest period of the day, he is constantly raising his hat, revealing the full outline of the red zuchetta. Strangest of all, he calls the names of a great proportion of those whose salutes he receives and seems to be an intimate part of their joys and sorrows, their daily lives—a fountain from which a thousand streams flow. He steps into an office or store, chats a moment, smiles and departs, swinging his cane and resuming his interminable task of bowing to each acquaintance. Visitors from other cities are surprised, but to the cardinal's neighbors it is all a matter of course.

True to his habit of regulating everything with precision, he returns at twenty minutes past one and ten minutes later is at dinner. This simple meal being over, he pauses for the first time in the course of the day to rest in the quiet of his room, and takes a nap of three-quarters of an hour, from which he arises refreshed for the newer occupations of the day. His afternoon repose is a habit with him, whether he is at home or abroad, and has had a great part in sustaining him through the physical ordeals which he endures.

At three o'clock he begins on his matins and lauds, having previously read the remainder of his office, and, at the conclusion of this long exercise, indulges in a cigar—often his first of the day. About half-past four o'clock he goes for another walk, lasting a little over an hour, often traversing several miles through the residential section of the city, even in the severest weather, and bowing, as before, to acquaintances seemingly without number. Before returning to his residence, he stops in the Cathedral for a visit of fifteen minutes to the Blessed Sacrament. At half-past six o'clock comes supper and then another cigar. The cardinal, now through with the heavier cares of the day and in the quiet of his study, seeks the solace of a book, or perhaps a chat with an intimate friend. At half-past seven o'clock he says his rosary, or, if he happens to be going out to supper, he performs this act of devotion before leaving the house; nothing is permitted to interfere with it. From half-past nine to a quarter before ten he recites his night prayers and at ten o'clock he is in bed, allowing nothing, unless some extraordinary circumstance, to interfere. Added to his numerous acts of daily devotion, he goes to confession once a week at St. Mary's Seminary and never fails to attend the quarterly conferences of the clergy or to make his annual retreat of one week.

CHAPTER XXIII.

Great Civic Celebration in His Honor.

After work, came reward; after service, gratitude even in a republic. History leaped ahead June 6, 1911, and the mists of past misunderstandings fled before the brilliant sunlight of a better day. It was as if the jarring din of centuries had blended at last in a sweet note of harmony and goodwill for all men. Europe had half learned, through blood and tears, that differences concerning religion need not be settled by violence of word or deed; but it remained for America to teach the sublimest lesson, to bring to perfect fruit the seed planted at St. Mary's in 1634, when Calvert's colonists, gathering around a rough-hewn cross, set up in the primeval wilderness a commonwealth dedicated to liberty of conscience.

On that June day Cardinal Gibbons stood in the Fifth Regiment Armory, a great public hall of Baltimore, and looked upon an extraordinary assemblage. It had met in honor of his golden jubilee as priest and his silver jubilee as cardinal, to attest the regard in which his public services were held by his nation, state and city. Near him, on a huge platform, sat the President of the United States, Mr. Taft; the Vice-President, Mr. Sherman; the only living ex-President, Mr. Roosevelt; the Chief Justice of the Supreme Court, Mr. White; the Speaker of the House of Representatives, Mr. Clark; the ex-Speaker, Mr. Cannon; the British Ambassador, Mr. Bryce; the Governor of Maryland, Mr. Crothers; the Mayor of Baltimore, Mr. Preston; the United States Senators from Maryland, Messrs. Rayner and Smith; the members of the House of Representatives from the

Cardinal's State, and a large number of the most prominent figures in both Houses of Congress, as well as leading men of the state and city, without regard to religious belief. The hall was densely crowded with 20,000 of the Cardinal's fellow-citizens, Catholics and non-Catholics, men and women, sharing alike the inspiring feelings of the occasion.

As the time of the jubilee drew near, this unique tribute had been suggested by the *Baltimore Sun,* whose columns had reflected during that pregnant half-century the labors and aspirations of the cardinal's life. The project was taken up with eagerness and soon the great celebration was arranged by committees headed by Governor Crothers, a Methodist, and Mayor Preston, the superintendent of an Episcopal Sunday-school. The committees included a number of Catholics, but a large majority of their membership was composed of Protestants. Bishop Murray, of the Episcopal diocese of Maryland, was one of the most active workers. The whole aspect of the tribute was non-sectarian in both conception and execution.

The governor, who presided, pointed out that the occasion was "typically representative" of Maryland.

"It is a gathering," he said, "embracing all religious denominations, without distinction or exception, assembled to do honor to a great standard-bearer of religion, who represents the highest purposes of church, state and society. While we have assembled to honor, as with one heart, a distinguished ecclesiastic, an incomparable citizen and a great and good man, the occasion is, in my mind, still more significant as a spontaneous union of men and women, holding every religious and political opinion, to tender the token of their esteem and affection to the head, in America, of a great church, which has now endured almost two thousand years, and whose influence is as wide as civilization itself.

"We salute you, Cardinal Gibbons, as a torch-bearer in our midst of religion, justice and patriotism. We acknowledge and celebrate before the country and the world your lofty devotion to religious faith and purposes, your unfailing and ceaseless activities in behalf of this State and Union and of all their spiritual and material interests, your encouragement and help in all good aspirations, your wise and beneficent counsels in times of difficulty and doubt, your elevating influence upon all the movements and concerns of this your own native land. The State of Maryland tenders you its warmest and deepest felicitations and most earnestly wishes you many more years of life and happiness."

President Taft, who, like not a few of his predecessors in office, looked on the Cardinal as both friend and adviser, spoke from a full heart when he said:

"We are here to recognize and honor in him his high virtues as a patriotic member of our political community and one who through his long and useful life has spared no efforts in the cause of good citizenship and the uplifting of his fellow-men.

"As American citizens we are proud that his prominence in the Church brought him twenty-five years ago the rank of cardinal. The rarity with which this rank is conferred in his Church upon bishops and priests so far from Rome is an indication of the position which he had won among his fellow-churchmen. But what we are especially delighted to see confirmed in him and his life is the entire consistency which he has demonstrated between earnest and single-minded patriotism and love of country on the one hand and sincere devotion to his Church on the other.

"One of the tenets of his Church is respect for constituted authority, and always have we found him on the side of law and order, always in favor of peace and good will to all men, always in favor of religious tolerance, and always strong in the conviction that complete freedom in the matter of religion is the best condition under which churches may thrive. With pardonable pride he points to the fact that Maryland under

SCENE AT THE CIVIC CELEBRATION IN BALTIMORE, JUNE 6TH, 1911

Catholic control was among the first to give complete religious toleration.

"Nothing could more clearly show the character of the man whose jubilee we celebrate than the living testimonial that this assembly is to his value as a neighbor in the community of Baltimore.

"In spite of the burden and responsibilities of his high position in the Church, he has taken part in the many great movements for the betterment of mankind and has shown himself not only a good Catholic in the Church sense, but he has been broadly catholic in the secular sense of that word, so that the affection felt for him by his co-religionists has spread to all denominations and to all the people, who are quick to perceive a disinterested friend.

"That he may long continue active in his present high position, that he may long continue in secular movements to take the prominent place he has always had in works of usefulness is the fervent prayer of Catholic and Protestant, of Jew and Christian."

Ex-President Roosevelt took occasion to say that it had been his "good fortune" to be associated on many different occasions with Cardinal Gibbons.

"Not only is this gathering characteristic of Maryland," he remarked, "but it is characteristic of our great Union, it is characteristic of America, because here in this republic, with all of our faults and shortcomings—and we have plenty of them— it is nevertheless true that we have come nearer than any other nation to solving the difficult problem of combining complete religious liberty and toleration with a devoutly religious feeling in the people as a whole.

"And we meet this afternoon to do honor in the name of all the American people, in the name of the American nation, to you, because while the American people may differ among themselves on questions of dogma, they are a unit in recognizing what accounts in civic affairs for so much more than dogma—conduct, in the churchman as in the statesman.

"Friends, we read now and then prophecies of woe about the churches in the future, complaints as to congregations growing smaller, complaints as to lack of belief among the congregations. There will be no trouble about the future of any American church if that church makes as its cardinal principle the rendering of service to the people.

"No church in the United States will ever have to defend itself as long as those standing highest in that church, as well as those under them, serve the people, devote their lives to the service of the men and women round about them, as you, Cardinal Gibbons, have devoted your life to the service of your fellow-countrymen and countrywomen. What we care for, what we Americans wish to see in the church, is service; what we wish to judge the man by is his conduct and character.

"If the church renders good service and if the man rings true when we apply the touchstone of principle to his conduct and his character, then the American people will be well content with both church and man. And, my fellow-countrymen, in spite of all the little things that divide us, think how blessed we are because we are united on an occasion like this without regard to past history and antecedents, without regard to differences of religious or political belief, to honor a good man, who in and through his church and as a citizen of this country has lived the life that a good man should live.

"It was my good fortune the other day to attend a meeting composed chiefly of Protestant preachers, where I was introduced by a Catholic priest and where we were led in prayer by a Jewish rabbi, and now we come together, Catholic and Protestant, as the president has said, to render honor to the man who is our fellow-citizen and in whom we all claim a certain proprietary right. And, friends, religious intolerance and bitterness are bad enough in any country, but they are inexcusable in ours.

"Our republic, mighty in its youth, destined to endure for ages, will see many presidents during those ages, and it will see presidents who are Catholics as well as presidents who are Protestants; presidents who are Jews as well as presidents who are Gentiles.

"The Cardinal throughout his life has devoted himself to the service of the American people. He has endeavored to work and he has worked steadily in the uplifting of the lowly; he has worked steadily to bring nearer the day when we should approximate better to the rule of justice and fair dealing as between man and man. His voice has ever been raised on behalf of the weak and the downtrodden, his hand ever stretched out toward those who may have slept, toward all those who are in suffering, who have suffered loss or were suffering pain. He has fought for the rights of the lowly, he has done all that he might to bring nearer the day when there should be a more complete reign of justice in this land, and he has shown by his life his realization of the truth that justice can come only through law and order; that disorder and lawlessness are the negation of justice and in the end deal most severely against the poor and the lowly.

"He has set an example to all of us in public and private life, both by that for which he has striven and the way in which he has striven to achieve it. He has striven for justice, he has striven for fair dealing and he has striven for it in the spirit of truth, in the spirit that has no relation to lawlessness or disorder, and at the same time with the fullest recognition that law and order, essential though they are, are primarily essential because on them as a foundation, and only on them as a foundation, is it possible to build the great temple of justice and generous fair dealing as between man and man. I am honored—we are all honored—that the opportunity has come today to pay a tribute to what is highest and best in American citizenship, when we meet to celebrate this occasion, Cardinal Gibbons."

Vice-President Sherman presented congratulations to the Cardinal in behalf of the Senate, and Senator Root, of New York, spoke of him as the "champion of ideals."

"It is because Cardinal Gibbons," said Mr. Root, "has illustrated in his life, in his conduct, in his arduous labors, in his self-devotion to all good causes, all that we would like to have our children admire and follow, all that we love to believe our country possesses, that America, through us, with sincerity and ardor, honors him today. And it is because he has been the champion of ideals, because he is a man not only of works but of faith that we who differ from him in dogma, who do not belong to his church, hold him as in his proper person illustrating the true union of service to State and service to God, the true union which makes the functional and ceremonial union of church and state unnecessary, the union in the heart of man of devotion to country and devotion to God.

"He is both a great prelate and a great citizen, and under his guidance his church, his people and his followers have always stood, and now stand, a bulwark against atheism and anarchy, against the tearing down of those principles of morality and of government upon which the opportunities of our country depend."

Speaker Clark brought greetings not only as presiding officer of the House of Representatives but as a citizen of Missouri when he said:

"Cardinal Gibbons stands here today honored by the entire American people, without respect to politics or religion or geographical lines. Among the men that have met here to do him honor, I live farther from this city than any other man here except the Ambassador from Great Britain; and the cardinal's words are quoted as often, his influence is as great, the affection for him is as strong, west of the great river as it is in the city of Baltimore."

Not a few of those in the vast crowd were unidentified with any church. These found a voice in ex-Speaker Cannon, who said:

"In the United States no man lives who has led in doing more to bring men together under the influence of a broad Catholic spirit in religion, in politics, than yourself. As a member of no church organization, one of the outsiders, so far as church membership is concerned, I tender to you my thanks for the great work that you have led in doing and for the great work that is being done, not only in the great republic, but in all the world, by those who live under and teach under, with a broad Catholic spirit, the precepts of the Master."

Ambassador Bryce, famous as a historian, took a characteristic view of the remarkable scene.

"Is it not a beautiful sight," he asked, "when we think of the ages of the past in which those of us who do not belong to the church which his Eminence represents, and those of us who do belong to that church, were divided by bitter antagonisms and mutual suspicions—is it not a blessed thing that today we can all meet without distinction of religious faith to pay honor to one who illustrates the fundamental principles of Christianity by his life as well as by his teachings?

"There are diversities of governments but the same spirit, and in his Eminence and in his life there is drawn out a beautiful example of those virtues which belong to our common Christianity and which we can all honor alike.

"And I may say to you, citizens of the United States, that if there is anything which we in Europe specially honor and admire in the great republic which belongs to you, it is this— that you have carried out consistently from the first that admirable principle with which you started, of making no distinction of religion and by teaching all men that their Christianity is a part of common citizenship. That is a great lesson which has been taught to the world by America and I do not think it could be taught in a more impressive form than it is taught when all religious faiths may gather to honor an illustrious prelate of the Catholic Church."

Mayor Preston spoke of the "exalted character and useful life" of Cardinal Gibbons and said:

"In the name of our city and of this vast assemblage of distinguished guests and home people I respectfully felicitate him upon this recognition by his fellow-citizens of his life and labors."

As the Cardinal arose, amid acclamations which in ruder ages might have been bestowed on a hero returning from the conquest of an empire, he beheld in the scene around him the justification of his faith in the American people. He who had trusted them in the anguish of war, the dark hours of labor riots, the scandals of polluted politics, the poisoned atmosphere of social vice and the malignant flames of prejudice, saw now that he had not labored in vain. He spoke simply and modestly, picturing frankly to his fellow-countrymen the strivings of his long career and his confidence in the future. His address was as follows:

"I am filled with emotions of gratitude by this extraordinary manifestation on the part of my fellow-citizens, without distinction of race or religion or condition of life, and I am overwhelmed with confusion by the unmerited encomiums which have been pronounced by the President of the United States, the Vice-President, the former President, the Speaker of the House of Representatives, the former Speaker, Senator Root, the Ambassador of Great Britain, the Governor of Maryland and the Mayor of Baltimore.

"Gentlemen, you have portrayed your subject not, I fear, as he is, but as he should be. But your portrait is so attractive to me that it shall be my endeavor to resemble it more and more every day of the few years that remain to me. One merit only can I truly claim regarding my civic life, and that is, an ardent love for my native country and her political institutions.   Ever since I entered the sacred ministry my aim has been to make those over whom I exerted any influence not only more upright Christians, but also more loyal citizens; for the most faithful Christian makes the best citizen.

"I consider the Republic of the United States one of the most precious heirlooms ever bestowed on mankind down the ages, and that it is the duty and should be the delight of every citizen to strengthen and perpetuate our Government by the observance of its laws and by the integrity of his private life. 'Righteousness,' says the Book of Proverbs, 'exalteth a nation, but sin is a reproach to the people.'

"If our Government is destined to be enduring it must rest on the eternal principles of justice, truth and righteousness, and these principles must have for their sanction the recognition of a Supreme Being who created all things by His power, who governs them by His wisdom and whose superintending Providence watches over the affairs of nations and of men.

"When the framers of our immortal Constitution were in session, Benjamin Franklin complained to his colleagues of the small progress they had made after several weeks of deliberation.   He used these memorable words: 'We have spent many days in fruitless discussion.   We have been groping in the dark because we have not sought light from the Father of Light to illumine our understanding.   I have lived,' he continued, 'for many years, and the longer I live the more convincing proofs I have that God governs the affairs of men.   And if a sparrow can not fall to the ground without His notice, is it probable that an empire can rise without His aid and co-operation?   We are told in the same sacred writings that 'unless the Lord build the house, he laboreth in vain who buildeth it.'

"Thank God, the words of Franklin did not fall on barren soil.   They have borne fruit.   Our Government from its dawn to the present time has been guided by Christian ideals.   It has recognized the existence of a superintending Providence.   This is evident from the fact that our presidents, from George

Washington to William Howard Taft, have almost invariably invoked the aid of our heavenly Father in their inaugural proclamations. Both Houses of Congress are opened with prayer. The Christian Sabbath is recognized and observed throughout the land. The President of the United States issues an annual proclamation, inviting his fellow-citizens to assemble in their respective houses of worship and thank the Almighty for the blessings vouchsafed to us as a nation.

"It is true, indeed, that there is no official union of Church and State in this country. But we must not infer from this that there is any antagonism between the civil and religious authorities. Far from it, Church and State move on parallel lines. They mutually assist one another. The State holds over the spiritual rulers the ægis of its protection without interfering with the sacred and God-given rights of conscience. And the Church on her part helps to enforce the civil laws by moral and religious sanctions.

"I fear that we do not fully realize and are not duly grateful for the anxious cares with which our Chief Magistrate and the heads of the co-ordinate branches of the Government are preoccupied in the discharge of their official duties. And these cares are the price which is paid for our domestic peace and comfort and the tranquility of the commonwealth. When the traveler in mid-ocean is buffeted by the waves he feels a sense of security, because he knows that the captain and his officers are at the post of duty. So do we securely rest on our pillows because we are conscious that our great captain and his associates in office are diligently steering the Ship of State.

"It is the duty of us all, churchman and layman, to hold up the hands of our President, as Aaron and Hur stayed up the hands of Moses. Let us remember that our Chief Executive and all subordinate magistrates are the accredited agents and ministers of God and are clothed with divine authority and therefore it is our duty and should be our delight to aid them by every means in our power in guiding and controlling the destiny of our glorious republic."

From one end of the country to the other there was a chorus of comment on this remarkable demonstration.   Catholics naturally rejoiced, and it was significant that some of the heartiest expressions of approval came from non-Catholics.   Men ransacked their minds in vain to find a parallel for it.

CHAPTER XXIV.

A Summary of His Labors.

The long and varied life of Cardinal Gibbons has been essentially one of achievement; and in such a career some great results must stand out. Most important of all, perhaps, is that he has made America better understood abroad. His speech at his installation in his titular church in Rome, in 1887, was timed at a moment when it was able to produce a profound and permanent impression on Europe. Its echoes radiated at once throughout the vast structure of the Catholic Church, and, from such a source, attracted equally the attention of Protestants. Europe had not conceived before that America had reached an era when there might be "liberty without license, and authority without despotism." Such utterances had been considered the exuberant fancies of emotional and shallow theorists. But here was the deliberate judgment of a prince of the Catholic Church, a leader of the greatest conservative force in the world, pronounced after full observation and under circumstances which bespoke the intensity of deep conviction.

The Cardinal also shattered at a blow the fiction that there was anything hostile to the Church in the American theory of separation of Church and state. He declared that the Church was attaining her greatest progress under this system, and that in its results it amounted to powerful protection instead of repression.

He forced on Europe a realization of the stability and soundness of the United States as a political organization, demonstrating that the stage of experiment had passed, and that

America must be admitted on an equal footing as a permanent member of the family of nations. The victories in the Spanish War, eleven years later, demonstrated his country's power, and proved that she was to be feared as well as respected. As human nature goes, the two lessons were corollaries, and both have been learned in a way that once seemed impossible.

Another great service performed by the Cardinal is that he has taken the bitterness out of religious life in America. He has not only made Catholics tolerant of Protestants, and vice versa, but he has made the different Protestant denominations more tolerant of each other. He has long since been accorded the place of the most representative churchman of America, and he has constantly used this prestige to widen the scope of forbearance among all men. This has been accomplished without the least modification in the orthodoxy of his belief; he has merely proved that being a devoted Catholic is entirely compatible with thorough Americanism and with the friendliest attitude toward adherents of other faiths. He has claimed for his Church and for himself only such privileges as he freely conceded to others under the Constitution and laws. In the court of public opinion the Catholic Church has been immensely a gainer by his attitude; this forum is open to all, and the Catholic advance has been chiefly due to the fact that he has warded off the effects of bigotry and misunderstanding, which were far too numerous in the early days of the country.

His life has been a standing refutation of the imaginative fear that the Church meditates some kind of assault on American institutions. Now and then, in the heat of the "A. P. A." agitation, someone was heard to say that the Cardinal so frequently declared his admiration for his country in order to bring about a false sense of security and make the way easier for a contemplated inroad. This reasoning failed to take into account that he reprehended defects in American political and social institutions as often as he bestowed praise. He was like a sentinel on the tower, always crying the alarm at the approach of danger.   Of all Americans, he has been, perhaps, the most outspoken in denouncing national faults, and he has not infrequently been the first one of prominence to expose them. Throughout his career, however, he has expressed faith in the future and in the capacity of the people to right their own wrongs by orderly means.   He has always held up an ideal and tried to guide the footsteps of the people toward it.

His prompt and vigorous action on the Cahensly question arrested the growth of what undoubtedly threatened to be a serious centrifugal force in the nation.   Even the most assertive of those who denounced the Catholic Church as being in some measure identified with foreign influence, were startled by the heroic figure of a prince of her hierarchy standing as a champion against the encroachment of European ideas in America.   No wonder that the "A. P. A." weed wilted in the sunlight of this experience.   It is due to him, more than to any other man, that the vast wave of emigration from Continental Europe in the last two decades of the nineteenth century commingled freely with the placid waters of American nationalism, and that the assimilative power of the people withstood a test which no nation in all time was ever before called upon to meet. The immigrant, while loving not less the land of his nativity, cherishes still more the land of his adoption.

Only by the most determined efforts was he able to place the Church in an attitude of friendship toward organized labor; but the task, if difficult, was well and thoroughly done.   His Knights of Labor letter, followed by an encyclical from Leo XIII, indorsing his views, obtained the highest sanction for the working people in the assertion of their economic rights, and has proved a bulwark for them ever since.   This the Cardinal has considered one of his most substantial achievements.   His courage in defense of principle was never better shown than in his struggle with the authorities at Rome in behalf of the Knights; this illustrated the extent of his resources when he called them into play.   He not only gave the cause of labor a tremendous prestige throughout the civilized world, but he won to the Church the love of tens of thousands who might otherwise have regarded her with far different feelings. Instead of promoting violence, his course has served to prevent it, as he predicted; the strike is declining and the peaceful settlement of wage disputes has made wonderful progress, nowhere greater than in the United States.

His work in North Carolina was arduous and full of picturesque episodes, and he has regarded this as one of the most important periods of his life. It was undoubtedly a great undertaking to erect a solid foundation for the Church in a State of more than a million population, where there were barely 800 Catholics. He was 34 years old when he went there, and brimming with constructive ideas, many of which his youthful energy and zeal enabled him to carry out. The people had been Presbyterians and Baptists and Methodists for centuries, with a sprinkling of other denominations, and his tact and liberality of view were drawn upon to the utmost in getting an audience for the faith he had come to spread. Measured by the physical obstacles which he overcame in his pioneer work over a large area, where the means of communication were poor, his accomplishments in North Carolina were the greatest of his life; estimated by the difficulty of his task of diverting the current of public opinion, they were also important. It was a purely apostolic labor, and as such he has found cause for rejoicing in its results ever since. Perhaps it is for this reason that he has always placed it so high among the fruitful periods of his life.

Gauged only by the standards of a churchman, his work in organizing and presiding as apostolic delegate over the Third Plenary Council of Baltimore is undoubtedly first. It was this which decided Leo XIII to create him a cardinal. Such a council must take into its purview the whole history and institutions of the Church, for its decrees, when approved by the Pontiff, succeed those of every previous council, and are a constitution and guide for all the manifold activities of the Church in the jurisdiction embraced. Everyone may speak his mind freely in a plenary council, and the diversity of view in a country like the United States is particularly wide. A secular parallel may, perhaps, be found in the convention which framed the National Constitution in 1787, which even Washington could scarcely prevent from breaking up in disagreement. The results of the Third Plenary Council of Baltimore established clearly the high order of ability, no less than the statesmanlike qualities, which its presiding officer possessed. It was hailed on all sides as a triumph of churchmanship and served as a model for subsequent councils in other countries.

But these conspicuous accomplishments, which have attracted the attention of the world, should not be permitted to cloud with an unfair estimate the more modest labors with which his life has been filled. He has been first of all the priest, laboring for the salvation of souls and never relaxing his self-discipline in the school of piety. The simpler and more spiritual duties of his office have always appealed to him most powerfully, and no entanglements with the great affairs of the world have been sufficient to divert him from the constancy and fervor of his devotions. With him religion has been a real thing—the greatest reality of life—and he has ever clung close to the rigorous Sulpician code he learned at the seminary, although engaged in manifold labors that have left an indelible stamp upon the fabric of contemporary history.

INDEX

INDEX.

Mediation, Offered by Leo XIII to Prevent War Betweeen the United States and Spain, 283, 284
Madrid, 284
Merry del Val, Cardinal, 315
Messmer, Archbishop, 333
Methodists, 65, 93, 203, 272, 276, 277, 397
Middleburg, Va., 68
Mill Hill College, England, 167
Milwaukee, Wis., 179, 225, 241, 244, 329
Minnesota, 229
Mississippi River, 9, 85
Modern Woodmen, Order of, 351, 362
Mohammedans, 270
Mohonk, Lake, Peace Conferences There, 362
Monastic Orders, 48
Moniteur de Rome, 151, 162
Monk, Dr. J. C., 36, 38
Monroe, President, 68
Montalembert, Vicompte, 206
Montez D'Oca, Bishop, 193
Montreal, Eucharistic Congress in, 368
Moore, Bishop, 79
Moore's, N. C., 43
Moral Theology, 113
Morgantown, N. C., 43
Mormonism, 189 201
Morris, Col. John T., 183
Morton, Levi P., 205
Mothers, Congress of, Cardinal's Letter to, 365
Mount St. Mary's College, Emmitsburg, Md., 109
Mt. Vernon Place Methodist Episcopal Church, Baltimore, 349
Muccioli, Count, 127, 129
Muller, Ury, 360
Murray, Bishop John G., 383
Music, in Church, 112, 200

Naples, 289
Napoleon I, 169
Napoleon III, 47, 57, 58
Napoleonic Wars, 237
Nassau, Island, 6
"National Bishops," 239, 240, 241
National League for the Protection of American Institutions, 252
Nation, Mrs. Carrie, 209
Naturalism, 48
Naval Academy, U. S., 285
Navarro, Mrs., 353
Navy, United States, 145
Neale, Archbishop, 3, 82, 133

Negro Question, Bishop Gibbons' Observation of "Reconstruction" Era in North Carolina, 32, 33; Education of Priests for Missionary Work Among Negroes, 167, 168; Attitude of the Church Toward the Slaves, 342, 343; Cardinal's Denunciation of Lynching, 349, 350; His Views on Aspects of Race Question, 361, 362
Newark, Bishopric of, 63, 126
New Bern, N. C., 32, 34, 40, 41
Newman, Cardinal, 87
New Orleans, Cardinal Gibbons' Early Life There, 6 to 9; Death of His Mother There, 90; Gifts Presented to Him at Public Reception, 181; Catholic Patriotism in, 199; Cardinal's Visits to, 339, 340, 344
Newton Grove N. C., 36, 37, 38
New York, See of, 63, 126, 367, 368
New Zealand, 300
Nihilism, 201
Nina, Cardinal, 87
Noble Guards, 127, 129
Norfolk, Duke of, 326
Norfolk, Va., 65
North American Review, 58, 295, 349, 361
North Carolina, Vicariate Apostolic of; Father Gibbons Selected for, 23, 24; His Labors and Experiences in, 29 to 45, 397; Administrator of, 63; Lack of Immigration to, 65; Bishop Gibbons' Work in, After His Elevation to the See of Richmond, 73 to 75; Work of Bishop Keane and Father Gross There, 86, 87
North Point, Battle of, 66
Northrop, Bishop, 34, 40, 87
Notre Dame College, Baltimore, 341
Nozaleda, Archbishop, 289
Nugent, Rev. James, 208, 300

O'Connell, Bishop D. J., 103, 107, 140, 141, 151, 183, 193, 256, 262
O'Connell, Daniel, 4
O'Connell, Rev. J. J., 44
O'Connell, Rev. Lawrence P., 34, 39, 40
Odd Fellows, 25
O'Ferrall, Bishop, 206
O'Gorman, James A., 314
O'Hagan, Dr., 35
O'Hara, Bishop, 29
Ohio River, 9, 85
Oreglia, Cardinal, 314
"Our Christian Heritage," Cardinal Gibbons' Second Book, 188, 189, 208
Our Lady of Good Counsel, Church, Baltimore, 15